The Certified Criminal Investigator Body of Knowledge

Center for National Threat Assessment

Certified Forensic Consultant Body of Knowledge
American College of Forensic Examiners Institute
ISBN: 978-1-4987-5207-7

The Certified Criminal Investigator Body of Knowledge
American College of Forensic Examiners Institute
ISBN: 978-1-4987-5205-3

Sensitive Security Information, Certified® (SSI) Body of Knowledge
American Board for Certification in Homeland Security
ISBN: 978-1-4987-5211-4

The Certified Criminal Investigator Body of Knowledge

American College of
Forensic Examiners Institute

CRC Press
Taylor & Francis Group
Boca Raton   London   New York

CRC Press is an imprint of the
Taylor & Francis Group, an **informa** business

CRC Press
Taylor & Francis Group
6000 Broken Sound Parkway NW, Suite 300
Boca Raton, FL 33487-2742

Printed on acid-free paper
Version Date: 20151110

International Standard Book Number-13: 978-1-4987-5205-3 (Paperback)

Visit the Taylor & Francis Web site at
http://www.taylorandfrancis.com

and the CRC Press Web site at
http://www.crcpress.com

Contents

SECTION III   CRIMINAL INVESTIGATIONS AND TRIALS

SECTION V INJURIES AND FATALITIES

SECTION VI THE PSYCHOLOGICAL AUTOPSY

Taking the Exam

The Certified Criminal Investigator, CCI® exam was created by subject matter experts and approved by the American Board of Certified Criminal Investigators. The examination tests an individual's knowledge in the field of criminal investigation. The individual must go into the exam with a basic set of knowledge of the field. Do not expect to pass an exam just from reading this material. To be a true CCI, one must have gained knowledge from education, training, and experience.

Steps to Taking the Exam

I. Apply for and Sign Up for the Program

This book is provided to all applicants of the CCI certification as study material. If you have purchased the book through a third-party company, you should contact our office at (800) 423-9737, and ask for member services to apply for the program.

II. Review the Material

This book does not guarantee your success in passing the exam—your education, training, and experience are crucial factors in becoming credentialed. However, this book is here to help you prepare for the exam. Focus your study on the sections you are weaker in to better prepare for the exam. There also are sample questions at the end of each section. You can use these as a pretest to gauge your current knowledge or to review what you learned from a chapter.

III. Take the Online Exam

After signing up, you will be issued a username and a password. This information will allow you to log on to your account at our website: www.acfei.com. Here you can access the exam.

Frequently Asked Questions

1. How many questions is the exam?

    The exam will include 200 questions.

2. What type of questions will be asked?

    The exams consist of multiple-choice questions with four possible answers to choose from. There are no true-or-false questions and no *all of the above* or *none of the above* options.

3. What kind of time limit do I have for the exam?

    Exams are limited to four hours.

Practice Questions

After each section, you will find questions pertaining to the text you just read. These questions are in no way affiliated with the actual CCI exam for which you are preparing, and are just meant to be a simple way to test yourself. The answers to these questions can be found at the back of the book.

Contributors

Larry Barksdale, AA, BS, MA, worked for the Lincoln, Nebraska, Police Department beginning 1971. He retired in 2012, when he was supervisor of the Crime Scene Tech Unit and case manager in criminal investigations. Barksdale earned a BS in criminal justice from the University of Nebraska at Omaha and an MA in political science from the University of Nebraska–Lincoln. He has lectured in crime scene investigation subjects at multiple universities and for numerous professional organizations. He is past president of the International Association of Auto Theft Investigators, past president of the Nebraska Chapter of the International Association for Identification (IAI), and a certified crime scene analyst, IAI. He is currently an assistant professor of practice forensic science at the University of Nebraska–Lincoln.

Martin A. Matisoff began his forensic career in the 1970s as a forensic toxicology technician with the Los Angeles County Coroner/ Medical Examiner. He specialized in organic extraction of diazapines from blood and liver bases. Matisoff was also a clinical laboratory technician who specialized in radioimmunoassay, cardiac isoenzymes, infectious diseases, and bacteriology. He earned a BA from Western Illinois University and an MSc in entomology with a subspecialty in forensic science from the University of Nebraska–Lincoln. Currently,

Matisoff is an insect anatomist and morphologist at Kentucky State University, where he studies pathogens that have been linked to colony collapse disorder. He is also the publications manager and technical editor for the *Journal of Terrestrial Observation* and the *Professional Agricultural Workers Journal*, published by Tuskegee University.

Dr. Katherine Ramsland has published more than 1000 articles and 47 books, including *The Mind of a Murderer* and *Beating the Devil's Game: A History of Forensic Science and Criminal Investigation*. Dr. Ramsland is a professor of forensic psychology at DeSales University in Pennsylvania and has been a member of the American College of Forensic Examiners Institute since 1998.

Dr. Greg Vecchi began his service with the FBI in Miami, Florida, in 1996, where he worked on a variety of organized crime and drug matters. Dr. Vecchi became an auxiliary negotiator in 1998 and was formally certified by the FBI in 2002. In 2003, Dr. Vecchi was promoted and transferred to the FBI's Critical Incident Response Group, where he was assigned to the Rapid Deployment/Logistics Unit (RDLU) and subsequently to the Crisis Negotiation Unit as a program manager. During his time at RDLU, Dr. Vecchi was deployed to Iraq in support of counterterrorism operations.

Prior to joining the FBI, Dr. Vecchi was a special agent/criminal investigator with the U.S. Department of Justice–Office of the Inspector General (OIG), U.S. Department of Agriculture–OIG, and the U.S. Army Criminal Investigation Division. Dr. Vecchi earned a PhD degree in conflict analysis and resolution from Nova Southeastern University, Fort Lauderdale, Florida, in 2006; an MS degree in criminal justice from the University of Alabama, Tuscaloosa, Alabama, in 1999; and a BS degree in human resource management from Park College, Parkville, Missouri, in 1991. Dr. Vecchi has conducted extensive research and is published in the areas of conflict and crisis management and communication. He also teaches, trains, and consults with executive law enforcement officers on the topic.

Major C. E. "Sonny" Wells is the chief administrative deputy at the Christian County Sheriff's Office located in Missouri. He earned his BA degree in criminal justice administration from Columbia College, where he graduated summa cum laude. Major Wells's law enforcement career spans nearly 35 years and includes municipal and county policing in addition to jail administration. He has served as a criminal investigator for the Webster County Prosecuting Attorney's Office, as the assistant police chief for the city of Marshfield, Missouri, and two terms as the elected sheriff of Webster County, Missouri. His jail administration experience includes serving as the director of the Christian County, Missouri, Detention Center and the director of the Greene County, Missouri, Detention Center. He is a graduate of the National Institute of Corrections Jail Administration Course with additional training in legal issues in today's jails through the American Jail Association. Major Wells served as a contractor in Afghanistan from 2008 to 2010 for the U.S. Training Center, Xe (formerly known as Blackwater). During that time, he was a trainer, a team leader, and, ultimately, the program manager for the Regional Training Team, a Drug Enforcement Administration–monitored project providing training to the National Interdiction Unit of the Counter Narcotics Police of Afghanistan. He is a Missouri Peace Officer Standards and Training generalist instructor for the Missouri Sheriffs' Association Training Academy.

American Board of Certified Criminal Investigators®

Joseph Alercia II is the owner and director of Lion Investigation Academy and a licensed and practicing private investigator in the states of Pennsylvania, New York, New Jersey, Nebraska, Massachusetts, North Carolina, and formerly the District of Columbia. His four decades of practical experience in the private investigation and security realm provide the student with the added advantage of a complete instructor who not only corrects exams, but can also give practical answers to the students' questions based on the knowledge he has acquired through work on thousands of cases. He is a graduate of many distance learning institutions and, as such, understands the need and direction of distance learning education.

Dilsher Ali is a seasoned law enforcement officer who is currently employed as a special agent in the Major Crime Unit at the Arizona Attorney General's office. He was previously employed as a law enforcement officer with the Virginia State Police. He has a combined 11 years of performing law enforcement and criminal and administrative investigations.

Ali is a certified anti-money laundering specialist and a professional certified investigator. His specialty is financial and money laundering investigations. He is an Education Task Force member of the Association of Certified Anti-Money Laundering Specialists and he enjoys teaching financial investigative techniques to law enforcement officers. Ali earned BS and MS degrees in electronics engineering from the City University of New York, and is currently enrolled in an MS degree program in accounting. He also has a graduate certificate in forensic criminology from the University of Massachusetts at Lowell.

Mark Boutwell's experience and expertise span 28 years in the Department of Defense, performing intelligence analysis and technical and forensic exploitation against counterterrorism, narcoterrorism, counternarcotics, human trafficking, counterproliferation, cyber and digital communications, and respective disciplines. He has in-depth experience with small group tactics, weapons, surveillance, mission planning, and target profiling and pursuit. His exceptional supervisory and leadership experience includes leading joint civilian and multiservice personnel conducting military and intelligence operations.

In 2011, Boutwell transferred to his current position in the Department of Defense (Alaska) as an intelligence liaison officer. His three previous positions with the Department of Defense (Georgia) included supervisor of cryptanalysis and exploitation, technical director, and senior forensic analyst.

Boutwell graduated in 2009 with an MS degree in information systems from the University of Phoenix and in 2003 with a BS degree in computer science from Hawaii Pacific University. He also holds a master certificate in forensic death investigation from the University of Florida and completed the Covert Electronic Surveillance and Advanced Forensics Techniques (CSI Level II) programs at the Federal Law Enforcement Training Center in 2009 and 2010, respectively. His professional certificates include those on research, development, test, and evaluation; contract management; and maintenance management from the U.S. Army's Logistics Management College. Boutwell has been an adjunct faculty instructor with the National Cryptologic School, Department of Defense, where he has instructed numerous technical and operational courses since 1997.

Robert D. Boyden, PhD, served as police officer for more than 21 years in the Philadelphia, Pennsylvania, area, holding positions as a criminal investigator, sergeant, and member and instructor of the Special Weapons and Tactics (SWAT) team, before retiring. He has been a member of the American College of Forensic Examiners Institute (ACFEI) since 1994, attaining the status of both fellow and diplomate. Dr. Boyden holds an MS degree in public safety administration from St. Joseph's University and a PhD in public policy and administration with a specialization in public safety leadership and disaster management from Walden University. He has written extensively on police and public safety issues for various trade magazines and newspapers and has just had his first book published, *Police Stress in Small Town USA* (Lambert Academic Publishing). Dr. Boyden currently has a private consulting firm called Public Safety Concepts Group.

Henry "Scott" Browne worked with the Wayne County Health Department as a public health sanitarian. He is currently serving as the environmental health specialist and assisting the faculty in the Forensic Investigation program for Wayne State University in Detroit. He has a postbachelor certificate in forensic investigations from Wayne State University, and a master's degree in forensic science from the University of Florida. He also holds a registered sanitarian certificate through the state of Michigan and a CHS-III level with American Board of Certification in Homeland Security (ABCHS). He is an officer in the United States Coast Guard Reserve, a licensed private investigator, and a member of the Michigan Council of Private/Professional Investigators.

Marvin "Gene" E. Bullington earned a BA degree in criminal justice from the University of South Florida. He began his career in forensics at the Pinellas County Sheriff's Department in Florida where he specialized in traffic homicide, burglary, and arson investigations. Bullington is currently the president, chief operations officer, and senior forensic analyst at Interscience, Inc., headquartered in Tampa, Florida. He is a Certified Forensic Consultant (CFC), life member and fellow in ACFEI, and a certified fire and explosion investigator through the National Association of Arson Investigators. In addition to performing forensic analysis of various types of evidence, Interscience is also one of the largest evidence collection, storage, and examination facilities in the southeast, and is responsible for the proper collection, preservation, and submission of thousands of items of evidence each year.

Dennis Chevalier, PhD, is eager to bring students and professionals into the 21st century using a unique combination of education and experience coupled with 26 years of experience in law enforcement in operations, academy, and Special Weapons and Tactics (SWAT) systems management. He holds a PhD in criminal psychology, an MS degree in management of criminal justice, and a BS degree in criminal justice, all from Colorado Technical University. Dr. Chevalier is dedicated to enthusiastic and dynamic teaching as means of creating and nurturing a lifelong love of knowledge in criminal justice professionals.

John Daab, PhD, MA, MBA, MPS, MA, CFE, CFC, CCI, CHS-I, IAC, CI, began work as a carpenter apprentice, and became a New York City (NYC) high-rise builder and construction manager executive, a professor of construction at New York University (NYU), owner of two schools, sculptor, writer, business consultant, and educational course and program developer.

A former NYC Transit police officer, Daab is currently a Certified Forensic Consultant (CFC), Certified Criminal Investigator (CCI), and certified instructor for teaching CFC and CCI courses with the ACFEI. Dr. Daab holds diplomate status and is a board member of the ABCCI. He is a Certified Homeland Security-I (CHS-I), a Certified Intelligence Analyst (IAC), and a member of the ABCHS.

Dr. Daab earned a BA and an MA degree in philosophy, an MBA degree in business, an MPS degree in industrial counseling, an MA degree in labor studies, and a PhD in business administration with a focus on the business of art. He is member of the Association for Research in Crimes against Art and Fine Art Forensics. He has won awards for teaching management and service to NYU. He has published more than 100 articles and recently authored *The Art Fraud Protection Handbook*. Dr. Daab has received certification in

Art Appraisal Studies from NYU, completed a docent program at Princeton, and written a second book, *Forensic Applications in Detecting Fine, Decorative, and Collectible Art Fakes*. Recently, he has provided lectures to third-year law students at the University of Pennsylvania; Princeton University Art Museum; the Grounds for Sculpture, Drumthwacket; Nassau Club; and Brookdale College. Dr. Daab has also given developed courses in art forensics. He is currently involved in ascertaining the use of crime scene concepts and processes in determinations of authenticity in works of art.

Joseph A. Juchniewicz is a senior security consultant at Accudata Systems, Inc., providing high-level consulting services to clients primarily in the area of security for more than 20 years. Juchniewicz has worked as a consultant for Accenture's Global Architecture and Core Technologies Security Technologies Practice and as a security specialist with Lockheed Martin Tactical Aircraft Systems.

His primary focus is providing security consulting services to clients, including the design and implementation of security solutions; conducting security assessments; and assisting with the alignment of operational procedures with information security best practices. Juchniewicz has extensive experience in penetration testing, social engineering, security assessments, investigations, and forensics within the Department of Defense, Department of Homeland Security, as well as in several of the top Fortune 100 companies.

Eric Lakes, a digital forensic expert, established Digital Forensic Examiner in Lexington, Kentucky. He has been in business since 1988 when he started a computer firm called MCA, Inc. (Micro Computer Analysts, Inc.). MCA, Inc., is also an Internet hosting company. His specialties include digital forensic examinations, expert witness, expert testimony, electronic discovery and litigation support, forensic training, and more.

Captain David Millsap, BS, MS, has 30 years of experience in the criminal justice field. Captain Millsap has commanded the Criminal Investigations Section, Special Investigations Section, Traffic Section, and Patrol Section of the Springfield, Missouri, Police Department. He has supervised the Community Policing Unit, Patrol Unit, and the

Training Academy. He has worked as a patrol officer, detective, and task force officer for both the Springfield Police Department and the Laclede County Sheriff's Department. He also spent 10 years as the juvenile officer in the 26th Circuit Court. He is currently the South Division commander for the Springfield Police Department. Captain Millsap is the current president of the Missouri State Investigators Association.

Thomas Price has more than 20 years of worldwide experience in law enforcement, security, and investigative operations. He has senior-level experience in executive decision making, policy direction, strategic business planning, and personnel management. Price began his career in the United States Air Force Security Forces in 1991, and was awarded an honorable discharge in 1999 as a staff sergeant. During his enlistment, he served both domestically and overseas in installation and forward deployed environments, where he provided security during low-, medium-, and high-threat levels; installation law enforcement; investigations; emergency service team functions; and critical resource/force protection. He then served as a deputy sheriff in North Carolina from 1999 to June 2002, providing law enforcement, investigations, corrections, special weapons and tactics, and high-risk inmate transport service. In June 2002, Price was in the initial hiring phase as a U.S. Federal Air Marshal (FAM). He served as a FAM until October 2006, providing counterterrorist protection of aircraft and resources domestically and abroad and investigative functions as well as operations officer duties. In October 2006, Price was hired by Accenture National Security Services (now Accenture Federal Services), where he provides senior level security management, internal investigations, physical security subject matter expertise, risk and vulnerability assessments, and policy/process/SOP development.

Harold F. Risk, PhD, graduated from Indiana State University, Terre Haute, Indiana, with a BS and an MS in the fields of health, safety, and physical medicine. He completed graduate work at the University of Illinois, Champaign, Illinois, in the field of medical science and transportation engineering and reconstruction. Dr. Risk earned his PhD degree from the University of Southern Illinois University,

Carbondale, Illinois, in the field of health and medical science. He has taught at Indiana State University, University of Illinois, and St. Cloud State University in St. Cloud, Minnesota. Dr. Risk was the assistant medical examiner for Stearns County, Minnesota, for nine years and is also a death investigator and accident reconstructionist. He is also a licensed paramedic and mortician.

Dr. Risk is the president of two companies: Risk's Safety Consulting Company and VENTUS LLC. He is also a member of DMORT V, which is a division of Health and Human Services (HHS), and has been deployed to various fatal disasters around the United States. Dr. Risk has published dozens of articles in the fields of rehabilitative medicine, accident reconstruction, drug-related deaths, motorcycle accidents, and driving assistive device design. He has presented numerous presentations at state, national, and international conferences.

Dr. Risk is on the editorial board for the National Safety Council and the *Journal of Alcohol and Drug Education*, and is a member of the American College of Forensic Examiners Institute.

Cyril Wecht, MD, JD, of Pennsylvania, is a nationally renowned forensic pathologist and has served as a consultant in numerous high-profile cases, but he is perhaps best known for his outspoken criticism of the Warren Commission's findings concerning the assassination of John F. Kennedy. He served as the county commissioner, coroner, and medical examiner of Allegheny County, Pennsylvania. He earned a BS from the University of Pittsburgh in 1952, an MD from the University of Pittsburgh School of Medicine in 1956, and a JD from the University of Maryland School of Law. After serving in the United States Air Force, he became a forensic pathologist. He formerly chaired the Department of Pathology and was president of the medical staff at St. Francis Central Hospital in Pittsburgh and is actively involved as a medical-legal and forensic science consultant, author, and lecturer. He also served as the elected coroner of Allegheny County for 20 years.

Dr. Wecht is the author or coauthor of 530 professional publications; an editorial board member of 16 national and international medical-legal and forensic scientific publications; and an editor or coeditor of 44 books, including the five-volume set *Forensic Sciences*

(Matthew Bender). Dr. Wecht has testified in more than 1000 civil, criminal, and workers' compensation cases in state and federal courts in more than 30 states. He has also testified in several foreign countries. During his career, Dr. Wecht has personally performed more than 14,000 autopsies.

SECTION I

INTRODUCTION TO FORENSIC SCIENCE

Section I, Introduction to Forensic Science, reviews ethics relating to criminal investigators as well as the skills and characteristics of successful investigators. It also goes into the history of forensics and gives background information on several different specialties within forensics. See page 83 for questions reviewing the material in Section I.

1

PROFESSIONAL CONDUCT

1.1 Ethics

Ethical behavior goes beyond simply knowing the difference between right and wrong; it is doing what is right. The purpose of promoting ethical investigation practices is to establish and promote clearly defined standards of conduct for all investigators. These standards assist in protecting the investigator and the public. While some practices may be legal, the investigator must ask if they are ethical. The conduct of an investigator must be ethical at all times if he or she is to be taken seriously as a professional. That means adhering to the following principles:

- Confidentiality
- Honesty
- Ethical investigation practices
- Avoiding conflicts of interest
- Supporting equal rights

1.1.1 Confidentiality

Confidentiality safeguards privileged information that is obtained. Disclosure of information is restricted to what is necessary, relevant, and verifiable with respect to the victim's and suspect's right to privacy. Professional files, reports, and records should be maintained in a secure manner or destroyed in an appropriate fashion. To ensure investigation techniques fall within the boundaries of the law, it is a good idea to become familiar with the privacy laws of the state.

1.1.2 Honesty

The first order of investigation is the commitment made to the interests of the victim. However, that does not eliminate the obligation to determine the facts of a case, giving an honest and unbiased report no matter how that report affects those involved. Investigators are dedicated to searching for the truth in each investigation. Investigators should strive to be honest, just, and courteous to everyone with whom they come in contact.

1.1.2.1 Misrepresentation Investigators must not misrepresent or embellish their services, but rather they should give a factual report or summary of services themselves. Do not knowingly misrepresent yourself, your duties, or your credentials at any time.

1.1.2.2 Reporting Ensure your reporting is based on truth and fact by only expressing honest opinions. The submission of reports should be provided in a timely fashion, should respond to the purpose of the investigation, and should include recommendations if appropriate. Reports should reflect objective, independent observations based on factual determinations within the provider's area of expertise and discipline. Reports of service and findings should be distributed to appropriate parties and be in compliance with all applicable legal regulations.

1.1.2.3 Testimony When requested, investigators have an obligation to provide truthful and objective testimony. Often investigators are called upon to testify to facts of which they have knowledge and provide professional opinions about a case. That testimony should be limited to the specific field of which an individual is considered an expert as dictated by training, experience, education, and the local judicial system.

1.1.3 Ethical Investigation Practices

The services of the investigators should be presented to the public as promoting justice for the overall good of the community. Using appropriate business conduct is a large part of doing that.

1.1.3.1 Professionalism Investigators should never be party to any practices that can damage their profession or the good of the public at large. Illegal and unethical practices as defined by law, professional organizations, and legal precedent in your jurisdiction should be avoided. Injuring, defaming, or harming in any way the professional reputation or practice of a victim, suspect, colleague, or employer is unacceptable practice and possibly illegal. Investigators should guard against using tactics that could harm others and carry professional liability insurance for his or her protection.

1.1.3.2 Qualifications Render only those services that you are competent in and qualified to perform. Do not accept assignments that require you to perform services that fall outside your field of expertise. Do not engage in the unauthorized practice of law unless you are licensed to practice law. Do not promise or offer services or results that you cannot deliver.

Stay informed of changes in legal matters, proposed legislation, public policies, and forensic or technical advances as they relate to the investigation field. Local, state, and federal levels of information must be current if an investigator is to offer an informed opinion and services.

1.1.4 Avoiding Conflicts of Interest

Investigators should not accept assignments if the mission will create a personal or professional conflict of interest. A conflict of interest is a real or apparent conflict between one's professional or official duties and one's private interests or a situation where one duty conflicts with another—for example, if an investigator were to work for both parties in a divorce proceeding.

Cooperation with other investigators and related professionals should be conducted in a way that does not violate the interests of anyone involved in the investigation. Respect the integrity of people with and for whom you work. When there is a conflict of interest, the nature and direction of loyalty and responsibilities must be clarified and all parties must be kept informed of that commitment.

1.1.5 Supporting Equal Rights

Do not deny professional services to any person for reasons of race, color, religion, gender, handicap, national origin, sexual preference, or age. Do not be party to any plan or agreement that discriminates against a person based on any of these characteristics. Do not allow personal feelings or prejudices to interfere with factual and truthful disclosure.

1.2 Attributes of a Successful Investigator

An investigator is a professional researcher. Using observation, inquiry, and examination, an investigator provides evidence and factual information upon which sound decisions are made.

1.2.1 Investigation Skills

1.2.1.1 Observation Good investigators use their five senses to obtain information about a case. Remembering details about a crime scene or an individual can be crucial to an investigation. Pay attention and make note of details even if they seem insignificant at the time.

Work with the evidence you find at the scene. Examine all evidence carefully, such as pieces of paper, printed documents, tools, fragments of cloth, or personal items. Any physical evidence can provide an important lead in the investigation. You can never gather too much information. It is easier to eliminate nonessential information than to obtain additional information later on.

1.2.1.2 Listening Skills Ask as many questions as possible, repeating questions and asking follow-up questions as necessary. This helps uncover discrepancies and obtain details. In order to communicate effectively and be a good interviewer and listener, you must be able to understand the person whom you are questioning. This takes good listening skills—not just hearing the words but understanding them and the meaning behind them. Words, tone, inflection, and expression all play a part in how a message is conveyed. To be a good listener, you must use more than just your ears.

1.2.1.3 Patience Do not jump to conclusions. Do not take things for granted. Make no assumptions about how much information is needed before you begin searching for facts. False assumptions lead to the loss of valuable information. When investigating a crime, do not commit yourself to the guilt or innocence of anyone whom you may question at the scene. Your purpose is to gather facts. Judgments are not made at the beginning of an investigation; they are made later.

1.2.2 People Skills

1.2.2.1 Unbiasedness Bias and prejudice bring about poor investigation results. The biased investigator can end up clouding the facts of a case and may treat suspects unfairly. This does very little to uncover the truth, which is the job of the investigator. Do not let personal likes and dislikes interfere with your job. It is important to recognize that suspects, criminals, and other subjects of investigation come from all walks of life and are represented by all races, both sexes, and an endless variety of lifestyles.

1.2.2.2 Persuasiveness Investigations require investigators to interact with others to discover information. These contacts are essential to the job. Clients, witnesses, suspects, and others can provide valuable information if they are properly motivated. A good investigator is able to obtain cooperation from as many people as possible, even when they do not want to cooperate. This can lead to the vital facts needed to conclude an investigation.

In order to be persuasive, an investigator must be able to convince people to submit to interviews. The ability to comfort people and put them at ease is an essential skill needed to do this.

The art of persuasion requires patience, courtesy, tact, and understanding. In spite of what is shown in the movies or on TV, suspects who have been intimidated, frightened, or angered are not likely to provide the needed information. The information they provide is usually of little value.

Another aspect of persuasion is the ability to speak to a person at his or her level. No one wants to talk to someone who speaks condescendingly or in language that is difficult to understand. Investigators must be able to talk to anyone from the high school dropout to the doctor of philosophy in language that is appropriate and understandable.

1.2.2.3 Intuitiveness   Investigators must understand basic human nature. Investigators often see people while they are experiencing extreme emotional distress. The ability to recognize this and proceed with caution can greatly help in an investigation.

It is also important to be tuned in to how a person responds to questions. The investigator, from various telltales, may infer that the person is lying. To know if a person is truthful in an interview situation, you must be able to read body language. At the end of an interview, you must be able to gauge the person's honesty and credibility.

1.2.2.4 Manners   Good manners can open more doors than rude behavior ever will. Being rude will hurt your investigation. No one wants to talk to or give information to a rude investigator.

1.2.3 Intelligence

1.2.3.1 Cautious   Being suspicious of obvious things and wary of people who are quick to provide alibis and identification is essential to a thorough investigation. Verify facts whenever possible. Caution can also protect an investigator from getting caught in a dangerous situation. Whether on a stakeout or in an interview with a witness, investigators must always be on guard and wary of potential difficulties.

1.2.3.2 Curiosity   Investigation by its very definition requires a certain amount of curiosity. Good investigators learn to harness and develop their own natural curiosity. A desire to learn the truth and do what is necessary to find it can drive an investigator on when an investigation grows stale. An inquisitive mind is essential to the investigator.

1.2.3.3 Good Memory   The ability to accurately recall the facts of a case, events that transpired, and the characteristics of a suspect is a valuable skill. This can be developed somewhat, but a natural ability is extremely helpful. Forgetting important details is not an option when conducting an investigation of any kind. Take copious notes at all times.

1.2.3.4 Common Sense Understanding the way the world works and how people behave is an important attribute to have. This can be developed or refined. More time spent interacting in the world can sharpen your street sense. This can be learned over time as you work as an investigator.

1.2.4 Work Ethic

1.2.4.1 Persistence Investigators often find themselves working late nights following a promising lead. Stick with the job until the end can pay off, whether on a stakeout or trying to persuade a valuable witness to cooperate.

1.2.4.2 Resourcefulness An investigator must be able to adapt to all types of stressful situations. Quick thinking and ingenuity can make a difference on the field.

1.2.4.3 Interest in the Work True success in any profession is based on sincere interest in the work and pride in a job well done. Knowing that your efforts can bring a criminal to justice, locate a missing person, or save a business is a great motivator in this profession.

1.2.4.4 Discipline Investigation requires the ability to stick with it to the end. Investigators must have self-discipline to sit through an 18-hour stakeout, read through stacks of public records, and control their temper when being hassled by a suspect.

1.2.4.5 Flexibility On top of hard work and lots of practice, being able to adapt to new situations is key. Maybe you are an introvert who feels uncomfortable in crowds, but need to be in a large event. Pretend to be an extrovert for the day. Learn to blend in by watching others around you. The faster you learn how to be flexible, go with the flow, and adjust to whatever situation you are in, the faster you will find the right groove.

1.2.4.6 Self-Confidence   Optimism and assertiveness play a part in investigations. This can include assertiveness of an individual who depends on his or her knowledge of how to handle a difficult situation.

1.2.4.7 Integrity   Falsified facts and incomplete information can spell disaster for an investigator. It is absolutely essential that investigators double-check all facts and do not misrepresent themselves to others. A reputation for honesty and integrity can keep you out of trouble.

Bibliography

McMahon, R.J. (2001). *Practical handbook for private investigators.* New York NY: CRC Press LLC.

2

HISTORY OF FORENSIC SCIENCE

2.1 A History

On June 13, 1994, someone attacked and killed Nicole Brown Simpson and Ronald Goldman outside Nicole's home. Since Nicole seemed the likely target, her estranged ex-husband, O. J. Simpson, was arrested. His televised trial brought to the public's awareness the nature of evidence handling and scientific analysis in a criminal investigation. The public watched crime scene specialists, crime lab personnel, pathologists, investigators, DNA analysts, blood spatter pattern analysts, and other experts who used physical evidence to reconstruct what had happened. Not only did millions of laypersons learn intimate details about the investigative process, but they also witnessed its limitations. In the end, Simpson was acquitted, while investigators, scientists, and lab personnel were left to ponder their costly errors. The forerunner to American College of Forensic Examiners Institute was founded less than 2 years before the murders.

The story of forensic science is an exciting and dramatic tale involving people who, against all odds, have improved crime investigation in the interest of justice. Toxicologists, pathologists, and trace experts were among the earliest pioneers, and they exemplified the tenacious temperament often required for making a significant historical mark. Then, as experts specialized in forensic application, improvements occurred in the development of technologies for detecting poison, perfecting microscopy, and analyzing bullets and wounds. Anthropology joined psychology to address criminal origins, and the science of identification changed the course of investigative history.

2.1.1 Early Forensics

The earliest crime labs were self-funded by earnest men such as Edmond Locard and Jean Servais Stas, who were intent on applying science to law enforcement. Since judges disliked when science challenged common sense, scientists strove to give compelling demonstrations. Parallel with the tumultuous rise of science in intellectual discourse, forensic applications profited from new discoveries and persistent thinkers willing to gamble on innovation. By the time the 20th century arrived, bold pioneers had cleared the way for science to become vital in solving crimes and bringing offenders to justice.

Although ancient Rome grounded the Western practice of criminal and civil law, China made the earliest strides in death investigation. In the middle of the 13th century, Sung Tz'u, a Chinese lawyer, was featured in the first work of forensic science, *The Washing Away of Wrongs*. However, China was a closed society and this work had limited international impact.

During the Renaissance, educated men turned to experimentation and measurements, and the human body was further explored—often illegally—to learn its function. In 1560, the first scientific society was organized in Italy, and by 1642, the University of Leipzig offered a course for doctors in forensic medicine. During this same century, Anton van Leeuwenhoek invented the precision microscope, allowing forensic pioneers to better see such things as blood cells and disease in organs.

The first documented evidence of an investigator using logic to match physical evidence from a crime to a specific criminal occurred in 1784, with a torn piece of newspaper that implicated a shooter named John Toms in a murder. Part of the newspaper had been used as wadding for the gun and part of it was in his home. It took a quick-thinking officer to place them side by side, with ragged edges matching, to show the court that both pieces were from the same paper.

Eugène François Vidocq, once a criminal, pioneered undercover investigations in Paris in the early 1800s and formed the world's first detective force, the Sureté. As he succeeded in catching criminals, he also invented a number of forensic techniques, such as matching bullets to guns, analyzing handwriting, cleverly interrogating suspects, and creating methods for undercover operatives. In 1811, pediatrician and chemist Pierre-Hubert Nysten formulated Nysten's law, which is about the progress of rigidity in a cadaver, and other physicians first used mercury-based thermometers to check postmortem body temperature.

Not far away in Germany, the first questioned document analysis occurred with the application of a chemical test for ink. It was applied to a document known as the *Konigin Hanschritt*, which helped to develop a means of distinguishing between forged and authentic documents. Yet it was the field of toxicology that made the most dramatic progress during this era, thanks to the increased reliance on poison as the murderer's weapon of choice. Mathieu Orfila became the father of toxicology as he published the first systematic treatise on known poisons.

In an 1836 trial, Scottish chemist James Marsh wanted to prove he had detected arsenic in the organs of a potential murder victim. He found that he was unable to explain it easily to the jury and felt frustrated with his inability to persuade, so he invented a device to show his detection method that would be more visually appealing, and it worked.

In America, medical testimony was first used in the trial of John Webster for the murder of prominent Boston citizen George Parkman. Physicians, dentists, and anthropologists were able to tell the jury the age, sex, physical dimensions, and time of death of the victim, whose parts were not all there, as well as the effect of fire on the victim's charred remains. It was an impressive demonstration and, thereafter, such professionals were not only welcomed by judges but also expected in murder trials.

With the rise of modern science and the emphasis on natural law, a person's external appearance became fodder for ideas about how body dimensions revealed criminality. Phrenology assigned specific brain functions and personality temperaments to the various bumps and depressions on a person's skull, while some physicians decided that criminals could be detected by facial characteristics.

By 1876, Italian anthropologist Cesare Lombroso, a professor at the University of Turin in Italy and in possession of the world's largest collection of skulls, published *L'uomo delinquente* (*Criminal Man*). Believing that human behavior could be classified with objective tests, Lombroso was convinced that certain people were born criminals, identifiable by specific physical traits, such as bulging brows, long arms, and apelike noses. Striking a social chord, Lombroso's ideas spread across Europe and America, supported by the new evolutionary thinking, and they dominated ideas about criminals for two decades.

In addition to criminality, the cause of insanity continued to interest investigators. A specific type of criminal, who showed extreme brutality and no remorse, received some attention as well. To classify such people, Philippe Pinel introduced *mania without delirium* in 1809, and more than two decades later British physician James Prichard used *moral insanity* to label a corrupted faculty for inappropriate behavior. These were the precursor labels to the psychopath— the person who had no conscience about his cruel and destructive acts.

While science was improving methods of investigation and prosecution, the need for identification of repeat offenders inspired several innovations. Alphonse Bertillon organized the chaotic collection of police photos and files in Paris, inventing anthropometry. As offenders were arrested, he took 14 measurements from the length of the foot to the width of the jaw, classifying each person and recording the measurements on cards. In 1883, after measuring almost 2000 men, he succeeded in identifying a repeat offender strictly by measurements. His technique became more precisely known as bertillonage and quickly became the method for identification. However, it proved to be difficult to apply.

In 1877 in the United States, Thomas Taylor proposed that skin ridge patterns on palms and fingertips be used for identification. Three years later, Scottish physician Henry Faulds, who discovered how to make fingerprints visible with powders, had successfully eliminated a suspect and helped to convict the true offender in a burglary. Other researchers discovered the significant fact that fingerprints were unchanging over time, and getting a set of prints from an arrested criminal proved much easier than taking measurements.

The first trial that actually included fingerprint evidence in its crime reconstruction occurred in Argentina in 1892. Francesca Rojas accused a man named Velasquez of murdering her two children with blows to the head. However, rumor had it that Rojas had a young lover who had said he would not marry her because of her children. So she had a motive. Juan Vucetich, who had formulated an identification system from fingertip ridge patterns, went over the crime scene and found what appeared to be a thumbprint in a spot of dried blood. He compared this pattern with both suspects and identified the mother as the person who had placed her thumb in blood and thus had murdered the children. She confessed and was convicted.

Austrian lawyer Hans Gross, who was versed in a variety of sciences from physics to psychology, opened the Criminalistic Institute at the University of Graz, offering it as a police science that called for a collaboration of diverse specialists. In 1891, he published *Criminal Investigation*, the first comprehensive description of the use of physical evidence in solving crime, which influenced the methods of England's early murder squad, a group of men who brought new integrity to law enforcement and efficiency into investigation. By the end of the century, these detectives were categorizing criminals by modus operandi, and would soon emphasize the value of preserving crime scenes and properly handling evidence.

Alexandre Lacassagne, a professor of medicine at the Institute of Forensic Medicine, was so committed to new discoveries that he burned his fingertips to see whether fingerprints could be altered. He also influenced the direction of forensic medicine as he developed more careful methods for examining wounds and body changes during death. Pathologists during those days believed that the time of death could easily be determined by measuring body temperature and stages of rigor mortis and lividity, but the more homicide cases they saw, the more they realized it was not that simple.

By this time, the popularity of the fictional world's first consulting detective, Sherlock Holmes, had grown. He inspired the idea of a supersleuth type of detective who could use logic and empirical methods to solve seemingly unsolvable crimes. The series of short stories by Sir Arthur Conan Doyle had created not just a beloved character but also a role model for real-life detectives.

2.1.2 Forensics in the Early 1900s

The early 1900s was a heyday of scientific invention for forensic purposes. Pathologist Karl Landsteiner first detected distinct human blood groups in 1900. The next year in Germany, Paul Uhlenhuth devised the precipitin test to distinguish primate blood from that of other animals. He then found a way to detect the difference between human and animal blood.

In 1902, R. A. Swiss created the first academic curriculum in forensic science. During this era, detectives working with fingerprint evidence sought ways to get acceptance for their methods, which they believed were much more manageable, scientific, and accurate than bertillonage. The case of Will West in Leavenworth Penitentiary in 1903 made the difference. There were two inmates with this name who shared physical measurements so similar they were mistaken as the same person. This proved a blow to anthropometry, but there was one thing that did distinguish these men: their unique fingerprints.

British investigators succeeded with fingerprint evidence in a precarious case that drew the world's attention. A book about the method by Sir Francis Galton had already been published in which he proposed that fingerprints bore three primary features and from them he could devise 60,000 classes. He had worked with Sir Edward Henry, head of Scotland Yard, who had created a classification system based on five pattern types. Henry established the Fingerprint Office, and then Assistant Commissioner Melville Macnaghten from Scotland Yard's Criminal Investigation Department proved the method's value when he used a thumbprint found on a cashbox at the scene of a double homicide to persuade a jury that fingerprinting was a credible and accurate method for identification. Agencies around the world took note, and most quickly replaced their reliance on bertillonage. In the United States, based on expert testimony about a fingerprint left in wet paint in a criminal case, an appeals court declared that fingerprint technology had a scientific basis.

In Germany, George Popp used botanical material as evidence for the first time in 1904, and Oskar and Rudolph Adler developed a presumptive test for blood. During this decade, the Bureau of Investigation—the forerunner of the Federal Bureau of Investigation (FBI)—was established under the presidency of Theodore Roosevelt, and U.S. physiologist Thomas Hunt Morgan demonstrated that chromosomes carry inherited information—a discovery that would one day have implications for crime investigation. In 1910, Albert S. Osborn published *Questioned Documents* to show the forensic value of document examination. Frenchman Edmond Locard set up the first forensic police lab by using scientific analysis on trace evidence to solve crimes. Inspired by Sherlock Holmes, Locard bought microscopes and studied forensic techniques. He believed that criminals had to leave traces of their presence at a crime scene, developing his *exchange principle*. Few people listened to him until he took on a case in 1911 that involved finding the fine dust from counterfeit coins in a perpetrator's pocket and showed that even the smallest traces can help to solve crimes.

During World War I, Albert Schneider of the United States developed a vacuum apparatus to collect trace evidence. Directly after the war, Luke May demonstrated the value of striation patterns for comparisons between specific tools such as screwdrivers and the marks they made. Charles E. Waite took on the ambitious task of cataloguing all U.S. and European guns ever manufactured in terms of construction, date of manufacture, caliber, number, twist of the lands and grooves, and type of ammunition used. He observed that no type was identical to any other and was able to scientifically distinguish which type had fired a specific spent bullet. As Waite's work progressed, his associates invented the invaluable comparison microscope to make side-by-side identifications, along with the helixometer for examining gun barrels.

In Massachusetts, during the 1920s, two men robbed and gunned down two payroll delivery men in South Braintree. Investigators at the murder scene recovered six ejected shell casings and traced them to three manufacturers: Remington, Winchester, and Peters. They arrested Nicola Sacco, 29, and Bartolomeo Vanzetti, 32. Both men had pistols and Sacco's was the right caliber—a .32-caliber Colt automatic—to be one of the murder weapons. Sacco and Vanzetti were convicted of murder and sentenced to be executed, but during their appeals, a committee hired Calvin Goddard to reexamine the evidence. In the presence of defense experts, he fired a bullet from Sacco's gun into a wad of cotton and then placed the ejected casing on a comparison microscope. Next to it, he examined the collected evidentiary casings. Even the defense expert conceded the remarkable similarity. Both defendants went to the electric chair.

Around this time, John Larson and Leonarde Keeler built the first lie detector that measured blood pressure, but a case involving a blood systolic device for deception detection caused the results from using such devices to be barred from the courts. In 1923, *Frye versus United*

States set the first formal standards for admissibility of scientific evidence. Lie detectors were considered not sufficiently proven to the scientific community to be admitted as science.

Forensic evidence in the form of questioned document examination was highlighted in a famous case, that of Nathan Leopold and Richard Loeb. These wealthy young men decided that they could commit the perfect crime, so they murdered 14-year-old Bobby Franks. Forensic investigation based on document examination of their typed ransom note brought them down.

In 1929, Calvin Goddard used scientific analysis to identify the weapons used by Al Capone's hit men in the St. Valentine's Day massacre. This feat inspired the nation's first formal crime lab, the Scientific Crime Detection Lab, privately funded by area businesspersons.

At the Berlin Technical University in Germany in 1931, Max Knoll and Ernst Ruska developed the transmission electron microscope, patterned on the light transmission microscope, except that it relied on a focused beam of fast-moving electrons rather than light to see through a specimen. This enabled scientists to see much smaller objects, enhancing trace evidence examination.

The following year, Calvin Goddard advised the United States Bureau of Investigation, currently known as the FBI, on how to develop its crime lab, and their first pieces of equipment were a microscope and a helixometer. The bureau had set up a national fingerprint file 2 years earlier.

A sensational event in 1932 brought the country's attention to evidence analysis. On a blustery March evening, someone kidnapped Charles Lindbergh's infant son from his Hopewell, New Jersey, home. Lindbergh was an international hero for his historic flight from New York to Paris, so the kidnapping outraged millions. Two months later, the child's remains were found in the woods 2 mi from the home, and it took police 2 years to track down a suspect, Bruno Richard Hauptmann. Although he was in possession of marked bills from the ransom money, Hauptmann insisted he was innocent. When he learned about the polygraph while in prison, he begged to have one administered. But since a federal appeals court had already banned the results of systolic blood pressure deception tests, it seemed of little use to his attorney. After a sensational trial that relied on eyewitness and voice memory, and the analysis of wood grains and handwriting, Hauptmann was found guilty and executed.

Frits Zernike invented the first interference contrast microscope, and Alexander Mearns used the life cycle of maggots to estimate time of death in the trial of Buck Ruxton for the murder of his wife and house cleaner in England. By 1937, Walter Specht developed luminol, which detects latent bloodstains that criminals may have tried wiping away. The following year, at the University of Kharkov, Izmailov and Schreiber introduced simple, thin-layer chromatography. In 1940, Vincent Hnizda pioneered the forensic analysis of ignitable fluids, laying the foundation for arson research.

Bell Labs in the United States used L. G. Kersta's work to develop voiceprint identification. Their sound spectrograph analyzed the frequency and intensity of sound waves to produce a visual record of distinct voice patterns on a graph. Acoustic scientists used the technology to attempt to identify enemy voices on telephones and radios, and decades later, it proved useful for criminal investigation.

In 1967, the FBI started the National Crime Information Center, a computerized index that permitted state and local jurisdictions access to FBI archives on such items as license plate numbers and recovered guns, as well as the ability to post notices about wanted or missing persons. It provided a way to coordinate certain types of national investigations. The FBI also established a plan for the Automated Fingerprint Identification System, which it finally launched in 1975.

The gas chromatograph–mass spectrometer was first evaluated in the United Kingdom for forensic use in 1976. Chromatography was a method by which compounds could be separated into their purest elements, as inert gas propelled a heated substance through a glass tube where a detector charted each element's unique speed for a composite profile. The mass spectrometer linked to the mass detector affirmed the identifications via patterns of spectra. With this equipment, forensic scientists could analyze such items as hair samples for drugs or poison, charred remains for accelerants, and the composition of explosives.

In the late 1970s, the FBI also established the Behavioral Science Unit (BSU) at Quantico for a better approach to the investigation of serial crimes. By 1977, the BSU had a three-pronged purpose: crime scene analysis, profiling, and analysis of threatening letters. As the unit grew, these special agents developed better methods and helped to refine criminology.

Anthropologist William Bass established the Anthropology Research Center at the University of Tennessee in Knoxville to study the condition of corpses for more precise interpretations of time-since-death intervals. It was the only such facility of its kind in the world, bringing the developments in entomology together with anthropology and pathology into an integrated program.

The FBI funded a national computer database, the Violent Criminal Apprehension Program (ViCAP), slated to become the most comprehensive computerized database for homicides nationwide. Police departments around the country were invited to contribute solved, unsolved, and attempted homicides; unidentified bodies in which the manner of death was suspect; and missing-persons cases involving suspected foul play. The FBI then set up the National Center for the Analysis of Violent Crime. The Behavioral Analysis Unit (BAU) was spun off the BSU.

Around this time, a case in Narborough, England, precipitated one of the most dramatic contributions to law enforcement since the discovery of fingerprinting. In 1983 and 1986, two 15-year-old girls were raped and murdered on pathways in adjacent villages. Semen specimens showed the killer's blood type to be A. While a kitchen porter confessed to one incident, he refused to admit to the other, and no physical evidence implicated him in either. Not far away, in Leicester, geneticist Alec Jeffreys had used a process called Restriction Fragment Length Polymorphism (RFLP) to map human genetic profiles via markers in specific regions of the DNA. Since each map was unique to each person, aside from those for identical twins, he named his discovery DNA fingerprinting.

Hearing about this discovery, the Narborough police approached Jeffreys for help, so he put the semen samples through RFLP. There was no match to the suspect in custody, but the samples matched each other, so they were looking for a single suspect. When investigators asked the area's men for DNA samples, they were able to arrest Colin Pitchfork, and he was subsequently convicted of both rape-murders.

Pitchfork's conviction based on DNA evidence was a first for law enforcement. It was also the first DNA-based exoneration: the suspect who had falsely confessed. The rush was on worldwide to apply DNA technology to more crimes, but defense attorneys challenged it, citing contamination during evidence handling (which occurred in the O. J. Simpson trial).

2.1.3 Modern Forensics

By the 1990s, forensic science had become a high-tech arena, with more exacting ways to analyze evidence in many different areas. In 1991, Walsh Automation developed an automated ballistics system, and the following year the FBI commissioned the Drugfire database to store details on the markings of spent bullets and cartridge cases. Other databases were developed for tire prints, paint chips, soil, and nearly any other type of physical evidence commonly found at crime scenes.

DNA also served another unexpected benefit. On June 28, 1993, after nearly 9 years served in prison (including death row) for an act he did not commit, Kirk Bloodsworth was released. Later that year, he was granted a pardon and the State of Maryland paid him $300,000 based on 10 years of lost income. Despite collective eyewitness testimony offered twice, Bloodsworth became the first person who had been sentenced to death to be exonerated with DNA technology. There would be more, eventually shocking the governor of Illinois so much that he placed a moratorium on the death penalty in his state for further review. Defense attorneys Barry Scheck and Peter Neufeld set up the Innocence Project in Manhattan to assist falsely imprisoned inmates. Eventually, every state had a branch.

In 1998, the FBI established CODIS, the Combined DNA Index System, and as the century and millennium turned, the FBI and the Bureau of Alcohol, Tobacco, Firearms and Explosives merged their respective firearms databases to create the National Integrated Ballistics Network. *Cold Hits* entered the terminology as fingerprints from years earlier and DNA from cases with preserved biological evidence were entered into systems and matched to convicted felons.

The BAU evolved once again into the Behavioral Analysis Unit, East and West, divided geographically east and west of the Mississippi River. Then in 1999, based on the Protection of Children from Sexual Predators Act of 1998, the FBI received some mandates related to crimes against children and serial murder. The bureau created the Child Abduction and Serial Murder Investigative Resource Center.

This was the status until after the terrorist attacks on U.S. soil on September 11, 2001.

At this point, the BAU became the Behavioral Analysis Unit 1 (counterterrorism and threat assessment), Behavioral Analysis Unit 2 (crimes against adults), Behavioral Analysis Unit 3 (crimes against children), and the ViCAP Unit, which had broken off from the Profiling and Behavioral Assessment Unit. By restructuring in this way, the BAU developed a concentration of personnel in each unit that possess specialized training and experience in specific areas of responsibility.

The pace of development was so fast and multifaceted that in 2005, Congress directed the National Academies to assess the resource needs of the forensic science community. The National Academy of Sciences (NAS) formed a distinguished committee to hear presentations from relevant organizations, and on February 18, 2009, its members issued a sweeping report, Strengthening Forensic Science in the United States: A Path Forward. While the report acknowledged the many dedicated professionals in the community, it also noted cause for concern. There was too much variability across the disciplines in terms of expert qualifications, reliability of findings, and downright proof of claims. In short, forensic science should develop a better foundation in education, mandatory accreditation, a national oversight agency, and higher standards.

The report became more prominent when Casey Anthony went on trial in 2011 in a media circus nearly as chaotic as the O. J. Simpson trial. The decomposed remains of her 2-year-old child, Caylee Marie Anthony, had turned up in a bag in the woods. The prosecutor believed the remains had been stored for a brief time in the trunk of her car, which had emitted a foul smell when opened. The defense said the odor was from trash. Both sides clashed over an odor identification method, with claims of "junk science" and "fantasy forensics" flung about like rotten tomatoes. Forensic scientists testified on both sides in several different areas, including the emerging discipline of digital forensics. Anthony was eventually acquitted.

2.1.4 Summary

Forensic science has come a long way since its 19th-century practitioners began collaborating with police and testifying in court. Mistakes were made then, as they are now, but these errors only strengthen the determination to get things right. The DNA exonerations have shown that many assumptions about such things as eyewitness testimony and confession evidence are not as reliable as was once believed, and in light of the NAS report, many agencies have reexamined their claims and methodologies. With so many different disciplines involved, and with the increased threat of terrorist incidents, the need for solid science and investigative integrity is paramount.

2.2 Locard's Exchange Principle

This principle, briefly mentioned in the previous section, outlines the exchange of materials between two objects that occurs whenever two objects come into contact with one another. Locard is attributed with the important basic principle of forensic science: "Every contact leaves a trace." As interpreted, this principle means that when a criminal comes into contact with a person or object, there is a cross transfer of evidence. Therefore, a criminal can be connected to a crime by particles on his or her body that originated at the crime scene.

Bibliography

Beavan, C. (2001). *Fingerprints*. New York: Hyperion.

Brown, D. & Tullett, E.V. (1952). *The scalpel of Scotland Yard: The life of Sir Bernard Spilsbury*. New York: E. P. Dutton and Company, Inc.

De River, J.P. (1949). *The sexual criminal*. Springfield, IL: Charles C. Thomas.

Edwards, S. (1977). *The Vidocq dossier*. Boston: Houghton Mifflin Company.

Friedman, L.M. (1993). *Crime and punishment in American history*. New York: Basic.

Fridell, R. (2000). *Solving crimes: Pioneers of forensic science*. New York: Grolier.

Frye versus United States, 293 F. 1013 (D.C. Cir. 1923).

James, S.H. & Nordby, J. (2003). *Forensic science: An introduction to scientific and investigative techniques*. Boca Raton, FL: CRC Press.

Lee, H.C., & Tirnady, F. (2003). *Blood evidence: How DNA revolutionized the way we solve crimes*. Cambridge, MA: Perseus.

Mohr, J.C. (1993). *Doctors and the law*. Baltimore, MD: The Johns Hopkins University Press.

Morton, J. (2001). *Catching the killers: A history of crime detection*. London, UK: Random House.

Owen, D. (2000). *Hidden evidence: Forty true crimes and how forensic science helped solve them*. Buffalo, NY: Firefly Books.

Roughhead, W. (2000). *Classic crimes.* New York: New York Review of Books.

Snyder Sachs, J. (2001). *Corpse: Nature, forensics and the struggle to pinpoint time of death.* Cambridge, MA: Perseus.

Stocking, G.W., Jr. (1987). *Victorian anthropology.* New York: Free Press.

Sung, T. (1981). *The washing away of wrongs.* (B.E. McKnight, Trans.). Ann Arbor, MI: Center for Chinese Studies, University of Michigan.

Symons, J. (1966). *A pictorial history of crime: 1840 to the present.* New York: Bonanza Books.

Thomas, R. (1999). *Detective fiction and the rise of forensic science.* Cambridge, UK: Cambridge University Press.

Thorwald, J. (1964). *The century of the detective.* New York: Harcourt, Brace & World.

Thorwald, J. (1966). *Crime and science.* New York: Harcourt, Brace & World.

Tullet, T. (1979). *Strictly murder: Famous cases of Scotland Yard's murder squad.* New York: St. Martin's Press.

Wilson, C. & Wilson, D. (2003). *Written in blood: A history of forensic detection.* New York: Carroll and Graf Publishers.

3

DEVELOPMENTS OF FORENSIC SCIENCE

In the investigation of crimes, various types of forensic science services can come into play. For the forensic investigator, there are two primary issues that must be addressed when reviewing how a crime scene was processed. First, how was evidence identified? Second, was evidence properly collected and preserved for later analysis? In addition, investigators must understand how different types of evidence are handled.

This chapter details some of the most prominent branches of forensic science that affect the direction of investigations and court proceedings.

3.1 Odontology

Odontology provides identification of unknown victims through teeth in terms of their alignment and the overall structure of the mouth. Odontologists also analyze bite marks left on a victim or on a substance at the crime scene, which might help identify the perpetrator. Since 1970, forensic odontology has been a recognized division of the American Academy of the Forensic Sciences.

3.1.1 History

Forensic dentistry relies on pattern recognition, documentation, and collection. A forensic odontologist, a dentist with training in forensic procedures and courtroom testimony, has two primary roles: identification and comparison analysis. In the former, people can be identified by dental work they had done while alive, as well as by how their teeth have acquired certain wear characteristics. In the latter, teeth are viewed as tools that leave a characteristic mark.

Silversmith and dentist Paul Revere has been called the father of American odontology. In 1776, he identified General Joseph Warren, killed at the Battle of Bunker Hill, from a false tooth he had made.

In Boston in 1849, a murder victim was identified as the missing George Parkman via his jawbone and three teeth. During the trial, Dr. Nathan Keep, Parkman's dentist, described how the jawbone found in a furnace with the false teeth still in it was that of George Parkman. Keep had made an impression of the jaw, and he showed how it fit the jawbone. A defense expert insisted there were no identifying features and placed false teeth of his own making into the mold. However, in rebuttal, three dentists testified that an artist knows his own work.

A landmark criminal case was *Doyle versus State of Texas* in 1954. A bite mark was spotted on a piece of cheese at the scene of a burglary. The suspect was asked to bite a similar piece of cheese and a dentist identified it as a match.

3.1.2 Charting Teeth

The American approach to charting teeth is called the universal numbering system. A number is assigned to each of the 32 adult teeth, beginning at one with the upper right third molar and ending with the lower right third molar. Each tooth has five visible surfaces, and the composite information about each surface makes it possible to make grids (odontograms).

The basic assumption in forensic odontology is that each individual's grid is unique and can thus be used for identification. If an individual has dental disorders, gum problems, chipped teeth, or a poorly formed bite, he or she will be easier to identify.

There are multiple factors to consider, including matching for striations, whorls, indentations, pitting, and abrasions. Over time, teeth can chip, fall out, or become worn. There are also additions, such as restorations, fillings, rotations, and breakage repair, that can make one person's teeth distinct from others.

3.1.3 Characteristics of Bite Marks

For forensic purposes (identification or prosecution), the physical characteristics of both a bite mark impression and the suspect's teeth are collected, including the following information:

- The distance from cuspid to cuspid
- The shape of the mouth's arch
- One or more teeth out of alignment
- Teeth width and thickness
- Discolorations from substances like tea or tobacco
- Spacing between teeth and missing teeth
- Partial or full restoration
- The curves of biting edges
- Unusual dental procedures
- Wear patterns such as chips or grinding

Odontologists learn that biting into fatty areas leaves a less-defined impression than biting into skin over muscle. Also, bite marks made on a victim prior to death have a different appearance from postmortem impressions, which have no associated bruising. Bite marks on a struggling victim will be less defined, which makes the identification tenuous.

3.1.4 Methods of Analysis

Generally, the teeth that leave the strongest impressions from humans are in the front, both top and bottom. Once a mark is considered of human origin, investigators look for a suspect to make a comparison.

The collection of bite mark impressions on human skin requires a specific procedure. First, form a ring around the bite area with a mix of powder and liquid acrylic. After it hardens, the investigator applies a high-resolution casting material. After this sets, another vinyl substance is applied, and then an acrylic layer. Finally, this material is removed and dental stone is poured onto the impression and allowed to harden. The material will capture the shape of the teeth that made the bite.

In the case of a bite wound with a suspect identification, once the suspect is identified, dental impressions or molds are made of his or her upper and lower teeth. From this, the odontologist creates a transparency or uses computer imaging. Photographs are taken of the maximum mouth opening and the way the suspect bites. The bone structure of the jaw is examined, along with the biting dynamics of the muscles and tongue. Sample bites are taken and master casts made. Saliva is also taken for DNA testing. If any of the teeth appear to be recently chipped, ground, or broken, the relative age of this condition is estimated. A continued dental history of suspects should be charted, especially post-incident, because they might attempt to change their bite profile.

During a bite mark analysis, all parts are examined in detail and compared, preferably in a blind test in which the odontologist is unaware of suspect information. (This can be difficult in a high profile case.)

Bite marks on living victims (such as with rape or assault) require special care. Photos should be taken over several stages as healing will change the color and shape of the mark, and eventually it will disappear. Ultraviolet light photography can illuminate details in ways that other light sources do not.

Experts seek a sufficient number of points of similarity between the evidence and a suspect to be able to say with a reasonable degree of certainty that a bite mark was made by the suspect. They identify patterns by examining either a whole or a partial set of teeth. They record every detail about size, appearance, color, and location of the bite on the body or substance, as well as the presence of other bites.

3.1.5 Expert Testimony

The American Board of Forensic Odontology sets guidelines for court testimony: An identification can be declared *positive, probable, possible, not possible* (the suspect is excluded), or *insufficient as evidence to make a definitive statement.* The highest standard is *reasonable medical certainty*, wherein an expert confidently identifies the perpetrator as the person who made a questioned bite mark.

Photographs for use in court involve using two rulers, one laid against the length and one against the width. Older techniques involved hand tracing on clear acetate, and some methods use infrared or filtered procedures.

Properly scaled photographs are important to the legal process, as is the type of equipment used. Cameras with close-focusing capability are best. The camera must be supported to hold steady, because the details must be clear and precise. A wound with a curving surface is photographed from several angles.

Forensic odontologists can also analyze bite marks on food in cases where a perpetrator might have taken a bite out of something in the victim's home and left it behind. Bite marks left on foodstuff offer a three-dimensional (3D) impression.

3.1.6 Status as a Science

In a 2009 comprehensive report for the NAS, the review committee for the forensic sciences stated that forensic odontology "might not be sufficiently grounded in science to be admissible under *Daubert*, but this discipline might be able to reliably exclude a suspect. Although the majority of forensic odontologists are satisfied that bite marks can demonstrate sufficient detail for positive identification, no scientific studies support this assessment, and no large population studies have been conducted. In numerous instances, experts diverge widely in their evaluations of the same bite mark evidence."

Although bite mark analysis has been pivotal in some cases, the science is based largely on anecdotal success rather than on a solid history of standardized testing. Of concern is that no error rate has been examined or identified. Thus, before a court considers bite mark analysis as significant evidence, the edges and shape of a bite mark should be clear, with several experts confirming the evidence independently, and without knowledge of the suspect.

3.1.7 Improvements

Researchers at Marquette University in Wisconsin claim they have developed a computer program that can precisely measure bite mark characteristics. If reliable, it could help build a database by means of which to narrow down suspects.

3.1.8 Conclusion

Although bite mark evidence has been under scrutiny, its founding assumptions are sufficiently sensible to improve its status as a science if controlled studies are undertaken, computers are employed for analysis, and a database is developed.

3.2 Anthropology

According to the American Board of Forensic Anthropology, "Forensic anthropology is the application of the science of physical anthropology to the legal process. The identification of skeletal, badly decomposed, or otherwise unidentified human remains is important for both legal and humanitarian reasons."

Anthropology deals with the identification and examination of human skeletal remains. It can reveal a bone's origin, sex, approximate age, race, and skeletal injury. It can also help in the process of facial reconstruction. Anthropologists have knowledge of biology, cultural diversity, and archaeological techniques in addition to skeletal anatomy.

3.2.1 Areas of Specialization

Anthropology consists of several subfields:

- Physical anthropology—This involves the study of the primate order, past and present, such as primate biology, skeletal biology, and human adaptation.
- Cultural and linguistic anthropology—This is the study of human society and language, both past and present.
- Archaeology—This is the study of past cultures via material remains and artifacts.

To some degree, forensic anthropologists draw on each of these fields, but they generally rely on knowledge from physical anthropology to apply their expertise to skeletal remains. They usually coordinate with others on investigation teams. They can be useful in either civil or criminal contexts and are especially valuable in mass disasters or excavating mass graves.

3.2.2 History

Anthropology crossed into the legal arena during the 19th century, developing the field of criminal anthropology. This involved proving criminality with body measurements. Italian psychiatrist Cesare Lombroso proposed that some people are closer to their primitive ancestors than others. He relied on the work of anthropologist Pierre-Paul Broca to develop his own methods. Lombroso took skull, facial, and bodily measurements from thousands of prisoners to identify anomalies. He believed there was a born criminal who was irresistibly compelled toward a life of crime, that this criminal was an evolutionary throwback to earlier hedonistic races, and that certain physical traits signaled those who belonged to this distinct species.

This theory was central to criminology for many years. The idea that criminal genetic patterns are outwardly manifested influenced film, novels, and real-life investigations, giving rise to the idea that a criminal can easily be spotted.

During the 20th century, anthropologists stopped relying on physical appearance to assess moral nature and leaned more toward a study of the physical and cultural differences among races, but they were still influential in the forensic field. In 1932, the FBI set up the first government crime lab in Washington, D.C., and about 5 years later, the agents discovered that at the Smithsonian Institution nearby were experts in bone analysis. These anthropologists were qualified to consult on the skeletal remains of victims that might otherwise go unidentified, so over the years a team was formed for this purpose.

As the demands grew and many investigative officials asked for assistance from university-affiliated anthropologists, these experts honed their methods for detecting past injuries to bone. They noted indicators of illness or occupation and provided whatever information they could about time-since-death estimates. In 1972, the Physical Anthropology Section of the American Academy of Forensic Sciences was established.

During the late 1970s, Dr. William Bass created the Forensic Anthropology Center at the University of Tennessee at Knoxville, a protected 2-acre field dedicated to the study of decomposing human remains after death that is truly unique. He realized that there was no scientific research establishing time lines for various conditions in which skeletal remains were found. The researchers in this facility analyze soil samples as well as bodies and body parts because by-products of decomposition generally seep into the ground. Thus, scientists can determine how long a body was lying in a particular area or whether it had been placed somewhere else and then moved. The facility is also a teaching center for entomologists, FBI agents, homicide investigators, anthropologists, archaeologists, coroners, and medical examiners.

3.2.3 The Human Skeleton

The fully mature adult human body has 206 bones. They weigh about 12 lb for the average male and 10 lb for females. Aside from sex, height, and age, anthropologists can identify from a set of skeletal remains things such as race, previous trauma, body type, and possible cause of death via poison, knife wounds, blunt force, or bullet holes.

To calculate factors about the bones, they are laid out on an osteometric board and measured with calipers. The basic identifying factors in bones include the following:

- Gender—The male pelvis is narrower than the female, and certain features of the skull are larger in males. The bones tend to be heavier as well.
- Age—In younger people, the stages at which bones are uniting show advancing age. For older people, calcium and other mineral deposits help as well, along with successive changes in the pelvis or evidence of bone diseases like arthritis. Other clues come from the developmental stages in the teeth and from worn areas in enamel.
- Previous trauma—If a bone was broken and there are hospital records, this can help with identification.
- Race—One of three races can be determined from variations in the facial structure, especially the nose and eye sockets. In Negroids and Mongoloids, the nose ridge is broader than in Caucasians.
- Height/stature—An intact corpse can be measured, but a disarticulated or incomplete skeleton has to be pieced together. A program called Fordisc 3.0 provides formulas.
- Body type—Tables provide an estimate based on bone characteristics for determining whether the person was slender, of medium build, or heavy.
- Cause and manner of death—This might be evident in the skull or some of the bones—a knife cut, bullet holes, a blunt weapon fracture, or even a saw to dismember the bones.

Sometimes bones will yield evidence of poisoning as well. Knowledge of biomechanics and bone fracture assist in this process.

3.2.4 Methods

Many of the determinations in forensic anthropology derive from the area of osteology or the study of bones, although some forensic anthropologists specialize in entomology and its relationship to body decomposition. Anthropologists will first determine if a bone is of animal or human origin. If it is human, they will try to determine the gender, age, height, race, trauma, body type, and cause of death.

Forensic anthropologists work on bones that the police bring to them, go out into a field to examine skeletal remains lying in the open, and coordinate archaeological digs. Skeletal remains are sometimes identified by context, using missing persons reports, along with clothing and personal items that might be among the remains.

Careful excavation and accurate mapping of discovered or buried remains can assist in trace evidence collection. If flesh remains on the bones and there is no critical reason to retain it, the anthropologist might x-ray the remains and then boil off the flesh. They might help to interpret outdoor death scenes, provide an interpretation of bone damage, lead a team in the recovery of the remains, and assist in getting remains identified via a biological profile. Aside from serving as consultants, they may also testify in court as experts.

3.2.5 Facial Reconstruction

A forensic anthropologist or forensic artist may also be called in to do a facial reconstruction, known as a forensic sculpture. The skull must first be prepared. Cotton wadding works to support fragile bones and sometimes certain parts of the skull, such as the eye sockets or a bullet hole, can be taped for protection.

Before the physical work begins, the artist or anthropologist gathers all of the information about the case. Artists study various parts of the skull, such as the teeth, to determine how a person had looked before death. Missing teeth are evaluated for whether they fell out before or after death. If after, dentures or partial dentures may be used for the restoration.

One technique involves making a two-dimensional blueprint before making a skull cast. Then holes are drilled in strategic places for inserting thin wooden or vinyl pegs for developing skin and muscle depth. With modeling clay, the muscles and features around the nose, mouth, cheeks, and eyes are carefully built up along the bony structure and a thin layer of plastic or clay goes over the skull. The neck is developed and then ears are formed and attached. Individual features are created from educated guesses about idiosyncrasies; eyebrows and textures are added to humanize the face. If glasses, jewelry, or items of clothing were found with the skeleton, these can be added, along with a wig and prosthetic eyes. Photographs and/or drawings are made for use on posters and in the newspaper.

With the anatomical method, muscles are created individually for making a face. The tissue depth method relies on data about the depth of facial tissue on different faces, collected from 21 points for both genders and all three racial groups. Some approaches combine both methods. No matter which method is used, the artist needs to know a lot about facial anatomy.

At the Forensic Anthropology and Computer Enhancement Services Laboratory, anthropologists use computer-enhanced age progression. A photo of a missing person is scanned into the software, which then predicts structural changes that the face would undergo during specific ages. It morphs the photo into those changes.

3.2.6 Conclusion

Physical anthropologists apply knowledge of osteology and biometrics to found skeletal remains in order to assist law enforcement with recovery, time-since-death estimate, and identification of possible homicide victims. Today, forensic anthropologists are engaged in a diverse array of casework and expert testimony.

3.3 Entomology

Forensic entomology studies the developmental stages of insects and their relation to a criminal investigation. The insects provide indicators about the time that has passed since the person's death, although this is not an exact science. They also indicate something about the climate and locale in which the death may have occurred. The job of the forensic entomologist is to interpret these relationships in order to offer information to law enforcement officers that will assist in leads and to trier of fact in their search for truth in a criminal case.

3.3.1 History

The first documented use of insects in a death investigation occurred in China during the 13th century. After a murder, the culprit was identified by flies alighting on his hand sickle, the murder weapon.

In 1848, Mathieu Orfila had listed the types and succession of insects and arthropods that visited a decomposing corpse to feed and lay eggs. When a couple moved into an apartment in Paris around this time, workers discovered the mummified corpse of an infant lodged between the walls. In their defense, Dr. Marcel Bergeret found that a specific type of fly, *Sarcophaga carnaria*, had deposited larvae on the dead baby. He determined that the child had died before the couple moved in.

This case inspired widespread interest among pathologists, notably Edmond Perrier Mégnin in France. He regularly visited morgues and cemeteries, recording eight distinct stages of necrophilous insect infestation. He published *Fauna of the Cadavers* in 1894, which offered his findings about insects that assisted in estimating the postmortem interval over the course of 3 years.

3.3.2 Characteristics of Insects

Insects are the largest groups of arthropods, characterized by having six legs and a body that is divided into three regions. Spiders, mites, ticks, centipedes, and scorpions are arthropods but not insects. Around 900,000 insect species have been described; only some have forensic application.

3.3.3 Insects and Decomposition

Decomposition consists of two primary processes: putrefaction and autolysis. Bacteria and fungi break down tissues during decomposition;

insects are processors of decomposing tissues and are attracted to cadavers in predictable ways. In some areas, insects can cause a carcass to lose 90% of its weight in 1 week during the summer.

Forensic entomologists analyze insect colonies within a corpse as decomposition progresses. It is also based on the development rates of the various stages of particular insect species. Entomological evidence can help determine the cause of death, movement of a body, and the length of the postmortem interval. For instance, body lice can outlive their host by 3 to 6 days. If body lice are found, either alive or dead, this can give investigators a time line.

As time passes after a death, different groups of insects come and go in the process of assisting corpse decomposition. As each feeds on the body, it changes the body for the next group, which is attracted to those particular changes. Entomologists agree that there are five types of relationships occurring in a specific order:

- The necrophagous species (blowflies and beetles) that feed directly on the corpse and their stages of development over about 2 weeks helps to indicate how long the person has been dead. Blowflies arrive within minutes after death. A female blowfly can lay its eggs immediately after feeding on protein-rich fluids of the body. Blowflies lay their eggs in the body's natural openings, such as the eyes, nose, and mouth, as they offer moist settings that enhance egg and larval survival.
- After the body bloats and active decay begins, beetles are typically the most predominant insects on the remains. Beetle larvae become more predominant over time. These beetles feed on the eggs and larvae of earlier arriving flies, and some beetle species feed directly on the decomposing tissues. Different types of beetles eventually colonize a decomposing carcass. This includes burying beetles, rove beetles, clown beetles, ham beetles, or scarab beetles.
- Predators and parasites of the flies and beetles arrive next. One type of blowfly can feed on either body tissue or maggots. Wasps are also parasitic on the maggots, and since they tend to specialize, it is easy to tell from them what kinds of flies had been on the body.

- Then come wasps, ants, and beetles that feed on both the body and the maggots. (Wasps that capture too many flies can actually delay decomposition.)
- Spiders use the body as a habitat to prey on other insects.

The relationships of the insects to the body are determined by the biology of the insect, although habitat and climatic factors can alter their periods of activity. If the particular insect feeds on dried tissues, it may appear earlier in a hot, arid habitat and possibly not appear at all in a moist habitat. These changes can affect the pattern of succession.

Insects are valuable for other calculations as well. They assist in determining many factors such as the following:

- Determining if the body has been moved following death
- Assessing wounds in terms of before, during, or after the death took place
- Serving as alternate specimens for toxicological analysis
- Providing DNA materials from gut contents
- Supporting or contradicting an alibi

3.3.4 Collection and Preservation

All vials and containers of both preserved and living specimens should include two labels. One label is written in pencil on plain paper and is placed inside the container or vial. The second label is written on adhesive-backed paper and affixed to the outside of the vial. All labels should state the following identifying information:

- Date and time collected
- Case number
- Agency
- Name of collector
- Geographic location of the body
- Location on the body from which the insects were collected

The adult insects should be collected and preserved in ethyl or iso-propyl alcohol. Then investigators should turn their attention to the collection of basic climatological data that will be needed for the ento-mological analysis. The following temperatures should be recorded:

- Ambient air temperature taken at a height of about 4 ft
- Air temperature 1 ft above the upper body surface
- Body surface temperature
- Maggot mass temperature
- Body–ground interface temperature
- Soil surface temperature
- Soil temperature at a depth of approximately 1 in.

All temperatures should be taken with the thermometer shielded from the sun.

The larvae to be collected and kept alive must be placed in a temporary rearing container. A rearing pouch can be made out of an 8 in. sheet of aluminum foil. This sheet is fashioned into a pouch in which a palm-sized piece of beef liver is placed and can sustain 50 to 60 larvae overnight. Once the larvae are on the beef liver, the edges of the foil are crimped together to prevent spillage. The foil pouch is then placed into a container with a tight-fitting lid. Marine plants and animals are best preserved in 10% neutral buffered formalin.

Finally, entomologists search for migrating or wandering larvae, as this can help to establish when they were actually on a body. Migrating larvae are generally older than those on the body. If the remains are indoors, investigators search along baseboards and under rugs, carpet, furniture, and other objects in contact with the floor.

Shipped specimens are packaged in containers and vials in well-cushioned boxes and shipped expediently.

3.3.5 Insect Rearing

Collected maggots are kept alive and can be reared on diets of pork, chicken, beef liver, and pieces of musculature obtained from the corpse. Larvae are transferred with forceps from the temporary rearing containers onto the dietary material and placed on a 4 to 8 cm deep container filled with coarse soil or vermiculite. Each lab culture contains 25 to 50 larvae.

Larval activity and size are recorded daily. Once the adult flies have emerged, they are fed on a cotton pad or ball soaked with sugar water or Gatorade. This provides flight energy and ensures that their exoskeletons will harden and allow for positive species identification.

Emerged adults can be pinned and stored in insect boxes. The adults can also be placed in a 75% ethanol solution.

3.3.6 Climatic Information

Obtaining accurate climate conditions from the location of the corpse is of critical importance. Entomologists record the maximum and minimum temperatures at the scene for three to five days after the discovery of the remains. They also obtain climatic data from the nearest weather station for the entire estimated postmortem period, as well as from the 2- to 3-week interval before the estimated time of death.

3.3.7 Collection Equipment

The following equipment might be needed to collect insects:

- Small toolbox or tackle box
- Collapsible insect net or standard student net
- Trowel
- Plastic evidence or specimen bags
- Fine-point forceps
- Featherweight or soft-touch forceps
- Four-draw vials with Polyseal caps
- Surgical gloves
- Thermometer
- Paper labels
- Adhesive labels
- Yogurt containers for live specimens
- Aluminum foil (potato wrappers are best)
- Vermiculite
- 75% to 80% ethyl alcohol
- Small funnel

3.3.8 Entomotoxicology

Entomotoxicology uses insects as toxicological indicators and the impact of toxins (poisons and drugs) on insect development. Entomotoxicology can give an estimation of the time of death, movement of the remains, postmortem injuries, and the presence of drugs or toxins.

Toxins and contaminants in the tissue have an impact on the development of immature insects. Larval and adult carrion-feeding insects can be used as alternative sources of toxicological information.

However, in studies on the effects of cocaine on the development of the sarcophagid fly, researchers demonstrated that this might not always be the case. In one study, maggots were reared on tissues receiving known dosages of cocaine. Two patterns of development were noted: control and sublethal dosage colonies developed at about the same rate. The colonies that fed on tissues from the lethal and twice-lethal dosages developed more rapidly.

In studies on methamphetamine, there were increases in the rates of development for colonies fed on lethal dosages of methamphetamine. There was also increased puparial mortality in the half-lethal and lethal dosage colonies, and both median-lethal and twice-median-lethal dosage colonies failed to produce viable offspring by the second generation.

3.3.9 Conclusion

Insects may serve as reliable alternative specimens for toxicological analyses in the absence of tissues and body fluids normally sampled for such purposes. In cases of badly decomposed or skeletal remains, analyses of carrion-feeding insects may provide the most accurate qualitative sources of toxicological information.

3.4 Engineering

Forensic engineering is the legal application of mathematical and scientific principles involved in mechanical, chemical, electrical, and metallurgical engineering. These experts deal with failure analysis, accident reconstruction, bioengineering incidents, and causes or origins of fires and explosions. The majority of investigations occur during civil litigation.

3.4.1 The Science of Buildings

Forensic engineers analyze buildings after fires, explosions, collapse, damage from natural disasters, and damage due to neglect or poor construction. They engage in an incident reconstruction based on what they know of a building's behavior under diverse conditions.

Engineers are responsible for determining how a building might have brought harm or death to a victim (or victims), or why it was compromised. Engineers must know the various technical disciplines involved in construction so whenever a failure or catastrophic incident occurs, they can analyze it from every angle. They must understand the design, the composition of materials used, the reputation of the engineers and building companies who were engaged in the construction, the types of errors that could have occurred at different stages, the way a computer simulation might have been used during development, and even the geological surveys for the area. After extensive examination, with mathematical calculations, they can see specifically how a building failed and determine whether there was intentional criminal damage or criminal malpractice.

For example, the Kansas City Hyatt Regency skywalk collapse in 1981 resulted in 114 deaths and 200 injuries. An investigation showed that the original suspension rods had been poorly designed, the result of neglecting to fully evaluate a change in design in order to meet a construction deadline.

3.4.2 Instrument for Analysis

Engineers use instruments like the dielectrometer to locate imperfections inside a structure's walls. It works with an electronic impulse and records the absorption of energy to indicate significant changes in some part of the structure not readily visible. From sophisticated calculations in any crimes involving a building, they can estimate potential damage from different distinct forces. Thus, they can supply a prosecution team with accurate information in cases where the attempt to damage a building was thwarted. They can also advise on how to provide protection in new buildings against future attacks.

3.4.3 Accident Reconstruction

This activity encompasses all types of accidents, including vehicular, electrical, chemical, fire, and industrial.

The most common causes of death by automobile accident include excessive speed, failure to yield the right of way, disregard of a sign or signal, use of substances while driving, and improper passing. Accident reconstructionists apply engineering to an investigator's facts and photos to make an accurate calculation of what happened between two (or more) vehicles or a vehicle and an object. The tool kit might include many different types of screwdrivers, an extendable machinist's mirror, a set of sockets, different types of metric and Allen wrenches, a jackknife, a 3-4-5 triangle, a pad and drawing pencil, chalk, depth gauges, vehicle motion rods, and a tape measure.

For calculations, engineers rely on items such as pre- and postimpact skid marks, road and weather conditions, the final positions of the vehicle or vehicles, mechanical condition of the vehicle, the point and depth of impact, the type of damage to the vehicles or objects, tire conditions, and the travel direction. They will also collect eyewitness accounts, what to expect in terms of performance from the vehicle models, the date of the accident, and the placement of roadway markers that may have been implicated. The best information is the vehicle itself and where it came to rest. Thus, investigators often work backward to establish the incident chronology, including all other known facts. Then an engineering analysis is done to derive the speed at which the vehicle was traveling.

Engineers apply three laws of physics (conservation of energy, conservation of momentum, and equivalency) to organize one of two approaches: the work–energy principle and the impulse–momentum principle.

The first law states that in a physical process, the total energy of the system at the start of the process is equal to the total energy at the end (force = mass times acceleration). The vehicle in motion has kinetic energy, and reducing it to zero when the vehicle is stopped requires that the kinetic energy take another form of energy. Kinetic energy is calculated according to the vehicle's mass and velocity, and reducing it to zero requires energy from brake friction, skidding, or hitting an object. There are equations available for a variety of scenarios.

The momentum method relies on the law that defines momentum as velocity times mass, and adds that for every action there is an equal and opposite reaction. When vehicles collide, they exert opposing forces. Net momentum prior to the impact equals the net momentum after. The accident reconstructionist determines how much momentum was transferred from a vehicle in motion to something against which it impacted.

There is also a calculation of *kinematics*, or the way a person moves in a crashing vehicle. This is related to the injuries sustained. Thus, engineers must also know how accidents impact human biological systems (the application of Newtonian mechanics to biology). To learn about how cars impact pedestrians, cadavers have often been used in impact studies. Injury correlations involve statistics with an error rate. They are not absolute.

3.4.4 Terrorism

With damage from an act of terrorism, forensic engineers rely on blast physics to determine the extent and pattern of the damage, as well as the precise reason for the building's failure. After the terrorist strikes against the World Trade Center in Manhattan in 2001, for example, a committee of experts examined every aspect of the building design to understand how it had collapsed after a commercial airliner strike on the upper floors. The report was issued in 2005, stating that the buildings had withstood the impacts, but the impacts had knocked out the fireproofing, and the subsequent fire had caused the progressive collapse. This analysis was part of the investigation and was also a means for improving design in the future.

Forensic engineers were instrumental in the investigation of the most destructive act of domestic terrorism on American soil, the bombing of the nine-story Alfred P. Murrah Federal Building in Oklahoma City, Oklahoma. Timothy McVeigh had loaded a 5000 lb ammonium nitrate-based bomb into a Ryder rental truck, leaving it parked on the north side of the building on the morning of August 19, 1995. When the bomb exploded at 9:02 a.m., one-third of the building collapsed, killing 168 men, women, and children and injuring another 800.

The resulting crater on that side of the building was 30 ft wide and 8 ft deep, and the blast damaged more than 300 other buildings in the general area. Once the dust was clear and the scene secured, forensic engineers determined which areas were still unsafe and the full extent of the bombing. Working with the FBI Explosives Unit, they evaluated, from the way the building had collapsed, the type of bomb used and whether there had been more than one.

The initial step is to talk with the building engineer of record to learn about the building's design and construction, and then conduct a comprehensive visual inspection (after the building is declared safe to enter). The Alfred P. Murrah Federal Building had been designed and constructed in the mid-1970s, with the involvement of several companies, but the structural engineer and general contractor were located, along with original drawings and plans. They found that, although the building met state codes for wind resistance and loads from normal office use, there had been no consideration in the design for extreme conditions such as an earthquake or explosion. The collapse appeared to have been initiated when two or more bomb-damaged columns on the north side failed. In essence, the building was ordinary reinforced concrete framing with reinforced columns, girders, and beams. The team concluded that crushing had caused the majority of injuries.

The Federal Emergency Management Agency (FEMA) assembled a Building Performance Assessment Team (BPAT), which included civil, government, and U.S. Army engineers. They created 157 architectural drawings from which to work and collected samples from different areas of the blast site. In such incidents, forensic engineers look for ground zero, the point of origin of the collapse, and the BPAT found that in the exploded truck. Checking around, they learned that an audiotape existed from a meeting conducted in a building across the street, with which they could do an acoustic analysis. Construction Technology Laboratories in Illinois analyzed sections of concrete and structural bars to provide information about the building's physical properties.

To develop a plan for a new building that would have reduced the progressive collapse by 95%, thereby reducing fatalities and other collateral damage, they utilized FEMA's 1994 report about reducing earthquake hazards in new buildings. When the investigation was completed, the building was demolished.

3.4.5 Product Safety

This area examines whether a product was defective in relationship to injuries or death. There are three types of defects:

- Design defects
- Manufacturing defects
- Failure to warn or instruct a user in safe use

Identification procedures during design include examining a system via component parts, examining an undesirable outcome in relation to the item, and a product safety audit checklist to minimize probability of an injury.

Workplaces also are examined for safety issues to avoid slip and fall accidents. Biomechanical research is at the forefront of research for slip resistance and predictable movement across a surface.

3.4.6 Conclusion

Forensic engineering is a rapidly growing field of research and application, especially for building evaluation and product safety. Engineers must have a solid background in physics and mathematics. They must also know about laws that apply to areas such as accident reconstruction, building failure, and biomechanics.

3.5 Pathology

Forensic pathology is a medical specialty that determines cause and manner of death in situations falling under the jurisdiction of the local medical examiner or coroner.

3.5.1 History

The early anatomists who dissected corpses gained support when the Emperor Charles V decreed in the 1500s that medical expertise be relied upon in all trials involving suspected murder or abortion. They noticed how things like rigor mortis (state of muscle rigidity) and algor mortis (the body's cooling temperature) worked, and to the list, they also added the progressive changes in coloration known as livor mortis or lividity (blood settling at the lowest point of gravity).

In the late 1700s, French physician Pierre Nysten provided Nysten's law to the effect that the decomposition process begins in the face and neck and moves downward through the body. In England, Dr. John Davey added a scientific time clock with thermometers to measure the diminishing body temperature.

Medicolegal death investigation in the United States today is carried out by coroners or medical examiners. The coroner system derives from the British *Charts of Privileges*, as the office of crowner or tax collector. They summoned inquest juries for people who were seriously wounded or had died from misadventure. Eventually the office evolved into that of a death investigator.

Beginning in the 19th century in the United States, some states replaced the coroner with a medical examiner (ME), who was usually a physician. The duties of any death investigator are to determine the cause and manner of death and, if possible, the time of death. A coroner will generally bring a discovered body to a forensic pathologist for an autopsy unless a treating doctor acknowledges that the individual was ill and the death was from natural causes. The ME, with medical background, can perform an autopsy.

In 1959, forensic pathology was formally acknowledged as a subspecialty of pathology.

3.5.2 Death Investigation

Only licensed physicians with training in forensic pathology should perform medicolegal autopsies. One year of training in forensic pathology and a full pathology residency are the minimum requirements.

Death investigation involves reconstructing an incident, with the manner of death being the result of a homicide, suicide, accident, or natural causes. (Sometimes the manner of death cannot be clearly determined.) Thus, forensic pathologists would assist with violent, unexpected, unexplained, or suspicious death incidents.

A reconstruction is the process of determining the events and actions that occurred during the death event, including the examination and interpretation of physical and behavioral evidence. This process follows the scientific method. Experience, sound logic, and careful observation are necessary for an accurate reconstruction.

Until the coroner or ME arrives at a scene, no one should move the body. The ME may perform certain initial examinations to acquire information that might otherwise be lost.

Many deaths that occur outside the presence of another person are categorized as *unattended*. In other words, the person died in a place other than a hospital, hospice, or long-term care facility, and no physician had recently examined that person for some illness. Generally, any deaths not the result of natural causes, such as a disease or old age, are investigated. Even natural deaths may be subject to investigation when the cause is in doubt. The laws (and economics) of the jurisdiction in which the death occurred govern the methods and means, including how extensive an investigation can be.

At the scene, death investigators make preliminary notes and direct the photographer to take specific photographs. They may also take the body temperature and examine the eyes. They should also note the presence of blood at the scene and whether it approximates the amount of bleeding that would ensue from a specific type of wound. If insects are present on the body or the remains are skeletal, the ME may call in a forensic entomologist or anthropologist.

3.5.3 The Autopsy

The ME or coroner decides if there will be an autopsy, which is generally the practice for any unattended death and always for a homicide. An autopsy is a postmortem medical examination of a corpse to determine the manner and cause of death for an official report. Around one out of four deaths are thus investigated. The autopsy may be partial, selective, or complete. A partial autopsy examines only the injured part of the body, while a selective autopsy may only involve one specific organ.

Although the autopsy suite might differ from one place to another, it will often include a steel autopsy table equipped for draining away liquids. Next to it is a smaller dissection table for cutting up and examining organs. Near that is a hanging scale for weighing them as they are removed. A large tank on the floor collects fluids.

Before anything is done to it, the body gets photographed, both clothed (if it was clothed when found) and unclothed. Then it is x-rayed, weighed, fingerprinted, and measured, and any identifying marks are recorded. Old and new injuries are noted, along with tattoos and scars. Trace evidence, such as hair and fibers, is collected off the body and from under the fingernails before it is cleaned. Even the nails are clipped. The wrapping sheet, along with clothing and trace evidence, is sent for analysis. In cases of suspected suicide by gunshot, hands are swabbed for gunpowder residue.

A crime scene photographer may also take photographs (or videotape) during the autopsy. Generally, the pathologist will direct the photographer as to what photos are needed, and color film is always used. Close-ups are made of all wounds, tattoos, scars, or bruises, and these are framed with a ruler laid next to the wound or mark. Photos are taken again after a wound is washed or a body part is shaved.

The clean body is laid out on the steel table with a stabilizing block placed under the head. The pathologist makes a Y incision, which is a cut into the body from shoulder to shoulder, meeting at the sternum and then going straight down the abdomen into the pelvis. This exposes the internal organs.

The pathologist uses X-rays of injuries or a lodged bullet as a guide. The next step is to take a blood sample and remove the organs to weigh them. Samples are taken of fluid in the organs, and the stomach and intestines are slit open to examine contents. Samples of everything that seems relevant to the case are taken and sent to the lab for further analysis.

The last step is to examine the head. An incision is made in the scalp behind the head and the skin is peeled forward over the face to expose the skull. The skull is opened and the brain is lifted out, examined, and weighed.

3.5.4 Virtual Autopsies

Virtual imaging can produce a 3D image without cutting the body open. A combination of CT scans for an overview of the body and magnetic resonance imagining can detect many ailments in the organs and muscles. With imaging, pathologists can go right to the problem without having to slice up everything else. Interpretation requires a radiologist trained in forensic procedure. It is easier on juries to see computer images than actual autopsy photographs, and this technique eliminates the destruction of forensic evidence. In addition, the digitized images can easily be stored or sent to other pathologists for consultations.

3.5.5 Death Certificate

On the official form, when the death is not natural, the coroner or ME records the circumstances surrounding the death, along with all available information about the deceased person. They include the results of the external examination and a list of physical characteristics. When the examination is complete, they include the cause of death and sign the form. This is presented as the official statement to families and the court.

3.5.6 Conclusion

Forensic pathology is a subspecialty of medical pathology specific to a medicolegal investigation. Some pathologists can conduct their own investigations. Their analytical and scientific focus is the human corpse with the intent of determining the manner of death.

3.6 Psychology

Psychologists and psychiatrists work with individuals who have a variety of mental illnesses within the context of the criminal or civil arenas of the law. It also focuses on the many intersections of mental health and law, including policy, and assists with interpreting behavioral evidence at a crime or death scene.

3.6.1 Areas

The discipline of forensic psychology concerns any arena in which the legal system requires services or testimony from a behavioral scientist. While most practitioners are clinicians with knowledge of forensic issues, this discipline involves a range of specialties in both the civil and criminal arenas. These areas include consulting on criminal investigations, assessing threats of violence, determining the fitness of a parent for guardianship, developing specialized knowledge of crimes and motives, evaluating the effects of sexual harassment, consulting on sentencing guidelines, developing prison programs, and conducting research that has forensic implications.

For the legal arena, forensic psychologists most typically evaluate a defendant's present psychological state for competency to participate in some area of the legal process, or they assess a defendant's mental state at the time of an incident in which he or she was allegedly involved. In addition, psychologists appraise behaviors such as malingering, confessing, deception, or acting suicidal.

Outside the courtroom, psychologists have some presence in emergency service fields such as fire control, corrections, and law enforcement. They may be asked to provide assessments on preemployment exams for police officers, fitness for duty evaluations, and special unit evaluations. In addition, they might assist in mass disaster training and counseling.

As a consultant, psychologists might assist a forensic artist to get an accurate facial reconstruction, help with finding motive in an incident, or advise an attorney on jury selection. They can defuse a potentially violent situation with negotiation or risk assessment and aid death investigators with reducing ambiguity in a death determination. Some forensic psychologists work for police departments, while many others are employed in prisons or forensic hospitals. Quite a few have private practices and consult or perform assessments on the side.

3.6.2 Qualifications as Experts

Forensic psychologists must know the expectations of the court, so as to offer information that will facilitate the decision making of the trier of fact (judge or jury). They must be aware of landmark cases relevant to the issue on which they offer expertise, learn proper courtroom protocol, and fulfill the requirements to be qualified as experts. They also must be fully prepared to explain to a jury how they arrived at their findings. This most often involves a firm grasp of psychological assessment instruments, the procedures for making a standard diagnosis, or methods of statistical analysis in the behavioral sciences.

An important qualification is to be an excellent psychiatrist or psychologist. A person who is certified in forensic psychiatry or psychology but does not practice in a treatment setting cannot represent that he or she is as qualified to assist the court on mental illness issues as a person who regularly makes diagnostic and treatment decisions.

The forensic psychologist or psychiatrist should assist the court or hiring attorney in all aspects of case management from recommending sources of information to training for deposition to offering input on prospective jurors to preparation for trial.

3.6.3 Clinical Forensic Evaluations

Unlike therapeutic contexts, the forensic evaluation recognizes the agendas of opposing parties and the interest of the defendant. Approaching the evaluation involves the presumption of skepticism versus the acceptance of face value in a regular clinical consultation. The clinician must also address the subject of the lack of confidentiality and ask for a signed acknowledgement of understanding.

Standardized psychological assessment is central to a broad spectrum of clinical-forensic contexts. Assessments can be done for the court, the government, insurance companies, or any other decision-making fact finders involved in legal issues.

Psychologists present results from test data and clinical interviews. Forensic assessment instruments measure intelligence, personality traits, motor skills, neurological conditions, potential for deception, and inclination for criminal behavior. A common battery includes the Wechsler Adult Intelligence Scales, the Minnesota Multiphasic Personality Inventory, the Rorschach inkblot test, and, when organic damage is suspected, neuropsychological testing. The diagnostic question is the primary guide for selecting assessments. Some assessments serve clinical more than forensic purposes because they lack scientific methodology.

3.6.4 Competency

In *Dusky versus United States* in 1960, the Supreme Court set standards for defining mental competency. Accordingly, to be judged competent, defendants must show a rational and factual understanding of the charges: They must possess sufficient present capacity to understand the criminal process, to function in that process, and to consult with counsel. They must show that they understand the roles played by the various participants and must be able to plan or assist in the planning of their defense.

Competency examinations are performed in both criminal and civil cases, most often concerning competency to stand trial. However, there are other competencies that can affect different stages of the criminal process: competencies to waive one's Miranda rights (right to silence and to legal counsel), to confess, to understand the nature of the crime committed, to testify, and to refuse an insanity defense and even competency to be executed. In civil cases, competency screenings cover things such as parenting capacity in child custody suits, guardianship, and consent to treatment.

A judgment of incompetency prompts the court to transfer the defendant to treatment facilities charged with restoring competency. Sometimes competency can be restored with education about the legal process, but more often treatment involves psychoactive medication.

3.6.5 Insanity and Responsibility

Forensic psychologists also assess a defendant's state of mind during the commission of a crime, referred to as the mental state at the time of the offense (MSO). A finding of insanity aims toward an acquittal or mitigating a sentence. The legal system recognizes that responsibility for committing a crime depends on two things: *actus reus*, evidence that the accused engaged in the act, and *mens rea*, the mental state required to have intended to commit the act and foreseen its consequences.

The standard for determining criminal responsibility varies by state, but in the concept of a trial, insanity is not a diagnostic but a legal concept. It is not synonymous with serious mental illness. One can be psychotic and also be judged sane because he or she understood that the nature of the act was wrong. One can also be judged temporarily insane while having no mental illness.

To make a determination of the MSO, the clinician must examine the defendant's actions, circumstances, and perceptions leading up to the crime and coordinate these findings with law enforcement reports. Mental health defenses to crime include insanity, automatism, diminished capacity, battered woman defenses, delirium from medical conditions, and involuntary intoxication.

The MSO evaluation invariably appraises the motive behind a crime; the more absent a rational motive, the more readily a psychologist may consider an irrational motive that may herald impaired appreciation of wrong, inability to conform conduct, or impaired appreciation of the nature and consequences of actions. MSO also encompasses temporary insanity and other mental impairments such as extreme emotional disturbance.

There is an exception to lack of appreciation for a finding of insanity: the deific decree. When defendants claim that God told them to do it, they do know it is wrong. However, in their minds, God's law supersedes social rules. Thus, they can know that an illegal act is wrong but still be eligible for an insanity defense.

3.6.6 Corrections

In prison, psychologists assist to classify prisoners for mental health programs or medication, assess mental illness, treat it, consult on program design, assist with crisis intervention, and conduct research. They may also be called in for risk evaluation during parole and probation hearings.

3.6.7 Behavioral Evidence

Among the most popular arenas of forensic psychology is profiling, or the method the FBI's BAU utilizes to link serial crimes and to discern motive and offender personality issues. Private forensic psychologists may also consult on the behavioral analysis of crime scenes. A profile is an educated attempt to provide investigative agencies with parameters about the type of person who committed a certain crime or series of crimes, based on the idea that people inevitably will leave behavioral evidence. From a crime scene, a profiler can assess whether the person is an organized predator as opposed to committing an impulsive crime of opportunity, or observe if an offender used a vehicle, shows criminal sophistication, pays attention to the investigation, or is acting out a particular type of sexual fantasy.

Behavioral evidence is also important for psychological autopsies, in which psychologists can assist to disambiguate a death incident with psychological factors. This often involves expertise in suicidology.

Psychologists also may be involved in risk assessment, which can be part of a parole hearing or a potentially explosive situation at a workplace or school. This area of the discipline has improved over the past two decades, although it still is quite tricky to know just how great a risk an individual might be to become violent. There must be a balance between recognizing when threats are just venting or when they may be rehearsals for a likely scenario.

3.6.8 Research

Academic psychologists take on research issues that apply to the legal system, such as eyewitness memory, false confession, deception detection, neuropsychology and violence, post-traumatic stress disorder, and repressed memory. If they have sufficient expertise in a given area that is relevant to a case, they qualify as expert witnesses.

3.6.9 Conclusion

Forensic psychology covers a broad spectrum of issues in the investigative and legal system. Although these matters are primarily clinical, they can also encompass other behavioral contexts, especially for research and consulting.

3.7 Botany

Botany is the application of plant science to legal questions. Trace botanical evidence can give vital information about a crime scene or a suspect because a plant's anatomy and its ecological requirements are, in some cases, species specific.

Becoming a forensic botanist requires education in botany and/or biology, with expertise in subdisciplines of anatomy, ecology, systematics, molecular biology, and plant chemistry.

3.7.1 History

Forensic botany got a start in 1873 when a pathologist, Dr. Alfred Swaine Taylor, found microscopic plant life in the lungs of a drowning victim. He examined the diatoms and realized that they were from a body of water other than the one in which the deceased had been found. This discovery flagged the death as a homicide.

Although plants are ubiquitous, their morphological diversity makes it possible to compare among them and make matches between samples. Similar to the uniqueness of a fingerprint, plant material is often unique to certain species or ecological areas. Developments in DNA analysis have made this identification more precise. Plant material that can be useful for forensic botany includes seeds, flowers, leaves, wood, pollen, spores, twigs, cells, and hairs. Ecological and molecular factors assist a forensic botanist to narrow the possibilities of crime times and locations and, in some cases, a suspect. Aquatic species are helpful to determine a death by drowning in a type of water other than in which the victim was found.

Assessment of evidence frequently requires access to databases and reference collections. For these reasons, investigative laboratories have generally relied on botanists who are employed by universities, museums, or botanical gardens.

3.7.2 Plant Typology

Plants are either vascular or nonvascular. Vascular plants have evolved specialized tissues: xylem is involved in structural support and water conduction, and phloem functions in food conduction. They possess roots, stems, and leaves, representing a higher form of organization that is characteristically absent in plants lacking vascular tissues. Nonvascular plants are more dependent on the environment that surrounds them to maintain appropriate amounts of moisture and tend to inhabit damp, shady areas.

3.7.3 Plant Cell Structure

Plant cells have a membrane-bound nucleus, and the DNA is housed within the nucleus. Plant cells also contain other membrane-bound organelles, or cellular structures, that carry out specific functions necessary for cellular operation. Plant cells are generally larger than animal cells and are typically rectangular or cube shaped. There are at least 260,000 species of plants in the world today.

3.7.4 Applications

Botanical evidence has helped to identify clandestine graves. After soil has been dug up and replaced, certain plants quickly spread on the surface, making it distinct from surrounding plants of the same type. Other species follow in succession as the area recovers. However, to the trained eye, the plant composition and distribution is different from the original plant growth in the area. In addition, body decomposition can affect the soil and either promote or inhibit growth.

Analysis of plant materials for forensic purposes requires expertise in one or more of several plant science subdisciplines such as anatomy, palynology, ecology, molecular biology, or plant chemistry.

For example, forensic palynology is the study of pollen and spores in criminal investigations. Pollen and spores are seasonal and often geographically specific, so they can help to link a suspect, victim, or object to a particular place. The seasonal production of certain pollens can help investigators develop a time line for a particular event. The production and dispersal patterns of spores and pollens are known as pollen rain. Anemophilous, or wind pollinated, are the most common type. Palynology can be important in drug detection, since substances such as cannabis and cocaine are derived from plants. Techniques may be able to link drug samples to a specific batch or location.

It may also be possible to obtain trace evidence from plant cells found in gastric contents. These materials may help investigators pinpoint the rough time of the victim's last meal.

3.7.5 Essential Evidence

A famous criminal case involved the wood analysis in the trial for the kidnapping and homicide of Charles Lindbergh, Jr., in 1935. Arthur Koehler, an employee of the Forest Products Laboratory at the United States Forest Service, testified for the prosecution that wood from the kidnapper's ladder matched a piece of flooring cut from the kidnapper's attic. He had identified the plant species (birch, pine, and Douglas fir) and structural patterns, as well as tool marks left on the wood.

In the 1960 kidnap and murder case of 8-year-old Graeme Thorne in Australia, seeds from a rare type of cypress found in pink mortar on the body told investigators that the body had been moved from the murder site (no such mortar was present where the body was found). A cypress tree found in a garden of a house that also had been built with pink mortar pointed the police in the right direction. Inside, they found a tassel from a rug that had belonged to the boy's family. Further evidence, including hair analysis from a dog, built a case against Stephen Bradley, who was convicted and sentenced to life imprisonment.

Plant DNA was first analyzed in a 1992 murder case in Arizona. Denise Johnson was found on May 2, strangled, bound, and left nude near a cluster of Palo Verde trees in a remote part of Maricopa County. A pager belonging to Earl Bogan lay nearby and a witness had seen a specific type of white truck leave the area—the same type driven by Bogan's son, Mark. The truck was seized for a search, which turned up seedpods in the back area from a Palo Verde tree. However, there was no trace of Johnson inside the cab. Still, Brogan admitted that he had picked her up for consensual sex. He also said that he had dropped her off. When confronted with the pager, he said that Johnson had stolen it from him. Investigators looked for a way to use the pods as evidence.

Dr. Timothy Helentjaris, a professor of molecular genetics, tested the pods from the truck with Randomly Amplified Polymorphic DNA, a technique known for several years among plant geneticists. He compared other trees in the area and matched the crime-related pods to a specific tree, which was near where the body was found. This tied Brogan's truck to the crime scene area. This tree also bore a recent gash, which was the height of the truck's back bumper. The collection of evidence suggests that Bogan had killed Johnson, dropped the pager, backed into the tree (shaking pods into the back), and left. He was convicted of first-degree murder, upheld on appeal against the unique new method.

3.7.6 Time-since-Death Estimates

Trees and roots are useful for determining how much time has passed since a death, or the postmortem interval. Many plants and trees grow in annual cycles that vary with environmental conditions, so growth rings can be counted, especially if the roots grow through clothing or bone. Even partial damage to root growth can suggest the period since an interruption occurred. It also can help to establish the age of a grave.

Cher Elder had been missing since March 31, 1993. A suspect was identified in Tom Luther, a man who was seen with her at a casino in Central City, Colorado, before she went missing. He was a convicted sex offender who had nearly killed a woman after a brutal rape. An informant told police that Elder had been buried off Interstate 70, near a stone marker. An independent team of specialists called NecroSearch went to the area, but was unable to locate the grave.

In 1995, another informant described an area that Luther had pointed out to him. With a hand auger, the team drilled a deep hole and found adipocere, a soap-like substance made from body fat. After 2 days of painstaking archaeological work, they located the skeletal remains of Cher Elder. A botanist helped to determine from plant roots the age of the grave, which matched the time that a witness placed Luther in the area, and bullet fragments were found in Elder's skull that matched to a gun Luther once had owned. A jury convicted him of second-degree murder.

3.7.7 Forensic Limitations

Some plant materials are too common for unique identification. Pollen, for example, can be found wherever one finds plants, and if fresh pollen falls on an unprotected crime scene or half-dug grave, it cannot be distinguished from evidential pollen.

With postmortem interval estimates, false or distorted rings can result in a faulty calculation. Also, if a body has been covered under vegetation from the area at the time of burial, the plant could influence a longer postmortem interval estimate than the body does. In contrast, decomposition processes may delay the growth of a plant and cause a plant younger than the burial to be present on the surface.

3.7.8 Conclusion

Although botany is considered a minor area of forensic science, experts in this area can assist with different aspects of death investigation, particularly time since death estimates.

3.8 Serology

Serology involves the analysis of the properties and effects of serums—blood, semen, saliva, sweat, and fecal matter. Biological evidence is often found at crime scenes. It might be fresh liquid, coagulated, dried, or in the form of spatters, a small drop, or a stain. Since the advent of DNA analysis, more laboratories rely on it than on past serological markers.

3.8.1 Blood Properties

Human bodies contain about 10 pt of blood, which is a multicomponent fluid that circulates through the body to distribute oxygen and nutrients and collect waste. When wounded, the heart's pumping action makes bodies leak or spray blood, and its behavior in flight tends to remain uniform.

One of the earliest ways to link a suspect to the victim was through the analysis of blood types. In 1901, Karl Landsteiner named and standardized the different blood types. Separating red blood cells from the plasma in a centrifuge, he added red blood cells from other subjects and found two distinct antigen reactions—clumping and repelling. Landsteiner labeled these reactions type A (antigen A present, anti-B antibody present, antigen B absent) and B (antigen B present, antigen A absent). When he found both antigens A and B absent, the blood became type O. Another serum discovered later was labeled AB (both antigens present). In the human population, types A and O are most common, and AB the rarest. With only four categories, finding a specific type at a scene does not identify a suspect but it can eliminate those who have other blood types.

As it evolved over the next few decades, blood typing involved identifying many different enzymes and proteins that perform specific activities in the body. More than 150 serum proteins and 250 cellular enzymes were isolated, as well as many more antigens. Identifying them helped to individualize a sample, but as markers, they are less stable than their DNA counterparts.

Serology also made another important discovery for forensic investigation. Around 80% of the members of the human race were found to be secretors, which means that the specific types of antigens, proteins, antibodies, and enzyme characteristic of their blood can be found in other bodily fluids and tissues. By examining saliva, semen, and even teardrops, analysts can tell the blood type.

3.8.2 Biological Identification Methods

Forensic serologists now focus on identifying biological stains, documenting them, determining their origin, and preserving them as potential evidence. Before applying typing tests, it must first be determined that a stain is blood or that blood was once present. Investigators use a presumptive test that will differentiate between blood and other substances. A positive result is an indication to use other tests to confirm.

The first test involves moving a powerful light, such as a laser, across every surface. Most screening tests for blood are color tests, based on the property of the heme portion of hemoglobin in the red blood cells to catalyze the release of oxygen from hydrogen peroxide. Chemicals, such as o-tolidine, phenolphthalein (Kastle–Meyer test), tetramethylbenzidine, and luminol have been used.

The Kastle–Meyer color test relies on a solution of phenolphthalein and hydrogen peroxide. First, a cotton swab is rubbed through the area suspected to be blood. Then a drop of phenolphthalein is applied, followed by a drop of hydrogen peroxide. If blood of any quantity is present, it turns pink or red within about 15 seconds. However, it also turns pink in the presence of potatoes or horseradish.

A positive screening test should never be considered conclusive for the presence of blood. A confirmatory test is required to show that blood is present. Manufactured test strips are used in most labs for this process. The stain is soaked in saline and a few drops are added to the strip. Within 10 minutes, the human bloodstain will give a positive result.

Investigators may also use the precipitin test to determine whether the blood is of animal or human origin. Either a sample of the questioned blood is put into a test tube over the rabbit serum or it is used in the gel diffusion test, where it is placed in gel on a glass slide next to a sample of the reagent (anti–human serum). By stimulating it with an electric current, the protein molecules filter toward each other. If a line forms where they meet—called a precipitin line—the sample has a human origin.

If blood is suspected but not observed, a chemical reagent called luminol can be sprayed across the scene because it reacts to blood and makes it luminescent. It only takes about 5 seconds to produce a bluish glow when the area is darkened. The intensity of the glow increases proportionately to the amount of blood present. However, a limitation of luminol is that it can destroy the blood's properties. It also reacts to other substances that are not blood, such as bleach.

Another technique uses the fluorescein reagent. It works like luminol, although it requires two successive coatings of different solutions. Fluorescein is illuminated with a UV light, and since it persists much longer than luminol, it can be better for photographs.

3.8.3 Bodily Fluids

With the advent of DNA testing during the 1980s, some serological techniques were discarded. In recent years, serological analysis has been limited to identifying the type of biological evidence that might be present in a sample.

Statistics show that the greatest number of crimes against persons in which DNA is used is that of sexual assaults. The most common screening method for semen is the acid phosphatase test. Acid phosphatase is usually present in high levels in semen but can also be found in other substances such as plant matter, so the presence of semen in a stain must be confirmed. This is easily done by identifying spermatozoa under a microscope or by using test strips to detect the human seminal protein, p30, also called prostate-specific antigen.

Tests may also be conducted to identify other biological substances such as saliva, urine, gastric fluid, and fecal matter. After biological evidence has been characterized, DNA analysis may be conducted. However, only about 30% to 40% of forensic cases contain biological materials that may be suitable for DNA analysis, and not all DNA test results provide information for case investigation.

3.8.4 Pattern Interpretation

With violent crimes, blood is the body fluid most likely to be encountered. Bloodstain patterns can offer crucial evidence in the reconstruction of a crime scene. When blood flies through the air, the pattern in which it lands can determine its track as well as the location and position of the weapon that inflicted the blow. When layered, one spatter atop another, it can also provide an estimate of how many blows were struck and how much momentum a murder weapon may have been given.

Blood pattern experts examine many different things, including the type of injuries on a body, the order in which the wounds were received, whose blood is present and in what locations, the type of weapon that caused the injuries, whether the victim was in motion when struck, whether the victim was moved from one spot to another, and where blood spray or drops landed in terms of travel distance and patterns.

The most essential aspects of the bloodstains at a scene for interpretation are size of spots and velocity of drops at impact with a surface that can record them. In the 1930s, Scottish pathologist John Glaister classified blood splashes into distinct categories, based on the energy needed to disperse it and on projectile angles, which many experts still rely on today:

- Circular marks come from blood ejected with relatively little force that strikes a surface at right angles.
- Crenellated marks are made by blood flying at a good clip or falling a distance to a surface below.
- Elliptical blood drops strike a surface at an angle, and their degree of elongation can help to calculate the area of origin.
- Splashes with long tails come from blood flying through the air and hitting a surface at an angle of 30% or less. The tail points back in the direction from which the drop came.
- Spurts that come from a major artery or vein produce a strong blood spray.
- Smears left by pressing a bleeding body part against a surface leave a transfer pattern.
- Trails may take the form of smears when a bleeding body is dragged, or droplets when someone wounded walks or is carried for some distance.

Assuming blood generally moves in a straight trajectory with a slight arc and a fine mist indicates more force than large droplets, bloodstain patterns can assist investigators to figure out the positions and the means by which the victim and suspect interacted and possibly struggled through a crime scene.

3.8.5 Conclusion

Many violent incidents involve bodily fluids, particularly blood, and the field of serology has contributed to forensic investigations for over a century. Refinements in blood analysis have yielded to the more precise DNA analysis for identification, but blood spatter pattern analysis remains a key part of homicide investigations.

3.9 Toxicology

Toxicology is the detection of substances in human tissue that can have a noxious effect, and forensic toxicology has a medicolegal application. Investigation requires knowing what substance is present and in what amounts.

3.9.1 History

Toxicological analysis for investigative purposes goes back to more than 200 years. The first person to suggest a chemical method for the detection of poisons was Dr. Herman Boerhaave. It consisted of placing substances suspected of containing poison like arsenic on red-hot coals and then testing the odors.

In 1787, Johann Daniel Metzger discovered that when arsenious oxide was heated with charcoal, it formed a black mirrorlike deposit on a cold plate held over the coals. That substance was arsenic. Then in 1806, Valentine Rose showed how to detect arsenic in human organs. Around the same time, in 1813, Mathieu Joseph Bonaventure Orfila published *Treatise of General Toxicology*, a classification of the known poisons. Orfila was further assisted by the work of the next prominent chemist, James Marsh, who created the Marsh test to help jurors see and understand the testing process.

As killers learned that arsenic was easily detected and prosecuted, they turned to other substances to achieve their goals. Scientists had to develop new tests for law enforcement.

Another major development was the need for methods for detecting the presence of vegetable alkaloids, such as caffeine, quinine, morphine, strychnine, atropine, and opium. These poisons affect the victim's central nervous system.

3.9.2 Areas of Analysis

Forensic toxicologists most often engage in postmortem analysis, human performance analysis, and drug testing interpretation. The toxicology (tox) section is standard to any crime lab since so many victims have drugs or poisons in their systems or have been exposed to environmental hazards. Examples of poisons that have been commonly used in murder include aconitine, atropine, strychnine, thallium, antimony, arsenic, and cyanide. Toxicology analysis also covers alcohol, industrial chemicals, poisonous gas, illegal drugs, or drug overdoses.

Sometimes, a procedure involves analyzing a blood, hair, or urine sample; other times, it requires a full autopsy in which tissue samples are removed from various organs. A living person might be tested for a suspected substance with a basic kit, such as a breath test for detecting alcohol levels. If the test registers a positive result or if symptoms show something different, a more sophisticated analysis may be required.

3.9.3 Need for Analysis

The American Chemistry Society indicates there are around 21 million registered compounds, but there are screening tests for only a fraction of these. The four basic types of situations that require toxicological analysis are the following situations:

- The cause of death is known but drug findings are needed to clarify the circumstances.
- Drugs are the suspected cause of death.
- Negative results permit the pathologist to rule out drugs or poison and concentrate on disease.
- Someone dies with no obvious trauma and no medical history or trouble.

For example, a healthy middle-aged man in Brooklyn who won the lottery died suddenly the following day. A toxicology screening would be justified. (In fact, he had been poisoned with cyanide.)

Human performance toxicology, or behavioral toxicology, deals with a person's ability to perform. This is used for blood alcohol screenings and drug concentrations in the blood. Toxicologists must know about the pharmacology of ethyl alcohol and drugs. For example, they must know about the concentration of alcohol in a specific beverage in order to interpret the effect of quantities consumed over specific periods of time (absorption rates). A person's blood alcohol content can be estimated with specific formulas. The estimate is based on the time between the arrest and blood testing.

3.9.4 Methods of Analysis

Postmortem analysis involves removing samples of bodily fluids (blood and urine) and organs during an autopsy, especially for unexplained deaths. They may also test stomach contents and bile. The tests can detect many kinds of poisons, the presence of a drug overdose, or environmental poisoning. However, the testing is limited to a basic tox screening unless there is reason to include a specific test.

For example, when Marilyn Monroe was found dead from an overdose of Nembutal and chloral hydrate in 1962, a toxicological screening was done. She fit the profile for frequent suicidal depression, so accidental overdose was ruled out. The drugs she had taken appeared to be obvious, since the packages were on her nightstand and the pills were in her stomach. Yet in light of conspiracy theories that arose at once about murder, Monroe was thoroughly tested for the levels of these and other drugs.

A significant concern during the industrialized era was the production of synthetic alkaloids, developed with the growth of pharmaceutical chemistry, which required entirely new methods of identification. A. S. Curry proposed the use of column, or paper, chromatography for analyzing a substance based on molecular size or polarity. This method makes colorless alkaloids visible and easily separable onto filter paper.

For both alcohol and drugs, analysis involves spectrometry and some form of chromatography. Toxicologists dissolve tissues for analysis in an acidic or alkaline solution and then perform high-pressure liquid or gas chromatography with mass spectrometry (LC/MS, GC/MS). Most things encountered at a crime scene are complex mixtures, and this method can separate them into their purest components.

A small amount of the suspected substance or unknown material is dissolved in a solvent and then injected by needle into a hollow tube. A flow of inert gas (helium or nitrogen) propels the heated mixture through the coiled glass tube, where a highly sensitive, computerized detector identifies the separate elements at the other end. Since each element moves at its own speed, it can be identified as it crosses the finish line. The amount of pure substance in the mixture is measured as well, producing a chart that offers a composite profile (via measured travel time). Comparison—or control—substances also are put through GC/MS.

The mass spectrometer bombards samples with electrons produced by a heated cathode, breaking the samples into electrically charged fragments. These fragments pass through the spectrometer accelerated by an electric field. A magnetic field deflects them onto a circular path, the radius of which varies according to the mass of the fragment. As the magnetic field is increased, a detector linked to a computer records the energy spectrums. The position of each fragment on the spectrum measures its mass, and its intensity indicates its proportion in the sample. This comes through as a printed readout.

Thin layer chromatography is also used where a sample is placed in a vertical gel film and is subjected to a liquid solvent that identifies its constituent parts.

3.9.5 Terrorism

Among the most worrisome situations in toxicology is the anonymous person who attempts to poison a supply of food, medicine, or water, or the terrorist who uses lethal substances to hold communities or countries hostage. In the United States, the first such case involved product tampering.

In the Chicago area in 1982, people suddenly began to die in a mysterious manner. There were seven victims in all. The police eventually discovered that each victim had purchased a bottle of Extra Strength Tylenol and had consumed capsules laced with cyanide. The problem was the random nature of the product tampering. No specific person or store had been targeted, and there appeared to be no motive. No one was using it to blackmail a company into paying a ransom. Despite all efforts, the Tylenol Killer was never identified.

3.9.6 Cold-Case Investigations

Toxicological analysis often figures into cold-case resolutions, if biological samples allow for testing. In 1871, Charles Francis Hall led an expedition in search of the North Pole. He set anchor for the winter about 500 mi from their goal in a harbor in Greenland. On October 24, after drinking coffee, Hall became ill. Dr. Emil Bessels gave him medications, but he only grew worse. Hall believed he was being poisoned, but before anyone could do anything for him, he died.

Nearly a century later, Professor Chauncey C. Loomis and pathologist Dr. Franklin Paddock formed a team and went to Greenland to exhume Hall's remains. The body was well preserved. In Hall's fingernail, they found evidence that Hall had received a large amount of arsenic during the last 2 weeks before his death. Since the nail had shown differential growth, its condition undermined the idea that arsenic had leeched through the coffin into the body. Those involved in the investigation agreed that the chances were good that Hall had been murdered.

3.9.7 Conclusion

Toxicology is essential to forensic investigations, whether for a suspected poisoning or an incident involving drugs. From cold cases to terrorism, the ability to detect foreign substances in the body or in consumer products continues to be refined and broadened as new products with potentially lethal effects are developed.

3.10 Nursing

Nurses trained in forensic procedures combine nursing skill and knowledge of the legal system with clinical information about criminology.

Any time nurses treat a crime victim, a suspect in a crime, a person suffering bodily harm that involves liability, or a person involved in an accident with criminal implications, they are involved in a forensic case. There will be a legal as well as a medical investigation.

The American Academy of Forensic Sciences formally recognized the specialty in 1991, and the International Association of Forensic Nurses (IAFN), with the support of the American Nurses Association (ANA), has developed its standards and scope of practice. In 1996, the ANA formally recognized the forensic specialty.

3.10.1 History

In 1992 in Minneapolis, Dr. Linda Ledray organized a group of 72 nurses with experience in sexual assault cases to improve recognition for what they did. She believed the best way to be a complete patient advocate was to meet with others and devise protocols to improve their work. She asked them how they performed rape examinations and about their success and failure rates in terms of convictions of perpetrators. Ledray learned that nurses who had specialized training and expertise in the criminal justice field best handled the types of problems faced by victims of sexual assault. This meeting led to the founding of the IAFN to serve the needs of sexual assault nurse examiners (SANEs).

3.10.2 Forensic Nurses Today

Today, forensic nursing includes more than just the subspecialty of SANEs. The IAFN describes forensic nursing as the application of nursing science to public or legal proceedings. In other words, it is also the application of the forensic aspects of healthcare combined with the biopsychosocial education of the registered nurse in the scientific investigation and treatment of trauma and/or death of victims and perpetrators of abuse, violence, criminal activity, and traumatic accidents. The forensic nurse can work in many fields, including becoming a death investigator, a nurse coroner, a forensic nurse consultant, a nurse attorney, a correctional nurse, or a legal nurse consultant. He or she also can train to be part of a mass disaster team or assist with community antiviolence programs.

3.10.3 Skills for Forensic Nurses

Victims of violence (domestic violence, sexual assault, child abuse, neglect, or intentional injury) who need medical care require handling by someone who knows about criminal and legal issues. Forensic nurses are trained to understand these issues. Yet since most nursing curricula lack a forensic component, few nurses today are trained to be aware of this dimension. Forensic training develops skills such as evidence handling and documentation, documentation at a crime scene, photo documentation, computer forensics, chain of custody issues, and ways to bridge the gap between law enforcement and healthcare.

Forensic nurses can be adjuncts to a medical examiner or coroner. As emergency room attendants, they see victims first and know the importance of recognizing wound patterns and preserving evidence. They can also investigate unnatural deaths.

Forensic nurses are also trained in courtroom procedures and can give testimony to assist triers of fact with complex medical concepts or procedures. They can fill in for doctors, thereby offering less expensive experts and less disruption of hospital services.

3.10.4 SANEs

SANEs are registered nurses who have completed specialized education and clinical preparation in the medical forensic care of patients who have experienced sexual assault or abuse. They also are referred to as sexual assault forensic examiners, and they may be part of a sexual assault response team. Training is extensive for learning how to take a patient's history, interview the patient for facts about the incident, and conduct the time-consuming and sensitive examination. They must be able to handle the instruments used for examining genital injury, recognize different types of sexual injury, take appropriate photographs, write detailed reports, and even be prepared for false victim reports.

The exam involves taking a medical forensic history, performing a detailed physical and emotional assessment, collecting and managing forensic samples to ensure chain of custody, and providing emotional and social support and resources. The SANEs can also testify in any legal proceedings, particularly with regard to victim trauma and integrity of the evidence.

Methods for performing the exam vary from one place to another, but the priority is to collect the facts, protect the evidence, and work with law enforcement. They know that clothing must be preserved and the test kit must not be exposed to contamination. More than 80% of victims who receive a proper exam from a SANE have a successful prosecution of the rapist.

SANEs also learn about victimology and linkage analysis, so that in the event of a serial rapist, they can assist to identify connections among cases. They also understand the differences between stranger and date rape, as well as rape from incest.

3.10.5 Risk Management

Protection of patients requires coworkers to be observant of fellow staff, especially in light of cases of healthcare personnel abusing or killing patients. The role of the nurse as a patient advocate mandates the nurse take action to report behavior that is consistent with a deliberate attempt to harm or kill a patient. These concerns should be carried up the chain of command and ultimately to the risk manager (if the facility has one).

With no data bank available at this time, and little or no forensic training offered in nursing curricula today, the responsibility to develop a pathway for reporting suspicious activities by the professional staff falls on the risk management departments. Nurses with forensic training are invaluable assets because they can recognize a possible forensic situation.

Their skills include understanding the protocol of a crime scene, recognizing what constitutes potential evidence, and knowing how to preserve it properly. Their attention to detail and ability to recognize the possible importance of every piece of evidence may lead to a suspect or solve a crime. They know that a body is a crime scene. They recognize the importance of documentation of findings, and they are aware of the significance of the absence of findings. In addition, they know when to call in law enforcement. Their skills come into play as well in taking histories to get a full and accurate story or determine a discrepancy among several narratives.

3.10.6 Nurses and Law Enforcement

Forensic nurses have knowledge of legal issues and investigative protocol and, thus, are able to speak to detectives who arrive on the scene. They understand what may constitute as evidence and can assist in describing potential contamination of the scene. Additionally, they will inform police about who may have handled potential evidence. In addition, forensic nurses can educate potential witnesses in courtroom protocol.

3.10.7 Conclusion

Although not readily recognized as a distinct field, forensic nursing has quickly proven itself highly beneficial to both the legal and medical communities. Nurses who understand evidence collection and preservation, as well as courtroom protocol, offer a great deal to rape, assault, and homicide investigations.

3.11 Accounting

Forensic accounting applies accounting, auditing, and research skills to investigations and the formation of legal opinions. Such professionals can be involved in both litigation support and investigative accounting. Being engaged by an attorney can protect the accountant's communication as a work product.

3.11.1 Roles

Accountants can serve as consultants to attorneys, expert witnesses to assist judges or juries, mediators between parties in dispute, or arbitrators. Most often, they clarify financial matters related to a case and help attorneys prepare appropriate questions for jury candidates and for cross-examination. In court, as experts, they explain specific financial concepts or calculations. Accountants can spot falsified books, overinflated records, falsely stated profits, and overstated costs. They can also help to estimate damages to businesses.

3.11.2 Skills

Forensic accountants are bound by legal rules versus general auditing standards set by the American Institute of Certified Public Accountants (CPAs). Forensic examiners are largely concerned with investigating theft, infringement, and fraud. Forensic reports are written more definitively than normal auditing, in part to resist challenge. Forensic accountants must know what business losses are permitted by law, how to calculate losses, and how to convey these complex items accessibly to triers of fact.

Forensic accountants typically have acquired skills in analytical thinking, interviewing, forecasting, and investigation. They understand financial data and can quickly analyze records for anomalies. To supplement what they see in the data, they can devise appropriate questions for personnel. They can watch someone explain concepts or reconstruct a data sheet that they already understand, just to see how the person responds. Interviewing assists accountants to reconstruct the facts to uncover the source of the fraud.

The skill of auditing, in which accountants are trained, involves examining facts, analyzing data sets, drawing conclusions, and confirming information from several sources. They must understand balance sheets, income statements, earnings statements, and cash flow statements. They can also anticipate financial trends, which can be useful in determining damages in civil proceedings.

3.11.3 Types of Services

Forensic accountants can work in either the civil or the criminal arena for any party. If a matter in dispute is financial, generally both sides will hire forensic accountants as either experts or consultants. They can assess damages to businesses from interruption, a breach of contract, and torts associated with fraud and theft.

Tort law deals with situations where a person's behavior has unfairly caused someone to suffer loss or harm. The law allows those who are harmed to recover their loss. Accountants must determine what the revenue would have been. Often, tort damage involves infringement on a copyright, patent, or intellectual property.

For damage review, forensic accountants calculate what an injured party would have made, in terms of lost profit or reasonable royalty, had the infringement never occurred. This can involve lost revenue, increased expenses, and costs associated with offsetting the loss. Market trends and length of time of the interruption or infringement figure into the calculations.

The forensic accountant identifies the illegal issue and gives a report to management, letting management decide the next step.

3.11.4 Fraud

Fraud can be civil or criminal. In a business setting, it usually involves false statements, theft, and embezzlement. The fraud triangle results from a combination of pressure, opportunity, and ability to rationalize.

Embezzlement typically involves diverting cash receipts, opening false checking accounts, creating fake vendors, removing minor amounts from expense reports, altered checks, cash register thefts, and making fraudulent payments.

In divorce cases, one party may try to hide assets, which is a form of fraud, so the other party might hire an accountant to go through the records to evaluate suspicious or illegal activity.

3.11.5 Bankruptcy

The Federal Bankruptcy Court administers bankruptcy hearings. A Chapter 7 proceeding liquidates a business to pay creditors. A Chapter 11 proceeding helps to reorganize a business so that it can settle its debts and get a fresh start. Forensic accountants help to establish the financial status of a business going through either proceeding, as well as to protect the business's interests.

3.11.6 Personal Damages

Individuals suffer personal damages, such as in a wrongful death, discrimination, defamation, wrongful termination, or personal injury. Any suit brought for personal injury involves liability and damages. A finding of liability precedes a valuation of damages. Such valuations combine several factors, depending on the damages, such as work life expectancy, personal consumption expenses, or future income projections.

3.11.7 Taxes

Accountants may serve as experts on matters such as tax collection, tax disputes, estate valuations, and tax violations. The failure to pay or collect tax, the failure to file a tax return, filing an untruthful return, and evading taxes altogether are criminal matters. Accountants are often used in defending against charges brought by the Internal Revenue Service (IRS).

3.11.8 Arson for Profit

The investigation of outright criminal activities, such as burning a building in order to profit from insurance, could involve the expertise of a forensic accountant. During periods of decreased value, property fires for those who hold mortgages greater than the property is worth should always be treated as suspicious, especially if attempts to sell the property have been unsuccessful. On the defense for such alleged crimes, the accountant may seek to show that the property was easily sellable or is profitable.

3.11.9 Murder for Profit

Similar to arson, some criminals insure a person in order to benefit from the person's death, usually by murder. For the prosecution, the accountant would help show that the defendant needed money, but on the defense, the accountant would attempt to do the opposite. In either case, the account must research the defendant's income, bank accounts, and debts.

3.11.10 Forensic Analytics

Analytics in the digital age involves procuring and analyzing electronic data in order to support or reconstruct a claim of financial fraud. In a business, for example, investigating employees who use digital means to keep records would require an accountant versed in computer data.

3.11.11 Litigation Support

Attorneys engage accountants to review accounts and explain their importance to specific parties. Accountants may also tell attorneys about items important to a case that the attorney may not realize due to lack of expertise. The accountant can also assist with decisions about how well financial evidence supports (or does not support) a case.

3.11.12 Conclusion

Although not actually a science, forensic accounting supports the other forensic sciences for investigations requiring knowledge of financial records and transactions.

3.12 Digital Forensics

The Scientific Working Group on Digital Evidence defines it as information of potential value stored or transmitted in digital format. Digital forensics is the methodology for preserving, retrieving, analyzing, and interpreting these data from various storage and transmittal devices. This includes (but is not limited to) cell phones, desktop computers, laptops, USB drives, tablets, CDs, DVDs, webcams, DVRs, digital readers, RFID tags, pagers, iPods, mp3 players, digital memory cards in cameras, digital recorders, digital games, global positioning systems, card readers, and digital assistants.

Digital forensics was formerly called computer forensics and often involves cyberinformatics. Most crimes today have a digital component.

3.12.1 Basic Data

Digital evidence is volatile. It can be easily contaminated, altered, or destroyed. Examiners go through special training to learn specific tools for different devices and situations. Stored as 1s and 0s, digital data are found in one of two forms: static (stored in a fairly permanent location) or streaming (in motion from one device to another). Data are typically organized in documents, files, and folders. Data communication protocols dictate how data are or can be transferred.

Criminals hide data with encryption (scrambling) or steganography (planted inside larger innocuous files such as photos). These data can be used as direct or corroborative evidence.

3.12.2 History

Computer crime began with pranks and simple theft, but it has progressed into more sophisticated and destructive forms. During the early 1970s, offenders sought unauthorized access to computers, stealing time for which others had paid. Later, computer hackers looked for bigger fish in the form of corporate, bank, or government computers, in which lay the data of power and wealth. The Internet also became a networking arena for sexual predators, terrorists, organized crime, and identity thieves.

Lawmakers soon realized the need for formal regulations and penalties, but initially, these measures were weak and ineffective. The FBI and IRS organized a unit to seize computer records from mainframe computers, but they largely ignored the personal computer, which became increasingly popular throughout the 1980s. As serious criminals realized the Internet's potential, as well as the dearth of law enforcement, the crimes grew more malicious.

Law enforcement slowly caught up, instituting training sessions during the 1990s for federal, state, and local agencies and establishing regional centers for digital evidence processing. Around the United States, predator sting operations netted numerous pedophiles, child porn users, and child molesters, while intelligence gatherers learned the codes of terrorism. The International Association of Computer Investigative Specialists formed in 1991. Soon, the FBI instituted the Automated Computer Examination System. A program of best practices and standard methods was organized along with certification courses.

In 2000, commercial software became available for forensic examiners, including Encase, P2 Commander, Device Seizure, and Forensic Toolkit. Later open-source software such as Sleuthkit and DEFT also became available. However, criminals kept introducing a range of methods to deflect these efforts. The National Institute of Science and Technology initiated validation testing on the software and established digital labs began to achieve accredited status. Today, individual examiners are periodically tested for skills proficiency.

3.12.3 Areas

Digital forensics has many subspecialties, any of which can involve gathering, storing, classifying, and retrieving information. Examiners recover digital evidence from almost any device, track identity theft or piracy, bait and ambush Internet-based offenders, track cyberstalkers, identify network trespass, and explore computer fraud or extortion. Some examiners are dedicated to detecting terrorist cells that pass information via the Internet.

3.12.4 The Digital Lab

The tools needed for analysis include a device for recovering intelligence, appropriate software, nonmagnetic hand tools, proper cables, remote proof evidence bags, external hard drives, storage CDs and DVDs, write blockers, adapters, inventory logs, and a secure lab.

The digital forensics section resembles the other sections in a crime laboratory, with desks and chairs. Different stations within this area are set up for examining different types of equipment/media. This would include disk duplicators and disk erasers. There must also be security for storing devices, especially those that hold evidence for a court case. Examiners must also have access to a separate stand-alone network for the lab.

Lab design should ameliorate noise, provide cooling mechanisms in high–computer use areas, and allow for airflow into spaces where small parts and pieces are being manipulated.

3.12.5 Investigations

In incidents involving devices with digital data, time is of the essence, since offenders can try to remotely erase or destroy digital data. Examiners must look for signs that the target device is connected to wireless access points or is in active communication with other users. The offenders may use a logic bomb, or delayed-action virus code designed to execute under specified circumstances, such as the failure of a user to respond to a program command.

Once a data source is secured, examiners can recover some deleted data, sometimes decode encrypted files, and restore many corrupted files, as well as determine which websites were visited to acquire information or make contacts. They should handle the original source material delicately, forensically imaging it before any examination or analysis.

Examiners work with a device's hard drive and operating system, which interfaces the software with the hardware. They look for the file storage system and the data itself. Their primary task is to identify the relevant data and separate it from all the rest (which can be considerable). They must be careful to maintain context and not cherry-pick to support an investigative hypothesis. They should clearly document their plan for examination, in order to demonstrate the process to other investigators, attorneys, or in court, if necessary.

The role of the computer as a repository and organizer of information can be tricky. Once power is removed, data in the memory chips are lost. This can include user names and passwords, encryption keys, instant-messenger chat sessions, open e-mails, unsaved documents, and other items that can serve as evidence. Traditional cyberforensics has focused on dead-box analysis, but the demand today is for live-box analysis, which preserves and harvests vital evidence from a computer's memory. Static forms (i.e., saved files) are retrieved by confiscating the computer's hard drive and/or making an image (exact copy) of the contents. Live-box investigations give investigators access to the entire running system. The issues with a live-box examination would be the tainting of potential evidence. Depending on the operating system, information can be found in the operating systems cached files.

Digital examiners rely on equipment that can duplicate whatever is on a computer's hard drive without having to turn the computer on, so as to prevent any loss of data from programs that may activate to erase it. When faced with a machine that is still on, they must handle it without turning it off, so as to preserve the live data. Streaming data capture involves duplicating the packets while in transit, arranging them in the right sequence, and examining both the metadata and the contents.

Once data are acquired, examiners select appropriate software to first document the contents of the device or medium. Using the case, plus legal guidelines (the specific legal issue), examiners look for relevant data that can serve as evidence. The final step is to export the data for further analysis and presentation in court. Examiners must be able to explain the notions of data recovery and content searches that match strings of data, codes, and key words.

The major dangers when retrieving data are the potential loss of information and data distortion or alteration. To be admissible in court, computer data must be handled with proper protocol with the information gathering method and chain of custody invulnerable to challenge.

3.12.6 Admissible Evidence

Federal Rules of Evidence apply, as do stipulations from *Frye* or *Daubert*, depending on the jurisdiction. Under *Daubert*, the tools used to gather the data must be accepted as standard by the forensic informatics community and peer-reviewed; they must also be capable of producing replicable results, and the results must be relevant to the issue under consideration. With chain of custody issues, examiners must be able to prove that the evidence is an accurate representation of the data on the computer.

3.12.7 Digital Crime: Identity Theft

Identity theft is the use of someone's personal records, from bank accounts to social security numbers to home addresses, in order to purchase large items, reappropriate debt, or divert law enforcement. Thanks to cloud technology, online participants are especially vulnerable. Crimes like this have a high probability of going cold, in part because such criminals can be difficult to catch and in part, because victimized institutions are reluctant to report or challenge it. Identity theft is the primary way terrorist groups that have targeted the United States have managed to get professional training, driver's licenses, banks accounts, and access to sensitive information.

3.12.8 Digital Crime: Cyberpredators

It is easy for participants on the Internet to present themselves in any way they deem attractive, including false photos, names, and profiles. Cyberspace has become a sinister playground for predators. People desperate for love or connection may believe whatever they are told and are often willing to meet strangers in person. This can result in being conned, robbed, raped, kidnapped, stalked, or murdered.

Cyberpredators who seek the young and vulnerable look for kids with low self-esteem, family troubles, uncertainty about their sexuality, frustration about parents or teachers, and other issues common to the transitions of adolescence. Online, predators can achieve a quick intimacy as they have more time to calculate. They study children to get the right phrasing so they can come across as an equal in the child's cadre of friends. They also develop a relationship prior to any visual interactions, which can establish a degree of trust that undermines basic gut instinct.

At first, it seemed to be an overwhelming task for law enforcement to attempt to go in and out of chat rooms to find these offenders, but they devised a way to turn the modus operandi back on the predators. They too posed as teenagers to lure the pedophiles to meet them at a specified location, where they would be waiting with an arrest warrant. Some departments assign such officers to full-time computer policing.

3.12.9 Terrorism

To improve real time intelligence gathering for evaluating security threats, the FBI is developing a web app that can continuously monitor social networks, including Facebook, Twitter, and various news feeds. The app would provide an automated search and scrape function; a filter; instant notifications; a geo-locator; an archivable database; coded maps; the ability to create, define, and select parameters/key word requirements; and the ability to define and select radius search functions. Although this app is meant for national security, its basic design could become useful for identifying sexual predators as well.

3.12.10 Summary

Digital forensic investigation is a fast-growing field. Digital predation involves sophisticated offenders seeking ways to use the digital arena to exploit or harm others, and digital investigators must constantly monitor these crimes and devise ways to target and stop them.

Bibliography

Baden, M. & Roach, M. (2001). *Dead reckoning: The new science of catching killers*. New York: Simon & Schuster.

Bass, W. & Jefferson, J. (2003). *Death's acre: Inside the legendary forensic lab the Body Farm*. New York: Putnam.

Benedict, J. (2003). *No bone unturned.* New York: Harper Collins.

Bowers, C.M. & Johansen, R. (2000). Forensic dentistry: An overview of bite marks. In Human and Animal Bitemark Management. Forensic Mailing Services.

Casey, E. (2004). *Digital evidence and computer crime: Forensic science, computers and the Internet* (Second ed.). San Diego, CA: Academic Press.

Cummings, R. (2008, November–December). Computer Forensics. *Evidence Technology Magazine,* Vol. 6, No. 6. Retrieved from http://www.evi dencemagazine.com/index.php?option=com_content&task=view&id=1 16&Itemid=49.

Daubert versus Merrell Dow Pharmaceuticals (92–102), 509 U.S. 579 (1993).

Doyle versus State of Texas. 159 TEX, Crim. 310, 263 S.W. 2d 779 (1954).

Dusky versus United States, 362 U.S. 402 (1960).

Fisher, B. (2000). *Techniques of crime scene investigation* (Sixth ed.). Boca Raton, FL: CRC Press.

Guide to litigation support services. (2003). Forth Worth, TX: Practitioners Publishing Company.

Kiely, T.F. (2006). *Forensic evidence: Science and the criminal law* (Second ed.). Boca Raton, FL: CRC Press.

Lee, H.C. & Harris, H.A. (2000). *Physical evidence in forensic science.* Tucson, AZ: Lawyers & Judges Publishing Company.

Mandia, K. & Harms, K. (2013, January 30). Don't forget your memory. *DFI News.* Retrieved from http://www.dfinews.com/article/dont -forget-your-memory

Marcella, A. & Menendez, D. (2008). *Cyber forensics: A field manual for collecting, examining, and preserving evidence of computer crimes* (Second ed.). Boca Raton, FL: CRC Press.

National Academy of Science. (2009). *Strengthening forensic science in the United States: A path forward.* Washington, DC: National Academies Press.

Platt, R. (2003). *The ultimate guide to forensic science.* London, UK: DK Publishing.

Pollitt, M. (2006). Digital forensics. In Wecht, C.H. & J.T. Rago (Eds.), *Forensic science and law: Investigative applications in criminal, civil, and family justice* (pp. 495–503). Boca Raton, FL: CRC Press.

Ramsland, K. (2001). *The forensic science of C.S.I.* New York: Berkley.

Ramsland, K. (2004). *The science of cold case files.* New York: Berkley.

Randall, B. (1997). *Death investigation: The basics.* Tucson, AZ: Galen Press.

Rhine, S. (1998). *Bone voyage: A journey in forensic anthropology.* Albuquerque, NM: University of New Mexico Press.

Saferstein, R. (1995). *Criminalistics: An introduction to forensic science* (Fifth ed.). Englewood Cliffs, NJ: Prentice Hall.

Steadman, D.W. (2003). *Hard evidence: Cases studies in forensic anthropology.* Upper Saddle River, NJ: Prentice hall.

Stevens, S. (2004). *Forensic nurse: The new role of the nurse in law enforcement.* New York, NY: St. Martin's Press.

Trestrail, J.H. (2000). *Criminal poisoning.* Totowa, NJ: Humana Press.

van Dam, C. (2006). *The socially skilled child molester*. New York: Haworth Press.

Wecht, C.H. & Rago, J.T. (Eds.) (2006). *Forensic science and law: Investigative applications in criminal, civil, and family justice*. Boca Raton, FL: CRC Press.

Welner, M. & Ramsland, K. (2006). Behavioral science and the law. In Wecht, C.H. & J.T. Rago (Eds.), *Forensic science and law: Investigative applications in criminal, civil, and family justice* (pp. 474–494). Boca Raton, FL: CRC Press.

Wolak, J., Finklehor, D., Mitchell, K. & Ybarra, M. (2008). Online "predators" and their victims: Myths, realities, and implications for prevention and treatment. *American Psychologist*, Vol. 63, No. 2, pp. 111–128.

SECTION I
PRACTICE TEST

1. Ethical behavior goes beyond simply knowing the difference between right and wrong; it is doing what is _____.
   a. honest
   b. diligent
   c. right
   d. discreet

2. Investigators should not allow personal feelings or _____ to interfere with factual and truthful disclosure.
   a. anger
   b. hatred
   c. laziness
   d. prejudices

3. In 1994 in the O. J. Simpson murder trial, not only did millions of laypeople learn intimate details about the investigative process, they also witnessed its _____.
   a. limitations
   b. influence
   c. importance
   d. complexity

4. Believing that human behavior could be classified with objective tests, _____ was convinced that certain people were born criminals, identifiable by specific physical traits such as bulging brows, long arms, and apelike noses.
   a. Vidocq
   b. Pinel
   c. Lombroso
   d. Prichard

5. Colin Pitchfork was the first person convicted for rape and murder based on _____.

   a. fingerprints

   b. DNA evidence

   c. blood typing

   d. bite mark evidence

6. A forensic odontologist, a dentist with training in forensic procedures and courtroom testimony, has two primary roles: identification and _____.

   a. comparison analysis

   b. reconstruction

   c. testifying

   d. collection

7. The bones of an average, fully mature adult male weigh about _____ lb.

   a. 20

   b. 15

   c. 12

   d. 16

8. _____ is a medical specialty that determines the cause and manner of death in situations falling under the jurisdiction of the local medical examiner or coroner.

   a. Forensic investigation

   b. Forensic autopsy

   c. Forensic medicine

   d. Forensic pathology

9. _____ states that the decomposition process begins in the face and neck and moves downward through the body.

   a. Hick's hypothesis

   b. The principle of masticular rigidity

   c. Raoult's law

   d. Nysten's law

10. A Chapter 11 bankruptcy proceeding helps to _____ a business so that it can settle its debts and get a fresh start.

   a. reorganize

   b. dissolve

   c. liquidate

   d. inventory

See page 521 for answer key.

SECTION II
CRIME SCENES AND EVIDENCE

Section II deals with proper protocol of investigating and searching crime scenes and dealing with victims, suspects, and witnesses on the scene. It also details the various types of evidence that might be present on a crime scene, such as physical evidence, trace evidence, DNA evidence, and digital evidence. Procedures for collecting each type of evidence are presented. See page 229 for questions reviewing the material in Section II.

4

CRIME SCENE INVESTIGATION

4.1 Types of Investigations

There are two types of investigations: complaint driven and intelligence driven.

4.1.1 Complaint-Driven Investigations

Complaint-driven investigations are reactive in nature and can be generated by either individuals or entities. Individual complainants can be victims of crimes, witnesses to crimes, informants, or perpetrators. Entity complainants include law enforcement agencies, healthcare institutions, or victims of property crimes. Victims of property crime are the most common type of complainant.

4.1.2 Intelligence-Driven Investigations

Intelligence-driven investigations are proactive in nature. It requires investigators to hunt out the individual aspects of the crime themselves. These crimes are often victimless and covert. Intelligence-driven investigations are often investigations over drugs, gangs, organized crime, vice, terrorism, or foreign counterintelligence. Investigators obtain information about such crimes through witnesses, informants, and assets.

4.2 Initial Response

This section details the investigator's first actions when responding to a crime scene.

4.2.1 Note the Dispatch Information

The first step is to log the dispatch information. Investigators can get this information from the dispatcher, the person making the complaint, or their own observations. The following list details what needs to be noted:

- Address
- Date
- Parties involved
- Specific location (e.g., storefront, second-floor rear, mile marker)
- Time
- Type of call
- Type of scene (ongoing/dangerous scene or currently safe)
- Weapons involved

4.2.2 Watch Persons at the Crime Scene

The investigator's initial observation of people at the crime scene can provide important clues to a case. The following list details what investigators should document:

- Investigator's time of arrival
- Vehicles present—Know the make, model, color, condition, license plate number, and age of the vehicles. Descriptions should be vague if anything about the vehicle is unclear. For example, a black Nissan could be a dark blue Toyota, so *a dark color compact car* might be a better description. Investigators must note any vehicles leaving the scene.
- Individuals present—List and describe anyone at the scene. Descriptions should include the person's height, weight, race, age, clothing, gender, and any distinguishing features.
- Direction of travel—Directions always should be described with terms such as north, south, east, and west. Left and right could be many directions depending on the viewer's location, so investigators should avoid using them.

4.2.3 Assess the Crime Scene

Investigators approach a crime scene attentively and make careful observations. Upon arrival, they scan the entire area to thoroughly assess the scene. From this assessment, investigators note any possible secondary crime scenes. If there is activity other than in the main crime scene area, this may indicate a secondary crime scene. Finally, investigators scan the area for any vehicles or people who might be involved.

4.2.4 Approach the Scene Cautiously

Investigators approach the scene cautiously to ensure their own safety. This can begin before the investigator has even arrived. Investigators should use logic in how they approach the scene in their vehicles. Information known about the crime can help investigators decide how to approach. Crime scene personnel should always park with room around their vehicle in case they must make an emergency exit. If the crime is in progress, investigators should consider the noise their vehicles make. Measures may need to be taken to guard against the perpetrators hearing the investigators as they approach.

Upon arrival, investigators assess the scene for any ongoing dangerous activity. Using their senses, investigators watch out for downed power lines, dangerous animals, or the presence of biohazards, chemicals, or weapons. If an investigator believes a situation to be very dangerous (e.g., anthrax attack or bomb scene), he or she should not enter the scene. Safety of the investigators must be ensured before proceeding.

If investigators do proceed with entering the scene, they do so with caution. As they enter, investigators look for possible protective cover in case they come under attack and must either engage or retreat. Remaining alert and attentive throughout this process is essential. Investigators always act as if the crime is ongoing until they know it to be otherwise. The location is treated as a crime scene until investigators have determined it to be otherwise. The scene may not be what it initially appears to be.

It is also important to preserve the scene. It should remain in the same condition as when the investigator first arrived. For instance, if a light is on when investigators arrive, it should be left on.

4.2.5 Form an Investigative Plan

The criminal investigator's ultimate goal is to find the truth. Forming an investigative plan can assist in this goal. The investigative plan describes investigative goals and techniques and involves a list of the resources needed to meet the goals. The investigative goals should be logical, objective, and unbiased. They should remain flexible, as they may need to change as new information is discovered. Investigative resources may include labor, compensation, equipment, and supplies.

4.3 People at the Scene

At this point, officers start thinking about the people at the scene. This includes offering emergency care for injured victims and evaluating whether the other people present should be at the scene.

4.3.1 Emergency Care

Offering emergency care to the injured is the investigator's first priority. Investigators must remain alert throughout this process. Investigators cannot help anyone if they are injured. If there are at least two investigators present, one stands guard and keeps the scene safe while the other administers medical assistance to the victims. Investigators follow the steps outlined below in offering emergency care.

4.3.1.1 Assess Victims for Injury The first step in offering emergency care is to assess the victims' injuries. Investigators try to discover the medical needs of victims. They also look for signs of life in the seriously injured or possibly deceased. They administer emergency first aid if it is needed. Investigators also look for anything that may have been disturbed or changed by those who arrived on the scene before them.

4.3.1.2 Request for Medical Personnel The next step is to request for medical personnel if they are not already on the scene. Investigators follow departmental guidelines and practices for notifying medical personnel while they continue to assist victims as necessary until medical professionals arrive.

4.3.1.3 Guide Medical Personnel to Victims When medical personnel arrive, investigators need to be prepared. First, investigators will choose a pathway for them to follow that minimizes contamination and alteration of the crime scene. Once the medical personnel have arrived, they are directed along this chosen pathway. If possible, investigators remain with emergency medical personnel as they assist the injured.

4.3.1.4 Protect Evidence It is vital that crime scene personnel do what they can to protect the physical evidence on the scene. They can do this by pointing out potential evidence to the emergency medical personnel, instructing them to avoid contact with such items if at all possible. Medical personnel may need to be reminded to preserve all clothing of the victims, especially bullet holes and knife tears.

Medical personnel must not clean up the scene or any potential evidence. This means they should not remove items from the scene. This includes trace evidence that can adhere to emergency medical equipment or a victim's skin. They should also avoid altering items originating from the scene, including anything they brought in such as bandages or wrappers.

During this process, investigators document the movement of injured people and objects on the scene. Everything is potentially important, so investigators document the movement of everything, including furniture, blankets, or weapons.

4.3.1.5 Document Medical Personnel Investigators record the medical responders who are present. The medical personnel can provide information about scene alteration and elimination or standard/reference samples that will help the investigation. The following information about the medical personnel is documented:

- Name
- Unit
- Agency name and phone number
- Name and location of the medical facility to which the victim is being transported

4.3.1.6 Document Statements and Comments Documenting statements made by victims, suspects, and witnesses is crucial to any investigation. When documenting a statement, investigators include the statement itself, who made it, to whom it was made, and the circumstances surrounding it.

Taking statements includes obtaining dying declarations when necessary. Investigators should have an understanding of the jurisdictional law regarding dying declarations. Investigators take dying declarations of anyone who has been gravely injured. This includes acquiring statements from the injured and establishing that the victim is coherent and acknowledges the fact that his or her injuries are fatal.

If there is an injured person, investigators accompany him or her to the medical facility and document statements and comments made during transport. If law enforcement is unavailable to do this, the accompanying medical personnel can document the person's statements and comments.

4.3.2 Security of Individuals at the Scene

It is the responsibility of the present investigator to secure the individuals at the crime scene. The two major aspects of this responsibility are outlined below.

4.3.2.1 Control All Persons at Scene Controlling the people at the scene is vital to maintaining order and preserving the crime scene. Investigators do this by restricting people from moving around the scene. This prevents them from altering or destroying physical evidence. Safety is maintained by having investigators at the scene.

4.3.2.2 Identify All Persons at Scene Investigators identify all the people at the scene and remove them if their presence is unnecessary. Investigators identify individuals by obtaining verifiable personal information.

Investigators secure and separate suspects and witnesses until they have been interviewed by law enforcement. Investigators obtain and document valid forms of ID from the witnesses and suspects. Investigators should remain compassionate toward victims and their family and friends while controlling their actions. They cannot be allowed to alter anything. Victims should be assisted and moved from the scene as quickly as possible. Medical personnel will be present, but as long as investigators direct their actions and document information about them, as is stated above, this should not be a problem.

Investigators should remove any unauthorized or nonessential people from the scene. This includes bystanders, law enforcement officials not working on the case, and any other nonessential personnel.

Politicians and media should not be allowed on the crime scene. A staging area can be set up close to the scene for politicians, media, and investigators to make any public information releases. In the aftermath of working a crime scene, prohibiting the media from a crime scene can have a negative impact; therefore, do not remove them completely.

4.4 Crime Scene Assessment

Assessing the crime scene is the next step in the investigation. The crime scene is the physical area where the crime took place. This is to be extended to every area that may have played a role in the crime. For example, a death crime scene in a rural area could include the area of a roadway where a vehicle could have been parked as well as the areas around the body.

Once victims have received medical attention and the scene is secure, it is time to begin assessing the crime scene. There are many steps included in this; they will briefly be discussed.

Throughout this process, investigators continue to evaluate the safety of the personnel entering the scene. If necessary, they modify their current safety practices to keep all personnel safe. This may mean obtaining and using personal protective equipment (PPE).

4.4.1 Information from First Responders

The first step is to talk to the first responders about their initial observations of the scene and any actions they took. Investigators do this first by introducing themselves and explaining their roles within the investigation to the first responders. Then they ask for information first responders have about the incident. The first responders are asked about the scene boundaries they established and the pathways in and out of the scene they have been using.

4.4.1.1 Scene Boundaries   Investigators evaluate the first responders' choices in the scene boundaries. To evaluate the scene boundaries, they must identify the focal points of the scene. Investigators should be aware of trace and impression evidence and include the areas where these are present within the boundaries. The secure area includes all areas where the victims or evidence were moved, the place where the crime occurred, and potential points of entry or exit of suspects and witnesses.

Once it has been determined what should be included within the scene, investigators ensure that all of those areas are secure. They can secure these areas by setting up physical barriers with crime scene tape, rope, cones, vehicles, or personnel. Existing structures such as walls, rooms, or gated areas can also be used as barriers.

After securing the crime scene, investigators canvass the surrounding area. Appropriate personnel are chosen to conduct the canvass and ensure that the canvass is properly documented.

4.4.1.2 Pathways   Investigators evaluate the pathways the first responders have been using to enter and exit the scene, modifying them as necessary. All authorized personnel must be notified of the changes. Once established pathways are accepted or modified, unauthorized people must be prevented from accessing the scene. All people who enter and exit the crime scene are documented.

4.4.2 Resources

The second step is to determine what is needed for the investigation. First, investigators evaluate search and seizure issues. They determine if they need to obtain consent to search, a search warrant, or prosecutorial resources. If these need to be obtained, investigators begin to do so. An entire investigative team rather than the first investigator on the scene will likely make these decisions.

However, in some jurisdictions, the first investigator may be the one to conduct the entire investigation; in this case, the first investigator would apply for any necessary search warrants or ask for consent to search.

Once this is established, investigators move on to other resources. They must determine if they need additional investigative resources, specialized units, legal consultation, or specialized equipment and supplies. If these are needed, investigators must request them.

4.4.3 Prioritization of Crime Scenes

The third step is to prioritize the scene investigations. Investigators determine the number and size of scenes and prioritize assessing them. Investigators allocate resources to the scenes based on their priorities. If there are multiple scenes, investigators need to establish communication between individuals at each scene. When selecting the type of communication, investigators must ensure the communication is secure before updating those at other scenes with current information as necessary.

4.4.4 Scene Areas

The fourth step is to establish two different areas around the crime scene: a staging area and an area for evidence storage. The staging area is an area for consultation and equipment. It is close to the scene but not in an area actually involved in the incident or included in the crime scene. This area is secured and access to it is limited. The evidence storage area should be protected from the weather and other environmental factors that could cause degradation or loss of evidence. Investigators must consider rules of evidence and chain of custody laws when choosing this area.

4.4.5 Protection and Documentation of Evidence

Crime scene personnel identify and protect any fragile or perishable evidence. This includes the evidence that is documented. Investigators should take the weather and any other environmental factors into account to keep evidence safe while protecting evidence from human-made intrusions as well. For example, investigators could protect a shoe or tire impression from mechanical devices such as sprinklers and from animals. Investigators also evaluate any crowds of people who may be present. If there is a hostile environment, investigators take the necessary steps to ensure all evidence is safe.

Next, investigators ensure documentation and photography of the scene. When documenting the crime scene, investigators take care to document factual observations and not their opinions. They document the scene as it was first observed using preliminary photographs, rough sketches, and notes. Investigators document the point of origin of evidence and persons at the scene. They must pay particular attention to items, persons, and conditions that are likely to be lost if they are not immediately documented. They photograph or document items, conditions, or persons (including injuries or lack thereof) that may change over time.

Note: More information about how to document the scene is provided later—this is just a rough estimate of what is done initially.

4.4.6 Contamination Control

There are several small steps investigators take to eliminate any contamination:

- Limit access to the crime scene to people directly involved in processing the scene.
- Remove any nonessential personnel from the scene.
- Use the established entry and exit pathways.
- Consider collecting elimination samples from involved parties (first responders, victims, etc.).
- Identify an area far from the evidence storage area for trash generated in the investigation, assigning someone to remove the trash as needed.
- Assess potential hazards and use PPE to protect personnel if needed, disposing of the PPE in a biohazard receptacle when finished.
- Clean reusable equipment before collecting each new piece of evidence and before storing it.

- Use single-use tools or equipment for biological samples—tools can include swabs, swatches, gloves, forceps, scalpels, and pipettes.
- Package each sample individually.

4.5 Scene Documentation

Properly documenting evidence at a crime scene is essential to the success of an investigation. The first step of proper documentation is to coordinate the documentation. Investigators decide which types of documentation are needed and assign each type to an individual, ensuring that each separate documentation bears the unique identifier assigned to that case. Investigators obtain and use the necessary forms, such as photo logs, checklists, evidence logs, and chain of custody forms. There are several types of documentation, such as photos, videos, sketches, notes, and observations.

4.5.1 Photographs

Photographs should be taken of the entire crime scene. First, investigators take entry photos, or overlapping shots of the entire crime scene. This is before evidence is touched and before the crime scene is searched. Then, investigators take individual, close-up photos of each item of evidence from several angles. They try to include a ruler or some other scale to establish the size of the item. Exit photos are taken after processing the crime scene to demonstrate that the scene was processed properly and to show that no unnecessary damage occurred. Investigators also take photos of victims, suspects, witnesses, crowds, and vehicles that may be relevant to the investigation.

Maintaining perspective is the most important aspect of photography. Perspective should reproduce the scene as it appeared to a person standing there. Distortion can diminish or destroy the evidentiary value of photographs. Investigators take photographs from various perspectives, such as an aerial view, the witness's view, and the area under a body once it is removed.

In approaching the scene, a logically organized photographic record is far more informative than random photographs taken of features as they are encountered. Investigators include a scale and some means of relating the photographs to the scene for later orientation.

Distance photographs can assist in documenting the location of the scene by including landmarks and unique features. Medium-range photographs are used to record the relative positions of related items and larger stain patterns within the scene itself. Close-up photographs of individual items will establish the nature of the items found and the presence of bloodstains or stain patterns.

A photo log, the photography equivalent of notes, should accompany crime scene photography. A photo log includes the following information:

- Photographer's name and agency
- Date and time
- Case number
- Type of camera and film
- Filtration
- Number of exposures
- Shutter speed

The photo log is important in organizing the prints. Organization is key to using photographs as evidence. If using a film camera, photos from multiple investigations should not be on the same roll of film. Investigators must ensure that there are no missing prints from a roll of film. Missing prints from a roll of film may cause an attack from the opposing legal counsel, providing an insinuation that something from the investigation is missing or being hidden. It is also important to organize digital photography. With digital photography appearing more frequently in criminal investigation, personnel must follow due diligence to properly sort and organize photos from multiple investigations into their proper case files.

4.5.2 Videos

Videos are useful evidence in a case that has a large amount of evidence such as a homicide, a large scene, or an officer-involved incident. Investigators should use a new tape for each investigation. Once an investigator has taken the video, he or she breaks off the write-protect tab to prevent accidental overwrite of the tape. Investigators should carefully monitor what is being said by those at the crime scene as well as what is said by the one taking the video. Comments including profanity or the investigator's opinion may cause concerns at the trial. In fact, investigators may consider turning off the audio according to jurisdictional requirements.

4.5.3 Sketches

Sketches complement both notes and photographs and are used to focus in on the most essential elements of a crime scene. Sketches can also be used to question people, prepare reports, and present evidence.

There are two different types of sketches: rough sketches and smooth sketches. Rough sketches are sketches that are drawn at the crime scene to portray information; they are not drawn to scale. Smooth sketches are sketches that can be made from a rough sketch and are usually drawn to scale by a skilled draftsperson.

When making a rough or preliminary sketch, there are several steps to take:

- Measuring the immediate area of the scene
- Indicating *north* on the sketch
- Indicating that the sketch is *not to scale*, if necessary
- Measuring the relative location of evidence for future correlation with evidence records
- Measuring the evidence prior to movement
- Measuring rooms, furniture, and other objects relevant to the scene
- Measuring the distance to adjacent buildings or other landmarks, such as mile markers, bridges, manhole covers, and silos
- Considering additional sketches that may be useful to focus attention on a particular area or item

4.5.4 Notes

Notes are taken because they are the most readily available record of the crime scene. Notes should be sufficiently detailed with as few people as possible taking notes for consistency purposes. Investigators write notes in blue or black ink. When mistakes are made in taking notes, investigators do not erase or tear out notes; instead, they cross out and initial them. Notes are kept in a secure location and archived or destroyed according to department policy when they are no longer needed. Notes are taken on loose-leaf paper for better organization, to reduce the chance of unrelated notes being disclosed in court, and because missing pages from a notebook can raise questions concerning integrity.

Notes should include the following items:

- Date
- Agency
- Case number
- Name of investigator and the investigator's initials
- Documentation of photo logs, checklists, evidence logs, and chain of custody forms
- A detailed description of the condition of each item
- Scene location
- Time the investigator arrives and departs from the scene
- Scene appearance
- Environmental conditions (weather, temperature)
- Transient evidence (smells, sounds, sights)
- Circumstances that require departures from usual procedures (safety, environmental, and traffic issues)

4.5.5 Observations

Each investigator documents observations of the crime scene. These should include the following:

- Conditions of the scene—These include descriptions of the weather and temperature, lighting (light or dark, artificial or natural), fixtures (doors, windows, etc.), odors, furniture placement, personal items, changing or deteriorating items (tracks in snow or sand, etc.), appliances (on or off, hot or cold, functional or broken), and vehicles (hot or cold, mileage, radio station, presence of cigarette butts or gum, position of driver's seat).

- Personal information and statements—These are recorded from witnesses, victims, and suspects, and should include personal identifying information.
- Investigator's actions and actions of others—These include all actions performed and who performed them; tasks delegated; areas entered and who entered them; dispatch arrival and departure times; and items that were moved or changed, who did this, and for what purpose.
- General observations—These include the location, appearance, and condition of persons and items within the crime scene.
- Descriptions of people—These include the person's age, gender, height, weight, race, hair color, eye color, scars, tattoos, and mannerisms.
- Descriptions of objects—These include the type, color, and size of an object, plus any details that sets it apart from other similar items.
- Possible hypostasis—If there is a dead body at a crime scene, hypothesize about possible hypostasis, or the pooling of blood as it accumulates at the lowest parts of the body due to decreased blood flow. This is a method of determining the position of the body at or after death.

4.6 Crime Scene Search

Collecting evidence properly is the next step in managing a crime scene. Investigators begin this process by searching the crime scene. The most important part of collecting evidence is to be methodical so that nothing is left out or forgotten.

4.6.1 The Search

More often than not, an investigator has just one chance to properly search the crime scene. Before the actual search, a preliminary survey is taken to consider all the information and opinions that preceded the investigator to the scene. Investigators should take notes of items, conditions, and locations. They take photographs, obtain statements from witnesses, and decide the order in which to process and collect evidence.

Before the search takes place, investigators determine the number of personnel available to help in the search. They take time to prioritize processing and collection methods in such a way that their initial actions do not compromise subsequent collection methods. For example, collecting biological or trace evidence should be performed prior to the use of powder or chemical enhancement techniques.

As the search takes place, crime scene investigators decide what constitutes evidence. Every piece of is evidence needs to be collected. There are four types of crime scene searches that can be utilized: circular, zone/sector, strip, and grid.

4.6.1.1 Circular Search The circular search, also known as a spiral search or concentric search, is useful when an item is missing from the center of the scene and investigators must conduct the search quickly, such as in inclement weather. A circular search will usually suffice for small areas. Investigators start in the center and move out in an ever-widening circle. Searchers can reverse the process and wind into the circle (contracting circle). The circular search is most appropriately used for exterior searches and large interior areas.

4.6.1.2 Zone/Sector Search The zone search, also known as a sector search or quadrant search, is effective for indoor and outdoor scenes that have regularly defined borders or regular patterns. A zone/sector search can be used for both small and large areas where searchers divide the area into sections and search each section. This search method also permits different types of searches in different sectors. For example, investigators can divide a building into rooms and search each one separately.

Even single rooms can be divided into zones for detailed searches:

- Zone one—The floor and all furniture on it
- Zone two—The walls from the floor to waist high
- Zone three—The walls from waist high to shoulder high
- Zone four—The walls from shoulder high to the ceiling
- Zone five—The ceiling and attached fixtures

The zone search can be appropriately used for both interior and exterior searches.

4.6.1.3 Strip Search   The strip or line search is among the most effective outdoor searches. Searchers go back and forth across the scene using stakes and lines to set up the lanes in which to narrow the field of search. Investigators can also use natural landmarks as boundaries or lane markers. The strip search is most appropriately used for exterior searches and large interior areas.

4.6.1.4 Grid Search   The grid search is similar to the strip or line search except all four compass directions are used. For example, after completing a search in a north-to-south direction, the search team will then go back over the same area in an east-to-west direction. The grid search is most appropriately used for exterior searches over large areas and larger interior areas.

4.6.2 Tips for Searching

When searching a crime scene, investigators focus first on easily accessible areas in open view and proceed to out-of-view locations. They must first identify areas that need to be processed immediately due to safety, weather, security, scene integrity, or high traffic. Then they identify areas that can be processed at a later time, such as vehicles, additional scenes, or areas protected from threats above. As investigators search, they must continually assess environmental and other factors that may affect evidence.

They can reprioritize collection, if warranted, based on these conditions. Investigators identify the present types of evidence (e.g., biological, latent prints, trace evidence) and consider potential evidence collected prior to this stage by first responders or medical personnel that may have been moved or removed from the scene.

4.7 Final Steps

In the final steps, the investigation focuses on identifying, collecting, and processing evidence. These things will be discussed in detail in the next chapter. Before an investigator can leave the crime scene, there are some final steps that must be taken. This section discusses composing an investigative team, composing a debriefing team, transferring control of the scene, surveying the scene for a final time, and creating the crime scene case file.

4.7.1 Composing an Investigative Team

Investigators begin composing an investigative team by assessing the need for additional personnel. If there are multiple scenes, multiple victims, numerous witnesses, or a need for additional resources (such as lighting and ladders), then investigators may need more personnel. Some people or vehicles may have been transported to a different location, such as a hospital or law enforcement facility. This may require additional personnel to recover evidence from them. Some crimes may require specialized personnel.

Investigators may need a specialist in a specific forensic area. If in doubt, investigators can consult with or call in outside sources to determine if they need a latent print analyst, bloodstain/blood spatter analyst, forensic anthropologist, accident reconstructionist, or someone else. There may also be a need for special equipment depending on the nature of the crime scene.

Investigators identify other needs they may have, such as specific photographs (aerial or underwater), specific sketch needs, or special evidence collection needs (latent prints, firearms, blood spatter, trace evidence, arson/bomb, or forensic anthropology). Once investigators have identified their needs, they select personnel to complete these specialized tasks.

After investigators have identified the investigation needs and the personnel to fill these needs, they establish a list of priorities. It is important for investigators to document each team members' responsibilities and ensure that the tasks are completed.

Throughout this process, investigators must maintain scene security by making sure someone is still responsible for maintaining entry and exit documentation. Investigators must keep the scene boundaries secure.

4.7.2 Debriefing the Team

The next step is to compose a debriefing team and summarize what has been learned at the crime scene.

4.7.2.1 Compose a Debriefing Team First, investigators determine the individuals who may participate in the debriefing. This team may consist of just one investigator, but it can include many others:

- Initial responding officer
- Additional police personnel—Other investigators, canvassing investigators, perimeter security, dispatchers, interviewing investigators, investigators controlling and assisting victims, witnesses, and suspects
- Evidence collection personnel—Photographers, evidence technicians, latent print personnel, and specialized personnel
- Emergency services personnel—Fire, medical, and search and rescue
- Prosecuting attorney

4.7.2.2 Discuss the Findings The debriefing team discusses the evidence that was collected and the preliminary scene findings. The team reviews evidence documentation and communicates with evidence collection personnel to discuss what was collected. The goal is to communicate with personnel regarding what they observed, what they were told, and the actions they performed—essentially, summarizing what everyone learned at the crime scene.

4.7.2.3 Discuss the Investigation The team discusses potential forensic evidence testing and how these tests should be prioritized. Discussion should be topic specific, depending on the personnel to whom the investigator in charge is speaking. In some jurisdictions, depending on the evidence in question and the nature of the crime, the investigator in charge should communicate with the prosecuting attorney's office before making decisions that may potentially compromise the evidence. The team communicates with evidence collection personnel, other specialized personnel, and the prosecuting attorney (when appropriate).

4.7.2.4 Complete the Crime Scene Investigation The debriefing team identifies actions necessary to complete the processing of the crime scene. They should consider areas that may not have been searched or processed and confirm that all assigned tasks have been completed.

Actions necessary to protect the crime scene and complete the investigation must be identified and initiated. Responsibilities are assigned to appropriate personnel. This may include personnel who are not present at the scene or debriefing.

Then the person who will be in charge once the assigned tasks are complete is briefed. Investigators communicate with team members, superiors, and the prosecuting attorney (when appropriate) to elicit advice and instruction for crime scene evaluation.

4.7.2.5 Establish Post-Scene Responsibilities The debriefing team assigns final tasks to law enforcement personnel and to other responders. They should avoid unnecessary communication with individuals not directly involved in the investigation. Investigators in charge must use caution in releasing any information that may compromise the investigation or potential prosecution.

4.7.3 Transferring Control of the Scene

When transferring control of a scene, the new person in charge is thoroughly briefed on what has happened thus far.

Investigators brief the investigators taking charge by introducing themselves and explaining their roles in the investigation. Investigators point out the established scene boundaries and pathway. They relay information about the incident, including roles and identities of the involved parties, facts about the incident, observations that have been made, comments made by involved parties, and information given by other responders.

Investigators also assist in controlling the scene as the transfer takes place. Part of this is transferring control of the entry/exit documentation to a designated person. The person doing this must understand his or her responsibility in documenting the people entering and leaving the scene.

Crime scene personnel are to remain at the scene until they are relieved of duty. They should contact the investigator in charge for instruction. When investigators do leave, they should document their scene departure time.

4.7.4 Surveying the Scene

Before leaving the scene, crime scene personnel should make one final survey. They perform a visual inspection of each area of the crime scene, determine the need for PPE upon reentry to the scene, and conduct a walk-through examining each area of the crime scene with the individuals processing the scene. Investigators look for evidence not collected previously, investigation equipment or materials left behind by crime scene personnel, or dangerous materials or conditions.

If an investigator sees any evidence remaining at the scene, he or she should collect it. Investigators assign appropriate personnel to collect evidence identified during the debriefing or during the walk-through. The same personnel might not be present in both.

If there was any equipment or material left behind that was generated during the investigation, it should be removed. Investigators assign appropriate people to do this from either the debriefing or the walk-through.

If there were dangerous materials or conditions discovered during the walk-through, crime scene personnel should report it to appropriate individuals or agencies for corrective action. They must notify individuals who may have been exposed to dangerous conditions at the scene and take preventative measures to minimize the danger to others. One simple way to do this is to lock the doors of a building to prevent unauthorized access.

The final step in the survey is to release the crime scene. Investigators should observe jurisdictional requirements for release. When the release is complete, investigators notify the people involved that the scene has been released and remove crime scene barriers, such as crime scene tape or cones.

4.7.5 Creating a Crime Scene Case File

The final step to crime scene investigation is to create a crime scene case file. It will include the following items:

- Initial responding investigators' documentation
- Emergency services personnel documentation

- Entry and exit documentation
- Photographs and videos
- Crime scene sketches and diagrams
- Evidence documentation
- Other responders' reports
- Record of consent forms or search warrants
- Other reports, such as forensic/technical reports

Investigators are to ensure preservation of case file documentation by reviewing and adhering to department guidelines or policies and procedures. It is recognized that some departments do not have written policies. While not encouraged, in such cases the routine practices of the department in maintaining records is, in essence, a policy.

Bibliography

Anonymous. (n.d.). *Unreliable or improper forensic evidence.* Innocence Project. Retrieved from http://www.innocenceproject.org/understand/Unreliable -Limited-Science.php.

Christianson, S. (2006). *Innocent: Inside wrongful conviction case.* New York: New York University Press.

Fisher, B.A.J. (2000). *Techniques of crime scene investigation* (Sixth ed.). Boca Raton, FL: CRC Press LLC.

Lee, H.C. (2002). *Cracking cases: The science of solving crimes.* New York: Prometheus Books.

Saferstein, R. (2004). *Criminalistics: An introduction to forensic science* (Eighth ed.). Upper Saddle River, NJ: Prentice Hall.

Scene of crime. (n.d.). *Forensic science: Let evidence reveal the truth.* Retrieved from http://library.thinkquest.org/04oct/00206/index1.htm.

Technical Working Group on Crime Scene Investigation. (2000). *Crime scene investigation: A guide for law enforcement.* Washington, DC: U.S. Department of Justice Bureau of Investigation. Retrieved from http:// www.fbi.gov/about-us/lab/forensic-science-communications/fsc /april2000/twgcsi.pdf.

Westveer, A.E., Jr. (2002). *Managing death investigations* (Vol. 1, Fifth ed.). Washington, DC: U.S. Department of Justice Federal Bureau of Investigation. (Used with permission.)

White, P.C. (Ed.). (1998). *Crime scene to court: The essentials of forensic science.* Cambridge, UK: The Royal Society of Chemistry.

Vecchi, G.M. (2010, Spring). Principles and approaches to criminal investigation (Part 4). *Forensic Examiner*, Vol. 19, No. 1, pp. 10–15.

Vecchi, G.M. (2009, Summer). Principles and approaches to criminal investigation (Part 1). *Forensic Examiner*, Vol. 1, No. 2, pp. 8–13.

Vecchi, G.M. (2009, Fall). Principles and approaches to criminal investigation (Part 2). *Forensic Examiner*, Vol. 18, No. 3, pp. 8–12.

Vecchi, G.M. (2009, Winter). Principles and approaches to criminal investigation (Part 3). *Forensic Examiner*, Vol. 18, No. 4, pp. 10–15.

5

EVIDENCE

5.1 Evidence and Information

Understanding the types of evidence that might be found for different types of cases is important before beginning an investigation. This section discusses sources of information that investigators commonly use and types of evidence found at a crime scene.

5.1.1 Information

Investigators use documentary sources and human sources to gather information to close a case.

5.1.1.1 Types of Documentary Sources　The types of documentary sources are listed below:

- Criminal and Department of Motor Vehicles (DMV) histories documents
- Old case files
- Court testimonies
- Medical records
- Licenses
- Telephone records
- Financial documents
- Court files
- Transcripts
- Trash pulls
- Psychological records
- Corporate indices
- Utility records

5.1.1.2 Human Sources   The most valuable sources in an investigation are people who provide specific information that is useful for an investigation. These people might be classified as informants, assets, or cooperating witnesses.

The most important consideration with human sources is reliability. Many cases have been lost due to an unreliable source. To test the reliability of a source, ask him or her questions to which the answer is already known. *Trust but verify* should be used with all human sources.

An investigator should also figure out the motives of human sources. The most common motivator is money. Other motivations include politics, altruism, and information on their competition.

When dealing with confidential human sources, an investigator should protect his or her identity. Protecting the source's identity also protects the integrity of the investigation and provides safety to the source.

The control investigator (primary handler) or alternate investigator (secondary handler) is the one to handle human sources. The control and alternative investigators provide control, confidentiality, integrity, rapport, and cooperation. To maintain rapport with a source, investigators should keep appointments, avoid being anxious, show appreciation, and only make promises they can keep.

5.1.2 Types of Evidence

There are two kinds of evidence: physical evidence (including direct and circumstantial evidence) and testimonial evidence. This section will focus on physical evidence.

Physical evidence alone can establish the guilt of a person in a court of law. Typically, a person cannot be convicted on confession alone as suspects can recant their confessions later. Also, the circumstances (coercion or duress) leading up to a confession can be questioned in court, sometimes resulting in the confession being overturned or excluded from evidence. Therefore, physical evidence is needed to confirm the truth of the facts within a confession.

Physical evidence is any tangible object that can establish that a crime has been committed. It can be anything that can be seen, touched, smelled, or heard. Even things that seem trivial may be important. Crime scene investigators should collect it all.

There are two types of physical evidence: direct evidence and circumstantial evidence. Direct evidence is evidence that stands on its own in proving or disproving facts. Circumstantial evidence is evidence that indirectly proves facts through inference.

Here are some common types of physical evidence:

- Blood
- Documents
- Drugs
- Explosives
- Fibers
- Fingerprints
- Firearms and ammunition
- Glass
- Hair
- Impressions
- Insects
- Organs and physiological fluids
- Paint
- Semen
- Saliva
- Soil and minerals
- Tool marks
- Wood and other vegetative matter

Trace evidence may also be found. Trace evidence is physical evidence found at the crime scene in small amounts. It is often found on clothing, footwear, the body, tools, and weapons. Here are some common types of trace evidence:

- Building materials (wood, cement, brick, etc.)
- Paint
- Glass
- Rust
- Metals
- Textiles and fibers
- Hair
- Oils, greases, and waxes

- Cigarettes and tobacco
- Matches
- Soil and vegetation

Circumstantial evidence is the most common type of evidence in a forensic crime scene.

There are many possible ways to use physical evidence. Here are some examples:

- A tool mark from a crime scene can be compared with a tool or other tool mark found on the property of a suspect.
- A laundry mark may lead to identifying a suspect from torn pieces of clothing left at a crime scene or identifying a victim through matching laundry marks found on the victim at the crime scene.
- Soils, rocks, and minerals from the crime scene can be compared with like samples on the suspect's clothes.

Investigators may also find substrate control near physical evidence. Substrate control is uncontaminated surface evidence close to an area where physical evidence has been deposited.

The following section goes into detail about three specific types of physical evidence: fingerprints, blood, and firearms.

5.1.2.1 Fingerprints   Fingerprints can be incriminating physical evidence. Here are some important terms to know:

- Arch—A class of fingerprints characterized by ridges lying one above the other in a general arching formation
- Loop—A class of fingerprints characterized by a pattern of one or more free recurving ridges and one point of delta
- Whorl—A class of fingerprints characterized by a pattern of one or more free recurving ridges and two points of delta
- Ridge characteristics—Patterns that must match in two fingerprints for their common origin to be established
- Latent fingerprint—An accidental fingerprint impression left by friction ridge skin (and made by the deposit of oils and/or perspiration) on a surface

5.1.2.2 Blood Knowing the type of blood found at a crime scene can help lead to the identification of both living and deceased people. Blood type cannot conclusively identify an individual, but it can eliminate him or her as a suspect. The ABO system is most commonly used for blood typing and divides blood into four different groups: A, B, AB, and O. Blood samples are preserved in ethylenediaminetetraacetic acid.

The discovery of DNA has been a tremendous stepping-stone in the field of forensic science as well as in the identification of individuals. It has allowed scientists to conclusively link pieces of evidence together and to an individual.

DNA typing is based on an individual's genetic makeup. DNA is the biochemical key to differentiating uniqueness among individuals. DNA is present in blood, seminal fluid, tissues, bone marrow, hair roots, saliva, urine, and tooth pulp.

Forensic scientists are able to unravel the DNA code and examine pieces of DNA to look for similarities and differences between individuals. DNA is probably the most accurate evidence for identification.

Here are some terms to know:

- Buccal swab—A swab of the inner portion of the cheek to collect DNA from an individual
- Chromosome—A circular strand of DNA in the cell nucleus that contains hereditary information
- Cortex—The external layer of the hair shaft
- Cuticle—The scale structure covering the exterior of the hair
- DNA—The abbreviation for deoxyribonucleic acid, a nucleic acid that carries the genetic information in a cell
- Follicular tag—A translucent piece of tissue near the root of a hair that contains an excellent source of DNA
- Medulla—A cellular column that runs through the center of the hair
- Mitochondrial DNA—DNA present exclusively in mitochondria; it is maternally inherited
- Multiplexing—A technique that simultaneously detects more than one DNA marker in a single analysis
- Nuclear DNA—DNA present within the nucleus of a cell

- Sequencing—A procedure that determines the order of the base pairs comprising a DNA sample
- Restriction fragment length polymorphism (RFLP)—A technology based on the fact that certain regions of DNA consist of repeated sequences of units
- Polymerase chain reaction (PCR)—A technology that has allowed forensic scientists to copy small quantities or broken pieces of DNA found at a crime scene; as a result, the sample size is no longer a limitation in characterizing DNA
- Short tandem repeats—A technology that combines RFLP and PCR technologies and is used on larger segments of DNA

5.1.2.3 Firearms   The analysis of firearms can be an important part of forensic investigations. Here are the classes of firearms:

- Shotgun—A smooth-barreled firearm intended to be fired from the shoulder and designed to discharge pellets
- Rifle—A firearm with a long barrel, designed to be fired from the shoulder; the barrel of the rifle is cut with spiral grooves (called the rifling), which cause the bullet to spin as it travels
- Pistol—Any firearm designed to be discharged from the hand with a much shorter barrel than a rifle; typically equipped with magazines holding up to 10 cartridges
- Submachine gun—A pistol designed to be fired using both hands that has a longer barrel and a larger capacity magazine

Investigators can make bullet comparisons, which can be useful as evidence. As a bullet passes through the barrel of a gun, the inner surface of the barrel leaves markings on it. These markings are specific to each individual gun. Thus, if a bullet found at the crime scene shows the same markings as a bullet fired from the suspect's gun, the suspect can be linked to the crime by use of the comparison microscope.

Interior ballistics is the study of events that occur between the trigger being pulled and the bullet leaving the muzzle of the firearm. This period is estimated to be less than 1/10 of a second. The forensic scientist can measure the striker impact on the cartridge, the cap explosion, and the line of the bullet through the barrel.

Exterior ballistics is the study of the bullet's flight from the moment it leaves the muzzle of the firearm until it comes to rest. This period is estimated to vary from a fraction of a second to several seconds depending on the type of firearm and range of fire. Forensic examiners do not deal much with exterior ballistics; their focus is more on interior ballistics.

5.2 Evidence Collection

Collecting evidence properly can be difficult. This section outlines how to do it effectively.

To retain evidentiary integrity, crime scene personnel strive to keep the items in their original conditions. A chain of custody must accompany evidence from the time it is collected to the time it is no longer considered evidence. Physical evidence also must be collected skillfully, handled carefully, preserved for laboratory analysis, and stored properly. These steps will help maintain evidence integrity.

When collecting evidence, investigators give top priority to fragile evidence, such as evidence that could be altered, damaged, or destroyed by changes in the weather. This includes items that may have DNA evidence on them and all types of biological evidence. Next, investigators collect items that could hinder continuing the search. Then they collect, examine, photograph, sketch, and record remaining evidence in a logical order. Consider consulting with forensic personnel for additional technical advice on how to collect evidence. Assess the scene to determine if other methods or resources are needed to aid in scene processing. This may include an alternate light source, blood pattern documentation, etc. In death scenes, crime scene personnel process the evidence between the point of entry to the scene and the body. After processing major evidence, it is important to search for and collect trace evidence.

The following evidence collection techniques are meant to be illustrative and are not meant to be exhaustive or exclusive.

5.2.1 Impression Evidence Collection

Impression evidence has two types: macroscopic evidence that is visible with the naked eye (footwear and tire) or microscopic evidence that may need magnification (latent prints, tool marks, cartridge cases, weapons, bullets, bite marks, fingernails). This evidence is located by using visual observation techniques or by using lighting techniques (oblique, alternate light source) or chemical enhancement techniques (powder, superglue, dyes, luminol).

Investigators develop impression evidence by using photography, which includes filters and an alternate light source or chemical enhancement. This evidence can be collected in three ways: by using photography; by using physical lifters such as gel lifters, dental stone, electrostatic lifters, molding materials, and lifting tape; or by taking the actual item. Consider collecting elimination samples.

Proper packaging of individual items of evidence includes documenting the location of evidence at the scene, the date of collection, the identity of the individual making the collection, and the description of items to be collected.

5.2.2 Latent Print Evidence Collection

To collect latent print evidence, investigators follow the techniques listed below.

First, they locate fingerprints, palm prints, and footprints by using visual observation techniques, lighting techniques (oblique, alternate light source), and chemical enhancement techniques (superglue, dyes, luminol, powders). Next, investigators develop latent print evidence collection by using photography (using filters and an alternate light source), chemical enhancement techniques, or powder enhancement techniques. Then, they collect print evidence by using photography, physical lifters (electrostatic lifters, lifting tape/adhesive, or silicon casting material), or by taking the actual item. Investigators also collect elimination samples to know if the evidence came from any law enforcement personnel.

Proper packaging of individual items of evidence includes documenting the location of evidence at the scene, the date of collection, the identity of the individual making the collection, and the description of items collected.

Locating and collecting fingerprints, a common type of latent evidence, is covered in detail below.

5.2.2.1 Fingerprints A few key areas to look for prints are the perpetrator's point of entry, broken glass, dishes, beverage containers, light switches, circuit breakers, tools, and other objects left at the scene. A flashlight is an excellent tool in the search for fingerprints. The investigator must always wear gloves during the fingerprint search or risk destroying any prints.

5.2.2.2 Fingerprint Development Techniques Many techniques have been developed to visualize fingerprints and use various chemical reagents that react with substances present in the print. Advances in fingerprint technology continue to emerge. The following are different powder techniques:

- Amido black—A stain that turns proteins in the blood a blue-black color
- DFO 1,8-diazafluoren-9-one—A stain that reacts with proteins and results in a fluorescent red color; often used in conjunction with ninhydrin
- Lasers and ultraviolet lamps—Find prints through fluorescent examination
- Gentian violet or crystal violet—Exposes fingerprints on the sticky side of adhesive tape
- Iodine—One of the oldest techniques for exposing prints; simple to use but its vapors are toxic, and the reaction is not permanent
- Ninhydrin solution—Reacts with amino acids to form a purple compound called Ruhemann's purple
- Physical developer—A silver-based solution used in place of the conventional silver nitrate procedure; a good procedure for photographing prints
- Silver nitrate—Reacts with chlorides in prints; has been widely replaced by physical developer
- Small particle reagent—A wet process for developing latent prints on wet surfaces; prints can be effectively photographed
- Sudan black—Used on nonporous articles; it turns prints blue black and works well on oily or greasy surfaces
- Superglue or cyanoacrylate fuming—Produces white prints that can be dusted with powder, photographed, and lifted or washed with dyes

- Vacuum metal deposition—The most effective technique for smooth, nonporous surfaces; evaporates gold or zinc in a vacuum chamber and deposits a thin film of metal on the print

Nonpowder techniques include the following:

- Lasers and alternative light sources—Give location and visualization of latent fingerprints
- Digital imaging—Enhances fingerprint evidence by converting photographic evidence into pixels
- Automated fingerprint identification systems—Compare latent fingerprints found at a crime scene with those in a database
- Photography—Preserves fingerprints when possible; fingerprint impressions can also be preserved with a casting material
- Transparent cellophane tape—A common collection method; after lifting the fingerprint powder onto the sticky surface, the tape is placed onto a card that contrasts with the powder used

5.2.3 Biological Evidence Collection

Visual observation techniques, lighting techniques (oblique or alternate light source), or chemical enhancement techniques (luminol, presumptive tests) are used to locate biological evidence.

Evidence is collected by using single-use equipment (swabs, threads, or gauze patches) and by taking the actual item (scrape with scalpel or cut out portion of substrate). Investigators also collect the whole item (stained door, clothing) or a representative sample (portion of blood trail, pooling of blood). Control/blank samples are also collected.

Proper packaging of individual items of evidence includes documenting the location of evidence at the scene, the date of collection, the identity of the individual making the collection, and the description of the items collected.

5.2.4 Arson/Explosive/Bomb Evidence Collection

Following an explosion, crime scene personnel should be aware of the possibility of secondary explosive devices. They should request that subject-matter experts respond to the scene. If some types of evidence are present, specialized personnel with protective equipment and training (arson investigators or an accelerant detection canine team) are needed. These types of evidence include accelerants, burn patterns, explosive residue, bombs, and explosives. When it is not possible for a specialized team to conduct the investigation, there are steps that can be taken. However, only bomb disposal personnel should investigate unexploded bombs or handle live explosives.

Visual observation techniques and smell are used to locate evidence. Investigators use photography, videography, written notes, sketches, and diagrams to document this evidence.

Investigators collect evidence by scooping ignitable liquid residues with a noncontaminated shovel, taking and packaging exploded bomb components, and taking sources of ignitable liquid residues. Handle these with gloves to avoid leaving fingerprints on the evidence. Consider collecting control samples. In arson, in addition to control samples, also take a burned sample from the point of origin of the fire.

Ensure proper packaging of individual items of evidence, with nonporous containers to prevent loss of volatile evidence and that the location of evidence at the scene, the date of collection, the identity of the individual making the collection, and that the description of items collected is documented.

5.2.5 Trace Evidence Collection

Visual observation techniques, lighting techniques (oblique or alternate light source), and taping techniques are used to locate trace evidence. Trace evidence is commonly located on clothing, footwear, the body, tools, and weapons.

Investigators collect trace evidence by using manual methods (tweezers, forceps, or gloved hands), taping techniques, scraping techniques, and vacuum techniques (last resort), and by taking the whole item on which the trace evidence is located (rock with hair, bumper with paint, carpeting). Collecting control and standard/reference samples should be considered. Trace evidence can also be collected by shaking a garment, brushing a surface, taping to recover fibers and hairs, vacuuming gunshot or drug residues, swabbing to recover smeared material, handpicking, and extracting.

Proper packaging of individual items of evidence includes documenting the location of evidence at the scene, the date of collection, the identity of the individual making the collection, and the description of items collected.

5.2.6 Questioned Documents/Electronic Evidence Collection

A document may be significant because of what it states (ransom notes, suicide notes, forged documents) or because of the nature of the physical evidence found in the document (ink, handwriting, or paper). Standard or reference samples are collected for comparison purposes in the later cases.

Visual observation techniques and lighting techniques are used to locate evidence. Investigators take the whole item as evidence. Standard or reference samples are also collected.

Proper packaging of individual items of evidence includes documenting the location of evidence at the scene, the date of collection, the identity of the individual making the collection, and the description of items collected.

5.2.7 Reconstruction Evidence

Investigators must determine the usefulness of reconstructive techniques. This can be helpful to demonstrate a sequence of events or the location and characteristics of the parties involved or to corroborate or disprove statements.

If reconstructive techniques may be useful, investigators locate evidence by applicable methods (visual observation, lighting, lasers, and chemical enhancement). They document evidence by applicable methods (photographs, videos, sketches with measurements).

Crime scene investigators recognize the significance of blood spatter interpretation, projectile trajectory reconstruction (glass fracture, laser, bullet path, stringing techniques), accident reconstruction, excavated human remains, a burial site and the surrounding area, skeletal remains, and preserving evidence specialists may use for reconstructive techniques—facial reconstruction, postmortem interval (time of death) determination, detection of administered chemicals/poisons, and forensic odontology for bitemark identification or identification of human remains.

5.2.8 Controlled Substances/Chemicals Evidence Collection

If dangerous substances, such as clandestine laboratory evidence, chemicals/poisons, industrial waste, or acids are present, specialized personnel with protective equipment and training should collect them. When it is not possible for a specialized team to conduct the investigation, there are steps that can be taken.

First, investigators reevaluate safety issues, and then, if it is safe, locate evidence by using visual observation (paraphernalia, pipes, glassine packets), alternate light sources, drug-detecting animals, field-testing techniques, and being aware of and noting odors that could indicate the presence of chemicals and/or reaction mixtures. Next, investigators collect samples of clandestine laboratory chemicals and take items of evidence. Last, investigators ensure proper packaging of individual items of evidence. This includes documenting the location of evidence at the scene, the date of collection, the identity of the individual making the collection, and the description of items collected.

5.2.9 Collection of Other Types of Evidence

All other types of evidence related to the crime may not fit into one of the above categories. This may include car parts, botanical evidence, physical matching evidence, toxicological evidence, or poisons. Investigators locate and collect these unique types of evidence. Collection of control/blank, standard/reference, and elimination samples is also considered. Proper packaging of individual items of evidence includes documenting the location of evidence at the scene, the date of collection, the identity of the individual making the collection, and the description of items collected.

5.3 Evidence Preservation

It is the lead investigator's responsibility to ensure that the evidence is preserved in its original state. The list below explains how to do this:

- Minimize its potential for change.
- Wear protective gloves.
- Handle evidence as little as possible.
- Use clean containers.

- Avoid cross contamination of evidence.
- Execute a chain of custody.
- Store the evidence in clean, proper evidence containers.

5.4 Evidence Processing

This section focuses on preserving, inventorying, documenting, packaging, identifying, securing, transporting, and submitting evidence. Processing begins immediately after collecting evidence. Crime scene personnel must avoid excessive handling of the evidence after it has been collected. They must also maintain scene security throughout the evidence processing. As always, this means removing nonessential personnel from the scene and documenting the entry and exit of all people at the scene.

5.4.1 Documenting Evidence and Gathering the Chain of Custody

The first step in processing evidence is to properly document the evidence and establish a chain of custody. Investigators document the evidence, including the location of the evidence at the scene, the date of collection, the identity of the individual making the collection, and the description of items collected.

The chain of custody is a list of all people who have had possession of the evidence. This list is kept to ensure the physical security of the evidence. To establish a chain of custody, investigators document who has had custody of the evidence by using evidence identifiers, chain of custody forms, and clear labeling of evidence. This list includes the collector's initials, the location where the evidence was found, and the date it was collected. When evidence is transferred to another person, it is recorded on the chain of custody form. This is important because it is typical for individuals involved in evidence handling to be called to testify in court.

5.4.2 Taking Samples

There are three kinds of samples that may need to be collected along with evidence: standard/reference samples, control samples, and elimination samples.

Standard/reference samples are samples of physical evidence taken from a known source, such as a victim, a suspect, or a suspect's belongings. These are to be compared to the crime scene evidence. These samples are collected at the same time as the evidence unless they are blood standards or hair exemplars from the victims or suspects. First, investigators determine if these samples are needed, then they identify and collect the samples. Control samples may not always be needed, but if it is determined that they are needed, investigators obtain them when they collect the evidence. These samples are packaged individually.

Elimination samples are samples from investigation personnel at the scene. This can show whether or not investigators or someone present at the crime unwittingly left evidence. First, investigators determine if these samples are needed, then they identify and collect them. Each sample is packaged individually.

5.4.3 Identifying and Securing Evidence

Identifying and securing evidence is the next step in processing evidence. This section will first address securing physical evidence in general and then focus on two specific types of evidence: electronic evidence and weapons and firearms.

5.4.3.1 Physical Evidence
Physical evidence should be identified and secured in proper containers. First, investigators identify the characteristics of evidence to be packaged. This will affect what type of container is used. Liquids, volatile substances, and powdered substances are placed in nonporous containers. Dried biological evidence and trace evidence are placed in porous containers. Glass fragments, sharps, and pills or capsules are placed in crushproof containers. Some substances may need to be packaged in more than one way. For example, a paint sample would need to be in a porous container first, and then that is placed in a crushproof bag. Drugs should be placed in either a plastic bag or a crushproof container. Trace evidence would need to be placed in a porous container and then a crushproof container, while blood would need only a porous container.

After deciding what type of container is needed, investigators ensure that the evidence is in proper condition for packaging. If biological or organic evidence is not completely dry, it is packaged in a temporary container until it can be dried. If it is dried, it can be packaged and sealed. Some items may need to be packaged separately to minimize cross contamination. If items are wet, they are double or triple bagged. If items are found in contact with one another, they are packaged together. This might include things such as clothing, trash, or weapons next to blood or hair. Once investigators have decided how to package the evidence, they place it in the container and seal it. Investigators avoid reopening the sealed evidence and avoid handling evidence as much as possible.

As evidence is packaged, crime scene personnel make sure to label, date, initial, and seal all evidence containers. They begin and maintain an inventory list of items of evidence that has been or will be collected. They also include information on all persons having custody of the evidence as it is transferred from person to person or place to place. It is best to limit the number of people in the chain of custody. During this time, investigators use a secure area to store the evidence. Keeping the evidence secure in a safe storage area can diminish degradation or loss of evidence. Evidence is kept in a cool, dry environment. It should be protected from temperature extremes and other environmental insults, such as an air-conditioned vehicle or building or a cooler. The evidence is kept here until it is ready for transport.

5.4.3.2 Electronic Evidence   Electronic evidence can include things such as answering machine tapes, voice mail messages, surveillance camera videotapes (including those of neighboring businesses), computers, cell phones, pagers, caller IDs, fax machines, e-mail messages, and peripherals. The first step is determining if any electronic evidence is present. If it is, electronic evidence should immediately be secured. It may be necessary for personnel trained in electronic crime investigation to collect electronic evidence. Even something as simple as unplugging or disconnecting an electronic device could result in the loss of electronically stored data.

5.4.3.3 Weapons and Firearms Before rendering them safe, investigators document the description and condition of firearms and weapons. It is necessary to gather this information before anything about the weapon is changed.

First, investigators identify the type of weapon. If it is readily observable, they document the make, model, caliber, and serial number of all firearms. Close-up photography is used to document any evidence that may be on or near the weapon. Investigators record the physical condition of the weapon including any markings on it and the state the weapon is in. For instance, if the firearm is cocked or cocked and locked or if there is a magazine in the weapon, these conditions are recorded. Investigators also record whether there is any trace or biological evidence adhered to the weapon and the location of any spent or live shell cases under the hammer or any cartridge or cartridge cases (live or spent rounds) in the firearm.

Once investigators have recorded all the information available about the firearm or weapon, they determine the best method for rendering the weapon safe. For firearms, the safety should be on and it should be unloaded. If it is found in water, it should be kept immersed in water. Sharps should be packaged in puncture-proof containers. Document any actions taken to render the weapon or firearm safe.

5.4.4 Transporting and Submitting Evidence

Using the proper procedure for transporting and submitting evidence is important. Investigators check inventory of evidence prior to transport to ensure that all evidence is accounted for. This is done without compromising the integrity of individual items that may not be processed yet (such as latent prints on a physical item).

After the inventory has been taken, investigators determine whether specialized equipment is needed to transport unusual items of evidence. Evidence is transported to an appropriate facility as soon as possible. When this is impossible due to weather or other delays, investigators maintain the chain of custody.

All evidence is submitted to an appropriate laboratory for processing. Evidence is usually submitted via personal delivery or mail. However, live ammunition, explosives, and some chemicals are restricted by postal regulations.

5.4.5 Completing Lab Analysis

The following terms will be useful to know when evidence is undergoing analysis:

- Serology—The science of antigen–antibody reactions; focuses largely on blood serum
- Toxicology—The study of the nature, effects, and detection of poisons and the treatment of poisoning; detects the presence of drugs and poisons in the body
- Acid—A compound capable of donating a hydrogen ion to another compound; also acts as a proton donor
- Base—A compound capable of accepting a hydrogen ion; also acts as a proton acceptor
- Catalyst—A substance that modifies and increases the rate of a reaction without being consumed or permanently changed in the process
- Microcrystalline tests—Drug identification tests that use crystal formation patterns to determine the presence of substances
- PH—A symbol used to express the basicity or acidity of a substance
- Polymer—Any natural or synthetic compound substance composed of a large number of atoms in a repeating pattern

Bibliography

Anonymous. (n.d.). Unreliable or improper forensic evidence. *Innocence Project*. Retrieved from http://www.innocenceproject.org/understand/Unreliable-Limited-Science.php.

Christianson, S. (2006). *Innocent: Inside wrongful conviction case.* New York: New York University Press.

Fisher, B.A.J. (2000). *Techniques of crime scene investigation* (Sixth ed.). Boca Raton, FL: CRC Press LLC.

Lee, H.C. (2002). *Cracking cases: The science of solving crimes.* New York: Prometheus Books.

Saferstein, R. (2004). *Criminalistics: An introduction to forensic science* (Eighth ed.). Upper Saddle River, NJ: Prentice Hall.

Scene of crime: Glossary. (n.d.). *Forensic science: Let evidence reveal the truth.* Retrieved from http://library.thinkquest.org/04oct/00206/index1.htm.

Technical Working Group on Crime Scene Investigation. (2000). *Crime scene investigation: A guide for law enforcement* (Research Paper). Washington, DC: U.S. Department of Justice Bureau of Investigation. Retrieved from http://www.fbi.gov/about-us/lab/forensic-science-communications/fsc /april2000/twgcsi.pdf.

White, P.C. (Ed.). (1998). *Crime scene to court: The essentials of forensic science.* Cambridge, UK: The Royal Society of Chemistry.

Vecchi, G.M. (2009, Summer). Principles and approaches to criminal investigation (Part 1). *Forensic Examiner*, Vol. 18, No. 2, pp. 8–13.

Vecchi, G.M. (2009, Fall). Principles and approaches to criminal investigation (Part 2). *Forensic Examiner*, Vol. 18, No. 3, pp. 8–12.

Vecchi, G.M. (2009, Winter). Principles and approaches to criminal investigation (Part 3). *Forensic Examiner*, Vol. 18, No. 4, pp. 10–15.

Vecchi, G.M. (2010, Spring). Principles and approaches to criminal investigation (Part 4). *Forensic Examiner*, Vol. 19, No. 1, pp. 10–15.

6

DNA Evidence

6.1 DNA

DNA, or deoxyribonucleic acid, is the fundamental building block for an individual's entire genetic makeup (Figure 6.1). It is in every cell in the body. The DNA, or genetic code, is passed through the sperm and the egg to the offspring. This code is packaged tightly in bundles inside a person's paired chromosomes.

The locus is simply a location in the DNA. These are at specific places in the chromosome. Chromosomes are bundles of DNA (Figure 6.2). There are consistently 23 pairs of chromosomes in humans. Each pair is consistent in size and shape. One of the 23 pairs of chromosomes is the sex chromosome. In females, the sex chromosome is a pair similar in size called the X chromosome. In males, there is one X chromosome and one small Y chromosome.

Alleles are variations at a particular site on a chromosome that can vary or be similar in each duplicated locus. Each locus is duplicated since each chromosome has a partner. The mother determines half of the human code and the father determines the other half. If the parents share similar codes in a locus, then the site is referred to as homozygous. If the codes vary, the site is referred to as heterozygous.

6.2 Identification of DNA Evidence

DNA is contained in blood, semen, skin cells, tissue, organs, muscle tissue, brain cells, teeth, hair, saliva, mucus, perspiration, fingernails, urine, and feces. Forensically valuable DNA can be found on evidence that is decades old.

Review Table 6.1 to see types of DNA evidence and where they may be found.

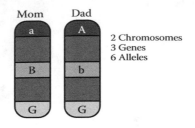

Figure 6.1 Illustrated DNA strand.

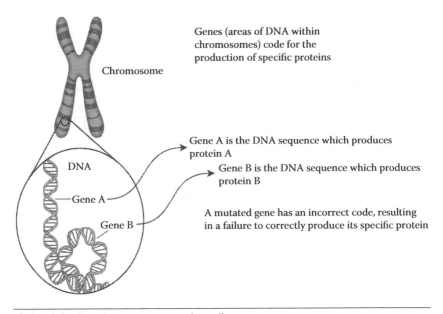

Figure 6.2 How chromosomes appear in a cell.

6.2.1 DNA Evidence

There are three types of evidence that may contain DNA: physical, trace, and biological.

6.2.1.1 Physical Evidence Physical evidence is tangible material, fibers, or latent prints. They are often considered silent witnesses.

6.2.1.2 Trace Evidence Trace evidence is small but measurable evidence that is discovered upon examination of larger physical evidence in the laboratory. It includes fibers, hair, paint chips, glass, plant material, and stains on clothing. Trace DNA evidence can be found virtually anywhere:

Table 6.1   Identifying DNA Evidence

EVIDENCE	POSSIBLE LOCATION OF DNA ON THE EVIDENCE	SOURCE OF DNA
Baseball bat	Handle, end	Sweat, skin, blood, tissue
Hat, bandana, or mask	Inside	Sweat, hair, dandruff
Eyeglasses	Nosepiece or earpiece, lens	Sweat, skin
Toothpick	Tips	Saliva
Tape or ligature	Inside/outside surface	Skin, sweat
Bottle, can, or glass	Sides, mouthpiece	Saliva, sweat
"Through and through" bullet	Outside surface	Blood, tissue
Bite mark	Individual's skin or clothing	Saliva
Fingernail, partial fingernail	Scrapings	Blood, sweat, tissue
Used cigarette	Cigarette butt	Saliva

Source: U.S. Department of Justice, National Institute of Justice, National Commission on the Future of DNA Evidence. *What Every Law Enforcement Officer Should Know about DNA Evidence.* Washington, DC, 1999.

- On the handle of a baseball bat
- Inside a hat or mask
- On the surface of soiled clothing or dirty laundry
- On the sides and openings of bottles, cans, and cups
- In bite marks on a person's skin or clothing
- In scrapings of fingernails

Maintaining trace evidence integrity is crucial. The primary source of compromise for trace evidence comes from the collector. To prevent contamination, crime scene personnel should wear gloves and use trace-contaminant-free implements for collection of evidence.

6.2.1.3 Biological Evidence   Biological evidence is not always visible to the naked eye. According to Locard's exchange principle, every time a person enters an environment something is added or removed from the environment. This applies to contact between individuals as well as between individuals and the physical environment.

All biological evidence is regarded as potentially infectious. Investigators follow all universal precautions for protection against infections. This means investigators wear PPE (gloves and masks), avoid eating and touching their faces, and identify biohazard evidence material and package it in containers with appropriate labeling.

Biological evidence can significantly degrade before or after collection due to the effects of the environment. Time, living organisms (bacteria, insects, and animals), weather, and the chemistry of the environment itself (chemicals and pH of the soil) can diminish evidentiary value. Very small amounts of material are required to obtain sufficient amounts of DNA. Conversely, very small amounts of material can contaminate a crime scene, which is more likely if the number of people inside the scene is not limited to only those necessary. All responders, investigators, and examiners are potential sources of contamination and loss of evidence.

6.2.2 Latent Prints and DNA

Latent prints, a potential source of DNA, must be packaged in a way that prevents smearing, smudging, or the further depositing of other latent prints. The destructive nature of some processing techniques should be considered prior to deciding whether to process for latent prints or swab for DNA. Investigators and laboratory personnel consider the quantity and quality of additional sources of evidence present at a crime scene. In some cases, laboratory personnel may need to be consulted on the sequence of evidence examination. Some latent print processing techniques can cause damage or loss of DNA evidence. Conversely, DNA analysis will eliminate any latent print evidence.

6.3 Crime Scenes and DNA Evidence

6.3.1 Types of Crime Scenes

There are three types of crime scenes: outdoor, indoor, and conveyance. DNA evidence can be found in each of these.

6.3.1.1 Outdoor
Outdoor crime scenes are the most vulnerable to loss, contamination, and damage in a short period. Heat, rain, wind, snow, and cold can all play a role in rapid degradation of biological evidence. Evidence that cannot be quickly protected in these conditions should be quickly collected in an effort to reduce degradation.

When a crime scene involves both indoor and outdoor areas, the outdoor area should be processed first. Nighttime crime scenes are problematic as the lack of sunlight can increase the potential to miss or damage evidence. When possible, secure a nighttime crime scene until daylight.

6.3.1.2 Indoor DNA evidence in an indoor crime scene is less susceptible to environmental loss and damage. The possibility of loss and contamination increases when multiple people enter the crime scene. Thus, limiting access to the crime scene is important.

6.3.1.3 Conveyance Conveyance is a means of transportation. Conveyance crimes are generally involved with vehicle burglary and car theft. Physical evidence can be recovered from the conveyance and well beyond. Suspects leaving in a hurry may carelessly leave traces of DNA evidence behind.

6.3.2 Location of DNA Evidence

Items of physical evidence (especially biological or DNA evidence) may not always be visible to the naked eye. A methodical approach to identifying and collecting DNA evidence is essential except when evidence integrity is at risk. In that situation, rapid decision making is important to prevent degradation and loss of evidence.

Alternate lighting may be needed to identify some types of biological evidence. For example, blood can be detected with chemical interactions. For example, luminol is used in detecting the presence of human and animal blood even when cleaning has occurred. The substance reacts with iron in blood, resulting in a blue green luminescence as a result of luminol treatment.

6.3.3 Evidence Priority

Prioritizing evidence collection is necessary. Investigators always collect DNA evidence and trace materials of the most fragile nature first, including the following items:

- Blood
- Cigarette butts
- Toothpicks
- Cups
- Cell phones
- Items that may have semen on them
- Partially eaten food (with bite marks)
- Hairs found at a point of entry

Second, investigators collect all swabs from handled items that may have been moved, appear to be out of place, or do not belong to the resident. This includes tools, pry bars, computer connectors and cables, frames, and boxes. Next, investigators collect lower quality biological evidence. This includes swabs of exterior doors and latches or handles of gates left open as well as smudged fingerprints.

6.3.4 DNA Samples

Control samples are taken on a surface or material next to a stain. These are packaged separately from the original stain where samples are taken. Control samples are useful in ensuring results were brought about by the stain and not the material on which the stain was deposited.

Reference samples are used for elimination or comparative purposes and are collected from all individuals who may be linked to a crime scene where DNA evidence is found. These are taken in the form of buccal swabs, a method involving swabbing the inside of the cheek area of an individual until moist. These are then compared to biological evidence found at a crime scene to place or eliminate them at the crime scene. Collection should be taken from possible suspects, victims, known references, and those with access to the scene (such as the homeowners). Investigators collect two swabs from each cheek for each reference sample. The donor name is identified on the swab box. The swab is allowed to air-dry before it is packaged.

6.4 DNA Evidence Collection

Before any evidence is collected at a crime scene, crime scene personnel secure a place for temporary storage. The location selected should be in a cool, dry environment that is out of direct sunlight. In warmer conditions, avoid the trunks of patrol cars as a storage place.

6.4.1 Equipment for Collecting DNA

A preassembled kit for collecting DNA evidence includes many items:

- Sterile wooden swabs
- Swab boxes or containers suitable for packaging swabs
- Tweezers
- Disposable razors or scalpel
- Scissors
- Distilled water
- Bleach solution (1:10 solution made fresh daily)
- Alcohol pads for cleaning
- Envelopes or bindle paper
- Paper wrapping
- Paper bags
- Pens/markers
- Evidence tape
- Biohazard labels

PPE should always be used when collecting DNA. PPE is used to maintain safety and to prevent cross contamination. PPE items include the following:

- Latex or nitrile gloves
- Eye protection
- Paper mask
- Tyvek white body suit
- Sleeve protectors
- Shoe covers
- Hair nets

6.4.2 Collection of Swabs and Stains

Properly collecting DNA evidence is important. When collecting evidence, investigators use clean, dry implements. When possible, they submit the entire item. A clean or disposable razor blade or scalpel is used to cut or scrape stains. Investigators do not use double tipped swabs for collecting evidence. Stains or swabs are allowed to air-dry before they are packaged. Heat and sunlight are not used to dry samples because these elements can aid in degradation and can contaminate the samples. All swabs are stored as soon as possible per agency protocol. All metal and glass items collected are labeled *room temperature storage*. Cold or frozen conditions can cause condensation, which could compromise evidence. All evidence is labeled as *biohazard*. Control samples are collected by the same method for the same type of evidence and surface. Each sample should be packaged separately with the proper identifying information and biohazard designation (when appropriate).

All evidence recovered is packaged and identified individually. The package is marked as well as the item of evidence inside. Anytime a transfer of evidence occurs, there is a risk of diluting or contaminating evidence. Any evidence that cannot be tagged should be placed in an appropriate container or envelope. Items that cannot be tagged include soil, hair, or stains. Investigators tag each sample using the agency case number, the item number, and the date the evidence was recovered.

6.4.3 *Collection of Blood and Bodily Fluid Stains*

There are different ways to collect stains from blood or other bodily fluids:

- Cutting—To collect blood or bodily fluid on an item, the section of the item containing the stain is removed using a sterile or clean cutting device.
- Wet absorption—A stain is absorbed using a sterile swab, gauze pad, or threads moistened with distilled water. The stain is concentrated on a localized part of the swab or gauze pad. The collection medium is then pressed or rubbed onto the stain and allowed to air-dry.
- Scraping—To use this technique, investigators scrape the sample with a clean razor blade or scalpel into a clean paper that can be folded and packaged in an envelope. Scraping

should be done where no wind or traffic is present to prevent contamination of the evidence.

- Tape lifting—This is an optional method for collecting dried bloodstains on a nonabsorbent surface. Clear fingerprint lifting tape may be used over the stain and lifted off. The stain is then transferred to the adhesive side of the tape, which can then be secured on a clear piece of acetate for submission to the lab. Precautions are taken to ensure that no biological material has contaminated the fingerprint tape.

The type of stain determines the method that should be used.

6.4.3.1 Wet Stains on Absorbent Surfaces   When collecting a wet stain on an absorbent surface, investigators document that the stain was wet and then submit the entire item if possible. If this is not feasible, they use a sterile swab to soak up the stain. If the stain is small, only the tip of the swab is used to soak up the stain. The swab is allowed to air-dry completely. When the stains are on soil or sand, investigators scoop a thick layer with the stain and allow it to air-dry. When it is dry, it is transferred to bindle paper.

When presented with a container still containing liquid, investigators poke a hole in the bottom of container to drain the liquid. This keeps investigators from contaminating the evidence around the mouth of container. A request should be made to do both DNA and fingerprint analyses.

Containers are marked for *room temperature storage* as aluminum and plastic can condensate when refrigerated, risking dilution of biological evidence.

6.4.3.2 Dry Stains on Absorbent Surfaces   Dry stains on surfaces such as carpet or wood are cut away with a clean razor or scalpel and packaged in paper. A portion of the unstained area is collected as a control sample. These samples are labeled and packaged separately.

6.4.3.3 Dry Stains on Nonabsorbent Surfaces   When there is a dry stain on a nonabsorbent surface, the entire stain is submitted if possible.

If an item contains broken glass or something sharp, it is placed in a cardboard package and labeled *sharp object enclosed*.

If the entire stain cannot be collected, investigators use a new or clean scalpel to scrape stains from the surface. The flakes are collected onto clean paper and the paper is folded into a bindle.

Each sample is placed in a labeled envelope, noting the location of the sample collection. Control samples are taken using moist swabs of the nonstained areas and allowed to air-dry. Each sample is labeled and packaged separately in paper.

6.4.4 *Collection of Hair and Fiber*

There are three procedures for collecting hair and fiber:

- Visual—Some fibers and hairs are visible to the naked eye. Clean forceps are used to transfer these to clean paper that can be folded and packaged in a clean envelope.
- Tape lifting—Trace tape can be used to lift and transfer hair and fibers from a surface. Trace tape with evidence is placed in a clean package.
- Vacuuming—An entire area of suspected trace evidence can be vacuumed and caught in a filter trap attached to the vacuum. These samples are packaged in clean trace paper then submitted to the laboratory. This is the least desirable method of evidence collection because there is a greater risk of cross contamination.

6.4.5 *Collection of Samples from a Smear*

Sometimes evidence is smeared. When this happens, investigators lightly moisten a sterile swab with distilled water and concentrate the substance on the tip of the swab. Control samples adjacent to the smear are collected using the same technique. For a perspiration smear, a clean, sterile, moistened swab is used to collect the sample and followed with a second sterile, clean, dry swab. All swabs are allowed to air-dry. All evidentiary and control samples are labeled and packaged separately in envelopes, bindle paper, or swab boxes.

6.5 Submission of Evidence

6.5.1 Evidence Labels

Accurately identifying evidence is absolutely vital. Evidence should include documentation of the following identifying marks:

- Type of item
- Size of item
- Manufacturer markings or serial numbers
- Noticeable damage or alteration
- Unusual stains
- Unusual markings

6.5.2 Evidence Transportation

Paper packaging is used for biological evidence if saturation is not a possibility. Excessive body fluids need to be transported in plastic to avoid contaminating people and other items. Saturated evidence should not stay in plastic packaging for too long because this promotes bacterial growth and evidence contamination, which can lead to DNA degradation.

6.5.3 Chain of Custody

Chain of custody is a tracking record of all detailed notes that describe the scene and where the evidence was collected. The chain should be maintained when evidence is received from an officer, detective, property personnel, and laboratory personnel.

Chain of custody includes notes of the scene including recovery location, time and date of collection, condition of the item, and any unusual markings or alterations of the item.

Individuals assuming custody of the evidence from collection through analysis must sign the chain of custody document or conduct an electronic transfer of the evidentiary items. In order to maintain an accurate and complete chain of custody, the number of persons handling the evidence should be limited. Investigators must confirm all names, dates, and identifications listed on the chain of custody. Finally, all evidence packaging is properly sealed and marked prior to submission.

6.5.4 Preservation of Evidence

All evidence must be identified, inventoried, and secured to preserve its integrity. Effective evidence preservation includes all appropriate packaging with correct and consistent information on labeling and procedural documentation for all items. It is crucial to demonstrate that the evidence introduced at trial is the same evidence collected at the crime scene and that access to evidence was controlled and documented.

6.5.5 Elements for Evidence Submission

To submit evidence, investigators must have the following items:

- Agency identification
- Names of suspects and victims
- Case identification number
- Violation characterization
- Date and location of crime
- Investigative summary of the incident
- Crime scene documentation including video and photos
- Description of items of physical evidence including the corresponding item number
- List of requested examinations
- Notations of interrelated past or current cases
- Reference to any relevant previous submissions
- Chain of custody, including method of delivery

6.6 Combined DNA Index System (CODIS)

The CODIS is a computer software program that operates local, state, and national databases and is funded by the FBI. Laboratories throughout the country share and compare DNA profiles through the National DNA Index System (NDIS), also managed by the FBI. The CODIS software enables state, local, and national law enforcement crime labs to compare DNA electronically. CODIS allows for the opportunity to link an unknown sample to a convicted offender, a solved case, or an unsolved crime. This helps exclude suspects.

6.6.1 DNA Profiles

DNA profiles are entered into CODIS from laboratories at the local, state, and national (NDIS) levels. Within each level, there are multiple categories that include convicted offender DNA profiles and unsolved crime scene evidence (forensic profiles), among others. Individual state legislation determines the qualifying offenses for which a convicted person must submit a biological sample for inclusion in the database. Convicted offender profiles account for the majority of entries in the state's DNA database.

DNA profiles are developed from evidence in forensic cases and entered via CODIS to search for a match in hopes of generating investigative leads. A significant number of forensic profiles are from cases where the perpetrator is not known, commonly referred to as unsolved cases.

Some states also enter forensic evidence profiles that match the reference profile of a suspect in a case that has been solved. Other state agencies, based on state laws, maintain DNA samples from individuals arrested for certain offenses. This is known as a *suspect* database.

6.6.2 John Doe Warrants

DNA database hits have assisted thousands of investigators. Benefits of searching for and supplying DNA profiles to the database include the ability to link cases to one another and identify suspects. Issuing a John Doe warrant allows for the prosecution of a case, even if a suspect is identified after the statute of limitations time has expired.

A John Doe warrant is used when the suspect has not been identified, but the investigator has obtained some of the suspect's DNA. The prosecutor may then issue an indictment against the suspect's DNA, and when the suspect is identified the warrant transfers to that person.

Bibliography

Kaye, D. & Sensabaugh, G. (2011). Reference guide on DNA evidence. In Federal Judicial Center (Ed.), *Reference manual on scientific evidence* (Third ed.). Washington, DC: National Academies Press. Retrieved from http://www.fjc.gov/public/pdf.nsf/lookup/SciMan3D06.pdf/$file /SciMan3D06.pdf.

National Institute of Justice. (2009, July 21). *Crime scene investigation: Guides for law enforcement.* Washington, DC: National Institute of Justice. Retrieved from http://www.ojp.usdoj.gov/nij/topics/law-enforcement /investigations/crime-scene/guides/welcome.htm.

National Institute of Justice. (2012, August 9). *DNA evidence basics.* Washington, DC: National Institute of Justice. Retrieved from http://www.nij.gov/nij /topics/forensics/evidence/dna/basics/welcome.htm.

Riley, D.E. (2005). DNA testing an introduction for non-scientists. *Scientific Testimony: An Online Journal.* Retrieved from http://www.scientific.org /tutorials/articles/riley/riley.html.

Ryan, S. (2009, January 12). *Transfer theory in forensic DNA analysis.* LawOfficer.com. Retrieved from http://www.lawofficer.com/article/needs -tags-columns/transfer-theory-forensic-dna-a.

The DNA Initiative. (2010, July). U.S. Government. Retrieved from http:// www.dna.gov.

Thompson, W.C. (2008, June 19–20). *The potential for error in forensic DNA testing (and how that complicates the use of DNA databases for criminal identification).* Paper produced for the Council for Responsible Genetics (CRG) and its national conference, Forensic DNA Databases and Race: Issues, Abuses and Actions, New York University. Retrieved from http://www .councilforresponsiblegenetics.org/pageDocuments/H4T5EOYUZI .pdf.

U.S. Department of Justice. (n.d.). *What every law enforcement officer should know about DNA evidence.* Washington, DC: Department of Justice. Retrieved from http://www.ncjrs.gov/pdffiles1/nij/bc000614.pdf.

U.S. Department of Justice Federal Bureau of Investigations. (n.d.). Combined DNA Index System. Retrieved from http://www.fbi.gov/about-us/lab /codis/codis.

7

BLOOD SPATTER
PATTERN ANALYSIS

7.1 Understanding Bloodstains

Bloodstain pattern work will provide probative information and aid the investigation, thus allowing the prosecutor to arrive at a well-founded decision. Understanding bloodstain patterns may be achieved by direct scene evaluations and meticulous study of scene photographs with a measuring device in view. The best method for analysis is to actually visit the scene.

7.1.1 Bloodstain Patterns Analysis

Bloodstain patterns can determine a lot about a crime scene, including the following:

- Source of the bloodstains
- Direction and type of impact
- Items that created the pattern
- Number of impacts
- Nature of the impact
- Location of the victim, assailant, and objects
- Position of the victim or suspect: sitting, standing, lying down
- Movement of the victim, assailant, and objects
- Signs of a struggle
- Blood smears or trails
- Footprints
- Fabric impressions
- Blockage of blood path
- Blood thrown from an object being swung

- In-line stain patterns
- Order of events
- Consistency in each person's story

Because bloodstain patterns can give so much insight into a crime scene, it is important to thoroughly analyze them.

7.1.2 Blood at a Crime Scene

Blood is a fluid mixture that contains cellular components and plasma. If blood is subjected to the external environment and various forces as the result of trauma, it will react in a predictable manner according to the principles of physics.

When blood is found at a crime scene, it is important to pay attention to the thickness, specific gravity, and surface tension. How investigators interpret the location, shape, size, and distribution of blood can help them discover the force or forces that produced it. When blood is found at a crime scene, investigators record the shape, size, location, and direction of the stain, as well as the surface area of impact.

Blood found at a crime scene can reveal whether it is human or animal blood, the blood type (A, B, AB, or O), the presence of drugs, and the DNA present in the blood. It can also help investigators reconstruct the events to discover what actually happened.

7.1.3 Necessary Equipment

When analyzing a bloodstain, the following items are necessary:

- Lights
- Light stands
- Protractor
- Compass
- String
- Tape
- Ring stands
- Magnifier
- Reticule

- Meterstick
- Tape measure
- Workshop manual
- Graph paper
- Ruler
- Tripod
- Camera
- Camera lens
- Extra film

7.1.4 Bloodstain Analysis Terms

Understanding the following concepts is necessary to complete a bloodstain analysis.

- Surface tension—Surface tension is the molecular cohesive forces that cause liquid to oppose penetration and separation. A sphere-shaped drop will not separate while falling unless it comes into contact with a force. The size of the drop depends on the balance of gravity and the object from which it drops. The texture of the surface that falling blood strikes dictates the degree of distortion of the bloodstain.
- Bloodstain diameter—The diameter of the bloodstain depends on the volume of blood that was spilled, the distance of the fall, and the texture of the surface on which the blood fell.
- Terminal velocity—Blood drops can typically reach terminal velocity of 25 ft per second (fps) after falling a distance of roughly 20 ft. The smoother the surface, the more uniform the edge character of the bloodstain. Blood dropping on non-horizontal surfaces or striking surfaces at an angle will produce a more oval, elongated bloodstain. The greater the angle of impact in which the blood hits, the greater the elongation of the bloodstain. The end of the bloodstain displaying the greatest degree of distortion will point in the direction of travel. Dividing the length of the bloodstain into the width of the bloodstain and consulting a sine table can determine the angle at which blood struck a surface.

- Point of convergence—This is a common point to which individual bloodstains can be traced.
- Point of origin—This is the location from which the blood producing the bloodstain originated.
- Energy and blood spatter—The greater the energy, the smaller the blood spatter.
- Blood spatter size categories—If the blood spatter is just a misting, the blood spatter is less than 1 mm. If it is fine, the blood spatter is less than 3 mm. If it is medium, the blood spatter is 3 to 6 mm. If it is large, the blood spatter is greater than 6 mm.
- Forces greater than gravity—Some forces are greater than gravity and can affect bloodstains. Vomiting, gunshots, and arterial gushing are forces greater than gravity.
- Blood transference—Blood can be transferred by swiping, wiping, and smudging.
- Splashed blood—Splashed blood happens when an abundant quantity of blood falls to a surface. It has a large central area with elongated rather than round peripheral spatter.

7.2 Documenting Bloodstains

Close-up photographs of individual items establish the nature of the items as found and the presence of bloodstains or stain patterns.

Photographs are taken perpendicular to the surface with the stains whenever possible. Investigators include a scale in the photograph. Flashes should be used carefully. If a flash is used sloppily, it can wash out stain pattern details or cause a reflection.

A body is photographed from all angles before it is moved. Any movement of the body is documented with photography. Bloodstains on the surface of the body or in the immediate vicinity of the body may be the result of blood dripping from a weapon or from an injured attacker.

Investigators should not overlook places that appear empty at first glance. In-line, cast-off stains such as stains that may be thrown from a blood-bearing object being swung may be present on walls or ceilings. Investigators should remember to look overhead.

7.3 Measuring Bloodstains

Bloodstain analysts measure the length and width of each bloodstain, taking tremendous care in the process. Figures 7.1 through 7.3 show how to measure bloodstains and what these measurements mean.

7.4 Mathematical and Statistical Analysis of Bloodstain Pattern Evidence

Note: The remainder of this chapter is based on an article originally appearing in the Spring and Summer 2012 issues of *The Forensic Examiner®*.

Statistics is the application of mathematical principles to the collection, analysis, and presentation of numerical data. Statistics relies on a set of mathematical procedures to organize, summarize, and interpret data. This section focuses on the application of statistical methods in the interpretation of bloodstain pattern evidence. This section reviews the most common mathematical methods for measuring bloodstains;

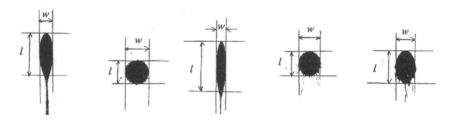

Figure 7.1   Measuring length and width of bloodstains.

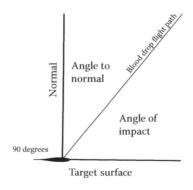

Figure 7.2   Angle of impact.

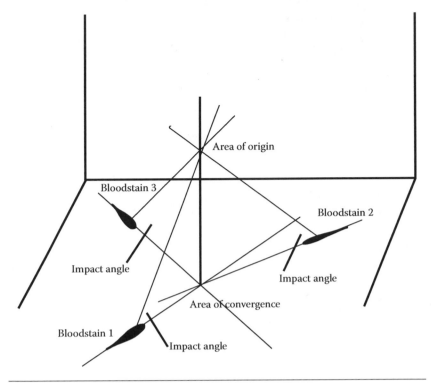

Figure 7.3   Area of origin determination.

explains the importance of formulating a hypothesis; discusses methods for minimizing errors in hypothesis testing; and explains standard and relative error, uncertainty analysis, types of error, and common sources of error. Since the O. J. Simpson trial, the public's craving for forensic science has increased dramatically, as evidenced by the number of crime dramas (e.g., *CSI*, *Law & Order* and *Criminal Minds*) and real-life crime shows (e.g., *American Justice*, *The F.B.I. Files*, and *Trace Evidence: The Case Files of Dr. Henry Lee*). Crime scene investigators must employ sophisticated techniques, including scientific explanations and statistical analysis, to solve crimes and to convince the public. The importance and prevalence of mathematics and statistical analysis in criminal investigations and trials has never been more critical.

7.4.1 It Is All about the Blood

Blood is a specialized form of connective tissue that consists predominantly of three distinct types of cells: red blood cells (RBCs;

erythrocytes), white blood cells (WBCs; leukocytes), and platelets (thrombocytes), all of which are suspended in plasma. The body contains approximately 5 L of blood, which equates to approximately 8% of an average male's total body weight (assuming a weight of 154 lb). There are about 30 trillion erythrocytes and 430 billion leukocytes circulating in the blood at any given time. Platelets play a major role in blood clotting, or hemostasis, by blocking breaches in damaged blood vessels. Plasma consists of 92% water, 7% protein, and various other substances including sugars, salts, clotting factors, minerals, hormones, and carbon dioxide. Plasma makes up about 55% of the total blood volume.

7.4.1.1 Behavioral Properties of Blood The qualities of blood are important from a forensic standpoint because the way blood reacts in response to a violent force largely determines how the resulting bloodstain pattern will form. When blood leaves the body, it behaves as a non-Newtonian fluid. Unlike Newtonian fluids such as water, inks, and alcohols that form a drop, based upon the strength of the surface tension and weight of the drop, non-Newtonian fluids separate into drops based on internal cohesion. Their flow properties are not described by a single constant viscosity value. Therefore, the mechanical behaviors of blood cannot be described using classical Newtonian mechanics (Wonder, 2007).

Blood is described by its rheological properties, which describe the relationships between stress and strain rate tensors under different flow conditions (Fung, 1971). These characteristics contribute to the unique bloodstain patterns that are deposited when blood leaves the body under gravitational, internal, or impact forces.

An important difference between blood—a non-Newtonian fluid—and water—a Newtonian fluid—has to do with the relationship between the stress and strain under different flow conditions. In Newtonian fluids, the coefficient of viscosity is constant at all shear values (Misra, 2005). In contrast, non-Newtonian fluids do not maintain constant viscosity under shearing forces. Therefore, they react differently to a sudden application of force. For example, stabbing the surface of a non-Newtonian fluid with a finger leads to the fluid behaving like a solid rather than a liquid. This same fluid, however, reacts like a liquid when a finger is slowly inserted into the fluid. This property is called *shear thickening*, or, more correctly, *shear thinning*, when discussing the projection of blood as it leaves the body under violent forces.

Shear thinning is considered the most significant non-Newtonian characteristic of blood (Siebert & Fodor, 2009). This quality is important when analyzing how blood behaves when it is released from the body and what type of stain will be created as it impacts a substrate. At very slow shear rates, blood cells tend to aggregate, or clump, increasing viscosity. As the shear rate increases, these formations break apart, reducing blood viscosity. The flexibility of the RBCs is also a factor in shear thinning. RBCs become increasingly deformed as the flow rate increases, decreasing the apparent viscosity of blood. This enables large cells to enter very small capillaries. The blood viscosity decreases as the shear rate increases. Shear thinning describes how blood behaves in response to an applied force: i.e., it becomes runnier and less viscous.

Yield stress is a function of hematocrit and fibrinogen concentrations in plasma—both are important for blood clotting. Yield stress tends to inhibit flow under relatively low stresses induced by gravity. However, if the lateral force exceeds a certain magnitude, blood will not relax back to its original shape or position leading to permanent (plastic or viscous) deformation; i.e., the blood flows (Merrill et al., 1969).

RBCs tend to stay in the center of the path of flow in vessels because they are large (Zhang, 1997). When smaller vessels break off from a vessel, shear thinning occurs because more cells continue to go straight rather than enter the new vessel. This affects the hematocrit ratio in the vessels, which is lowest in capillaries and other small vessels because the RBCs take the path of least resistance. This can be an important factor when evaluating low-, medium-, and high-velocity bloodstain patterns, i.e., venous flow versus arterial gush/spray.

For example, deoxygenated blood is pumped through the heart to the pulmonary artery, and then to the lungs for reoxygenation. This pumping action forces blood through the arterial system. Arteries are thick and muscular. This is very important to understand, because as a volume of blood is pumped through the arteries, the blood exerts considerable pressure against the artery walls. When a victim's artery is damaged, the pressure exerted on the blood forces it to leave the body under the same high pressure it exerts in the closed circulatory system. When blood leaves the body under extreme pressure, it creates a spurt or gush pattern on the substrate it hits.

In contrast, venous pressure is created by muscle contraction. As the muscles contract, they must act against gravity, forcing the blood back to the heart. When the muscle relaxes, small valves close. These valves prevent blood from going downward in response to gravitational force. Veins are very thin and contain very little muscle. Vascular pressure, therefore, is much lower than arterial pressure. Except in rare instances, such as victims with high blood pressure, venous bloodstain patterns respond to gravitation effects. When blood spurts a long distance, there is a good possibility that there was an injury to an artery.

7.4.1.2 Bloodstain Patterns and Actor Behavior Bloodstain pattern analysts can sometimes state with a relative level of certainty that a particular sequence of events occurred at the time of bloodshed, i.e., position, movement, direction of persons or objects at the time of bloodshed, mechanisms or objects used to create specific bloodstain patterns, the minimum number of impacts that occurred at the time of bloodshed, and direction of travel when the bloodstain was deposited on the substrate. The characteristics of blood as mentioned above have some effect on making these determinations. The behavior of the persons and instruments involved in the bloodshed events are other important variables.

Blood is often not released from a single point source, i.e., blood is not released one droplet at a time; rather, it is released in multiple droplets at the same time, resulting in patterns that do not regress back to a single source point. Furthermore, the victim and the assailant are not fixed in three-dimensional space. Depending on the force(s) involved, the victim may fall dead away, bend down, fall backwards, twist, or turn. Any of these variables, acting alone or in concert with each other, determine how blood will be deposited on various substrates, such as the walls, floors, or ceiling.

For example, victims of violent injuries related to gunshot wounds, bludgeoning, and accidental or deliberate suffocation may twist or turn because of the force being applied to their bodies. If the killer uses a ligature, such as an electrical extension cord, to kill the victim, the victim may fall dead away once the ligature is removed from his or her neck, despite any ensuing struggle. In these cases, bloodstain patterns may help identify what instrument or tool was used to murder the victim.

7.4.2 Mathematics and the Interpretation of Bloodstain Evidence

Blood droplets in free fall are affected by several forces, the most important of which are gravity, air resistance, and extraneous forces such as from the wind or a fan. Blood that exits the body accelerates due to the force of gravity until it reaches terminal velocity—the point where the droplets are in equilibrium with wind shear and other forces. Terminal velocity affects the formation of bloodstain patterns. However, the terminal velocity point is a function of mass and composition. The mass of a blood drop is not uniform, except in a vacuum. Therefore, the mass and composition of the falling drop are not uniform, so the terminal velocity will vary (Wonder, 2007).

This action has a direct effect on the formation of bloodstain patterns. Dr. Herbert Leon MacDonell established that blood released from an eyedropper (0.05 mL) reaches terminal velocity (25.1 fps) at a height of 6 ft (MacDonell, 1971). He also found that the size of a round stain (90°) does not increase in size when blood is dropped from a greater height. In contrast, blood droplets that strike a surface at an angle less than 90° exhibit elongated, elliptical shapes. The angle formed by the blood droplets and the substrate determine the angle of impact (see Figure 7.4). Balthazard et al. (1939), and later Dr. Herbert Leon MacDonell, realized that the relationship of the width–length ratio of the ellipse was a function of the sine of the impact angle (James et al., 2005). This approximate angle can be calculated by accurately measuring the width (w) and length (l) of the bloodstain.

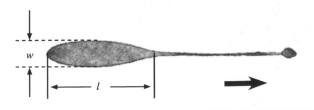

Figure 7.4 Direction of travel.

7.4.2.1 Angle of Impact   The angle of impact is the acute angle formed between the trajectory of the blood drop and the plane of the surface it strikes (see Figure 7.4).

From calculating the angle θ (see Figure 7.5), where *l* = length of ellipse (major axis), *w* = width of ellipse (minor axis), θ = angle of impact, the relationship between these variables is

$$\sin θ = w/l.$$

Therefore,

$$θ = \arcsin (w/l).$$

This calculation, the angle of impact, is a well-known technique to educated bloodstain pattern analysts. If the width of a well-formed bloodstain is 2 mm and the length is 4 mm, the sin of the angle of impact would be 2/4, which would be 0.5. The arcsin would be 30, indicating that the bloodstain impacted the substrate at an angle of 30°.

7.4.2.2 Accuracy and Precision   Bloodstain pattern measurements must be as accurate and precise as possible. Any error introduced by the

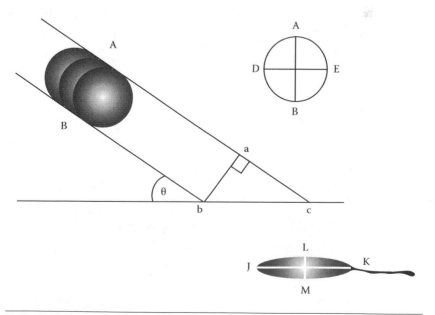

Figure 7.5   Angle of impact.

analyst while taking measurements increases the level of uncertainty (Bevel & Gardner, 2008).

Accuracy refers to how close one can measure to the actual value. For example, when calculating the angle of impact, the accuracy depends on accurate measurements of the length and the width. Precision refers to the repeatability of measurements time after time. For example, if the actual angle of impact was 10°, and an analyst made several measurements that result in a 1° difference, the accuracy would be ±1°. If an analyst measured 20 stains, all of which impacted at the same angle and the actual angle was 10°, but the analyst took measurements that calculated out to 6° for all 20, it could be said that the analyst was precise but not very accurate. The ideal is that the analyst takes measurements that are very close to the actual angle of impact and gets the same measurements each time. Hence, the analyst would be accurate and precise, and there would be a well-defined uncertainty such as ±1° in the above example. Error can be introduced, then, in the skill with which the analyst takes measurements.

Another source of error relates to the measurement instrument used and the number of significant digits. A basic rule is that one cannot accurately measure greater than the smallest value of the measuring instrument. If one is using a scale marked in millimeters, one cannot measure the length of a bloodstain in any smaller value than a millimeter. For example, one could say that the length is 2 mm or 3 mm, but not 2.5 mm length. That is because the instrument, the scale, does not allow for any smaller division of a measurement. If you would guess that it was about 2.5 mm, this is a guess and not a scientific measurement. Hence, one measures according to the capabilities of the instrument to be scientifically accurate and precise. If one wanted to be more accurate, one would get an instrument with smaller measurement units such as a micrometer that would measure in tenths of a millimeter. It is imperative that one follow the rules of significant digits.

The analyst is another very important instrument (Dror, 2010). Errors introduced by the analyst as a result of misreading the scale can lead to significant errors later down the line when the data are analyzed. Dror (2009, 2010) adds that cognitive biases and functions can also affect how an analyst reads the scale and determines the length and width. For these reasons, it is imperative that analysts be as precise and accurate as possible when taking measurements and record the actual measurements, not what the analyst thinks should be the measurements. They must be able to recognize potential sources of error as they take measurements and be able to account for them in the calculations. For example, analysts who have taken measurements over a period of years often can guesstimate the angle of impact simply by looking at the shape of an elliptical bloodstain. A very narrow bloodstain typically approximates a 10° angle of impact. Analysts know that certain measurement values result in 10° impact angles. Bias may be introduced by the analyst reading the measuring device in attempts to match the readings on the instrument to what is expected in the purported angle of impact.

7.4.2.3 The Area of Convergence: A Mathematical Application As previously acknowledged, projected blood strikes the target substrate at various angles and trajectory paths. That is, on a vertical surface, the blood drop may have been traveling through space on a line consistent with 20° from the horizontal (*x*) axis as defined by the standard Cartesian coordinates. A line drawn through a number of the well-formed bloodstains in the direction of the tails will project back to the area of location where the bloodshed incident occurred. Blood is not usually released from a single static point source, so oftentimes the actual point of convergence cannot be determined. Instead, the angles and directions of the impact bloodstain patterns can be used to determine the statistically probable area of convergence (AOC) where the original bloodshed occurred in two dimensions. This mathematical application is performed frequently by bloodstain analysts. AOC is determined by tracing the long axis of several well-formed bloodstains in the pattern back to a common AOC. The intersecting lines indicate the direction of travel, or the trajectory path, for each bloodstain, prior to it striking the substrate. The distance from the point of impact of the bloodstain and its distance to the AOC is an important value used to determine the area of origin (AO). Keep this value in mind. It will come into play as *distance* in the following model.

7.4.2.4 Following the Blood Evidence in Three-Dimensional Space The AO identifies the location in three-dimensional space where the blood source originated, i.e., the height (*H*) above ground level or

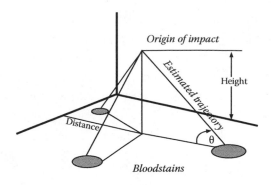

Figure 7.6 Bloodstain source in three-dimensional space.

the horizontal distance from a known point, such as a point on a wall. The height, also known as the third dimension, can be determined using the following formula:

$$\text{Height } (H) = \tan (\theta) * d,$$

where θ is the angle of impact and d is distance from the blood drop point of impact (represented by the head of the elliptical bloodstain and the selected point in the approximate center of the AOC).

The AO is the geographic location in three-dimensional space where the blood source was located at the time of the bloodletting incident (see Figure 7.6). The AO includes the AOC with a third dimension in the z direction. Since the z axis is perpendicular to the substrate surface, the AO is described by three dimensions. In the example, the z axis would be the height or the vertical distance from a fixed point. By applying the above formula to each well-formed bloodstain, it is possible to determine the AOC. The resulting range of values is defined as the AO. Just as with the AOC, the AO is not a single point in space; rather, it is the area defined by the parameters determined from mathematical calculations; i.e., it is a modeled geometrical entity.

7.4.3 A Consideration of Uncertainty

When collecting and analyzing data related to a blood source, remember that the sources are not fixed in three-dimensional space. Rather, they are dynamic. Victims move when struck. Skin elasticity affects how blood exits a wound, as do the positions of bones. Blood droplets collide and slightly alter their trajectories. Therefore, the forces related to projections can fluctuate. That is why most experts refer to an *area of origin*, rather than a single *point of origin*.

The variables in the bloodshed event can introduce uncertainty when calculating the AOC and AO values. These can be considered as inherent sources of uncertainty. Another source of uncertainty has to do with the line used to bisect the stain and the method for measuring the trajectory angle (see Figures 7.5 and 7.6). There is a certain amount of error in all measurement techniques used for measuring patterns due to the measuring instruments. There is also inherent error related to the instrument. Regardless of the instrument used, measurements are never absolute. Another source of error is related to the skill of the person taking the measurement. In other words, bloodstain measurements are as reliable as the person reading the scale. The most important thing to remember when measuring bloodstain patterns is that even the smallest, apparently inconsequential error resulting from inaccurate or imprecise measurement can lead to significant errors further on. This error is called the *butterfly effect*, or more appropriately the "sensitive dependence on initial conditions" (Lorenz, 1972). If the errors are serious enough, they can bias or skew the data, leading to a Type I error. Bloodstain measurements taken in two-dimensional space do not accurately represent the behavior of blood as it moves through three-dimensional space. In other words, the length and width measurements of an elliptical bloodstain can provide only a relative measurement of the angle of impact, not an absolute measurement. As with any statistical measurement, the more data you gather, the more likely you are to approach an absolute measurement.

7.4.4 Statistics, Hypotheses, and the Introduction of Error

7.4.4.1 The Vocabulary of Statistics   Statistics is a mathematical language that, as with any other language, consists of a specific vocabulary. The most important statistical concepts have to do with populations and samples. The set of all individuals or data of interest in a particular group is called the population. In comparison, the set of all individuals or items selected from that population, and that usually is intended to represent the population, is called the sample.

From the moment that investigators arrive at a crime scene, they start collecting information about the incident. These data are made up of measurements or observations that, when taken together, form a data set. Each specific measurement of the data set is called a score, or raw score. A numerical value derived from the population is known as a parameter, whereas a numerical value taken from the sample is referred to as a statistic. Bloodstain analysts are interested in specific characteristics in a population or sample that caused or led to a certain bloodstain. Bloodstain analysts are interested in constants and variables. Variables can have different values for different individuals. For example, bloodstain patterns from victims on blood thinners may be different from bloodstains from individuals who are not taking anticoagulants. A constant is anything that does not change. The atmospheric pressure at sea level is constant. A bloodstain made from a bloody shoe generally would be considered a constant in that it is a bloody shoe print impression and is anecdotally recognized as a representation of a shoe as the source of the geometric configuration. A variable is anything that can change. Repeated measurements of an elliptical bloodstain could change from examiner to examiner. Thus, the angle of impact could be a variable.

When working with statistics, analysts use two types of variables to describe what occurred at the crime scene. Independent variables can be manipulated by the perpetrator. They typically consist of the antecedent conditions that were manipulated prior to observing the dependent variable. In contrast, the dependent variable refers to a resulting or observed outcome of the perpetrator's actions.

For example, working backward, crime scene analysts discover a large, roundish mark (the dependent variable) on the concrete next to the victim. The analysts' goal is to discover what instrument (independent variable) was used to create that bloodstain, e.g., a hammer, a tube, or a pipe. When evaluating crime scene data, analysts typically compare their data to an exemplar, or model, of similar bloodstains in a database, not unlike Automated Fingerprint Identification System (AFIS) for fingerprints. This exemplar database is referred to as the control, whereas the physical evidence from the crime scene is referred to as the experimental, or test, value.

Bloodstain analysts are interested in discrete and continuous variables. Before performing any statistical analysis, it is important for analysts to know whether the variable is discrete or continuous. Discrete variables consist of separate, indivisible categories that exclude any values between the categories, i.e., types of bloodstains (see Figure 7.7). Continuous variables, on the other hand, offer an infinite number of possible values that may fall between any two observed values, i.e., AoI (see Figure 7.8).

It is imperative to understand the concept of constants and variables. This can be a critical source of uncertainty in bloodstain analysis. Certain geometrical patterns can be recognized based on experience. The bloody shoe pattern is an example. One can get numerous shoes, put blood on them, and press the sole to a surface. A certain geometric pattern always seems to form from the action. One can say, when the general pattern is observed, that it was made by footwear. This has nothing to do with individualizing the shoe. That is, one cannot say that a specific shoe made the pattern.

This process is a separate discipline called footwear identification. This information is referred to as anecdotal information. It is not really a descriptive statistic because there is not a definable change to the formation of the pattern. Different shoes make different patterns, but

Figure 7.7   Discrete variable.

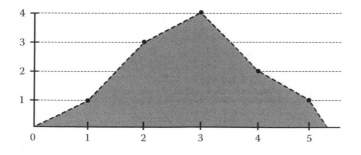

Figure 7.8   Continuous variables.

all shoes make generally the same pattern. One cannot tell if someone was wearing the shoe, if it was thrown and landed, or if it was staged by placing the shoe in one's hand and pressing it against a surface. A shoe pattern is relatively clear-cut in terms of a constant.

Other patterns are not as clear. Bloody hair along a surface makes a pattern with long thin lines. A piece of cloth with frazzled ends can make similar lines. We cannot say that 90% of the time hair will always make lines like frazzled cloth. We can only say that the lines are consistent with the lines made by frazzled cloth. This is still anecdotal information or information that is related to a constant. Uncertainty creeps in when analysts state constants as variables, such as stating that a certain pattern was made from hair dragging along a surface, or that 90% of the time such lines come from hair and not cloth. There is no way to count the formation of the patterns such that you can state a percentage with certainty. The pattern is either like or not like hair dragged along a surface. You should always compare your measurements with a known reference. Hence, uncertainty is the assumption that a pattern must be of a certain type, when in fact there is no way to establish this conclusively without additional information, such as witness testimony or an individual characteristic comparison.

Cognitive perception has been shown to have an effect on pattern recognition. If an analyst has a mental reference, there is a greater likelihood that the analyst will make an error.

This type of error is related to the uncertainty of the anecdotal information provided. For example, a frayed end of a piece of clothing or a long and flexible fiber brush often creates a pattern that is similar to that created by hair.

Discrete variables consist of separate, indivisible categories. No value exists between neighboring categories, for example, the number of sex offenders in a state, a person's race, a specific crime category, or the make and model of an automobile. Continuous variables, on the other hand, can have an infinite number of possible values that fall between any two observed values. Examples of continuous variables include age, measurements of bloodstains, or the time it takes for a drop of blood to fall from a certain height.

When collecting evidence, it is important to understand how to classify or categorize the data. Most data fall within one of four measurement scales: nominal, ordinal, interval, and ratio. Data that label or categorize observations but do not make any quantitative distinctions between the observations measure on a nominal scale. For instance, a steak knife, a hunting knife, and a paring knife are all knives, but none of them is better quantitatively than any of the other knives. Data that are sequenced in terms of order or magnitude are measured on an ordinal scale. Shirt sizes, for example, come in small, medium, and large. However, it is impossible to determine the magnitude of difference between individual sizes. The last two categories are quantitative scales that reflect differences in magnitude.

The interval scale consists of ordered categories of equal size. The differences between the numbers on the scale reflect equal differences in magnitude. The ratio scale and interval scale are the same with one important exception: The zero point on an interval scale is arbitrary; that is, it does not represent a zero amount. For example, Fahrenheit or Celsius on a thermometer makes it possible to measure magnitude and direction; however, the zero point does not imply a lack of temperature (as it is possible to have negative temperature). In contrast, the ratio (or zero) scale has an absolute zero point where the number reflects ratios of magnitude. For example, the Kelvin scale has an absolute zero—a hypothetical temperature characterized by a complete absence of heat energy.

The two most common types of statistical analysis used by bloodstain pattern analysts are descriptive and inferential statistics. Descriptive statistics organize, summarize, and describe data. Based on these data, analysts can use inferential statistics to make inferences or generalizations about a population based on data collected from a small group. Descriptive statistics use measurements of central tendency to describe the central position of a frequency distribution for a data group. The most common measurements are mode, median, and mean. The mode is the score or category that has the greatest frequency in a data set. It marks the midpoint of the most populous class interval, and it can have bimodal and multimodal distributions. The median is the score that separates the top 50% of the distribution from the bottom 50% of the distribution. The mean or arithmetic average of a distribution is the most commonly used measure of central tendency. It is computed by adding all of the scores in the distribution and dividing by the number of scores (i.e., $x_1, x_2, x_3, ..., x_n$) divided by the number of measurements in the sample (n).

The mean is a good measure of central tendency for roughly symmetric distributions. The mode is good for determining which category occurs most frequently among nominal variables. For example, in a sample of U.S. serial killers, the race with the highest frequency is white males with an average age of 28.7 years (Aamodt et al., 2008). The median is the best measurement when working with bad distributions, such as one or more outliers. It is good for measuring distributions with an arbitrary ceiling or floor. If 20 people measure 12 bloodstains, and the range was very large, the analyst could determine the measurements that occurred most often (the mode). Alternatively, the analyst could determine the middle measurement (median). When there are an odd number of measurements, the median is simply the number that has an equal number of measurements before the median value and after it. For example, if bloodstain measurements (in degrees) were 6, 7, 8, 8, 9, 9, 9, 10, 11, 12, 12, 12, and 17, then the median would be 9. If, on the other hand, the values 6, 7, 8, 8, 9, 9, 10, 11, 12, 12, 12, and 17, then the median would be (9 + 10)/2, or 9.5°. When calculating the central tendency where the sample is very large ($n = 40$), the mean, in conjunction with variance and standard deviation, provides the best measure of central tendency for continuous data. There are some situations, however, where the mean is not a good indicator of central tendency, such as when a distribution is skewed or when the number of subjects is small.

The last two terms are related to statistical analysis for samples and populations. Sampling error takes into account the fact that a sample is only a predictor of how a larger population behaves. It is not a perfectly accurate representation of a population.

Moreover, there is usually some discrepancy (or error) between a statistic computed for a sample and the corresponding parameter for the population. The standard error, on the other hand, is the standard deviation of the sampling distribution of a statistic.

All of these terms are important when evaluating bloodstain pattern evidence. Well-trained analysts know how the data were collected. Therefore, they can determine if there were any outliers or if the data were an even distribution—both of which can significantly affect the number of errors associated with a specific data set. Even the smallest error in a data set can lead to a high degree of uncertainty.

7.4.4.2 Formulating a Hypothesis Hypothesis testing is a statistical method that is used to determine the probability that a given hypothesis is true. It typically starts with an investigator positing a null hypothesis (H_0) regarding sample data that are randomly selected from a population. The null hypothesis always states that a variable will have no effect on the data being evaluated. For instance, the null hypothesis H_0 may state that the knife beside the victim was not the instrument that killed him. The alternate hypothesis (H_A) must then state that the knife was the instrument that killed him. H_0 and H_A are mutually exclusive. There is no gray area here; if a statistical analysis of the sample data suggests that the null hypothesis should be rejected, the alternative hypothesis must be accepted.

Note: Hypotheses do not state a fact. Rather, they state a condition, i.e., to reject the null hypothesis. Therefore, you have two options: you can accept the alternative hypothesis, or you can fail to reject the null hypothesis.

7.4.5 Outliers

Any time that measurements are taken from a random sample of bloodstains, the chance of obtaining one or more points that are outside the data range becomes greater. These distant points are referred to as outliers, and they can have a dramatic effect on the value obtained for a correlation. One way to quickly identify outliers in a data set is to create a scatter diagram from the available data (see Figure 7.9).

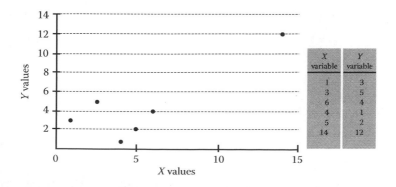

Figure 7.9   Scatterplot with outlier.

7.4.6 Errors in Hypothesis Testing

Researchers choose the number of data points that will be used to determine the likelihood that an event occurred. According to the law of large numbers, the larger the sample size (n), the more probable it is that the sample mean will be close to the population mean. The number of data points influences the size of the standard error in the denominator.

The standard error (SE) provides a method for determining and measuring sampling error, which is the error associated with a sample that does not accurately represent the sample population:

$$\text{Standard error } (\sigma_x) = s/\sqrt{n},$$

where σ = sample standard deviation and n = sample size.

As n increases, x decreases, thereby reducing the SE and increasing the likelihood that there will be a significant difference between the samples. A result is statistically significant if it is very unlikely that the result will occur if the null hypothesis is true; i.e., the result is sufficient to reject the null hypothesis.

In most cases, the population mean is unknown; therefore, a sample mean is used to approximate information about the unknown population mean. The SE is a method for defining and measuring sampling error. It gives a good indication of how accurate sample data represent population data. The sample mean is not a perfectly accurate representation of the population mean. There will always be some error between the sample and the population means; however, the SE does provide an indication of exactly how much error, on average, exists between the sample mean and the population mean.

When analyzing experimental data, it is important that you understand the difference between accuracy and precision. Accuracy refers to how closely a measured value is to a true or accepted value. Measurement error is the amount of inaccuracy between one or more measurements. It often is reported quantitatively as relative error (RE).

If the expected value for m is 80.0, then

$$RE = (78 - 80)/80 = -0.025, \text{ or } -2.5\%.$$

Note: The minus sign indicates that the measured value is less than the expected value.

Precision is a measure of how well a result can be determined (without reference to a theoretical or true value). It is the degree of consistency and agreement among independent measurements of the same quantity and the reliability or reproducibility of the result. Precision is often reported quantitatively by using relative or fractional uncertainty:

Relative uncertainty = |uncertainty (measured quantity)|.

For example, m = 75.5 g ± 0.5 g has a fractional uncertainty of |0.5 g/75.5 g| = 0.0066, or 0.66%.

Note: The uncertainty associated with a measurement should include any factors that affect the accuracy and precision of the measurement (see error propagation in the following).

There are different types of errors: measurement errors, random errors, and systematic errors.

Measurement errors are usually classified as random or systematic depending on how the measurement was obtained. For example, an instrument could cause a random error in one situation and a systematic error in another situation (Dunn & Brach, 2004).

Random errors are statistical fluctuations (in either direction) in the measured data due to the precision limitations of the measurement device. Random errors can be reduced by averaging the errors over a large number of observations.

Systematic errors are reproducible inaccuracies that consistently occur in the same direction. Systematic errors are difficult to detect and cannot be analyzed statistically. If a systematic error is identified when calibrating against a standard, bias can be reduced by applying a correction factor. However, unlike random errors, systematic errors cannot be detected or reduced by increasing the number of observations. The goal is to reduce as many sources of error as possible, and then keep track of those errors so they can be eliminated. It is useful to study the types of errors that may occur, so that you can recognize them when they arise.

Once all of the data are collected, the next step is to select the alpha level (α), or level of significance. The alpha level is the probability of attaining a Type I error, i.e., the probability value that defines the very unlikely sample outcome if the null hypothesis is true. The alpha level also determines the probability of obtaining sample data in the critical region even though the null hypothesis is true.

- Type I Errors

    Type I errors occur when a researcher rejects a null hypothesis that is true; i.e., the researcher concludes that there is a treatment effect when, in fact, there is no difference between the samples. In most cases, a Type I error can have serious consequences. If the researcher believes the data have a real effect, the study data may be published, leading to a false report that in scientific literature can be devastating.

- Type II Errors

    Type II errors (also known as beta [β] errors) occur when a researcher believes that the data have no effect when in reality there is a significant effect (see Figure 7.10). It is impossible to determine a single, exact probability value for a Type II error because it depends on a variety of factors including sample size and α. It only can be estimated as a function of the true population effect. The β error becomes smaller as the sample size increases or the number of end points increases. The relationship between Type I and Type II is such that when one increases the other decreases. Therefore, both errors cannot be controlled simultaneously. In most instances, Type I error is controlled by increasing the sample size and, therefore, minimizing the probability of obtaining a Type II error

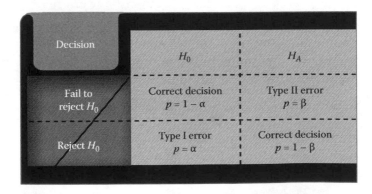

Figure 7.10   Logical possibilities in null hypothesis testing (TRUE STATE).

(Rangaswamy & Young, 1997). The decision to reject the null hypothesis when it is false is referred to as *the power of the test*, i.e., $1 - \beta$.

Generally, Type II errors are not as serious as Type I errors. The researcher must either accept the outcome or repeat the experiment to determine if there is a treatment effect. For example, we may want to know if a fan blowing in a room has an effect on the angle of impact. The null hypothesis states, "Wind blowing at an angle perpendicular to the trajectory of a blood drop will not have a significant effect on the angle of impact of that blood drop." To test our hypothesis, we place a fan at various distances from a known blood source. We use a device that consistently deposits blood drops at a 10° AoI.

We then measure 40 well-formed bloodstains. If our measurements indicate that the fan did have an effect on the AoI (i.e., AoI equals 6°), then we would reject the null hypothesis. In effect, we are saying that in all likelihood, we did not commit a Type I error; i.e., the fan has no effect on the AoI. Conversely, if the fan did have an effect on the bloodstain pattern and we stated that the fan had no effect on the pattern, we would have committed a Type II error; i.e., there was an effect and we stated that there was no effect.

Note: Recall that it is impossible to determine a single, exact probability value for a Type II error (Gravetter & Wallnau, 2008).

7.4.7 Common Sources of Errors Revisited

- Incomplete definition may be systematic or random. It occurs when measurements are not clearly defined. If two different people measure the length of the same bloodstain but the measurement method is not defined, it is very unlikely that they will get the same result. For example, we want to know the best method for determining the length of an elliptical bloodstain. Should the tail be included in the measurement? If not, what boundaries should we use to define the length? Definition errors can be minimized by carefully considering and specifying any condition(s) that may adversely affect the measurement.

- Failure to account for a factor is usually systematic. It occurs as a consequence of trying to control or account for all possible factors except for the one independent variable that is being analyzed. For instance, most bloodstain calculations ignore air resistance when measuring free-fall acceleration. The best way to account for this type of error is to consider all of the factors carefully that could affect the final measurements. Sometimes a correction can be applied to a result after taking data to account for an error that was not detected.

- Environmental factors can be systematic or random. This source of error is introduced by the immediate working environment, i.e., temperature, humidity, climate, weather, etc.

- Instrument resolution is a source of random error. All instruments have finite precision that limits the ability to resolve small measurement differences. For example, a meterstick cannot distinguish distances to a precision less than its smallest scale division, e.g., 0.5 mm. In most instances, however, whole numbers produce the same results when calculating angles of impact.

- Failure to calibrate or check zero of instrument is a type of systematic error. Instruments should be calibrated prior to taking measurements whenever possible. If a calibration standard is not available, the accuracy of the instrument should be checked by comparing it with another instrument that is at least as precise or by consulting the technical data provided by the manufacturer. When making a measurement with calipers or micrometers, the zero reading should always be checked before taking a reading. If the instrument is not zeroed, it should be zeroed, or the displacement of the zero reading from true zero should be measured and all measurements should be adjusted accordingly. It is good practice to check the zero reading before taking any new measurements.

- Personal errors are typically the result of carelessness, poor technique, or bias on the part of the analyst. Although personal error is usually unintentional, the analyst is responsible for ensuring that every effort has been made to identify potential sources of error and that all of the necessary steps have been taken to minimize them. In most cases, it is assumed that the measurements were obtained using correct procedures.

7.4.8 Estimating Experimental Uncertainty for a Single Measurement

All measurements, regardless of the instrument used to take the measurement, have some inherent uncertainty associated with them. This uncertainty is defined by the precision and accuracy of the measuring instrument, along with other factors previously mentioned. For example, if a bloodstain is measured using a standard ruler in millimeter increments, the uncertainty might be ±0.5 mm. If, however, the same bloodstains were measured using a vernier caliper, the uncertainty could be reduced to approximately 0.001 mm. In both cases, the uncertainty is greater than the smallest divisions marked on the measuring tool. Unfortunately, there is no general rule for determining the uncertainty in all measurements. The experimenter is the one who can best evaluate and quantify the uncertainty of a measurement based on all the possible factors that affect the result. Therefore, the person taking the measurement has the obligation to make the best judgment possible and report the uncertainty in a way that clearly explains what the uncertainty represents.

Measurement = (measured qty (x_i) Å} standard uncertainty) unit of measurement, where standard uncertainty is expressed as an estimated standard deviation, i.e., the one–sigma uncertainty.

For example, if the length of a 60° bloodstain is 6.7 mm and the precision of the rule is 0.5 mm, then the diameter would be written as 6.7 mm ± 0.5 mm.

The best estimate is the average, or mean, of N independent measurements:

$$\text{Average mean} = (x_1 + x_2 + \cdots + x_n).$$

Whenever possible, repeat a measurement several times and average the results. This average is the best estimate of the true value. The more repetitions made of a measurement, the better this estimate will be.

Note: Outliers have an effect on averages.

For example, an analyst measures a bloodstain using vernier calipers and determines that the length is 6.15 mm. The analyst takes four more measurements and then enters all of the results in a data table (see Figure 7.11). Precision calipers typically have an accuracy rating of ±0.001 mm. Although calipers give more precise measurements than a steel ruler does, they also can introduce error depending on the skill and experience of the person taking the measurements. To minimize the error rate, the analyst could take multiple readings and then average them to approach the true mean. A better estimate of the true value can be obtained if measurements from several analysts are collected and averaged together. This is called getting a second opinion or, in a purely scientific experiment, a peer review. This average is the best available estimate; however, it is not exact. Analysts would have to average an infinite number of measurements to approach the true mean value. Even then, however, there is no guarantee that the mean value is accurate because there will always be some inherent error associated with the measuring tool, which can never be calibrated perfectly.

One way to express the variation among the measurements is to use the average deviation. This statistic shows on average (with 50% confidence) how much the individual measurements vary from the mean:

Average deviation, $d = (|X_1 - X| + |X_2 - X| + |X_3 - \bar{X}| + \cdots + |X_N - \bar{X}|)/N$.

In contrast, the standard deviation characterizes the spread of a data set. The standard deviation is always slightly greater than the average deviation and is used because of its association with the normal distribution that is frequently encountered in statistical analyses.

Observation	Width (mm)
#1	6.150
#2	6.105
#3	6.180
#4	6.125
#5	6.155

Figure 7.11   Units of measurement.

For example, if 1000 (N = 1000) bloodstain analysts measured 40 bloodstains, a sample of the means from this relatively large population number should fit a normal distribution curve closely. If, however, only 100 (n = 100) analysts measure the same 40 stains, the mean of these samples is less likely to match a normal distribution curve, as the variation among the analysts is much greater (i.e., standard error). Therefore, a smaller sample size will result in a greater discrepancy, or sampling error, than a large sample size that more closely fits the normal distribution.

In most crime cases, a single person is responsible for measuring bloodstains. Depending on the level of experience and training, all of the measurements, regardless of the scale used, should be consistent. In other words, if an analyst uses a precision ruler to measure all of the stains, his or her error rate should be small. For example, prior to testifying in court, you should create 60 bloodstains on a surface that is comparable to the surface found at the crime scene. Once that is complete, you should measure at least 40 bloodstains carefully, and then calculate the range, error, and standard deviation for the samples. Only after you have performed this test can you testify that you have conducted individual research, determined the associated error, and expect all of the measurements to fall within the 95% confidence interval of your stated values.

Note: Your measurements should include several acute angles as well as several angles that are close to 90°.

7.4.9 Creating the Statistical Model

When evaluating evidence, analysts have a variety of tools in their statistical toolbox. Together, these tools provide a set of mathematical procedures for organizing, summarizing, and interpreting bloodstain evidence. When an analyst first arrives at a crime scene, there is typically an overabundance of bloodstain evidence. The total number of bloodstains represent the population (N), or set of all bloodstains at the scene. There are numerous values called parameters that describe the population. It is not possible (or realistic) for the analyst to measure all of the bloodstains; therefore, he or she chooses a representative subset of the population known as a sample (n). The different values in the sample are referred to as statistics. When performing calculations that involve angles of impact and AOs, the analyst must select well-formed bloodstains; i.e., the stains have clear elliptical definitions. Smaller stains tend to be more clearly defined than larger stains. Whenever possible, stains should be selected from various points around the circumference of the suspected AOC. In a cast-off event, stains should be selected from several points along the line of the cast-off stains. The variance of a distribution is a measurement of the amount of variation of all data points for a variable (not just the outliers that give the range). It is described by the following formula:

$$S^2_{N-1} \equiv \frac{1}{N} - \sum_{i=1}^{N}(x_i - \bar{X})^2,$$

where S^2 is the population variance.

A general rule of thumb is that for frequencies less than 40 (<40), the value for dividing the sum of the difference of the squares is $n - 1$. For frequencies over 40 (>40) the value is n. Generally, at least 15 data points should be collected for a significant statistic.

The standard deviation is the square root of the variance. For normally distributed data, approximately 68.3% of the data points should be within one standard deviation of the mean, 95% of the data points should be within two standard deviations, and 99% of the data points should be within three standard deviations.

Standard deviation is a useful measurement of spread because it is mathematically tractable (Lane, 2009). The formula for the standard deviation is

$$s = \sqrt{\frac{1}{N} - \sum_{i=1}^{N}(x_i - \bar{X})^2}.$$

The confidence level (confidence interval) refers to the likelihood that the true population parameter lies within the range specified as determined by the confidence interval expressed as a percentage.

For example, a 95% confidence level implies that the probability that the true population parameter lies within the confidence interval is 0.95. It does not imply, however, that there is a 95% chance that the population mean will fall between two specific values. The probability that a constant falls within any given range will always be 0.00 or 1.00. The confidence level only describes the uncertainty associated with a sampling method. When discussing the error rate at three standard deviations, crime scene analysts should not state that the error rate at 99% confidence level is 1%; rather, they should state that there is a reasonable expectation that the actual sample statistic will lie in the interval between –3 and +3. Any measurement that falls outside of this range would require additional investigation to determine if the outliers are significant or not.

Using the three-sigma, or empirical, rule for a normal distribution curve, nearly all values will lie within three standard deviations of the mean (see Figure 7.12).

The normal distribution curve is a function defined by the following equation and resembles a bell shape:

$$f(x) = 1/\sigma\sqrt{2\pi}e^{-(x-\mu)^2/2\sigma^2}.$$

A normal distribution has the following properties:

- It is symmetrical about the mean (m).
- It is unimodal.
- It extends to infinity in both directions.
- The area under the curve always equals 1.
- It is determined by its mean and standard deviation σ (or variance σ_2).

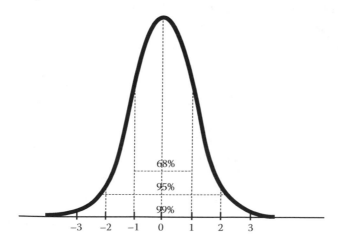

Figure 7.12   Normal distribution curve.

The normal distribution curve describes how a particular sample or population will behave under certain conditions.

All normal curves, regardless of the mean or standard deviation, conform to the following empirical rule, commonly known as the 68–95–99.7 rule:

- 68% of the area under the curve falls within one standard deviation of the mean.
- 95% of the area under the curve falls within two standard deviations of the mean.
- 99.7% of the area under the curve falls within three standard deviations of the mean.

Note: For most purposes, the outliers can be excluded from the probability calculations when measurements are based solely on the range.

7.4.9.1 Determination of the Range among Individual Variation in Measurements   Some variation should be expected in cases involving bloodstain evidence. The amount of variation, however, should be minimal assuming that all of the measurements that were taken are accurate (Barksdale, 2009). The error rate for bloodstain patterns is based on a simple frequency distribution. The probability that a particular event will occur is referred to as the relative frequency (RF), which is the number of times an event will occur compared with the total number of times that all possible events will occur over a long run of observations (conducted under identical conditions of all possible events). The RF measures the probability of that event; i.e., if n_x equals the number of trials where an event x occurred and n_t equals the total number of trials, the probability $P(x)$ of the event occurring can be approximated by the following formula:

$$P(x) \approx P(E) \approx n(E)/n(S),$$

where E = event and S = sample space.

In most cases, the determination of the variation in terms of range, or frequency, is sufficient for determining limits of error. For example, a bloodstain is dropped at an angle of 9.0°. Forty individuals measure the bloodstain and arrive at values ranging from 8.1 to 9.9. Using simple math, the error rate can be determined for the upper and lower range. The lower variation is calculated by dividing the lower data point (8.1) by the mean and then subtracting the result from one, i.e., $1 - (8.1/9.0) = 0.1$, or 10% error. Similarly, the upper variation is calculated by dividing the upper data point (9.9) by the mean and then subtracting one from the result, i.e., $(9.9/9) - 1.0 = 0.1$, or 10% error. Thus, the error rate for a bloodstain is written as 9.0 Å} 10%. That means that the range between the lowest value and the highest value is 20%. It is important to distinguish between the error rate, which is the variation in measurement among different analysts (i.e., the range including outliers) versus the standard deviation, which is a measure of central tendency.

Note: Analysts should undergo a periodic evaluation of their measurement techniques. As part of this evaluation, the analyst should measure 40 bloodstains at a known angle (e.g., 10°) and then calculate the standard deviation and the error rate as part of their personal research and expert data.

For example, the known value of a bloodstain is 10° and the analyst's measurements are between 8.5° and 11.5° (i.e., 10° ± 1.5°). If the standard deviation calculated from $n = 40$ bloodstains is ±0.05, then three standard deviations would be 1.5°. The error rate, on the other hand, would be ±15%, i.e., $1 - (8.5/10)$; and $(11.5/10) - 1$. Based on these findings, we would expect the analyst's measurement to be between 8.5° and 11.5°.

7.4.9.2 Incidence Rate Statistics and Associative Evidence   Edmond Locard (1877–1966) proclaimed, "Every contact leaves a trace." That statement forms the foundation of associative evidence, i.e., evidence that attempts to establish an association between people or between people, places, and things. Associative evidence is usually corroborative in nature—the evidence is weighed along with other evidence and has no substantial weight of its own. This associative evidence is particularly useful in crimes of violence, such as homicide, sexual assault, and aggravated assault, where physical contact may have occurred (Deedrick, 2000).

Associative evidence is sometimes accompanied by statistical testimony about the incidence rate of matching characteristics (Thompson and Schumann, 1987). Incidence rate statistics indicate the frequency of a trait or characteristic that is solely diagnostic of the target out-come. It is the percentage of some relevant population that possesses a characteristic trait linking the defendant to the crime. For example, the percentage of serial killers in U.S. prisons is a base rate statistic. The percentage of serial killers in U.S. prisons who use garrotes in the commission of their crimes is an incident-rate statistic. In criminal proceedings, the percentage of defendants in some relevant compari-son population who are guilty is a base-rate statistic.

7.4.9.3 Common Fallacies in the Presentation of Statistical Evidence A number of studies show that when jurors were asked to judge the like-lihood of an event, they tended to ignore or downplay statistics on the base-rate frequency (Bar-Hillel, 1980; Borgida & Brekke, 1981). This type of error is referred to as the base-rate fallacy. The following are some of the more common fallacies associated with the presentation of statistical evidence. The fallacy of suppressed evidence occurs when contradicting evidence is ignored or forgotten (Kahane, 1984). The fallacy of questionable causes occurs when a primary action is labeled as the cause of a secondary action, i.e., taking a statistical correlation as proof of a causal connection (Kahane, 1984). The two most com-mon fallacies associated with the presentation of statistical evidence are the prosecutor's fallacy and defense attorney's fallacy.

Prosecutors are guilty of fallacious reasoning when they draw con-clusions about the probability that a criminal suspect is guilty based on evidence of a match. This conclusion usually is drawn without con-sidering the percentage of people who would match the suspect as well as the a priori probability that the suspect in question is guilty. In contrast, defense attorneys are guilty of fallacious reasoning when they assume that associative evidence is irrelevant because it shows that the defendant and perpetrator are members of the same large group (Rossmo, 2009).

Historically, statistical evidence has posed a quandary for appellate courts that struggle over the competence of juries to understand sta-tistical inferences (Kaye, 1980). Some appellate courts have rejected the use of statistics on the grounds that jurors tend to overestimate the value of statistics (*People v. Robinson*, 1970; *People v. Macedono*, 1977; *State v. Carlson*, 1978; *People v. McMillen*, 1984). Most appel-late courts, however, admit statistical evidence, claiming that most jurors are unlikely to find it misleading and will give it the appropriate weight (Annotation, 1980; Jonakait, 1983).

When base-rate statistics are used in a criminal trial, they are often referred to as naked statistical evidence (Kaye, 1980). Naked statistics are probabilities that are not case specific to the events in question; rather, they are developed independently of the events in question (Wells, 1992). Courts generally treat naked statistical evidence differently than they do incidence rate statistics because naked statistical evidence tends to be of a very vague nature.

The classic example used to describe naked statistical evidence is the blue bus paradigm. In this scenario, a person is struck by a blue bus of unknown ownership. The evidence shows that a particular company operates 90% of the blue buses on that route. This evidence is referred to as *naked statistical evidence*. It associates the incident with the company that operates the majority of the buses in the area. Similarly, if a person possessing heroin is charged with concealing an illegally imported narcotic, evidence that 98% of heroin in the United States is illegally imported would be considered naked statistical evidence. In this case, the conclusion is based on the probability that the defendant's heroin was obtained most likely from an illegal source.

Historically, courts have treated naked statistical evidence differently than they have treated incidence rate statistics. Whereas the majority of jurisdictions will admit incidence rate statistics, most courts continue to reject naked statistical evidence (see *Smith v. Rapid Transit*, 1945). There are some notable cases, however, where naked statistical evidence admissibility was upheld (e.g., *Turner v. United States*, 1970; *Sindell v. Abbott Laboratories*, 1980).

7.4.10 Conclusion

Bloodstain pattern analysts follow strict protocols that dictate the best methods for collecting bloodstains: taking accurate and precise measurements, calculating angles of impact, determining areas of origin and convergence, and packaging and storing bloodstain evidence. These procedures are designed to ensure that evidence is not compromised during collection and processing, and that it represents an accurate portrayal of the original crime scene. When statistical evidence is used in tandem with a bloodstain pattern index, it may improve the credibility of bloodstain evidence. When preparing a bloodstain pattern index, it is critical to take precautionary measures to ensure all evidence intended for inclusion in the database is protected against the elements and prepared in accordance with long-term archival techniques. Statistics and probability are powerful tools that can significantly influence how bloodstain evidence is used in a criminal trial. Analysts use statistics to establish the reliability and validity of bloodstain evidence collected at the crime scene and to establish their own degree of accuracy and precision. Bloodstain pattern analysis is still more an art than a science. A large part of bloodstain analysis is pattern recognition. There is no statistical basis for determining the identity of a pattern. Investigators rely on logic, reasoning, and experience to link a particular bloodstain pattern to particular behavior, i.e., passive versus impact bloodstains. Likewise, prosecutors and defense attorneys rely on witness testimony, field research, and crime reenactment to support the proposed assumption. Anytime that investigators or attorneys posit a theory as to how a particular pattern was created, they increase the level of uncertainty. The application of statistical analysis to bloodstain pattern evidence is a relatively new field. Up until now, statistical techniques have been the purview of DNA experts. Better measurement techniques combined with more accurate measuring tools can help minimize the amount of error that creeps into bloodstain evidence analysis. Statistical methods used to link a suspect's DNA to a particular crime are now becoming more relevant in other forensic fields, such as bloodstain pattern analysis. Bloodstain pattern analysts should become adept at employing statistical analysis for reducing the level of uncertainty in criminal testimony.

Whenever human fallibility enters the equation, statistical uncertainty increases. Statistical error can lead to several fallacies of reasoning, mostly importantly, prosecutors and defense attorneys' fallacies. In any statistical analysis, one must use reasoning in making inferences. These inferences can mitigate or invalidate evidence that is presented in such a way that it assumes guilt in the absence of sufficient evidence.

Forensic DNA experts often use statistics to link a particular a DNA profile to a specific suspect in a certain statistical sample population. Today, forensic mathematicians are using those same principles in bloodstain pattern analysis. As analysts learn more about the rheological properties of blood outside the body, new methods for increasing the reliability and validity of bloodstain pattern evidence will be developed.

Bibliography

Aamodt, M.G., Henriques, K. & Hodges, C. (2008, October). *Profiling the age of serial killers*. Paper presented at the annual meeting of the Society for Police and Criminal Psychology, Walnut Creek, CA.

Annotation. (1980). Admissibility, weight and sufficiency of blood grouping tests in criminal cases. *American Law Reports*, Vol. 2, p. 500. Aspen Publishers Editorial Staff. 4th (ALR Series).

Balthazard, V., Piedelievre, R., Desoille, H. & DeRobert, L. (1939). Study of projected drops of blood. *Annales De Medecine Legale, Criminologie Police Scientifique Et Toxicologie*, Vol. 19, pp. 26–323.

Barksdale, L. (2009). *Origin determinations*. Unpublished manuscript.

Bar-Hillel, M. (1980). The base-rate fallacy in probability judgments. *Acta Psychologica*, Vol. 44, No. 3, pp. 211–233.

Bevel, T. & Gardner, R.M. (2008). *Bloodstain pattern analysis with an introduction to crime scene reconstruction* (Third ed.). p. 300. Boca Raton, FL: CRC Press.

Borgida, E. & Brekke, N. (1981). The base-rate fallacy in attribution and prediction. *New Directions in Attribution Research*, Vol. 3, pp. 63–95.

Deedrick, D.W. (2000). Hairs, fibers, crime, and evidence. *Masthead*, Vol. 2, No. 3.

Dror, I. (2009). How can Francis Bacon help forensic science? The four idols of human biases. *Jurimetrics*, Vol. 50, pp. 93–110.

Dror, I. (2010). *Why must forensic practice be based on cognitive research: Forensic science initiative training*. Unpublished manuscript.

Dror, I. and Cole, S. (2010). The vision in "blind" justice: Expert perception, judgment and visual cognition in forensic pattern recognition. *Psychonomic Bulletin & Review*, Vol. 17, No. 2, pp. 161–167.

Dunn, P.F. & Brach, R.M. (2004). *Uncertainty analysis for forensic science*. Tucson, AZ: Lawyers & Judges Publishing Co.

Fung, Y.C. (1971). Biomechanics: A survey of the blood flow problem. In C.S. Yih (Ed.), *Advances in applied mechanics*. New York: Academic Press.

Gravetter, F.J. & Wallnau, L.B. (2008). *Statistics for the behavioral sciences*, p. 783. Belmont, CA: Wadsworth Publishing Co.

James, S.H., Kish, P.E. & Sutton, T.P. (2005). *Principles of bloodstain pattern analysis: Theory and practice*, p. 576. Boca Raton, FL: CRC Press.

Jonakait, R.N. (1983). When blood is their argument: Probabilities in criminal cases, genetic markers, and, once again, Bayes' theorem. *University of Illinois Law Review*, p. 369.

Kahane, H. (1984). *Logic and contemporary rhetoric: The use of reason in everyday life* (Fourth ed.). Florence, KY: Thomson Wadsworth.

Kaye, D. (1980). Naked statistical evidence. *The Yale Law Journal*, Vol. 89, No. 3, pp. 601–611.

Lane, D. (2009). Hyperstat online contents. Retrieved from http://davidmlane.com/hyperstat/A16252.html.

Lorenz, E.N. (1972). *Does the flap of a butterfly's wings in Brazil set off a tornado in Texas?* American Association for the Advancement of Science. Presented at the Global Atmospheric Research Program 139th Meeting of the American Association for the Advancement of Science, Washington, DC. Unpublished.

MacDonell, H.L. (1971). *Flight characteristics and stain patterns of human blood* (No. PR 71–4), p. 77. Washington, DC: U.S. Government Printing Office. Retrieved from https://www.ncjrs.gov/pdffiles1/Digitization/1747NCJRS.pdf.

Merrill, E.W., Cheng, C.S. & Pelletier, G.A. (1969). Yield stress of normal human blood as a function of endogenous fibrinogen. *Journal of Applied Physiology*, Vol. 26, No. 1, p. 1.

Misra, J.C. (2005). Modern applied mathematics. In J.C. Misra & B. Pal (Eds.). *Modern applied mathematics* (pp. 56–82). India: Narosa Publishing House.

Rangaswamy, R. & Young, L.J. (1997). A text book of agricultural statistics. *Journal of Natural Resources and Life Sciences Education*, Vol. 26, No. 1, p. 82.

Rossmo, D.K. (2009). *Criminal investigative failures*, p. 400. Boca Raton, FL: CRC.

Siebert, M.W. & Fodor, P.S. (2009). Newtonian and non-Newtonian blood flow over a backward facing step—A case study. pp. 1–5. Presented at the *COMSOL Conference 2009*, Boston, MA.

Sindell v. Abbott Laboratories, 26 Cal. 3d 588 (1980).

Smith v. Rapid Transit, Inc., 317 Mass. 469, 58 N.E.2d 754 (1945).

Thompson, W.C. & Schumann, E.L. (1987). Interpretation of statistical evidence in criminal trials. *Law and Human Behavior*, Vol. 11, No. 3, pp. 167–187.

Turner v. United States, 396 U.S. 398 (1970).

Wells, G.L. (1992). Naked statistical evidence of liability: Is subjective probability enough? *Journal of Personality and Social Psychology*, Vol. 62, No. 5, pp. 739–752.

Westveer, A.E., Jr. (2002). *Managing death investigations*, Vol. 1 (Fifth ed.). Washington, DC: U.S. Department of Justice Federal Bureau of Investigation. (Used with permission.)

Wonder, A.Y. (2007). *Bloodstain pattern evidence: Objective approaches and case applications*. New York: Academic Press.

Zhang, Z. (1997). Parameter estimation techniques: A tutorial with application to conic fitting. *Image and Vision Computing*, Vol. 15, No. 1, pp. 59–76.

8

POSTMORTEM EXAMINATION

8.1 The Investigation

There are various stages that a person goes through during death. First, his or her respiratory system shuts down, and then circulation of blood stops. Last, the central nervous system ceases to function.

If possible, a medical examiner (ME) should respond to death scenes. A thorough investigation with an ME may exclude an innocent person from being a suspect. One of the most important purposes of an investigation is to establish the time of death versus the time of assault. Although this is important, the time of death is always an estimate. The only accurate method of determining time of death is to be there when the death occurs, and even then, there is a small margin of error. Currently, there is no 100% accurate marker to establish a time of death. Investigators should be extremely cautious when determining the time of death as different factors can enhance or impede the chemistry of death. The closer the examination is to the actual time of death, the greater the possibility of an accurate opinion from the scene and death markers.

8.1.1 Evidence about the Time of Death

8.1.1.1 Corporal Evidence Corporal evidence is evidence within the body. It may be useful in establishing the time of death. Here are some possible examples of corporal evidence:

- Stage of decomposition of organs versus exterior decomposition
- Soot in airway
- Medical conditions and previous surgery
- Alcohol and drug levels
- Beard, nails, and hair

8.1.1.2 Environmental Evidence   Evidence in the environment surrounding the victim may also be useful. For example, if there is uncollected mail or newspapers, the time of death might be before the mail was delivered. Here are some other pieces of evidence that might be useful in establishing the time of death:

- Sales slips or receipts
- State of lights, alarm, and oven (on/off)
- Food in the refrigerator
- Animals in the house
- Type of clothing (day or night)
- Indoors or outdoors
- Seasonal (remote deaths)
- Condition of clothing (mold, leached dyes)

8.1.1.3 Anamnestic Evidence   This is evidence based on the decedent's ordinary habits and daily activities, such as his or her usual activities, waking and sleeping patterns, eating habits (times and type of foods), and appointments.

8.1.1.4 Ocular Changes   Ocular changes can give an estimated time of death. This is not an exact science however; it depends on eyelid position, temperature, humidity, and air currents. Look at Table 8.1 for more information.

Table 8.1   Ocular Changes after Death

CHANGE	EYES OPEN	EYES CLOSED
Ophthalmoscopic exam	Within 1/2 hour (indication	Within 1/2 hour (indication
Boxcarring in vessels	of death) (Kevorkian; JFS,	of death)
Time interval changes	1961)	
Corneal film	Minutes	Several hours
Scleral discoloration "Tache noire"	Minutes to several hours	Minutes to several hours
Corneal cloudiness	2 hours or less	12–24 hours
Corneal opacity	N/A	Third postmortem day
Exophthalmos (bulging)	With gas formation	N/A
Endophthalmos (retraction)	Advaced decomposition	N/A

8.1.1.5 Food in the Stomach The investigator cannot rely on the amount of digestion of the food in the stomach as a time of death because there are too many variables. If the victim has a light meal, the food will be in the stomach for 1 1/2 to 2 hours. If the victim has an average-sized meal, the stomach will have food in it for 3 to 4 hours; with a heavy meal, the stomach will have food in it for 4 to 6 hours. The stomach will start to empty within 10 minutes. However, these times are general. Liquids are digested faster than semisolid food, which is digested faster than solid food. Also, the emotional state of the person can affect the digestion rate. Psychogenic pylorospasm can prevent the stomach from emptying for several hours, while hypermotility can cause diarrhea.

8.1.2 Range of Death

Once the evidence has been examined, investigators establish a window of death. They ask questions such as when the death could have occurred, when the deceased was last known to be alive, and when the body was found. These will help establish a time frame. The difference between when the person was known to be alive and when the body was found is the range of time wherein death could have occurred. Investigators use scene markers that allow some positioning of the death. Ask the following questions:

- When did he or she read the morning newspaper?
- When did he or she make phone calls?
- What type of meal did he or she consume?
- Where was he or she?
- In what state of dress was he or she?

The preliminary range of death is adjusted by these additional data. If the paper was available the night before or if the deceased worked nights could greatly affect his or her schedule.

Investigators also examine environmental factors such as if the sun was shining on the victim or if the air conditioner was on. They note the room temperature and the setting on the thermostat. An unusually cool thermostat setting is an indicator that someone intentionally wanted to impede postmortem changes of the body. Also, temperature affects the accuracy of the time of death estimation. If there are larvae present, it should be noted. This information is used to refine the investigator's opinion on the time of death.

When giving a time of death, investigators explain that it is a range and tell how they came to that conclusion.

8.2 Bodily Reactions to Death

8.2.1 Rigor Mortis

Rigor mortis is the result of chemical changes that occur within the body that cause stiffening of the body. It may be weakly formed in younger or older victims. The state of rigor mortis should only be used as a general determination of death. Rigor mortis is an unreliable method of indicating the time of death. It is affected by illness, temperature, activity before death, and the environmental and physical conditions where the body is placed or found.

Rigor mortis can affect the body immediately. It can be manifested within 1 to 6 hours. It will reach its maximum effect between 6 and 24 hours. It will disappear between 12 and 36+ hours after death. Cadaveric spasms are often confused with rigor mortis and are usually observed in sudden death.

8.2.2 Algor Mortis

Algor mortis is the gradual cooling of the body after death; it is one of the classic markers of death. It can be most accurately measured in the liver. The metabolism of the tissue generates heat, which is very tightly regulated by the body to a narrow range.

The body cools by radiation, convection, and direct transfer, so any factors that influence heat loss affect the rate. The scene, clothing, body size, activity, and physical factors have to be carefully considered in interpreting cooling rate. If the body always cooled at a uniform rate, that slope would enable an accurate determination of the time of death.

Over the years, there have been a number of formulas that would, in theory, allow the calculation of the time of death. One example is the idea that measured rectal temperature subtracted from 98.4 equals the hours since death. However, too many factors affect the temperature of the body for this to be reliable. Factors that can change the body's temperature after death include activity, sickness, decay, infection, and heat.

8.2.3 Livor Mortis

Livor mortis is the settling of blood to dependent parts of the body and has been recognized as a change of death. This is also sometimes called postmortem hypostasis, lividity, suggillations, and gravitation.

Livor mortis begins at or very soon after death, since it is a function of blood flow and, therefore, cardiac activity. When cardiac activity stops, the hydrostatic pressure of the liquid blood causes it to settle and distend the dependent capillary bed. The color of the dependent part will depend on the skin pigment and any additional compounds in the blood that may affect color, such as carbon monoxide, but it is generally dark blue or purple. Livor mortis is fully manifested within 8 to 12 hours after death.

8.2.4 Tardieu's Spots

Tardieu's spots are caused when capillaries rupture in circular areas of skin hemorrhage and are often confused with petechial hemorrhage. However, Tardieu's spots occur after the victim is dead and are found on the liver, while petechial hemorrhaging occurs when the victim is alive, is found in the lungs, and is suggestive of asphyxia. Tardieu's spots are usually 4 to 5 mm in diameter, while petechial hemorrhages are usually 1 mm or smaller in diameter.

8.2.5 Postmortem Tissue Changes

There is typically evidence of decomposition to the body when the time of death is more than 24 hours ago. Autolysis is the process after death in which the digestive enzymes in the body break down carbohydrates and proteins. For the sake of comparison to other cases, a crime scene investigator should collect hair, blood, and other bodily fluids.

8.2.6 Radiographic Film

Radiographic film obtained during life can be compared with postmortem film to find any foreign materials not observed during the postmortem examination. Dental radiographs may provide an estimate of age in children and young adults.

8.2.7 Fingers and Hands

If there is a glove-like separation of the epidermis of the hands, this may be used for fingerprints. If the epidermis is missing, it may be possible to fingerprint the stripped hands. If hands are damaged, they can be submitted to the FBI laboratory for further study.

8.2.8 Skeletal Remains

If skeletal remains intermix, they should be examined by shortwave ultraviolet light to be segregated and arranged in anatomic order. Photographs of bone lesions should be taken for comparison with antemortem films. Pubic bones should be examined for parturition pits, which indicate prior pregnancy.

8.2.9 DNA

Samples of known and unknown hair and fingernails can be compared by neutron activation analysis and microscopic examination of the linear striations of fingernails. If exhumation is necessary, investigators preserve the surrounding soil, water in the grave, and any fluids that may be in the casket for analysis.

When collecting DNA, it is essential to establish a chain of custody. Investigators request assistance of dentists, physical anthropologists, radiologists, and other specialists as needed. Photographs, X-rays, and other objects required for identification are acquired. Investigators obtain records for review and correlation with the investigative and pathologic findings. They examine, describe, record, and tabulate the results of examinations for comparison with known information.

8.3 Decomposition

When a body is decomposed, it may still be useful and contain evidence. Burned, decomposed, mutilated, or skeletal remains are still suitable for examination. Investigators look for artifacts and postmortem injuries. Commingled skeletal remains should not be examined together. The bones should be separated and arranged in anatomic order. Investigators should not rely on personal identification of the body by family or friends. Specimens for toxicological studies are not placed in formalin solution. Human remains should not be confused with the remains of animals.

8.3.1 Postmortem Decomposition

Postmortem decomposition can be affected by various things. First, environmental factors such as temperature fluctuations (freezing or thawing), insects, and microorganisms can change the rate of decomposition. Body habitus (the physique) can also affect the rate of decomposition. Deceased newborns, obese deceased, and thin deceased all decompose at different rates. Finally, the cause of death can affect decomposition. For example, death by exsanguination, or blood loss, may delay decomposition while anasarca, or generalized edema, accelerates it. An infection that causes death may also affect the rate of decomposition.

8.3.2 Decomposed and Skeletonized Remains

Decomposed and skeletonized remains should be treated like any other case. The best approach is to plan. Another day at this stage will probably not change the scene significantly but could make the conclusion better. For these cases, investigators use the services of a forensic anthropologist liberally and early.

Weathering of the bones may help investigators figure out what happened, but many things can affect it:

- Body placement (buried or not buried)
- Climate
- Moisture
- Elevation
- Terrain
- Protection
- Intervention by insects, animals, or people

When dealing with decomposed and skeletonized remains, investigators photograph, sketch, and document scene conditions as they would any other crime scene. Plants are collected when appropriate, and weather bureaus are checked for temperatures and rainfall amounts. These conditions are taken into account because they vary widely and have a major effect on the remains.

8.3.3 Insect Infestation (Fauna)

The presence of insects in a decomposing body may give a window of the time of death. Body lice outlive the host by 3 to 6 days. If lice are still alive, the time of death was within the past 6 days. Insects or arthropods are highly dependent on locale, temperature, and season. Representative samples are collected in preservative and taken to an entomologist. The preservative should be 85% alcohol.

8.3.4 Plant Life (Flora)

Grass or plants beneath an object wilt, turn yellow or brown, and die. The rate depends on type of plant, season, and climate. Seasonal plants or remnants may help indicate a range of time of death. Dead and dying grasses, twigs, and flowers are collected and taken to a botanist.

8.4 Identification of Human Remains

To identify unknown human remains, investigators compare known information derived from records with data gained by examination of the victim. Help from other forensic scientists, such as physical anthropologists, dentists, radiologists, criminalists, and serologists, is often required for identification.

8.4.1 Investigation of Human Remains

Identifying unknown human remains is important to complete official records, notify the next of kin, settle estates and insurance claims, and establish the corpus delicti after a homicide.

In investigating human remains, there are many types of records that may contain useful information:

- Missing-persons reports
- Fingerprints
- Dental records
- Health records
- Laboratory records, including blood type
- Antemortem X-ray
- Employment records
- Police records

Either the coroner or the medical examiner is responsible for determining the cause of death, identifying unknown human remains, and estimating the time of death.

8.4.2 Immediate Action for Postmortem Identification

To identify human remains, investigators immediately obtain all available records for comparison. Photographs of remains, clothing, and physical evidence are acquired. Selected X-rays, dental X-rays, or total body X-rays are obtained, as appropriate, for comparison with antemortem X-rays. Finally, investigators procure fingerprints for comparison with records.

8.5 Objectives of Medicolegal Examination

A medicolegal exam should answer the following questions:

- Are the remains human?
- What are the age, living stature, gender, race, and distinct characteristics of the individual?
- Is it possible to provide an estimate of the time of death and/or range of death?
- What is the cause of death?
- Were any of the injuries postmortem?
- Was there an interchange of physical evidence between the victim and attacker?

8.6 The Scene of the Investigation

As in any investigation, proper procedure at the crime scene is important. These steps ensure that proper procedure is followed:

- Create a perimeter around the scene to prevent any disturbances.
- Secure the area and require identification for personnel entering the area.
- Establish and maintain a chain of custody for all physical evidence.
- Assign consecutive numbers to bodies that are found.
- Provide a system for communication between investigators on the scene and central offices.
- Maintain the relationship between clothing and personal effects found at the scene and the respective remains.

8.6.1 Jurisdiction for Investigation

Jurisdiction of an investigating agency is generally determined by the geographical location of the crime and whether a state or federal law was violated.

8.6.1.1 State or Local Jurisdiction

- State law enforcement agencies—State investigations and state patrols, such as highway patrol
- Local law enforcement agencies—Sheriffs' offices, county police, medical examiner, and coroner

8.6.1.2 Federal Jurisdiction
The following are federal agencies that may be involved in a death investigation:

- Federal Aviation Administration
- National Transportation Safety Board
- Federal Bureau of Investigation
- FBI Disaster Squad

8.6.1.3 Military Jurisdiction

- Commanding officer of the nearest military installation
- Judge advocate of the nearest military installation

8.6.2 Facility Assistance

There are many logistical concerns with the facilities used in these investigations:

- Communications—Integration of adequate information and communications systems, both between agencies and throughout field operations, is an essential part of interoperability. Investigators must have the ability to communicate with one another and support services (Hawkins, 2006).
- Equipment—Investigators need consecutive numbered tags and disaster bags for remains as well as evidence collection and storage supplies.
- Transportation—It is necessary to have transportation for personnel to and from death scenes located in remote areas.

8.6.2.1 Facilities for Postmortem Exam and Preservation of Remains

- Refrigerated vans
- Building suitable for a temporary morgue

8.6.2.2 Laboratories or Examination of Evidence

Laboratories for evidence examination depend on jurisdiction, availability, exigency, and sometimes proximity to the death scene. Those that may be available are listed below:

- State crime laboratory
- Local crime laboratory
- FBI Laboratory
- Army Criminal Investigation Command Crime Laboratory
- Military hospital or area laboratory
- Civil Aeromedical Institute
- Armed Forces Institute of Pathology

8.6.2.3 Consultants   Some of the following people may be useful to an investigation:

- Medical examiner
- Coroner
- Physical anthropologist
- Forensic entomologist
- Radiologist
- Dentist
- FBI Disaster Squad
- FBI Criminal Justice Information Services—FBI Fingerprints

8.6.2.4 Other Needs   There are some other things that will be useful in the investigation:

- Black-and-white and color photography on the scene as well as during the postmortem examination
- Facilities for radiographic studies of remains, including dental X-rays and total body X-rays
- Facilities for special studies such as neutron activation analysis

Bibliography

Hawkins, D. (2006). *Law enforcement tech guide for communications interoperability: A guide for inter-agency communications projects.* In cooperation with the U.S. Department of Justice Office of Community Oriented Policing Services. Washington, DC: U.S. Department of Justice. Retrieved from http://ric-zai-inc.com/Publications/cops-p106-pub.pdf.

Westveer, A.E., Jr. (2002). *Managing death investigations,* Vol. 1 (Fifth ed.). Washington, DC: U.S. Department of Justice Federal Bureau of Investigation. (Used with permission.)

9
COMPUTER/DIGITAL FORENSICS

Computer/digital forensics is the collection and analysis of data from computers and other digital devices in the interest of obtaining evidence. Evidence obtained in a computer forensic investigation can be useful in criminal, civil, or corporate investigations, but different legal rules may apply.

9.1 The Importance of Digital Forensics

Here is an example of digital forensics assisting in the investigation of a serial killer. Dennis Rader was identified as the *BTK Killer* due to evidence that connected him to an incriminating Microsoft Word document e-mailed to a TV station. The evidence that led to Rader's conviction was actually contained within the metadata, or data about data, that is created by default in Microsoft Office documents.

According to some estimates, almost 95% of criminals leave evidence that could be captured and analyzed through proper computer forensic procedures. However, some criminals are getting smarter. Data-hiding techniques such as encryption and steganography can put evidence of criminal activity where traditional search methods cannot find it. Encryption is scrambling data, such as an e-mail message, so that these cannot be read if intercepted in transit. Steganography is hiding a message in a larger file, typically in a photographic image or sound file.

Computer forensics is not just about detective work—searching for and attempting to discover information. Computer forensics also is concerned with the following areas:

- Handling sensitive data responsibly and confidentially
- Taking precautions to not nullify findings by corrupting data

- Taking precautions to ensure the integrity of the data
- Staying within the law and rules of evidence

Evidence uncovered in a digital examination may be direct evidence of a crime or may simply corroborate other evidence or statements. The crime or incident being investigated may not necessarily be a computer-based crime.

True computer forensics should be performed by forensic experts specifically trained and experienced in the proper methodologies. System administrators and information security professionals should gain enough knowledge to know they do not have to be forensics experts. They should, however, work to minimize risk to their environment.

9.1.1 Investigations of Computer Forensics

The following list includes various types of crimes that are investigated using computer forensics:

- Identity theft
- Murder
- Sexual assault
- Fraud and embezzlement
- Software piracy and hacking
- Blackmail and extortion
- Child pornography and exploitation
- Prostitution
- Human trafficking
- Domestic violence
- Terrorism and national security
- Theft of intellectual property and trade secrets

9.1.2 Recovered Evidence

9.1.2.1 Computer Fraud   In cases of computer fraud, the following types of evidence can be recovered:

- Accounting software and files
- Credit card data

- Financial and asset records
- Account data from online auctions
- E-mails, notes, and letters

9.1.2.2 Child Exploitation   In cases of child exploitation, the following types of evidence can be recovered:

- Chat logs
- Photos and digital camera software
- Internet activity logs
- Movie files
- Graphic editing and viewing software
- User-created directory to classify images
- File sharing software
- Actual elements of the crime

9.1.2.3 Network Intrusion and Hacking   In cases of network intrusion and hacking, the following types of evidence can be recovered:

- Network usernames
- Internet protocol (IP) addresses
- Executable files (including viruses and spyware)
- Security logs
- Configuration files
- Text files and other documents containing sensitive information such as passwords

9.1.2.4 Identity Theft   In cases of identity theft, the following types of evidence can be recovered:

- Identification templates (birth certificates, drivers' licenses, Social Security cards)
- Electronic images of signatures
- Credit card numbers
- Credit card reader, writer, and scanner
- Online trading information

9.1.2.5 Harassment and Stalking   In cases of harassment and stalking, the following types of evidence can be recovered:

- Victim background research
- Maps to the victim's locations
- Photos
- Cell phone Global Positioning System (GPS) information
- Diaries
- Internet activity logs
- E-mails, notes, and letters

9.1.2.6 Software Piracy In cases of software piracy, the following types of evidence can be recovered:

- Software serial numbers
- Software cracking utilities
- Image files of software licenses
- Binary files for software installation
- Chat logs
- Internet activity logs

9.2 Evidence

An examiner must be able to identify the type of evidence and its characteristics, as well as apply it to the Federal Rules of Evidence and the *Daubert* or *Frye* test.

9.2.1 Types of Evidence

Evidence is something that tends to establish or disprove a fact. There are four types of evidence within digital forensics:

- Real—Real evidence is something that could actually be carried into court and shown to a jury. It is the most powerful type of evidence because it speaks for itself.
- Documentary—Documentary evidence is any evidence in written form (database files, server logs, e-mails, etc.). Documentary evidence can be faked by a skilled computer user and, therefore, must be authenticated to be admissible in court. Investigators always produce the original document rather than a copy.

- Testimonial—Testimonial evidence is the statement of a witness, under oath, either in court or by deposition. This type of evidence typically supports or validates other evidence.
- Demonstrative—Demonstrative evidence recreates or explains other evidence. It does not speak for itself and is used to illustrate and clarify previous points. This type of evidence is most helpful in explaining technical topics to nontechnical audiences.

9.2.2 Characteristics of Useful Evidence

For evidence to be useful, it must meet the following requirements:

- Admissible—If the evidence will not stand up in court, the investigator has wasted his or her time and possibly allowed a guilty party to go unpunished.
- Authentic—Evidence must be directly related to the incident being investigated. The digital forensic examination may reveal evidence that is interesting but irrelevant.
- Complete—The examiner should approach the case with no preconceived notions about someone's guilt or innocence. Forensic methods should eliminate alternative suspects and explanations until a definite conclusion is reached.
- Reliable—There should be no question about the truth of the examiner's conclusions. Reliability comes from using standardized and verified forensic tools and methods. Qualification (by a judge) of an examiner as an expert witness in a case will help to establish credibility and reliability.
- Believable—The examiner must produce results that are clear and easy to understand, even among the most nontechnical members of a jury. Have other examiners used the same forensic techniques and reached similar conclusions?

9.2.3 The Daubert Test

The case of *Daubert v. Merrill Dow Pharmaceuticals* (1983) established new criteria to determine the reliability, relevancy, and admissibility of scientific evidence. The theory or technique must meet the following requirements:

- Tested and that test must be replicable
- Subjected to peer review and publication
- Error rate associated with the technique that is known
- Accepted within the scientific community

9.2.4 General Rules of Evidence

The following are simple rules of evidence observed by digital forensic investigators:

- Best evidence rule—Evidence presented in court should be the actual item investigated or examined, which is considered best evidence. Federal Rules of Evidence consider a printout of computer data to be original if it can be read by sight and if it accurately represents the stored data. A proper forensic image can be considered best evidence if the original evidence has been returned to its owner.
- Relevance of evidence—Evidence is admissible only if it is relevant, and relevant evidence is admissible unless and until another rule says it is inadmissible. The judge presiding over a case can render evidence admissible or inadmissible.

9.2.5 Federal Rules of Evidence

Becoming federal law in 1975, the Federal Rules of Evidence are the most relevant legal rules for a forensic examiner. They pertain to evidence presented in federal courts. State courts may have their own rules of evidence, but they often use the federal rules as guidelines:

- Rule 401: Defining *Relevant Evidence*—Relevant evidence means any evidence having any tendency to make the existence of any fact that is of consequence to the determination of the action more probable or less probable than it would be without the evidence.
- Rule 402: Admissible Relevant Evidence; Inadmissible Irrelevant Evidence—All relevant evidence is admissible,

except as otherwise provided by the Constitution of the United States, by Act of Congress, by these rules, or by other rules prescribed by the Supreme Court pursuant to statutory authority. Evidence that is not relevant is not admissible.

- Rule 403: Exclusion of Relevant Evidence on Grounds of Prejudice, Confusion, or Waste of Time—Although relevant, evidence may be excluded if its probative value is substantially outweighed by the danger of unfair prejudice, confusion of the issues, misleading the jury, or by considerations of undue delay, waste of time, or needless presentation of cumulative evidence.

- Rule 601: General Rule of Competency—Every person is competent to be a witness except as otherwise as provided in these rules. However, in civil actions and proceedings, with respect to an element of a claim or defense as to which state law supplies the rule of decision, the competency of a witness shall be determined in accordance with state law.

- Rule 702: Testimony by Experts—If scientific, technical, or other specialized knowledge will assist in understanding the evidence or determining a fact in issue, a witness qualified as an expert by knowledge, skill, experience, training, or education may testify thereto in the form of an opinion or otherwise if the testimony is based upon sufficient facts or data, the testimony is the product of reliable principles and methods, and the witness has applied the principles and methods reliably to the facts of the case.

- Rule 703: Bases of Opinion Testimony by Experts—The facts or data in the particular case upon which an expert bases an opinion or inference may be those perceived by or made known to the expert at or before the hearing. If this is a type of case reasonably relied upon by experts in the particular field in forming opinions or inferences upon the subject, the facts or data need not be admissible in evidence in order for the opinion or inference to be admitted. Facts or data that are otherwise inadmissible shall not be disclosed to the jury by the proponent of the opinion or inference unless the court determines their probative value in assisting the jury to evaluate the expert's opinion substantially outweighs their prejudicial effect.

- Rule 1002: Requirement of Original—To prove the content of a writing, recording, or photograph, the original writing, recording, or photograph is required except as otherwise provided in these rules or by Act of Congress.
- Rule 1003: Admissibility of Duplicates—A duplicate is admissible to the same extent as an original unless a genuine question is raised as to the authenticity of the original or, if in the circumstances, it would be unfair to admit the duplicate in lieu of the original.

9.3 Governance of Evidence Collection

Investigators must abide by the laws that govern the collection of evidence.

9.3.1 Fourth Amendment

In criminal investigations, the rights of all citizens (including criminal suspects) are protected by the U.S. Constitution's Fourth Amendment and decades of legislation and case law. Failure to observe proper search and seizure procedure can ruin a criminal investigation no matter how incriminating the evidence.

The search warrant (required by the Fourth Amendment in most cases) should clearly state what investigators are searching for and the area in which they are authorized to search. It must be signed by a judge. Exceptions to the warrant requirement are listed below.

9.3.1.1 Plain View Doctrine The plain view doctrine says an officer can seize evidence that is in plain view as long as the officer is legally present at the site of the evidence, can legally access the evidence, and has probable cause to believe that the evidence or contraband is related to a crime. When applying the plain view doctrine, investigators must keep in mind the right to seize evidence gathered through the plain view exception does not necessarily imply the right to search that evidence.

9.3.1.2 Owner Consent If the owner of a computer or other digital evidence gives consent, the device may be seized. That consent should be given in writing and should acknowledge the possibility of future forensic examination by a trained computer forensic examiner or analyst.

9.3.1.3 Digital Privacy To determine whether an individual has a reasonable expectation of privacy in information stored in a computer, it helps to treat the computer like a closed container such as a briefcase or file cabinet. The Fourth Amendment generally prohibits law enforcement from accessing and viewing information stored in a computer without a warrant if it would be prohibited from opening a closed container and examining its contents in the same situation.

9.3.1.4 Corporate Responsibility Corporate (or private) investigations are not subject to the same search and seizure rules and Fourth Amendment issues. These types of investigations often involve misuse or abuse of company assets, falsification of data, discrimination, harassment, and similar matters likely to involve litigation.

A major threat to a corporate data network may be workers who violate the company's security or acceptable use policy, leaving the network vulnerable to attack. A skilled digital forensic examiner can often trace and neutralize these threats without the involvement of law enforcement. When the corporate investigation reveals illegal activity, however, police involvement may be needed. Investigators should proceed with caution and consult legal counsel if necessary. The Fourth Amendment does not apply to searches conducted by private parties who are not acting as agents of the government.

The Fourth Amendment "is wholly inapplicable to a search or seizure, even an unreasonable one, effected by a private individual not acting as an agent of the Government or with the participation or knowledge of any government official" *United States versus Jacobsen*, 466 U.S. 109, 113 (1984).

9.3.2 Evidence-Collection Laws

The following are other evidence-collection laws:

- The Wiretap Act
- Omnibus Crime Control and Safe Streets Act of 1968
- Electronic Communications Privacy Act
- 18 USC Section 2701
- USA PATRIOT Act
- Right to Financial Privacy Act
- Fair Credit Reporting Act

9.4 Laws and Ethics

The following are laws involving computer crimes and ethical issues that arise when investigating and prosecuting those crimes.

9.4.1 Title 18 U.S.C.

Much of U.S. federal law involving computer crime can be found in Title 18 of the United States Code:

- 18 U.S.C. § 1029—Fraud and related activity in connection with access devices.
- 18 U.S.C. § 1030—Fraud and related activity in connection with computers.
- 18 U.S.C. § 1030—Makes denial of service attacks a federal crime.
- 18 U.S.C. § 1030(a)(5)(A)—Transmission of program, information, code, or command, resulting in damage.
- 18 U.S.C. § 1030 makes substitution or redirection of a website a federal crime.
- 18 U.S.C. § 1030(a)(5)(A)(i)—Transmission of program, information, code, or command, resulting in damage.
- 18 U.S.C. § 1030(a)(5)(A)(ii)–(iii)—Accessing a computer without authorization, resulting in damage.
- 18 U.S.C. § 1030—Makes Internet fraud (phishing) a federal crime.
- 18 U.S.C. § 1030(a)(4)—Accessing a computer to defraud and obtain something of value.

- 18 U.S.C. § 2252B—Makes certain use of a misleading domain name a federal crime (using misleading domain name with intent to deceive a person into viewing obscene material or with intent to deceive a minor into viewing harmful material).
- 18 U.S.C. § 2261A—Makes cyberstalking a federal crime (using any facility of interstate or foreign commerce to engage in a course of conduct that places person in reasonable fear of death or serious bodily injury to person, person's spouse, or immediate family).

9.4.2 Ethical Issues

The digital forensic examiner must maintain absolute objectivity. It is not the examiner's job to determine someone's guilt or innocence. Rather, it is the examiner's responsibility to accurately report the relevant facts of a case. The investigator must maintain strict confidentiality, discussing the results of an investigation only on a need-to-know basis.

9.5 Forensic Hardware

9.5.1 Incident Response Tools

The hardware tools needed for a successful forensic analysis can be divided into two categories: incident response and laboratory. Incident response tools would include the hand tools, cabling, identification supplies, and other items necessary to perform an investigation at the scene of an incident.

Here are some necessary incident response tools:

- Laptop or notebook personal computer (PC) for data acquisition
- Write-blockers
- External hard drives
- USB drives, floppy disks, or external floppy drive
- Portable network hub or network switch
- Network cables
- Straight-through cable that will allow connection to a hub

- Crossover cable that will bypass a hub or switch in a direct PC-to-PC connection
- Evidence inventory logs
- Evidence identification tape, labels, and stickers
- Evidence bags (paper and antistatic)
- Crime scene tape
- Gloves
- Nonmagnetic hand tools
- Cameras (photo and video)

The following are some specific examples of incident response tools.

9.5.1.1 FREDL   The Forensic Recovery of Evidence Device–Laptop (FREDL), produced by Digital Intelligence, is an example of the modern mobile forensic workstation (Figure 9.1).

9.5.1.2 The Ultrakit   Also by Digital Intelligence, the Ultrakit includes write-blockers, cables, adapters, and power supplies necessary for obtaining evidence during an incident (Figure 9.2).

Figure 9.1   The FREDL. (Courtesy of Digital Intelligence, New Berlin, Wisconsin, www.DigitalIntelligence.com.)

Figure 9.2   The Ultrakit. (Courtesy of Digital Intelligence, New Berlin, Wisconsin, www .DigitalIntelligence.com.)

9.5.1.3 Faraday Cage   A practical item in the digital forensic tool kit is the Faraday cage, a container that isolates wireless devices from radio frequency signals that could compromise data. The Faraday cage can prevent some laptop PCs, mobile phones, and smartphones from being remotely wiped of data or otherwise locked down by wireless instructions.

9.5.1.4 Wireless StrongHold Bag   By Paraben, this bag is a Faraday cage built into an evidence bag for the safe collection of wireless devices in incident response (Figure 9.3).

9.5.2 Laboratory Tools

Laboratory tools would include the devices and accessories necessary to perform an analysis—under controlled conditions—of evidence retrieved from an incident scene.

Figure 9.3 Wireless StrongHold Bag. (Courtesy of Paraben, Ashburn, Virginia, www.Paraben.com.)

Forensic workstations are customized computer systems that contain the equipment necessary for analysis of suspect computers. In addition to standard PC components such as motherboards, hard drives, and memory, forensic workstations may include disk duplicators, disk erasers, and write-blockers.

The Forensic Recovery of Evidence Device (FRED), seen in Figure 9.4, is a modern forensic laboratory workstation by Digital Intelligence.

To avoid the possibility of data contamination, digital forensic workstations are typically not connected to the Internet or any computer outside of the laboratory's secure network. Investigators never check e-mail, surf the web, or perform typical IT duties on a forensic workstation. Viruses and spyware can seriously compromise an investigation. Under no circumstances should peer-to-peer (P2P) file sharing applications be allowed on the same network as a forensic workstation.

Figure 9.4 FRED. (Courtesy of Digital Intelligence, New Berlin, Wisconsin, www.DigitalIntelligence .com.)

9.5.3 Duplication of Hard Drives

In digital forensics, it is sometimes necessary to duplicate a hard drive. There are three generally accepted methods for duplicating hard drives:

- Disk imaging on a dedicated forensic system—This is a platform specifically built and designed to accommodate numerous types of hard drive connections. Specialized bit-level imaging software transfers an exact copy of the contents of the original hard drive (or other data source) to one or more blanks. Typically, an investigator makes more than one copy of the suspect hard drive using this method. If the forensic analysis is correct, the investigation should produce the same results on identical copies of the drive.

- System-to-system disk imaging—This method uses two separate computer systems: the suspect and a specialized forensics imaging system. Depending on the type of drives and connections available, both systems are booted from CD-ROM, DVD, USB drive, or floppy disk that loads the imaging software. Data are transferred between the computers using serial, parallel, Ethernet, or USB ports. This method can be slow, and is often not suited to on-the-scene incident response.

- Disk imaging on the original system—This method uses the original (suspect) computer to perform the disk imaging transfer process. A blank drive matching the original hard drive's capacity and configuration is added to the system, and a forensic boot disk is used to create a bit-level image of the original disk. This method is typically used in on-the-scene incident response when it is impractical to transport a computer to the investigator's laboratory.

9.5.4 Evidence on Removable Media

Removable media is normally imaged using a dedicated forensics system. This allows multiple images to be stored on a local hard drive. Duplicate copies can be burned from those images. As with any other kind of digital evidence, original source material should be handled as little as possible.

CDs and DVDs are the easiest and safest to handle since they are usually in read-only mode. When dealing with handwritten labels on CDs and DVDs, investigators must consider that the disk may be mislabeled, and they are actually dealing with a rewritable disk. With floppy disks, they must be sure the write-protect tab is set in the write-protect mode.

9.6 Forensic Software

Software used in digital forensic analysis comes in two varieties: commercial and open-source software. In either case, the software is typically used for copying data from a suspect's disk drive (or other data source) to an image file, and then analyzing the data without making any changes to the original source. Forensic software can also complete the following tasks:

- Disk imaging
- Data recovery
- Integrity checking
- Remote access
- Password recovery
- Permanent file deletion
- Searching and sorting

9.6.1 Commercial Software

Commercial software has both advantages and disadvantages. Here are the advantages:

- Proven admissibility in court (for major brands)
- Dedicated technical support
- Strict quality control for forensic accuracy
- Often has an easy point-and-click graphical user interface (GUI)
- Better documentation
- Greater availability of training and supplemental materials

Here are some disadvantages:

- High initial cost
- Cost of annual licensing/maintenance
- Licensing often done through USB keys or dongles that can be lost or damaged
- Customer may need to be a member of a restricted group of customers (such as law enforcement or academia) to receive best pricing and functionality

The following details some types of commercial software.

9.6.1.1 EnCase   Manufactured and sold by Guidance Software, this commercial software is a market leader and is widely recognized and accepted. Here are some of its key features:

- Court-validated logical evidence file format
- Advanced search options
- Internet and e-mail support
- Multiple viewers
- Instant message analysis
- Support for most system files
- Multiple acquisition options

9.6.1.2 Forensic Toolkit (FTK)   Manufactured and sold by AccessData, FTK has intuitive functionality, e-mail analysis, customizable data views, and stability.

9.6.1.3 P2 Commander   Manufactured and sold by Paraben, P2 Commander is a comprehensive digital forensic examination tool that includes these programs:

- E-mail Examiner
- Network E-mail Examiner
- Forensic Sorter
- Chat Examiner
- Advanced Registry and System Analyzer
- Text Searcher

9.6.1.4 Device Seizure   Manufactured and sold by Paraben, Device Seizure recovers data from more than 2200 mobile devices, including mobile phones, smartphones, and iPhones. It also collects the following information:

- Calls received, dialed, and missed
- E-mail
- Text message history
- Deleted text messages
- Contact lists

9.6.1.5 *Internet Evidence Finder (IEF)* Manufactured and sold by Magnet Forensics, IEF recovers data from forensically imaged mounted media or straight media. It also has the following features:

- Full search
- Quick search
- Unallocated search
- Sector level search
- Custom search
- P2P file sharing applications
- Cloud-based services
- Google Maps

It can also complete the following actions:

- Search entire logical and physical drives
- Search live memory or RAM captures
- Retrieve instant messaging chat history
- Retrieve web browser history
- Retrieve browser activity
- View activity on social networking sites
- Detect skin tone

9.6.2 Open-Source Software

Open-source software has both advantages and disadvantages. Here are the advantages:

- Lower initial cost (usually free)
- Possibility for an investigator to create his or her own forensic software from source code, incorporating only the features needed
- Fewer (if any) licensing issues

Here are the disadvantages:

- Little (if any) vendor support on free software
- Perceived as less standardized and reliable, and therefore, less likely to produce admissible results
- Often uses command-line interface instead of the point-and-click interface familiar to Windows users

The following details some types of open-source software.

9.6.2.1 Helix   Manufactured by e-fense, this Linux-based collection of forensic applications has a unique GUI. It can be used on computer systems running Windows, Linux, and Mac OS. Originally a free download, authorized copies of Helix are now available by subscription to the e-fense forum, which provides Helix support and training.

9.6.2.2 SleuthKit and Autopsy   SleuthKit is a set of Unix-based forensics tools. Autopsy is the graphical front end for SleuthKit. Download SleuthKit and Autopsy at www.sleuthkit.org.

9.6.2.3 dtSearch   The dtSearch product line can instantly search terabytes of text across a desktop, network, Internet, or Intranet site. It also highlights hits in HTML, XML, and PDF formats while displaying embedded links, formatting, and images. It is available from dtSearch Corp. at www.dtsearch.com.

9.6.2.4 Self-Monitoring Analysis and Reporting Technology (SMART)   SMART is another excellent Linux distribution designed for incident response and forensic analysis. When used as a bootable forensic CD, SMART will not mount file systems automatically, activate swap partitions, or otherwise change data on the target computer. SMART Linux is available at www.asrdata.com.

9.6.2.5 NFI Defraser   Defraser detects and restores complete and partial multimedia files from places that are typically invisible to the Windows file system (such as unallocated disk space). It was developed by the Netherlands Forensic Institute. Download it at www.defraser.sourceforge.net.

9.6.2.6 Guymager   A Linux-based forensic imaging platform, this has a user-friendly graphical interface, multilanguage support.

9.6.2.7 Digital Evidence and Forensics Toolkit (DEFT)   DEFT is a Xubuntu Linux-based live CD, which includes many popular and useful utilities for computer forensics, incident response, penetration testing, and security analysis. Download DEFT from www.deftlinux.net.

9.6.3 Standards and Testing

Through the Computer Forensics Tool Testing Project (CFTT), the National Institute of Standards and Technology (NIST) tests forensic software and hardware. Download CFTT test results and thousands of pages of related NIST research at www.cftt.nist.gov.

Whether commercial or open source, forensic software should meet the following criteria:

- Accepted by law enforcement, security professionals, and the legal community
- Able to export image files to multiple platform formats
- Have efficient storage capabilities
- Fully functional when launched from portable computing platforms (such as laptops)

9.7 Incident Response

Incident response is the response to a computer crime, a security policy violation, or similar events. It happens before the forensic analysis begins. Digital evidence is secured, preserved, and documented in this phase.

The incident responder is not necessarily the forensic specialist who will conduct the analysis of the digital evidence. In a large corporate setting, the incident responder may be a technician-level employee in security or information technology. In a smaller company, the network administrator or security officer may be the incident responder in addition to performing several other duties.

In the case of a criminal investigation, a sworn law enforcement officer or crime lab technician typically has incident responder responsibilities. There is always the possibility that law enforcement personnel will be called in after corporate personnel have done their own incident response. Investigators must be prepared to deal with an incident scene that may have been compromised.

Even a brief delay in the start of an investigation could give a criminal suspect time to erase, hide, or destroy digital evidence. In the workplace, delayed incident response greatly increases the likelihood of data being altered by another computer user or by background processes like automatic software updates, disk utilities, or data backups.

9.7.1 *National Institute of Justice Guidelines*

The following list is the National Institute of Justice's guidelines for dealing with digital evidence:

- Actions taken to secure and collect digital evidence should not affect the integrity of that evidence.
- Persons conducting an examination of digital evidence should be trained for that purpose.
- Activities relating to the seizure, examination, storage, or transfer of digital evidence should be documented, preserved, and available for review.

9.7.2 *Responder Responsibility*

Depending on the availability of investigative personnel, the incident responder may be called upon to complete the following activities:

- Recognize, identify, seize, and secure all digital evidence at the scene.
- Document the entire scene and the specific location of the evidence found.
- Collect, label, and preserve the digital evidence.
- Package and transport digital evidence in a secure manner.

Investigators must observe search and seizure laws. Unauthorized seizure can be a criminal offense. Before attempting a device seizure, investigators must have a search warrant or be covered by corporate policy or similar authority.

9.7.3 Guidelines for First Responders

Until the incident scene is secured, investigators do nothing that will alter the condition of any electronic device. If the computer is on, they leave it on. If the computer is off, they leave it off. Investigators should politely but firmly resist offers of technical help from anyone who is not authorized to assist in the investigation.

9.7.3.1 "Pull the Plug" versus "Shut Down"

Pulling the plug on a computer immediately halts processing, but destroys anything in memory and can corrupt files. Shutting down a computer protects files from corruption, but writes entries into the systems activity logs and, therefore, changes the state of the evidence. Forensic tools designed specifically for incident response may provide an option for a more reliable capture of digital evidence by keeping a computer's memory alive long enough to be analyzed.

9.7.3.2 Evidence Preservation and Safety

Investigators take appropriate measures to avoid compromising fingerprints, blood, DNA, and other physical evidence left on mice and keyboards. They must also protect their own health and safety by understanding these points:

- A crime scene may contain blood or other biohazards.
- Some electrical and electronic equipment can hold an electrical charge even when unplugged.
- Lasers in CD/DVD drives and laser printers can cause eye injury.

9.7.3.3 Network Activity

Investigators should look for signs of active communications with other computers, such as chat room activity or instant messaging. Network hardware such as routers or wireless access points may point to additional evidence elsewhere on the network.

9.8 Investigative Questions

The types of questions asked in a digital forensic investigation depend upon the scenario provided. Listed below are questions for some of the common crimes.

9.8.1 General

These questions should be asked in every case involving computers or electronics:

- When and where was the computer purchased? Was it new or used?
- Who has access to the computer hardware and software?
- Where are the removable media devices (CDs, DVDs, floppy disks, USB drives, backup tapes, etc.) stored?
- Whose fingerprints might be found on the removable media?
- How many people use this computer? Who are they? What are their usernames?
- At what times of the day do the individual users have access to the computer?
- If more than one person uses this computer, can all the users access every file, folder, and program?
- What is the level of computer experience or expertise of each user of the computer?
- How does the computer access the Internet (cable, DSL, dial-up, office LAN, etc.)?
- Does the suspect or victim have an e-mail account? What is his or her e-mail address?
- Who is the Internet service provider and/or e-mail service provider?
- Which e-mail client (such as Outlook) does the suspect or victim use?
- Does the suspect or victim use remote access software, such as PC Anywhere or GoToMyPC?
- Do any users of the computer use online storage or remote storage?
- Has any software (such as Evidence Eliminator or CCleaner) been used to clean the computer or wipe the hard drive?

- Does the computer contain encryption software?
- Is the computer always left on? If it is turned off when not in use, how often does that happen?

9.8.2 Identity Theft and Financial Crime

In cases involving identity theft and financial crime, investigators ask victims the following questions:

- Are you aware of any unusual activity on your bank accounts or credit cards?
- What accounts have been compromised?
- Have you given personal information to any person or organization?
- Do you pay your bills online?
- Have any bank statements or bills not arrived in regular mail when you expected them?
- Does the computer contain any software for making financial documents such as checks?
- Does the computer contain any software for making counterfeit drivers' licenses or other identification?
- Does the computer contain any software for scanning and manipulating photographs?
- Has the computer been used to purchase anything online?

9.8.3 Child Exploitation Victims

In cases involving child exploitation, investigators ask victims the following questions:

- Has the victim been in any online chat rooms?
- Did the victim give any information to anyone online indicating his or her true name, age, and location?
- Has the victim received any pictures or gifts from the suspect?
- Who is on the victim's chat room buddy lists?
- Does the victim use any social networking sites such as Facebook or MySpace?
- Has the suspect been in any online chat rooms?
- What is the suspect's chat room name or online identity?

- Who is on the suspect's chat room buddy lists?
- Does the suspect use more than one computer? Where are those computers?

9.8.4 Hacking and Intrusions

In cases involving hacking and intrusions, investigators ask victims the following questions:

- Who observed the illegal activity first?
- Are any employees or former employees considered suspects?
- Who is the network administrator?
- Is there a diagram of the network available?
- Are computer and server logs available? Are the logs current?
- Can the logs be immediately be secured to prevent access by suspects?

9.9 What to Look for

This section includes the different types of evidence that should be collected in a digital forensics investigation:

- Evidence on storage devices
  - Internal hard drives
  - External hard drives
  - USB drives (thumb drives)
  - Removable media
  - CD-ROM and CD-RW
  - DVD and DVD+R/DVD-R
  - Floppy disks and Zip disks
  - Memory cards
- Evidence on handheld devices
  - Mobile phones
  - Personal Digital Assistants or PDAs
  - iPod and other mp3 players
  - Pagers
  - GPS receivers

- Evidence on peripheral devices
  - Keyboards and mice
  - Webcams
  - Microphones
  - Memory card readers
  - USB and FireWire hubs
  - Voice over IP or VoIP devices (Vonage, Magic Jack)
- Evidence from media creation
  - Digital cameras
  - Video cameras
  - Digital video recorders (TiVo)
  - Digital audio recorders
  - Fingerprint/thumbprint reader
- Evidence from networks and the Internet
  - Satellite receiver and access cards
  - Network hubs
  - Network switches
  - Wireless access points
  - Modems (phone, cable, DSL, ISDN)
  - Wireless cards and antennas
  - Network information may be available from a network administrator
  - IP address (if this information can be obtained without compromising the suspect PC)
  - Domain name server or DNS information (if this information can be obtained without compromising the suspect PC)

9.10 Internet Abuse by Employees

Employees can abuse their Internet privileges at work in a variety of ways—surfing inappropriate websites, sending malicious e-mails, or using a company-owned computer during the workday for personal business. What if an employer suspects that an employee is using a workplace PC for more serious activity, such as stealing trade secrets or leaking confidential information via e-mail or blog posts? Assuming that a corporate security policy is in place warning employees that their computer use can be monitored and recorded, look for the following information:

- The offending e-mails, including headers
- E-mail server logs
- Web server logs
- Web URL information from browser history, bookmarks/favorites, and cache

9.11 Computer Examination Techniques

The goal of a successful computer forensics examination is to gather admissible evidence of a crime, security policy violation, or similar incident. This evidence may be located on a suspect's computer or peripheral devices, a network, or a combination of these.

A fundamental concept of digital forensics is to work from a copy of the data being investigated (whenever possible) instead of the original source. The ability to make an exact bit-for-bit copy of a hard disk or (similar storage device) is a common feature of forensic software packages such as EnCase and Helix.

9.11.1 Why Not Just Copy the Files?

For a forensically pure copy of the data, the examiner must use a process that does not write information to the suspect hard drive. The simple act of booting into Windows will alter the contents of the hard drive.

Working within Windows, Mac OS, or Linux/Unix operating systems will alter time stamps, logs, and other data, leaving clues that the investigator was there. Simply copying the files from the target computer will not capture data held in slack space or other areas not seen by the operating system.

9.11.2 The Association of Chief Police Officers (ACPO) Principles

The ACPO has outlined some guidelines for handling electronic evidence and offers good advice on digital forensics investigations.

- ACPO Principle 1—"No action taken by law enforcement agencies or their agents should change data held on a computer or storage media which may subsequently be relied upon in court."

- ACPO Principle 2—"In exceptional circumstances, where a person finds it necessary to access original data held on a computer or on storage media, that person must be competent to do so and be able to give evidence explaining the relevance and the implications of their actions."
- ACPO Principle 3—"An audit trail or other record of all processes applied to computer-based electronic evidence should be created and preserved. An independent third party should be able to examine those processes and achieve the same result."
- ACPO Principle 4—"The person in charge of the investigation (the case officer) has overall responsibility for ensuring that the law and these principles are adhered to."

9.11.3 Investigation Basics

The following list details basic investigative techniques that must be followed:

- Photograph and/or videotape the computer and surrounding area before unplugging any cables or power cords.
- Photograph whatever data are on the monitor.
- Draw a diagram detailing locations of peripherals and how they are connected to the PC.
- Look for removable media stored nearby, such as CDs, DVDs, and USB drives.
- Look for and document connections to networks, servers, and off-site file storage.
- Look for written notes containing passwords or website URLs.
- Note the presence of computer books, manuals, software packaging, and other items that may give a clue as to how the computer was used.
- Determine the time of the last access to the PC.

When completing these tasks, investigators should always think about admissibility—document everything, and record all actions, decisions, and results promptly and properly with the assumption that they may be called upon in court to explain and justify their findings.

The following actions can make the evidence inadmissible:

- Illegal or inappropriate seizure because of a lack of a proper search warrant or corporate authority
- Booting into the computer's operating system and "poking around" for evidence
- Violation of the chain of custody concept, causing doubts about who had access to the evidence at all times

9.12 Handling Digital Evidence

9.12.1 Team Effort

Digital forensic examiners should work in teams of two with one person performing analysis and the other handling documentation. One person is designated as evidence custodian and should know the location of evidence at all times and should be the keeper of locks, combinations, and other physical controls. The evidence custodian records all receipts and transfers; no evidence enters or leaves without documentation. When restoring evidence files, always restore to a hard drive or similar media with the same file system as the original drive (NTFS drive restored to NTFS, FAT 32 restored to FAT 32, etc.). Always be prepared to demonstrate, through MD5 or a similar hashing function that the examination/analysis has not added data to or removed data from the original source of evidence.

9.12.2 Chain of Custody

For evidence to be admissible, it must have a chain of custody. The chain of custody establishes the integrity of the evidence-handling process and proves continuity of the possession of evidence by means of a written record. The location of evidence should be traceable from its original point of seizure or collection through the analysis phase to the time it is presented in court or returned to its owner.

The chain of custody should answer these questions:

- Where has this evidence been?
- Who had access to this evidence?
- What has been done to this evidence?

- Has this evidence been left unattended?
- Has this evidence been subjected to tampering?

The following items should be documented in the chain of custody logs:

- Case number
- Item number (tag number)
- Date, time, and location the item was seized
- From whom the item was seized
- Who originally collected the evidence
- Full name and signature of the person who received the evidence
- Description of the evidence including brand name, model name or number, and serial number
- Hash values

Each link of the chain of custody must ensure that evidence remains unaltered. Standardized and repeatable processes and documentation must be used. And whether the investigation takes place in the field or in the lab, the goal is to leave the state of the target (suspect) computer as undisturbed as possible.

9.12.3 Documentation

When handling and processing digital evidence, documentation is critical. Evidence log entries should be written in ink, and logs should be kept in bound volumes to ensure pages are not removed. All evidence collection procedures are recorded in evidence logs at the time the evidence is collected. Investigators must not rely on their memories.

Examinations are always conducted with data integrity in mind. Investigators may be called upon to answer these questions about the evidence they have collected:

- How is the original source being protected?
- How was it acquired?
- How was it copied (mirrored)?
- Did you change the original data in any way? Are you sure?

Answering, *I do not know* to any of these questions may get evidence ruled inadmissible.

9.13 Network Forensics

Investigators must conduct systematic tracking of incoming and out-going traffic to ascertain how an attack was carried out or how an event occurred on a network. Then, they determine the cause of the abnormal traffic. There are two types of threats to networks: internal threats (system malfunction or bug) and external threats (attackers and hackers). External threats, or intruders, leave clues that can be uncovered with event logging and good audit procedures.

Defending the network is important. A well-defended network is arranged in layers. The most valuable data should be hidden in the innermost part of the network to deny easy access by attackers. With Defense in Depth, there are three modes of protection:

- People
- Technology
- Operations

9.14 Network Forensics Tools

9.14.1 Helix

Helix is an excellent choice for the bootable forensic CD used over the network. It operates in two modes: Windows Live (GUI or command-line interface) and bootable Linux. The Windows Live GUI version includes a runtime prompt for accessing the command line. The GUI will use more resources than the command-line interface.

9.14.2 Packet Sniffer

Also known as a packet analyzer, this can be either hardware or software that can monitor a network, identify network traffic, and analyze the content. Wireshark, a well-known packet sniffer, was formerly known as Ethereal. It was renamed due to trademark issues.

9.14.3 Sysinternals

Sysinternals is a collection of free tools for analysis of PCs running Windows. These Sysinternals tools (from the PsTools suite) may be of particular interest to the forensic analyst.

- PsPasswd changes account passwords.
- PsSuspend suspends processes.
- PsLoggedOn shows who is logged locally.
- PsGetSid displays security identifier or SID.

Bibliography

Association of Chief Police Officers. (n.d.). *ACPO good practice guide for computer-based electronic evidence.* Retrieved from http://www.7safe.com/electronic_evidence/ACPO_guidelines_computer_evidence_v4_web.pdf

Ciampa, M. (2009). *Security+ guide to network security fundamentals.* Boston, MA: Course Technology.

Daubert v. Merrell Dow Pharmaceuticals 509 U.S. 579 (1993).

Davis, C., Philipp, A. and Cowen, D. (2005). *Hacking exposed: Computer forensics.* Emeryville, CA: McGraw Hill Osborne.

Federal Evidence Review. (2009). *Federal rules of evidence 2009.* Arlington, VA: Federal Evidence Review. Retrieved from http://federalevidence.com/downloads/rules.of.evidence.pdf.

National Institute of Justice. (2008). *Electronic crime scene investigation: A guide for first responders.* Washington, DC: U.S. Department of Justice. Retrieved from http://www.nij.gov/pubs-sum/219941.htm.

National Institute of Justice. (2004). *Forensic examination of digital evidence: A guide for law enforcement.* Washington, DC: U.S. Department of Justice. Retrieved from http://www.nij.gov/pubs-sum/199408.htm.

National Institute of Justice. (2007). *Investigations involving the Internet and computer networks.* Washington, DC: U.S. Department of Justice. Retrieved from https://www.ncjrs.gov/pdffiles1/nij/210798.pdf.

Solomon, M., Barrett, D. and Broom, N. (2005). *Computer forensics jumpstart.* Alameda, CA: SYBEX, Inc.

United States Secret Service. (2009). *Best practices for seizing electronic evidence* (Third ed.). Retrieved from Forward Edge II: http://www.forwardedge2.com/pdf/bestPractices.pdf.

United States versus Jacobsen, 466 U.S. 109, 113 (1984).

United States v. Comprehensive Drug Testing, Inc., 2006 U.S. App. LEXIS 31850 (Ninth Cir. Dec. 27, 2006). Retrieved from http://www.ca9.uscourts.gov/datastore/opinions/2009/08/26/05-10067eb.pdf.

U.S. Department of Justice. (2007, February). *Prosecuting computer crimes.* Columbia, SC: Office of Legal Education Executive Office of Unite States Attorneys. Retrieved from http://www.justice.gov/criminal/cybercrime/docs/ccmanual.pdf.

SECTION II
PRACTICE TEST

1. Blood is a specialized form of _____ involving multiple cells suspended in plasma.
   a. connective tissue
   b. liquid that does not contain cells
   c. material that contains only red blood cells
   d. fluid that conforms to Newtonian physics

2. If a bloodstain on a vertical wall measures 3 mm wide and 6 mm long, the blood drop that caused the stain impacted the wall at an approximate _____ angle.
   a. 45°
   b. 30°
   c. 90°
   d. 60°

3. The pooling of blood as it accumulates at the lowest part of the body is known as _____.
   a. hypostasis
   b. plasmorphis
   c. gravitational coagulation
   d. convergence

4. A class of fingerprints that includes ridge patterns that are generally rounded or circular in shape and have two deltas is known as a _____.
   a. loop
   b. whorl
   c. bifurcation
   d. arch

5. The _____ should remain in the same condition as it was when the first officer arrived.

    a. victim's body

    b. suspect weapon

    c. suspected point of entry

    d. crime scene

6. Obtaining _____ samples is important to later use in comparison with crime scene evidence.

    a. standard/reference

    b. blood/semen

    c. hair follicle

    d. soil

7. When conducting a criminal investigation, ensure that witnesses of the incident are identified and _____.

    a. numbered

    b. interrogated

    c. separated

    d. catalogued

8. The ABO system is the most commonly used and divides _____ into four different groups.

    a. fingerprints

    b. blood

    c. crime scenes

    d. forensics

9. A _____ is a firearm designed to be fired using both hands and has a longer barrel and a larger capacity magazine.

    a. rifle

    b. pistol

    c. shotgun

    d. submachine gun

10. Which form of evidence can indirectly prove facts from inference?

    a. Physical evidence

    b. Testimonial evidence

    c. Direct evidence

    d. Circumstantial evidence

11. When searching a crime scene, a _____ search can be used for both large and small areas.

    a. grid

    b. strip

    c. zone/sector

    d. circle

12. When collecting evidence, what kind of evidence should be given first priority?

    a. Trace evidence

    b. Fragile evidence

    c. Evidence that could impede the search of the scene

    d. Circumstantial evidence

13. Blood from a victim who takes blood thinners may have a different hematocrit level from that of blood from a person who has just finished exercising in a gym. Blood thinners and exercise are known as _____ when doing a bloodstain pattern analysis.

    a. parameters

    b. variables

    c. raw scores

    d. raw values

14. You measure 40 well-formed bloodstains, calculate the angle of impact values, add them together, and divide by 40 to get a value known as _____.

    a. the standard deviation

    b. the regression coefficient

    c. mean

    d. mode

15. _____ evidence refers to evidence in written form.

    a. Text

    b. Graphical

    c. Documentary

    d. Binary

16. CDs and DVDs are the safest removable media to handle because they are usually in _____ mode.

    a. encrypted

    b. compressed

    c. rewritable

    d. read-only

17. _____ evidence is the statement of a witness under oath, either in court or by deposition.

   a. Documentary
   b. Testimonial
   c. Personal
   d. Verbal

18. What hidden area is typically missed by data-backup utilities?
   a. Metadata
   b. Slack space
   c. Spool space
   d. File index space

19. Which of the following is considered a responsibility of the coroner or medical examiner?
   a. Determining which items are considered evidence
   b. Determining who the murderer was
   c. Determining the cause of death
   d. Determining the next of kin

20. After eating, how long will food stay in the stomach before it starts to empty?
   a. 10 minutes
   b. 30 minutes
   c. 1 hour
   d. 2 hours

See page 523 for answer key.

SECTION III
CRIMINAL INVESTIGATIONS AND TRIALS

Section III details the management of investigations. It also covers how investigators interview witnesses and victims, interrogate suspects, and detect deception in everyone involved in a case. Finally, it discusses criminal trials and the investigator's role in them. See page 265 for questions reviewing the material in Section III.

Chapter 10: Management of Investigations
Chapter 11: Interview, Interrogation, and Detecting Deception
Chapter 12: Criminal Trials

10

MANAGEMENT
OF INVESTIGATIONS

10.1 Management and Organization

Properly managing and organizing an investigation can assist your
organization by minimizing any issues and leading to success.

10.1.1 Necessary Managerial Skills

The one managing an investigation must have skills to direct it properly. The following are managerial skills needed in an investigation:

- Technical skills—The ability to use knowledge, methods, techniques, and equipment as needed when performing specific
  tasks; skills obtained by experience, education, and training.
- Human skills—The ability to interact effectively with people by
  providing leadership, guidance, management, and motivation.
- Conceptual skills—The ability to understand the interre-
  lationship of ideas or elements in relation to the totality of
  the agency or organization. Using this skill will enable an
  individual to act within proper accordance of the agency's or
  organization's objectives and goals rather than acting only on
  behalf of his or her own individual goals.

10.1.2 Agency Organization

The organization of an agency itself is important to understand.

Managers and supervisors use specific selection criteria in giving
investigative assignments, including exams scores, aptitude tests,
ranks, recommendations, and board qualifications.

The managers must decide what type of and how much training to provide for the investigative team. They must also decide if they will be using specialization, generalization, or rotation assignments. Specialization is preferred if an agency can justify it based on case workload and needs. Generalization is ideal for departments that have manageable caseloads. Rotation can be demoralizing for an officer that is rotated out of a favored assignment without cause. This sort of rotation will also limit opportunities for career growth and professional ambitions.

Supervisors will be selected from within an investigation based on their qualifications. It is a waste of resources to give uniform assignments to recently promoted investigators. In selecting supervisors, experience is important to maintain properly delegated routine matters.

10.1.3 Organization of an Investigation

An investigation must be properly organized to run smoothly. Ensure the following items are organized:

- Evidence collection
- Procedural tactics
- Patrol officers' duties at a crime scene
- Proper preparation of forms and reports
- Ample allowance of overtime
- Individual responsibilities for case officers
- Budgeting for confidential informants

There are some things the leader of an investigation can do to ensure an investigation runs smoothly. The first is to meet the needs of the investigative team. This means giving access to all necessary equipment for an investigation, assigning duties to individuals, and properly notifying everyone of the status of the investigation and their own responsibilities within it.

The second thing that can be done is to facilitate teamwork—an absolute must for achieving and completing all investigational goals. It is the responsibility of both the detectives and the patrol officers to work together for a balanced and successful investigation. Management policies should always emphasize, encourage, and implement teamwork.

10.2 Cases

Managing a case is important. To do it effectively, you must evaluate the development of an investigation, commence with the initial report, and progress through all steps of the investigation until the case is closed.

10.2.1 Promote the Case

Resources are often limited and the competition for these resources can be rough. Agency managers are the gatekeepers of a thorough investigation, and investigators increase the likelihood of securing future resources and promoting cases by maintaining a positive track record of successfully conducted prior cases.

Having the resources necessary to properly investigate a crime is vital. To enhance the chances of obtaining resources, investigators must demonstrate an understanding of the nature of the investigation, the elements of the crime, the development of a well-conceived investigative plan, and what resources are needed.

10.2.2 Encourage Interagency Teamwork

All involved in an investigation need to establish a network of collaboration, trust, and respect. Those involved may include law enforcement personnel, prosecutors, medical examiners, and coroners.

Law enforcement personnel and prosecutors should work together and feel comfortable with sharing advice with one another during the course of an investigation. An investigator must be able to articulate the facts of the case to enable prosecution. Ultimately, prosecutors determine if a case is accepted, so an investigator must be able to coordinate and collaborate with them. The earlier an investigator involves the prosecutor, the easier it is to create a sense of ownership and participation for him or her. If the prosecutor becomes a stakeholder in an investigation, he or she will be more willing to see it through to the end.

Avoiding intraorganizational conflict is of great importance; do this by being aware of different opinions or perceptions and taking into account the needs of all stakeholders involved. One of the most memorable examples of intraorganizational conflict occurred in 1993 at the Mount Carmel Center in Waco, Texas, where two entities—the Hostage Rescue Team (HRT) and the Crisis Incident Negotiation Team (CINT)—responded to a hostile situation between law enforcement and the occupants of the David Koresh compound:

- HRT—In accordance with their training, the HRT responded by setting up snipers around the perimeter, entering the facility, and planning to make those inside uncomfortable.
- CINT—Their negotiators were not interested in putting more pressure on those inside. They also were negotiating with both the people inside as well as the HRT.

10.3 Supervisory Procedures

If you are assigned to supervise an investigation, understanding your role is absolutely vital. Here are the basic duties of a supervisor of an investigation:

- Be present at the scene for the preliminary investigation.
- Delegate specific investigative duties.
- Manage the crime scene search.
- Document all events.
- Conduct informational conferences for all active participants involved in the case throughout the course of the investigation.

10.3.1 On-Scene Supervision Responsibilities

The supervisor has many responsibilities at the crime scene itself.

First, the supervisor must document the details when responding to a crime scene. Include the date and the time notification of the incident was received, how the report was received, the name of the person or witness filing the report, and a complete account of all details.

When the supervisor is at the scene, he or she has the responsibility to record his or her exact time of arrival, just as all personnel do. The supervisor must also record the address of the crime scene and all present law enforcement personnel units. Also at the scene, the supervisor must verify that an investigator has been assigned to the case, establish cooperation with the patrol supervisor, and receive a briefing from the law enforcement personnel who arrived first to the scene.

Besides assigning tasks and properly documenting the crime scene, the supervisor should inspect and establish the crime scene boundaries. The supervisor should also delegate and assign duties as needed and coordinate and organize all assignments being performed.

Finally, the supervisor should develop an opinion or theory of what happened at the scene. It is okay to change your mind later; hypotheses are tentative at best. Remember things are not always as they appear. When creating a hypothesis, state whether the cause of death (if there is a fatality) was homicide, suicide, accident, or of natural causes. Determine this based on the crime scene, the statements, and the physical evidence. Include photos and sketches of the body before the examination and describe the body (including clothing).

10.3.2 Handling of Suspects in Custody

When the supervisor takes a suspect into custody, many steps need to be taken:

- Authenticating the warrant or the probable cause for arrest
- Determining the scope of the preliminary investigation
- Documenting all observations and statements, either acquired or overheard, and any information attained from family members, informants, or witnesses

10.3.2.1 Interviews and Interrogations   Document when the suspect was issued the Miranda warning and take a preliminary statement from him or her at the scene if the suspect is willing to cooperate. It is more useful to take this statement at the scene because it may assist in the recovery of evidence. The suspect may also become less than cooperative by the time he or she is transported to your office. If they are willing to talk, listen. Get his or her statement while you can—before they decide to engage their lawyer.

10.3.2.2 Suspect's Mental State   Evaluate and document the suspect's demeanor and mental capacity from the time of arrest to the time of accusation and/or during any interviews or interrogations. This procedure is necessary to prepare for a possible diminished capacity defense. Investigators may have evidence that corroborates diminished capacity defense.

10.3.3 Investigative Conference

This conference evaluates the investigation through an overall outline where everyone involved in the investigation shares their progress and thoughts. All developments in the investigation are shared through a general discussion. The conference gives daily updates of the investigation as a whole.

10.4 Special Investigations

Traditional crimes include murder, robbery, and arson. However, special investigations include analysis of drugs, organized crime, cybercrime, and terrorism. Drug trafficking criminal networks are the most common focus of special investigations.

10.4.1 Goals of Involved Parties

The goal of most criminal organizations is to make money. This can be achieved by selling illegal drugs or stolen property, laundering other people's money, and extortion.

The goal of special investigations is not to stop one criminal. With special investigations, the focus must be on the collective issue. To eliminate a single person will not stop further crimes from happening. The goals for special investigations are to disrupt, dismantle, and incapacitate the entire criminal network.

10.4.2 Conspiracy Laws

Conspiracy laws allow the prosecution of persons who are guilty based on conversations with others who actually commit the crimes. This allows prosecution of those who give orders to commit the crime, not only those who actually carry out the orders. This is useful in the special investigations. Some conspiracy laws used for special investigations include the following:

- Racketeer Influenced and Corrupt Organizations (RICO) Act
- The Continuing Criminal Enterprise Act
- The PATRIOT Act

Here is an example of the RICO Act in effect: If Dustin ordered Homer to murder Daniel, and Homer carried it out, both Dustin and Homer can be charged with the murder of Daniel. Without special conspiracy laws like RICO, Dustin would not likely be charged for his role in the crime.

10.4.3 Evidence-Gathering Techniques

Investigators use covert, undercover, and overt techniques to gather evidence. Covert techniques include pen registers and wiretaps. Undercover techniques include undercover informants, surveillance, and consensual monitoring. Overt techniques include the use of grand juries, interviews, interrogations, and search warrants.

10.5 The Investigator's Report

All of the important facts and conclusions from the investigation should be documented and clearly presented. This can include the following notes:

- What you learned in the investigation
- What the next steps are
- Discovery methods used
- Personnel involved
- Sequence of events
- System events
- Actions taken (with documented times)
- Preventative measures resulting from the investigation
- Recovery steps taken and further recommendations

Once the report is made, analyzing the completed investigation is the next step. This will help you improve the next investigation. Ask questions such as what went well, what needs improvement, and what the investigator's next steps are. Did the investigation reveal weaknesses in our network security or physical security? Are there regulatory issues? Did we break any laws or rules in this investigation? Will we be fined or penalized? Will more training, tougher standards, or better policy prevent a recurrence of the initial cause of the investigation?

Bibliography

Westveer, A.E., Jr. (2002). *Managing death investigations*, Vol. 1 (Fifth ed.). Washington, DC: U.S. Department of Justice Federal Bureau of Investigation. (Used with permission.)

11

INTERVIEW, INTERROGATION, AND DETECTING DECEPTION

An important skill is the ability to talk with people in different types of situations, some of which can be quite stressful. This could involve a crucial eyewitness, crime survivor, or prime suspect. There is a significant difference between interviewing a witness, survivor, or person of interest and the outright interrogation of a suspect.

11.1 Interviewing

11.1.1 The Basics

Interviewing witnesses—or even victims or complainants—is crucial to any investigation, but there are things to keep in mind. Just because they feel positive about what they are saying does not mean they are right. Confidence does not correlate highly with the truth, and people have been erroneously arrested (and convicted) as a result of confidence. Also, attentiveness varies according to different factors. Was the witness paying attention, fully conscious, and able to see clearly? Was the witness emotionally uninvolved? Does the witness harbor prejudices? Could lighting conditions or weather have affected the witness's perception? Is the witness fearful or anxious about answering questions?

11.1.2 Issues with Memory

If there is more than one witness, they must be separated to keep from corrupting the memory of a particular witness with what someone else might report. Each witness should be allowed to relate the account without interruption—especially an interruption that relies on information picked up from another witness.

In addition, the way questions are asked can influence how a story is told. All officers should learn about the way human memory works. There are many problems with the process of memory storage and retrieval, but investigations depend on getting information from both witnesses and victims of a crime. Either the witness or the victim may be dealing with trauma that can adversely affect the recall of accurate details. Thus, interviewers increasingly rely on the cognitive interview, which takes into account lessons from cognitive psychology.

The aim of this procedure is to mentally reinstate the context of an incident in order to better retrieve details from a person's memory. There are four steps:

1. The interview begins with an open-ended question, which urges the witness to try to recall everything in chronological order, starting with a physical description of the environment.
2. Then, the witness recounts the incident as fully as possible.
3. Following this, the interviewer asks the subject to change perspectives and describe the incident in this way.
4. In addition, the interviewer asks the witness how he or she was feeling at the time of the incident.

When the witness is done, the interviewer revisits specific aspects of the account to draw out more details, and may ask the witness to recount the event in a different order. The interviewer has a set of specific types of questions to ask, such as questions about names, numbers, conversations, and suspect descriptions. Once this process is finished, the interviewer summarizes the account. In addition, interviewers urge witnesses to contact them should any details surface later, as this is a common occurrence after such interviews.

Sometimes, a cognitive interview will involve inducing a light trance that might assist linking a memory to its original context. This raises the issue of forensic hypnosis, and most courts will not allow hypnotically refreshed testimony into a trial. There are many reasons for this, such as the induction of false memories. However, a light trance, which is nothing more than a technique for relaxation, is not the same as hypnosis.

11.1.2.1 Accuracy The accuracy of eyewitness reports relies on the quality of three different perceptual processes:

- Encoding (processing information)
- Storage (retaining information for short-term use or long-term recall)
- Retrieval (locating the stored information)

In turn, the quality of these processes depends on how many interfering factors are present and how strong they may be; it also depends on a witness's state of mind during the incident.

11.1.2.2 Distortion Memory is a process of construction organized via a cluster of related facts and experiences. Our memories can be distorted so that they are consistent with our prejudices and expectations. Exposure to new information between the time an incident occurred and the time when we try to retrieve the memory of it can also affect what is recalled, even if that new information contains errors.

Other factors affecting memory recall include how often an item is rehearsed, whether the encoding is mentally organized into meaningful patterns, whether the person was traumatized during the incident, and whether the person felt pressured to recall the incident in a certain way.

11.1.2.3 Encoding Specificity Principle The encoding specificity principle indicates that retrieval is more successful when retrieval cues match the situation in which the experience occurred. In summary, when we encode an experience we tend to select certain aspects and ignore others. We accept those things that make sense and reconstruct the memory to work for us. We all have internal scripts, widely held beliefs about sequences of actions that typically occur in a certain way. We get them from cultural narratives, and they affect how we remember something that happened.

11.1.2.4 Memory Studies Take the results of this research: Subjects were exposed to a film of a murder in a crowd. They then received written information about it, but half were misled about certain key details, such as describing a car that is actually green as being white.

Those who had been exposed to the erroneous information tended to report the errors rather than what they had actually seen with a rate of mistakes as high as 40%.

In similar studies, people have reported other types of errors, from broken glass they never saw to nonexistent signs and buildings. Our cultural plots train us to anticipate certain traits and behaviors, and we fill in gaps that occur during storage and recall to make a story work the way that makes most sense to us.

In truth, witnesses desire to tell what they remember. However, they cannot have a full narrative without some distortion. Then, there are those with something to hide, and for them, interrogation techniques may work better.

11.2 Interrogation

Interrogations are conducted with people believed to have information but who are unwilling to give that information or on people believed to have committed or helped commit an offense. Interrogation should be avoided with anyone who can be successfully interviewed.

Suspects are interrogated to obtain an admission of guilt or confession. The asking of questions is an interrogation if it can be shown that the officers knew the questions were likely to elicit incriminating statements—that is, they were guilt seeking.

Torturing a suspect is illegal. However, psychological pressure and deception are allowed in interrogations and sometimes this involves moderate sleep deprivation or solitary confinement. Some countries employ truth-producing drugs (narcoanalysis) in interrogations. All suspects are made aware that they have the right to say nothing. The Miranda warning, which must be read to and understood by all suspects, protects suspects from being forced to talk. When the Miranda warning is given, document it.

When you interrogate a suspect, first identify yourself as a law enforcement officer; have another officer present. If the investigator believes legal counsel has been retained or appointed for the suspect for the specific offense under investigation, that counsel should be notified immediately. During the interrogation, offer the suspect food and restroom breaks.

11.2.1 Reid Technique

One of the most utilized yet controversial interrogation approaches is the Reid technique, which develops via a series of calculated manipulations. Prohibited in some countries on vulnerable populations, the Reid technique has three components:

- Factual
- Interviewing
- Interrogation

Relying on what the investigation has turned up from a crime or crime scene (factual), investigators begin with a nonaccusatory interview to elicit more information and observe a suspect's behavior. They may also ask questions designed to provoke certain behaviors as a baseline for detecting deception. Typically, the questioner's demeanor is compassionate and understanding and designed to seem sympathetic. However, leading questions are embedded in the interview to try to get a guilty person to start the process of confession.

The interrogation stage, relying on moral justification, involves nine distinct steps. Interrogators directly confront suspects with an assertion of guilt, keeping up a monologue as they develop a theme that excuses the crime. At all times, they interrupt the suspect's effort to deny guilt and use whatever they can to overcome objections to what the interrogator is doing or saying. Interrogators try to prevent a passive suspect from withdrawing into silence or refusal; this may involve a false show of sympathy and understanding, or even a face-saving alternative ("We know you didn't mean to do it").

It may also involve intimidation or outright lies ("We have a witness who places you at the scene"), as well as an appeal to their best interest. However, interrogators are not allowed to threaten harm, promise leniency, use brutality, or continue with the questioning after the suspect has exercised the right to remain silent or see an attorney. Any admissions the subject makes are used to set up a choice between two incriminating alternatives or a set of alternatives that would likely pressure the suspect into accepting his or her guilt ("Either your father killed your sister or you did").

Essentially, the guilty person is steadily backed into a corner wherein the only perceived way out is to give the interrogators what they want. If there is more than one suspect, interrogators may try to play them off each other, scaring or enticing each into taking the deal first by turning on the other. The thrust of this technique is to get suspects to admit to details of the crime, and then to convert the oral statement into a written and signed confession.

However, getting an admission is not sufficient. It is also important to acquire details that can be corroborated with evidence. If a suspect should recant an admission, the investigation may stall unless the officers have developed more evidence. Thus, interviews should elicit methods, location details, and motives.

11.2.1.1 Interrogations Based on Personality Types   Some interrogation techniques follow from assessing the suspect's personality type. For example, psychopaths are insensitive to altruistic or interview themes (such as sympathy for their victims or guilt over their crimes), so interrogating them calls for different measures. Some interviewers have discovered that the psychopath's inherent narcissism, selfishness, grandiosity, and vanity can often be exploited by praising his or her intelligence or assuring him or her of attention or fame. Paranoid types need special handling, as do psychotic or transiently psychotic individuals.

11.2.1.2 False Confessions   Problems do arise from the firm presumption of guilt that grounds each interrogation session because it can create tunnel vision about other options or suspects and make the sessions so unrelenting that an innocent person could capitulate to the pressure. A negative result of interrogation techniques could be a false confession, or admitting to a crime that one did not commit. Some false confessions are voluntary, while others may be coerced. A coerced confession is usually offered when the person is exhausted, naive, frightened, or mentally impaired.

On rare occasions, a suspect may even internalize the incident and come to believe he or she actually committed a crime. This occurs when an interrogator seems confident of the suspect's guilt and uses several forms of manipulation over a certain period.

The characteristics of those most likely to falsely confess include the following:

- Young
- Low IQ
- Mentally instable
- High degree of suggestibility
- Trusting nature
- Low self-esteem
- High anxiety

11.2.2 PEACE Model

Some departments use an alternative to the Reid technique that is gaining ground among law enforcement in many countries: the planning and preparation, engage and explain, account, closure, evaluation (PEACE) model. The focus of the PEACE model is to gather information rather than obtain a confession. The first stage involves defining the objectives. This relies on knowing what the evidence may be, what evidence is needed, and making sure that interview exhibits are ready.

Engaging with a suspect involves forming the appropriate relationship; from there, the purpose and activities of the interview can be clarified. The interviewee is then invited to offer an account of the events of interest while the interrogator manages the conversation. The aim is to have the person mentally relive the event and perhaps recall it with different chronologies. The account is divided into manageable aspects and the interviewer maintains control over them. The C step is about providing closure so that both parties are on the same page and know what will happen next.

Then interviewers evaluate the material gained from the interview and may develop leads or decide that another interview is warranted; additionally, they may also use this opportunity to evaluate their own performance. While this method appears to minimize false confessions, all interrogators are faced with one of the trickiest aspects of any type of negotiation: spotting a liar.

11.3 Detecting Deception

Deception can take many forms and an important skill in forensic contexts is the ability to spot it. An offender might stage a crime scene, falsely accuse others, lie outright, or fake an illness. Despite some claims, there is no simple formula for catching a liar. Even people with repeated exposure to deception often perform no better than chance, but they can improve their skills with solid observation and sophisticated techniques.

11.3.1 Detection Techniques

Some detection techniques currently in use include examination of body language and behavior, statement analysis, and criteria-based content analysis.

11.3.1.1 Body Language   Researchers have found that lying requires more effort than truth-telling, so it produces physiological signals such as a heightened pulse rate, dilated pupils, twitches, and certain facial expressions, especially when the stakes are high. However, truthful but anxious people may also display such symptoms, while some types of liars might not. In fact, watching the face can be highly unreliable.

11.3.1.2 Behavior   The trick to accuracy is questioning persons of interest long enough to observe and recognize their default behavior. While there are no hard-and-fast rules, the types of behaviors that can signal discomfort, and thus potential deception, include the following behaviors:

- Language with more negative than positive statements
- Overgeneralizations
- Deflections
- Increased vocal pitch
- Hesitations and pauses in speech
- A lack of spontaneity
- Taking longer to respond to questions
- Appearing to plan what they will say
- Responses that seem too long or are irrelevant
- Increase in number of shrugs, blinking, and nervous habits
- Changes in the eye pupil
- Increased leg and foot movements in response to specific themes

- Venting the body, like pulling a shirt or collar away
- Pointing feet toward an exit
- Blanching
- Flushing
- Breath holding
- Sighing
- Reduced use of hand gestures
- Lack of head movement

None is definitive, but these behaviors occur more often in those with motivation to deceive, possibly because they are trying to plan and control what they say. Sometimes their deception will have a rehearsed quality, with the timing slightly off.

11.3.1.3 Statement Analysis   This is a common tool for interrogations and witness statements. An investigator asks an open-ended question and leaves the person to fill in the blanks in the form of a (recorded) oral or written statement. The subject picks the starting and ending points. Statement analysis focuses on what is said about events leading up to a crime, the crime itself, and the aftermath of the crime. Investigators watch for the distribution of detail in each area and note whether subjects provide more information than requested or skip something crucial.

Also, a change in tone or speed of delivery can reveal their comfort (or discomfort) with what they are saying. Another clue is a change in language regarding another person or sensitivity about some item, which may be apparent in a shift from first to third person. Information, about which investigators know the individual has some knowledge he or she left out, is a good source for follow-up questions.

11.3.1.4 Criteria-Based Content Analysis   A similar method called criteria-based content analysis closely examines how an incident is retold, comparing it against the typical method of recall in a truthful session versus fabricating a supposed recollection. Psychologist Aldert Vrij of the University of Portsmouth in England is among the leading figures in developing this method.

Accordingly, analysts look for specific features of a narrative: coherent and consistent but not strictly chronological, detailed with superfluous elements, reiterating dialogue and personal interactions including feelings and theories about a perpetrator, and spontaneous corrections. While telling the truth, people easily admit to memory gaps, vagueness, or contradictions and wonder if they are recalling an incident correctly. However, with an error rate of up to 30%, this method alone is unlikely to reveal a skillful liar.

11.3.2 Cognitive Load

Recognizing that half a century of research has shown that few people are good at spotting lies, the diagnostic approach to clues can cause a high percentage of false positives (erroneously identifying someone as a liar). Imposing a cognitive load involves several possible strategies for questioning a subject. Liars not only take on a cognitive load when they fabricate a story, but they are also typically looking for clues in the interrogator's behavior that affirms their success. They must also remind themselves to role-play.

For very good liars, this can become second nature. Thus, the interrogator must contrive a way to increase the cognitive load beyond the liar's typical strategy, which helps to discriminate more accurately between a liar and a truth-teller. One method is to ask interviewees to tell their story backward. This can disrupt the process of fabrication, which relies on a specific chronology that has no experiential basis for recall.

In addition, interviewers instruct subjects to keep eye contact at all times, because this form of concentration reduces the cognitive resources needed for lying. Research on these methods showed that they could increase the detection of lies from 42% to 60%.

Another strategy uses questions a subject would not anticipate; thus, they would not have planned lies with which to respond. The strategy requires some creativity on the part of interviewers, since they will have to think of a unique angle on the subject matter that can yield such questions. For example, instead of asking the typical "What was playing at the theater?" when a suspect offers "I went to a movie" as an alibi, the interrogator may ask how large the theater is, how many screens there are in the theater, or where the person was sitting. Asking an unanticipated question twice can also assist with deception detection because liars have a difficult time recalling lies they fabricated on the spot.

The interrogator may ask the suspect to draw a scene if such a visual construction is possible. Truth-tellers can achieve this more readily than liars (who often do vague drawings, get details wrong, or leave them out). Using these techniques, subjects in research conditions made the correct classification of liars about 80% of the time.

11.3.3 Strategic Use of Available Evidence (SUE)

The SUE approach also gets good results. Generally, guilty suspects will use more avoidance, deflection, or denial strategies under interrogation than truth-tellers do. Interrogators using SUE employ open-ended questions that elicit information; these are followed by specific questions strategically posed that suggest that they have evidence against the suspect.

Truth-tellers will spontaneously offer information, while guilty subjects will try to avoid it or will even contradict what the evidence shows. In research, interviewers untrained in SUE were correct in their assessment of a liar slightly more than 50% of the time, while SUE-trained interviewers obtained accuracy rates of up to 85%.

11.3.4 Physiological Measurement Devices

11.3.4.1 Polygraph Test   A polygraph test is only an investigation aid. Remember that it cannot detect truth or deception; it only measures bodily reactions. Before giving a polygraph test, investigators should have reasonable cause to believe that the suspect has more knowledge than he or she is sharing.

The polygraph in use today is a compact portable device that measures four key involuntary physiological responses to questioning: skin conductivity, abdominal and chest respiration, blood pressure, and heart rate. Some questions are designed to establish baseline responses, some are neutral, and others attempt to register guilty knowledge or at least a sense that the person knows something that confirms him or her as a suspect. The examiner must determine a baseline that tracks bodily measurements through regular question construction and delivery. Nonthreatening questions allow the examiner to adjust the machine for nervousness. Questions meant to be failed that also help establish a baseline may be something similar to the following: "Have you ever lied to anyone?" Testers often ask subjects obvious questions such as "Are the lights on in this room?" Results recorded from these questions provide a baseline for truth. The last questions of the polygraph test deal with issues of the case.

Although practitioners vouch for the accuracy of the polygraph test and investigators rely on it to intimidate suspects into providing information, research indicates polygraph tests do not offer certainty. The accuracy of a polygraph can be decreased by mental or physical fatigue, being overly emotional, mental or physical disabilities, and the presence of drugs or alcohol.

11.3.4.2 Psychological Stress Evaluator (PSE)   Advocates of the PSE, sometimes referred to as a Voice Stress Evaluator, claim that the voice itself reveals deception even if the subject is unaware of being evaluated. Supposedly, during a lie, the voice reaches a higher pitch than when someone is telling the truth. While the PSE does measure variations in emotional stress, it is not the same as detecting deception. The test is even less accurate than the polygraph, and there is little updated research.

11.3.4.3 Linguistic Inquiry and Word Count (LIWC)   The LIWC computer software analyzes written content. It is derived from the statement analysis approach and looks for three markers: fewer first-person pronouns, more words that convey negative emotion, and fewer exclusionary words (*except*, *but*). The software has been more effective than human judges, but the accuracy rate is still only about 67%.

11.3.5 Objective Assessments

Some psychological tests, which require a licensed clinician to administer and interpret, can pick up a specific type of deception: feigning a mental illness. Both the Minnesota Multiphasic Personality Inventory (MMPI-2), which picks up *faking bad* and *faking good*, and the Structured Interview of Reported Symptoms or SIRS specifically detect malingering. The MMPI-2 even has a built-in lie scale.

11.3.5.1 Facial Action Coding System (FACS)   Psychologist Paul Ekman created the FACS. He claims an accuracy rate of 90% when FACS is combined with measurements for voice stress and speech factors. He believes that the best cues are found in the voice and face for deception about feelings. Even slight gestures can leak emotional states that a person is trying to hide, providing a tell to a skilled and observant detector.

11.3.5.2 Perceived Credibility   Countering this idea, psychologists Charles Bond, Jr., and Bella DePaulo found that lie detection is not about the observer but the one being observed. A person's perceived credibility plays a strong role in whether someone judges him or her to be deceptive. That is not necessarily because a person is honest; it is because they comport themselves in a credible manner. These people appear to be honest right from the start, affecting gut instinct, while others appear to be dishonest. Averting one's gaze or having a long or wide face, as opposed to a more innocent-looking baby face or charming smile, can count against someone's general presentation.

Participants in the study more often believed liars with high credibility ratings than truth-tellers who were perceived as low in credibility. When Bond and DePaulo evaluated numerous other studies about deception, they realized individual differences among judges of deception hovered near the same rate as chance (50%).

11.3.5.3 Other Studies   Some researchers think that liars take slightly longer to start answering questions or show a rehearsed quality as if they have already thought about what they might say when questioned. If they have planned well, they actually might jump in more quickly than a truth-teller because they have their act in a nice package. Yet they are generally more negative and say less than truth-tellers. They will also repeat phrases more often and appear to be trying to manage the interviewer's perception of them.

In the real world, lies are often identified in context, when compared over a period to other behaviors or narratives. The judgment generally involves a number of factors, not just a response to some questions at the time a lie is told.

11.3.6 Neurology and Brain Scans

Psychiatrist Lawrence Farwell developed the brain fingerprinting process based on the notion that all experiences, including committing a crime, are stored in the brain. The electrical activity of a suspect's brain is monitored with sensors on a headband attached to a computer while the subject is exposed to words or images that are both relevant (probes) and irrelevant to the crime.

Certain information would be meaningful only to the actual perpetrator and would include such items as what was done to a victim, where the victim was taken, items removed from the victim, and items left at a scene. The subject would not see this list until the test itself was performed. Irrelevant stimuli may include a different type of weapon, different landscape or color of a room, a different modus operandi, or acts not performed during the commission of the crime.

If the brain activity shows recognition of relevant stimuli—a distinct spike called a MERMER or memory and encoding related multi-faceted electroencephalographic response—then the subject has a record of the crime stored in his or her brain. Innocent people will display no such response to crime-relevant stimuli.

11.3.6.1 Functional Magnetic Resonance Imaging (fMRI) Scans At the University of Texas Southwestern Medical Center, fMRI scans are used to detect differences in neural activity between lying and truth telling. In the experiments, subjects performed a theft of either a ring or a watch and concealed this information from the researchers.

First, each subject was asked neutral questions while being scanned, as well as questions about minor wrongful deeds commonly committed. This way, the researchers could identify typical neurological patterns during truthful responses. Then, each subject responded to questions in a way that was truthful about an object he or she did not steal, but was deceptive about the stolen object.

The rate of accuracy for the fMRI was around 90%. The trick lies in scanning brain regions that activate to suppress information and resolve internal conflicts; these regions are quiet when the person is telling the truth. However, neurological correlations remain vague in what they mean. At this stage, these results are merely suggestive.

11.3.6.2 Effectiveness of Brain Scans There is no one-size-fits-all signal in the neurocircuitry that a person is lying, but it does appear that brain scans are better at revealing tells than watching someone fidget and sweat under questioning. Identifying the right combination of brain signals for a high rate of accuracy when a person lies or hides the truth is still in the future.

11.4 Malingering

Lies are one thing, but faking a mental disorder is another, and when negotiators must deal with someone who appears emotionally unstable, they have to be able to spot malingering. Thus, they must be versed in psychological disorders and possess the skills necessary for dealing with both the real and fake presentations of mental disorders.

11.4.1 Dissociative Identity Disorder (DID)

Among the most often malingered disorders are DID—once called multiple personality disorder—and paranoid schizophrenia. Both are diagnosed in genuinely ill offenders, but many normal offenders with something to gain have learned how to mimic the symptoms. With DID, two or more subpersonalities reportedly develop within a single human being (a host body), each with its own identity, and each taking turns controlling the personality and behavior. The core person generally experiences periods of memory loss (amnesic barrier) and might even wake up in a foreign place with no idea how he or she arrived there. One person may have full access to the memory bank, while others only have partial access.

Experts believe that people with genuine DID develop it from an early childhood trauma, such as sexual abuse or violent, erratic beatings. They learned to mentally remove themselves from the situation, and this psychological flight then becomes their survival mechanism, disturbing the normal integrative functions of identity.

To confirm an alter personality, it is important to collect data from a variety of people who have seen evidence of it—friends, relatives, and coworkers. While alter personalities can be elicited through hypnosis, it is also possible to suggest them into existence. Malingerers mistakenly believe that this disorder involves a mere split personality.

As popular as the idea is, DID is not about a good person and an evil person living in the same body.

11.4.2 Detection Techniques

To detect the malingering of psychiatric symptoms, one may look for an exaggerated presentation, inconsistent information, a strangely deliberate manner, an attempt to display obvious (and stereotypical) symptoms, and an inconsistency with the person's past psychiatric diagnoses. Clinicians may check the defendant's past history of psychiatric confinement (if any) and any statements from witnesses (friends, family, prison guards, hospital staff) as to a person's condition, current and past. They may also observe the subject in various settings over a period.

Malingerers make a point of getting people to pay attention to their illness, while most truly mentally ill people would rather not be so visible. Sudden delusions or hallucinations are inconsistent with the clinical picture of mental illness, except for drug-induced psychosis.

Defendants who have a hard time retaining the voice and personality of the alter they blame for their crime are also suspect, as are defendants who appear to be not confused by their criminal behavior. Similar issues occur when offenders malinger schizophrenia, and many of the same techniques are used to detect a fraudulent presentation.

11.5 Summary

Questioning a person, whether they be a witness or a suspect, can be fraught with complexities, from suggestible memory to outright deception. Learning a good technique is a key to success, as is the development of solid observational skills. How much information can be gained for an investigation often depends on the way an interviewee is handled. Preparation, attention to detail, and the recognition that there are no shortcuts in this process are all necessary for becoming a good interviewer and interrogator.

Bibliography

Cooper, B. and Yullie, J. (2007). Psychopathy & Deception. In Hughes, H. and Yuille, J. (Eds.). *The psychopath: Theory, research and practice*, pp. 487–504. Mahwah, NJ: Lawrence Erlbaum Associates.

Ekman, P. (1992). *Telling lies: Clues to deceit in the marketplace, politics, and marriage* (Second ed.). New York: W.W. Norton & Company.

Feder, B. (2001, October 9). Truth and justice, by the blip of a brain wave. *New York Times.*

Givens, D. (2008). *Crime signals: How to spot a criminal before you become a victim.* New York: St. Martin's Griffin.

Gray, J.A. & McNoughton, N. (1996). The neuropsychology of anxiety: Reprise. *Nebraska symposium on motivation,* Vol. 43, pp. 61–134.

Inbau, F.E., Reid, J.E., Buckley, J.P. & Jayne, B.C. (2004). *Essentials of the Reid Technique: Criminal interrogations and confessions.* Boston: Jones and Bartlett Publishers.

Kassin, S. & Fong, C. (1999). "I'm innocent!": Effects of training on judgments of truth and deception in the interrogation room. *Law and Human Behavior,* Vol. 23, No. 5, pp. 499–516.

Lykken, D.T. (1978). The psychopath and the lie detector. *Psychophysiology,* Vol. 15, No. 2, pp. 137–142.

Navarro, J. & Karlins, M. (2008). *What every body is saying: An ex-FBI agent's guide to speed-reading people.* New York: William Morrow Paperbacks.

Vrij, A. (2008). *Detecting lies and deceit: Pitfalls and opportunities.* Chichester, UK: Wiley.

Vrij, A., Granhag, P., Mann, S. & Leal, S. (2011, February). Outsmarting the liars: Toward a cognitive lie detection approach. *Current Directions in Psychological Science,* Vol. 20, No. 1, pp. 28–32.

12

CRIMINAL TRIALS

12.1 Trial Basics

One of the first steps of a trial is selecting a jury. Both the prosecution and defense have opportunities to challenge prospective jurors. When the trial begins, the prosecution will usually begin presenting its case by calling witnesses who were initially interviewed by investigators. The prosecution may also have crime laboratory experts testify concerning physical evidence. The defense will then have the opportunity to outline its case, typically challenging the prosecutor's evidence. Both will attempt to point out the weaknesses of the other's case. The jury will render one of three possible verdicts: guilty, not guilty, or hung (they could not come to a consensus of the defendant's guilt or innocence).

Most challenges that occur during cross-examination are a result of improper collection efforts, missing links or mistakes in the chain of custody, a faulty method of analyses of the physical evidence, or a question of the accuracy of observations, interviews, affidavits, and rights waivers.

12.2 Expert Witnesses

After the crime has occurred and the investigation is complete, investigators often have another role—expert witness. It is the duty of the expert witness to remain impartial and present unbiased evidence to the court. The expert is expected to give information that falls outside the general knowledge of the judge or jury. One role of the expert is to offer an interpretation of his or her findings and express an opinion as to the significance of the findings. Only a judge can rule an individual as an expert witness.

Education, experience, and training are the most important areas evaluated when qualifying an expert witness. However, the witness's demeanor and communication abilities can also come into play.

When the prosecution hires witnesses, they are usually commissioned by the police as part of the investigative process. They are involved in the case from the beginning and often conduct an in-depth examination of the scene, which may take many weeks to complete.

When hired by the defense, witnesses are usually commissioned by the defense's legal team. They may have little or no involvement with the case until the prosecution's investigation is complete; they work from the information provided by the prosecution's expert rather than from the original evidence. They work on a much shorter time frame.

12.3 Investigator's Testimony

The result in bringing a case to fruition is the investigator's testimony. Investigators should prepare themselves thoroughly before testifying and work closely with the prosecution to avoid surprises in court.

Before testifying, an investigator should complete the following tasks:

- Review all statements for clarity.
- Review all waivers, affidavits, and search warrants.
- Review times, dates, and places of importance.
- Review and prepare notes for quick references.
- Review all evidence acquired in the investigation.
- Verify that the evidence is properly labeled.
- Review the chain of custody.
- Visit the crime scene.

During court, it is important for investigators to follow these tips:

- Establish themselves as credible witnesses.
- Present a clean, neat appearance.
- Be concerned with details.
- Refrain from distracting mannerisms or actions.
- Avoid using police jargon or technical language.

12.4 Innocent but Proven Guilty

America's justice system has taken numbers of guilty individuals off the streets; unfortunately, a number of innocent individuals have been wrongly convicted, stripped of the freedoms they deserve. It is the duty of the forensic examiner to help ensure that this does not happen by gathering and presenting accurate information.

Attorneys, forensic scientists, and students have teamed together and formed *innocence projects* around the nation. The purpose of these projects is to exonerate innocent individuals through the use of post-conviction DNA testing. The Wrongful Conviction and Imprisonment Act of 1984 permits suits against the state and damage awards if defendants can prove their innocence through clear and convincing evidence.

However, from 1985 to 2001, 165 claims were filed, 131 claims were dismissed, 22 claims were pending, and only 12 awards were made. New York is considered the most generous state in compensating wrongful convictions, holding no upper limit on the amount it will pay. In 36 other states, wrongfully convicted individuals are legally barred from recovering damages in a court of law. Voltaire said, "It is better to risk saving a guilty person than to condemn an innocent one." Blackstone wrote, "It is better that ten guilty persons escape than one innocent suffer."

Some leading causes of wrongful convictions include the following:

- Mistaken eyewitness identification
- Prosecutorial and police misconduct
- Fraudulent forensic science
- Inadequate or incompetent defense lawyering
- Jailhouse informants and snitches
- False confessions

Bibliography

Christianson, S. (2004). *Innocent: Inside wrongful conviction case.* New York: New York University Press.

Dictionary.com—Free Online English Dictionary. (n.d.). *Dictionary.com— Free Online English Dictionary.* Retrieved May 5, 2006, from http://www .dictionary.com.

FBI—Homepage. (n.d.). *FBI—Homepage*. Retrieved May 5, 2006, from http://www.fbi.gov/.

Fisher, B. & Fisher, D. (2000). *Techniques of Crime Scene Investigation* (Sixth ed.). Boca Raton, FL: CRC Press LLC.

Forensic Science: Let Evidence Reveal the Truth. (n.d.). *ThinkQuest: Library*. Retrieved May 5, 2006, from http://library.thinkquest.org/04oct/00206 /index1.htm.

Lee, H.C. (2002). *Cracking cases: The science of solving crimes*. New York: Prometheus Books.

Saferstein, R. (2004). *Criminalistics: An introduction to forensic science* (Eighth ed.). Upper Saddle River, NJ: Pearson Education, Inc.

The Innocence Project—Home. (n.d.). *The Innocence Project—Home*. Retrieved May 5, 2006, from http://www.innocenceproject.org/.

White, P. (1998). *Crime scene to court: The essentials of forensic science*. Cambridge, UK: The Royal Society of Chemistry.

SECTION III
PRACTICE TEST

1. The purpose of _____ is to exonerate innocent individuals through the use of post-conviction DNA testing.
   a. Operation Freedom
   b. wrongful justice
   c. the Innocence Project
   d. equal justice

2. In the courtroom, who is expected to remain impartial and present unbiased evidence?
   a. The prosecuting attorney
   b. The defense attorney
   c. The judge
   d. The expert witness

3. When is the interrogation process used?
   a. When people are believed to be not sharing information
   b. When you come across any person involved in an investigation
   c. When you are speaking with any witness of a crime
   d. The constitution protects any person from being interrogated

4. Who should you identify yourself as during an interrogation?
   a. Law enforcement
   b. Anybody you believe the suspect will talk to
   c. A fellow suspect
   d. Do not identify yourself at all

5. What does a polygraph measure?
   a. Truth
   b. Lies
   c. Deceptions
   d. Bodily reactions

6. Which of the following is one of the elements of case management?
   a. Commencing with the initial report
   b. Allocating supervisorial duties
   c. Giving proper notifications
   d. Dividing responsibilities for case officers

7. Which of the following is an exception to having a warrant?
   a. A canine alert
   b. Probable cause
   c. Intuition
   d. Consent

See page 527 for answer key.

SECTION IV

CRIME

Section IV details different types of crimes with which investigators may deal. It includes chapters on domestic abuse, homicide, child abuse, female sexual predators, and cyberpredators. Detailed information is given about each type of crime. For example, child abuse is broken up into infanticide, battery, sexual abuse, and more, while homicide is broken up into single homicide, mass murder, spree murder, and serial murder. See page 337 for questions reviewing the material in Section IV.

13

DOMESTIC ABUSE

Domestic violence is common against both men and women. These relationships continue because of the victim's dependency on the perpetrator. The control that both parties involved feel the abuser has is only illusionary. The victim may tolerate an abuser for fear that his or her situation would be helpless without the abuser. Also, an abuser will often apologize and promise not to become violent again, causing the victim to focus on how loving the abuser can be. This can also encourage the victim to tolerate abuse. There are many reasons people become violent, including the following:

- Feeling of freedom or control
- Punishment of others
- Image, status, role, or reputation
- Protection or survival reaction
- Threat reduction or aggressive precaution
- Self-punishment or guilt relief
- Civil or rationalized disobedience
- Exposure to violence and diffusion of individual responsibility
- Mental illness or medical condition

13.1 Gender Differences

There are both similarities and differences between the abuse of women and the abuse of men. Economic abuse is similar in both cases. Women seem to be more brutal than men with respect to mental or emotional abuse. Men are more brutal than women with respect to physical abuse.

13.1.1 Violence against Women

Battering is the leading cause of hospitalization in women, who are more likely to be victims of domestic violence than victims of burglaries and muggings combined. Approximately every 9 seconds, a woman is abused by her significant other. Nearly four million injuries are caused by domestic violence against women each year; 42% of murdered women are killed by their significant others.

13.1.2 Violence against Men

An estimated 300,000 to 400,000 men are treated violently by their significant others. However, reporting of physical abuse toward men is so low that it is difficult to obtain reliable estimates. Culturally, men are discouraged to report abuse, and the impact of domestic violence is less obvious in men.

13.2 Forms of Domestic Abuse

Domestic abuse includes physical, mental or emotional, sexual, and economic abuse and battering.

13.2.1 Physical Abuse

Physical abuse is hands-on violence and includes the following violent actions:

- Hitting
- Shoving
- Slapping
- Punching
- Burning
- Bruising
- Choking
- Pulling hair
- Using weapons
- Preventing access to an exit

13.2.2 Mental and Emotional Abuse

Mental and emotional abuse includes the following abusive acts:

- Harming the ability to think, reason, or have feelings
- Intimidating
- Humiliating
- Name-calling
- Threatening
- Refusing to talk
- Discussing love affairs
- Degrading
- Withholding affection
- Giving put-downs
- Abusing pets
- Expressing extreme jealously

13.2.3 Sexual Abuse

Sexual abuse can include both physical and mental aspects. Physical sexual abuse may include forced sex, attacks on the breasts or genitals, and rape with or without objects. Mental sexual abuse may include sexual name-calling, threatening remarks during sex, unwanted sexual advances, or forbidding the use of birth control.

13.2.4 Economic Abuse

Economic abuse may include the following actions:

- Preventing the victim from making financial decisions
- Forcing the victim to justify every expense
- Blaming the victim for financial problems
- Withholding access to financial resources
- Not allowing the victim to work outside the home

13.2.5 Battering

Battering can be divided into physical battery and psychological battery, both of which can be equally devastating. Physical battery includes hands-on physical and sexual assaults, while psychological battery comprises nonviolent abuse that can be mental, emotional, or economic in nature.

13.2.6 Reproductive Coercion

Reproductive coercion may include the following actions:

- Using pregnancy as a means of control
- Forbidding the use of contraception or protection
- Purposefully exposing partner to STIs or HIV
- Using pregnancy and then forcing abortion
- Forcing miscarriage (physical blunt force trauma [BFT])
- Preventing women's healthcare practices (prescription for STIs/HIV/prenatal care)
- Sabotaging birth control methods or practices

Bibliography

The American College of Obstetricians and Gynecologists. (2013). Reproductive and Sexual Coercion. *Committee Opinion*, p. 554.

Vecchi, G. (2009, Summer). Principles and Approaches to Criminal Investigation, Part 1. *Forensic Examiner*, Vol. 18, No. 2, pp. 8–13.

Vecchi, G. (2009, Fall). Principles and Approaches to Criminal Investigation, Part 2. *Forensic Examiner*, Vol. 18, No. 3, pp. 8–12.

Vecchi, G. (2009, Winter). Principles and Approaches to Criminal Investigation, Part 3. *Forensic Examiner*, Vol. 18, No. 4, pp. 10–15.

Vecchi, G. (2010, Spring). Principles and Approaches to Criminal Investigation, Part 4. *Forensic Examiner*, Vol. 19, No. 1, pp. 10–15.

14
HOMICIDE

14.1 Overview

Homicide is the killing of one human being by another. Although murder is a type of homicide, not all homicides involve murder. This can be confusing when popular media tend to use the terms interchangeably. There are justifiable and criminal homicides and single and multiple homicides, as well as different degrees of intent. There also are atypical homicides and staged homicides.

14.1.1 Classifications

There is no single classification system for all agencies and applications.

The FBI's *Crime Classification Manual* (Douglas, 1992) offers a standard system that delineates between criminal enterprise, personal cause, sexual cause, and group cause. The first category includes acts such as kidnap, murder, and contract killing. The second includes domestic homicides, conflicts, and revenge. The third category, sexual homicides, include sadistic murders and various types of aggressive intent, while group cause, the last category, includes homicide by cults, political extremists, and mobs.

The FBI's Uniform Crime Reports (UCR) classifies murder into five types: felony, suspected felony, argument-motivated, miscellaneous, and unknown. Individual criminologists might also stipulate typologies to accommodate specific research interests.

14.1.2 History of the Concept

In the United States, the approach to homicide in a forensic context is influenced by English common law. Early English common law divided homicide into two broad categories: felonious and nonfelonious. Historically, the deliberate and premeditated killing of a person was considered felonious and was classified as murder. This involved malice aforethought, or premeditation, and was usually punishable by death.

Nonfelonious homicide included justifiable and excusable homicides. Justifiable homicide was still a crime but had no punishment attached, whereas excusable homicide was not considered a crime. As U.S. jurisdictions adopted these concepts, various degrees of intent, mitigation, and justification were considered for sentencing.

14.1.3 Intent

Modern statutes generally divide criminal homicide into two broad categories: murder and manslaughter. Different states adopt different nuances, resulting in first- and second-degree murder (sometimes with third-degree) and voluntary and involuntary manslaughter.

The legal system recognizes that responsibility for committing a crime depends on two things: *actus reus*, or evidence that the accused engaged in the act, and *mens rea*, the mental state required to have intended to commit an act and to have foreseen its consequences. Mens rea determinations are relevant to degrees of intent. Where mens rea is absent, such as in a psychotic state, responsibility and punishment do not apply.

14.1.3.1 Murder

Murder—the unlawful killing of another person with malice—is further divided into first- and second-degree. First-degree murder typically involves a premeditated intent to kill. That is, the person had some time to think about it, however brief. Malice imparts the absence of all justification, excuse, or recognized mitigation, along with the presence of intent of the harm produced. First-degree also involves the intent to commit a dangerous felony or participate in an act that shows reckless indifference of a high rate to human life.

Second-degree murder occurs when harm but not death was intended, yet death ensued. For example, Prosenjit Poddar was obsessed with Tatiana Tarasoff. He went to her house with a pellet gun and knife, reportedly to kill himself or to make Tatiana believe that she was in danger. When she ran from him, he killed her.

Second-degree murder may also involve acts of dangerous negligence such as drunk driving (although this can also be designated as third-degree in some places).

14.1.3.2 Manslaughter   Manslaughter typically involves an unintentional killing that resulted from a person's criminal negligence or reckless disregard for human life. Voluntary manslaughter involves three distinct elements: adequate provocation, a heat of passion that suddenly comes on, and a connection between the provocation and the fatal act. A quarrel, an assault, and trespass are recognizable legal forms. Involuntary manslaughter includes a variety of killings not captured by other designations. For example, negligence that results in an unforeseen death, such as leaving a baby in a locked car that overheats, is manslaughter.

14.1.3.3 Case Complications: Intent   Sean Powell, 17, believed that his 30-year-old teacher, Erin McLean, loved him and wanted to marry him. On March 10, 2007, Sean showed up at her home. Her husband, Eric McLean, saw Sean sitting outside in his car. McLean called the police but then went out and shot Sean, killing him. McLean claimed he only wanted to scare the boy off. However, he had stolen the rifle and ammunition from his parents 2 weeks earlier, which suggested premeditation. He was charged with first-degree murder. At trial, McLean explained that he had felt powerless to stop his wife's affair. He had taken the rifle and three bullets with the intention to commit suicide, but when Powell arrived, it angered McLean. The gun was handy, so he had pointed it at the boy. Powell had grabbed the barrel, causing McLean to react. The shooting, he said, was impulsive and accidental. The jury convicted McLean of reckless homicide.

14.1.4 Noncriminal Homicides

14.1.4.1 Justifiable   A justifiable homicide is commanded or authorized by law. For instance, during wartime, soldiers may kill enemy soldiers. In addition, public officials may carry out a death sentence allowed by state or federal law. Police officers may use deadly force to stop or apprehend a fleeing felon, but only if the suspect is armed or has committed a crime that involved the infliction or threatened infliction of serious injury or death.

A person may also kill in self-defense or in the defense of others. The person must have reasonably believed that the killing is absolutely necessary to prevent serious harm or death. Most states do not require retreat in the face of deadly force if the individual was attacked or threatened in his or her home, place of employment, or place of business. In addition, some states do not require a person to retreat unless that person provoked the threat.

14.1.4.2 Excusable   Not commonly used, excusable homicide is sometimes distinguished from justifiable homicide on the basis that it involves some fault on the part of the person who ultimately used deadly force. For example, a person provoked a quarrel but then withdrew. The other party continued to attack, so the person had to act in self-defense, ultimately killing the attacking party.

14.1.5 Legal Issues

14.1.5.1 Other Defenses   Other legal defenses for criminal homicide include insanity, necessity, accident, and intoxication. The accused's mental state, or mens rea, will be a critical determinant of whether he or she had the requisite intent to commit a criminal homicide and the capacity to understand that it was wrong.

14.1.5.2 Euthanasia and Physician-Assisted Suicide   The killing of oneself is a suicide. If a person assists another person in committing suicide, this is considered a criminal homicide. (In some states, physician-assisted suicide is legal.) It does not matter if the other person was about to die or was terminally ill just prior to being killed.

14.1.6 Homicides by the Number

14.1.6.1 Single Homicide   A single homicide involves the killing of one person. For example, on December 9, 2001, Kathleen Peterson was found at the foot of a staircase in her home, with blood spatter all around her. Her husband, Michael, stated that she has slipped and fallen, but the jury determined that he had killed her during an argument, bludgeoning her with a fireplace poker. A single homicide may also be committed by a team or gang. The designation is decided based on the number of victims, not the number of perpetrators.

14.1.6.2 Double Homicide   A double homicide involves two victims in a single incident. An example is the murders of Nicole Brown Simpson and Ronald Goldman in June 1994 at Simpson's home. Both were killed in a single incident.

14.1.6.3 Triple Homicide   A triple homicide involves three victims killed during a single incident, although some criminologists have designated this number as the minimum count for a mass murder. For example, on November 12, 2010, in Ohio, Matthew Hoffman entered the home of Tina Herrmann, killing her, a friend of hers, and her son. Although the boy came home later, it was still considered a single incident.

14.1.6.4 Mass Murder   Mass murder is a focused and singular act, occurring in one basic locale, even if the killer travels to several loosely related spots in that general area. There are at least four fatalities involved, and the incident lasts no more than 24 hours. (Some criminologists define mass murder as having a minimum of three fatalities in a single incident, but most accept a minimum of four. Some criminologists also believe that a 24-hour period is too long, but there is no consensus on this.)

In 1966 in Austin, Texas, Charles Whitman murdered his wife and his mother one night, and the next day, he took food, supplies, and an arsenal into a clock tower at the University of Texas at Austin. From there, he shot people at random until police killed him. Whitman managed to murder 13 people and wound 30. He was angry and unhappy and had decided to make others pay a price for his own situation, although he knew he would die in the process. Whitman is often cited as an example of a classic mass murderer.

14.1.6.5 Spree Murder   A spree killing involves a string of at least three murders in several locations; it arises from a key precipitating incident that continues to fuel the need to kill. The murders occur fairly close in time but the locations change. The period is longer than that of a mass murderer—from several days to several weeks.

Charles Starkweather is considered a classic spree killer. On December 1, 1957, Charles Starkweather held up a gas station, abducting the attendant before driving him into the countryside to shoot him. Six weeks later, Starkweather shot and killed the parents of his girlfriend, Caril Ann Fugate, and murdered her 2-year-old sister. Fugate stayed with him, apparently without question, and after a week, they took off across Nebraska. Starkweather next killed a family friend and a pair of teenagers who gave them a ride. Then he and Fugate invaded a home where he murdered an older couple and their deaf house cleaner. Starkweather's final murder the next day was to kill a man for his car. The spree killer designation sometimes hazes into that of a serial killer, who has a hiatus—cooling-off period—between murders. For example, in 1984, spree killer Christopher Wilder murdered several women as he fled across the country, and yet he had time between homicides to reorganize and even attend some beauty contests. Likewise, Andrew Cunanan went on what seemed to be a spree that lasted several weeks, targeting acquaintances, strangers, and even a celebrity. He clearly had time to think about what he was doing before he finally killed himself.

The designation of spree killer rests heavily on motive, although a spree killer's motive is similar to that of a mass murder. While mass murderers remain in a single location—or closely associated locations—spree killers tend to move around. Spatial mobility may be important to them in ways that it is not to a mass killer because the spree killer may wish to extend his spate of killings while also achieving some other goal.

A spree killer stays on the move, killing along the way, until the spree ends with suicide, capture, or shooting by an officer. Mass murder incidents generally end quickly because the killer stays on location until law enforcement mobilizes or the perpetrator kills himself on site or goes home to await arrest. In both cases (mass and spree), the perpetrator's identity is generally known.

During an international conference in 2005, the FBI elected to drop the classification of *spree killer* because law enforcement officers thought it had little practical value. However, researchers who are interested in developmental and psychological issues that distinguish different types of killers recognize value in understanding how spree killers differ from other multiple murderers.

14.1.6.6 Serial Murder The earliest editions of the FBI's official *Crime Classification Manual* indicate that to be defined as a serial killer, there must be at least three different murder events at three different locations with a cooling-off period between events. However, the National Institute of Justice and some criminologists allowed for just two victims in two incidents. In addition, some killers brought their victims to the same location at different times, so having at least three distinct locations is clearly not necessary.

In 2005, the FBI simplified its definition to someone who commits murder twice in two separate incidents. Some criminologists add a requirement: the mental disposition or propensity to kill again. There is a psychological rest period between incidents, which could be considered a time of predatory preparation. Although the media still hangs onto the designation of three murders in three incidents, the FBI's definition has evolved.

14.1.7 *Typical versus Atypical Homicides*

14.1.7.1 Typical The typical homicide is situational; usually, the victim has a relationship with the perpetrator, such as in a domestic homicide or drug sale. Other typical homicides involve victims who took risks, such as in socially marginal activities like prostitution. These homicides are easier to investigate; leads to the perpetrator develop quickly because of the various connections between the victim and the perpetrator's associations. The perpetrator may have been a regular, paid with a credit card, or made traceable phone calls to the victim. There is a thread of logic that develops leads.

The most typical motives for homicide include anger, revenge, betrayal, profit, power play, and punishment. Typical murder weapons are guns, knives, poison, a bludgeoning implement, or a method of asphyxiation.

14.1.7.2 Atypical Atypical homicides include victims of psychotic killers, mass murderers, or serial killers. Despite media coverage, such murders are quite rare. They may involve an atypical location as well. Motives align with the singularity of the incident and/or perpetrator.

An example of homicide with atypical motives occurred in Sacramento, California, in 1978. Richard Trenton Chase, a man suffering from schizophrenia exacerbated by drug use, believed that on certain days his blood might turn to powder. To forestall this, he later told investigators that he had to have fresh blood. After reducing the pet population in his neighborhood, he entered a home and killed a pregnant woman. He shot and disemboweled her, then drank some of her blood. Chase went on to kill four other people, including a baby, before he was caught.

An ax is rarely used in homicides, although during the 19th century it showed up in many more homicides—probably because many more people had axes for their woodpiles. Other odd weapons include ice picks, teeth, screwdrivers, table knives, forks, homemade bombs, scissors, saws, frying pans, and corkscrews.

14.1.7.3 Overkill Another atypical aspect of any type of homicide is the notion of overkill. This means that the perpetrator inflicted far more damage to a body than was needed to take the decedent's life. Although found most often in criminal homicides, a case in Texas in 1980 ended in a verdict of self-defense and, therefore, was justifiable. It was the aspect of overkill that made the verdict controversial to the community at large. Candy Montgomery, a homemaker, had admitted to killing her neighbor, Betty Gore. The victim had sustained 41 ax wounds, some of which had severely mutilated her face. Skin had been sheared off, and the wounds were scattered all over the body. There were also massive gashes to the back of Gore's head, causing her brain to seep out. Supposedly, Montgomery had acted in a dissociative state after Gore had allegedly attacked her, swinging the ax over and over to strike numerous extraneous blows.

14.2 The Homicide Detective

14.2.1 The Basics

Uniformed police officers work through the ranks and many hope to become detectives. This is often in the form of a promotion achieved by passing a test after a specific number of years of service. Sometimes officers are rotated onto and off investigative assignments.

Detectives investigate a variety of crimes, and some departments are large enough for specialized areas such as homicide. The job of a homicide detective is to gather facts for incident reconstruction and eventual prosecution of a perpetrator. They conduct interviews with witnesses and persons of interest, as well as interrogations of suspects. They also examine documents, observe suspect activities, conduct searches and raids, and make arrests. They may also do follow-up investigation, such as for cold cases. Former homicide detective Lofland (2007) makes the following observation in *Police Procedure and Investigation*: "A good homicide detective is the chameleon of police officers. He can converse effectively with people from all walks of life. He knows the talk and the jive from the street, and he knows what it is like to wear a suit and tie while sipping the finest wine" (p. 83).

14.2.2 The Murder Squad

Scotland Yard's most elite department of detectives, the Murder Squad, was founded in 1907. At the time, there were many unsolved murders around England, so Home Secretary Herbert Gladstone decided to create an elite unit from members of the criminal investigation department. London had around 700 detectives, but provincial towns were lacking. London officials found that when cases with special circumstances arose, the local law enforcement officers generally muddled them. The home secretary gave Scotland Yard greater jurisdiction over serious crimes in locations outside London. The designated officers came to be known as the Murder Squad, although they received no such official title.

14.2.3 Training

Detectives are required to participate in regular in-service training to keep up with changes in law and developments in their field. They can also use the training to expand their skills and areas of knowledge, especially in response to criminal innovations. They receive intensive training in crime scene investigation, evidence collection, evidence preservation, bloodstain pattern analysis, crime scene photography, ballistics, and techniques of interview and interrogation. They may also receive training in reading people and detecting deception.

14.2.4 Role of Intuition

Intuition is the ability to understand something immediately without the need for conscious reasoning. The type of intuition employed for criminal investigations is based on experience, memory, and the ability to reason, which encourages mental agility and creative thinking. Years of experience and making good decisions can be the most formidable tools in the detective's arsenal. Nevertheless, a belief in gut instinct as an error-free guide makes investigators vulnerable to making serious mistakes.

14.2.5 Investigative Errors

Professional training in law enforcement does not include how cognitive processing influences perception, memory, and decision making. Homicide investigators often arrive at scenes with a specific mind-set that derives from experience, habit, and expectations. These mind-sets can help form a guiding hypothesis, but they can also result in a threshold diagnosis, reliance in stereotypes, and tunnel vision, which narrows the investigator's focus to a limited range of options.

Because humans have limited mental capacity, the mind is a cognitive miser. It relies on shortcuts to reduce complex information into simple rules of thumb, called heuristics. Because heuristics form automatically and without thoughtful consideration, they can lead to errors of thinking. Thus, they can result in poor decisions that negatively impact people's lives and can hinder—even damage—a criminal investigation.

Contexts influence the readiness to perceive something in accordance with expectations. Detective Kim Rossmo studied how certain cognitive processes affect investigations. He found that recall is more consistent with personal beliefs than with facts, especially as it supports a formulated hypothesis; he also found that contradictory information is generally ignored. In cognitive psychology, this is called confirmation bias.

Rossmo states from his own extensive experience with investigation, interpreted through what he has read in psychological research, that some information goes through rational channels and some through emotional or intuitive channels. Intuition, he says, is aligned with the automatic, subconscious judgment. Although reasoning is a slower process, Rossmo found that it opens the mind to a greater range of factors. The result, he found, is usually more reliable.

One influencing factor is the accessibility from memory of specific social constructs. A study involving detectives provided them with a scenario in which various murder suspects looked more or less guilty, based on social stereotypes. The detectives then received ambiguous evidence from witness statements. In the condition in which a suspect looked guilty, the detectives tended to interpret the ambiguous evidence toward guilt.

14.3 Databases

14.3.1 Uniform Crime Reports

The earliest classification system was the UCR, which the FBI prepared with the Department of Justice. Formed during the 1920s as the *Uniform Crime Records*, this annual roundup of statistics in the United States gives law enforcement, attorneys, researchers, and journalists perspective on the rates, volume, and locations of homicides.

The Bureau of Justice Statistics also offers U.S. homicide trends since 1976. Homicide rates are considered a reliable barometer of other violent crimes.

14.3.2 National Center for Health Statistics (NCHS)

The NCHS collects mortality data, which include those who have died by homicide. This information is available via a publication, *Vital Statistics*. It comes from coroner and medical examiner offices across the country. The accuracy is dependent on the thoroughness of the death investigations. Prior to 1968, undetermined deaths were not allowed, so deaths were assigned to a category into which they might not belong.

14.3.3 Violent Criminal Apprehension Program (ViCAP)

Prior to the FBI's first computerized database for homicide patterns and statistics, Special Agent Howard Teten, who worked for the San Leandro, California, police department at the time, had devised a rudimentary database method. "By about 1960," Teten said, "I had developed a hypothesis that in certain types of homicides, you'd be able to determine the kind of person you were looking for by what you could see at the crime scene. This was not really a new concept. If you dig into the research, you'll find that the more skilled the occupation, the lower the level of homicide. Suicides go up with greater skill, but homicides go down. That still holds true today. You can predict the number of homicides and suicides you will have by the average education and income of the population you're serving."

To compile a collection for analysis and comparison, Teten also reviewed unusual homicides from several police agencies, as well as from the California Identification Officers Association. To test himself and develop his approach, he set up an experiment. When he received the information, he would examine all the data and prepare a tentative description of the perpetrator. Then, he would look at the individual found to have committed the crime and compare the perpetrator to his description. This would become a basis for the approach undertaken by the FBI's BAU, which Teten founded.

In 1967, the FBI started the National Crime Information Center, a computerized index that permitted state and local jurisdictions access to FBI archives on items such as license plate numbers and recovered guns, as well as the ability to post notices about wanted or missing persons. It also provided a way to coordinate certain types of national investigations.

During the late 1970s, the FBI also established the criminal profiling unit at Quantico for a better approach to the investigation of serial crimes. By the mid-1980s, the bureau had developed a national computer database called the ViCAP, slated to become the most comprehensive computerized database for the investigation of homicides nationwide. Its purpose was to assist with linking cases across jurisdictions to a single offender. It is a pointer system that gives officers a chance to communicate with one another. Police departments from around the country were invited to contribute solved, unsolved, and attempted homicides; unidentified bodies in which the manner of death was suspect; and missing-persons cases involving suspected foul play.

The FBI then set up the National Center for the Analysis of Violent Crime and established the national DNA database, CODIS, that stores DNA profiles from every state. During this time, the FBI was also instrumental in developing the DRUGFIRE system, which was a computerized database of bullet and cartridge case evidence against which firearms evidence from unknown sources could be compared.

14.3.4 Local Databases

14.3.4.1 Homicide Investigation Tracking System Homicide Detective Robert D. Keppel chased down leads associated with Ted Bundy's serial murders in the Pacific Northwest. The overwhelming amount of information he had to keep track of inspired Keppel to design a database. To better serve Washington State, he and his colleagues developed a software program to assist them with a better understanding of the solvability characteristics of murder. They collected information from murder and rape cases from 274 law enforcement agencies, calling it the Washington Attorney General's Homicide Investigation Tracking System, or HITS. Later, they expanded to include information from agencies in Oregon. HITS was designed to improve the apprehension rate of violent offenders, specifically in the Pacific Northwest.

14.3.4.2 Trackers Trackers is a project out of Orange County, California. During a cold-case serial murder investigation, Deputy District Attorney Michael Jacobs was reviewing cases when he realized there was no local database for homicide and sexual assault. He found a good one in a nearby jurisdiction and borrowed it. He then worked to improve and expand it. Others got involved and made a searchable database accessible to any investigator from his or her computer. It allows cases to be revisited as new information is added and links incidents by geography and timing.

14.3.5 Historical Violence Database

Professor Randolph Roth founded a project called the Historical Violence Database, which has assembled reports of murders in several of the original 13 colonies; 19th-century records from five states, seven cities, and 34 counties; and a wealth of 20th-century statistics, chiefly from the UCR. Roth's work involves three steps: he counts murders, he calculates the homicide rate, and he identifies factors that correlate with that rate across four centuries.

14.3.6 United Nations Office on Drugs and Crime (UNODC)

In 2011, the UNODC issued a study on the worldwide trends in homicide rates based on data from 207 countries. The report estimated that in 2010, the total number of homicides globally was 468,000; 36% had occurred in Africa, 31% in the Americas, 27% in Asia, and just 5% in all of Europe. Since 1995, the homicide rate has been falling in Europe, North America, and Asia, but has risen in Central America and the Caribbean. About 82% of the victims were male, and of the female victims, 40 to 70% were linked to partner- or family-related violence. Forty-two percent of homicides around the world are committed with firearms.

Bibliography

Brown, M. (2001). *Criminal investigation: Law and practice* (Second ed.). Boston, MA: Butterworth-Heinemann.

Dietz, P. (1986). Mass, serial, and sensational homicides. *Bulletin of the New York Academy of Medicine*, Vol. 62, No. 5, pp. 477–491.

Douglas, J. (1992). *Crime classification manual.* New York: Lexington Books.

Geberth, V. (2006). *Practical homicide investigation: Tactics, procedures, and forensic techniques* (Fourth ed.). Boca Raton, FL: CRC Press.

Keppel, R.D. & Birnes, W.J. (2003). *The psychology of serial killer investigations: The grisly business unit.* Amsterdam, Netherlands: Academic Press.

Lofland, L. (2007). *Police procedure and investigation: A guide for writers.* Cincinnati, OH: Writers Digest Books.

Ramsland, K. (2005). *The human predator.* New York: Berkley.

Ramsland, K. (2006). *Inside the minds of mass murderers.* Westport, CT: Praeger.

Ramsland, K. (2007). *Beating the devil's game: A history of forensic science and criminal investigation.* New York: Berkley.

Ramsland, K. (2007). *Inside the minds of serial killers.* Westport, CT: Praeger.

Ramsland, K. (2011). Howard Teten: An FBI Visionary. *The Forensic Examiner*, Vol. 20, No. 2, pp. 22–27.

Rossmo, K.D. (2009). Cognitive biases: Perception, intuition, and tunnel vision. *Criminal Investigative Failures*, pp. 9–21. Boca Raton, FL: CRC Press.

Sachs, J.S. (2001). *Corpse: Nature, forensics, and the struggle to pinpoint time of death.* Cambridge, MA: Perseus Pub.

United Nations Office on Drugs and Crime. (2011). *2011 Global Study on Homicide.* Retrieved from http://www.unodc.org/unodc/en/data-and -analysis/statistics/crime/global-study-on-homicide-2011.html.

Weis, J.G. & Keppel, R.D. (1999). *Murder: A multidisciplinary anthology of readings.* Orlando, FL: Harcourt Custom Pub.

Zugibe, F.T. & Carroll, D.L. (2005). *Dissecting death: Secrets of a medical examiner.* New York: Broadway Books.

15
Child Abuse

15.1 Infanticide

Infanticide is the murder of an infant. For infanticide to take place, the infant must be born alive and the infant's death must be a result of violence or an act of omission. Infanticide must include an act or failure to act with the intention of harming the infant.

For a child to be considered alive at birth, there must be air in the stomach or lungs and food in the stomach. This is the absolute proof of a live birth. The cause of death in infanticide may include asphyxia, craniocerebral injury, or stab wounds. Asphyxia is the most common cause of death in infanticide.

15.2 Child Abuse

Child abuse can be physical, emotional, or sexual abuse or neglect. In most cases, child abuse begins at birth. If the child will die from abuse, it will likely happen before the child is 5 years old. Death from child abuse is sometimes mistaken for sudden infant death syndrome (SIDS), the most common cause of death in infants. Within 1 year's time, 1 million children will be abused; of these 1 million children, 1000 will die as a result of the abuse.

Physical child abuse often causes injuries to the head, abdomen, and skeleton. External injuries include burns, abrasions, bruises (often of varying ages), lacerations, and bite marks. Skeletal injuries include avulsion of the metaphysic, or meat torn from the bone, rib fractures, long-bone injuries, and skull fractures. Head injuries are the most common cause of death in child abuse. Eighty percent of all sexually related attacks on children are committed by the child's parents.

Educating the public on the common reasons for child abuse allows parents who believe they are prone to this kind of behavior to seek counseling. Medical and social welfare professionals should also be educated in identifying warning signs of child abuse.

15.3 Battered Child Syndrome

This is the premeditated, physical injury inflicted on babies or young children. It is typically done by the parents or caretaker. The most common form of physical injury is from mechanical force.

Associated forms of abuse that may accompany battering are emotional or physical neglect.

Battering has many factors that may lead up to it. The parents may have characteristics that are incompatible with raising a child contributing to the likelihood of their abusing a child. For instance, if the parent or caretaker was abused as a child or is currently undergoing abuse, it is more likely that the person will abuse a child. Environmental stresses also increase the likelihood of abuse.

Signs of battery include unexplained illness or injury, repeated physical abuse, and misleading statements to medical attendants. There may also be a delay in reporting injuries. Child abuse often has a pattern; there are frequent injuries, and there may be scars or X-ray evidence of old and healing fractures. There may also be a history of previous injuries in hospital records and a history of complaints and investigations in social service records.

An unsuitable explanation for the injuries suffered is often the first clue of battery. These discrepancies may involve the age and severity of the injury and the mechanism of injury.

15.4 Neglect

The neglected child is often the youngest in a family with three to seven children. If the child is going to die from neglect, the average age at death is 5 months. There are many signs of neglect. If there are environmental needs or a lack of adequate nutrition and the child is undernourished or dehydrated, the child may be neglected. Neglected children may also have poor hygiene with dirt or fecal matter dried on their skin. These children come to the hospital dead or, if living, weighing little more than their birth weight. Their homes are usually filthy. Autopsies of these infants must rule out a chronic debilitating disease, poisoning, and an overdose of prescribed medication.

15.5 Munchausen Syndrome by Proxy (MSBP)

MSBP is a criminal act in which subjects injure or induce illness in their children in order to gain attention and sympathy for themselves. It is mostly associated with mothers who induce breathing difficulties or poison or engineer illnesses in their children. They crave the attention given to them by relatives, doctors, and hospital personnel. Because the child's illness has no medical cause, doctors have difficulty making a diagnosis. As the baffling symptoms continue, doctors or hospital administrators may call on law enforcement to investigate the mysterious circumstances surrounding such cases.

There was a study of five families with a total of 18 children, many of whom were affected by MSBP. Of the 18 children, 72% were known MSBP victims. In each family, only 1 child was involved at a time; a total of 5 children seemed to be unaffected. Of those children affected, 31% died. In only one instance was there any other form of abuse present.

15.5.1 Perpetrators

In the standard offender–victim relationship, suspicion typically centers on the biological mother. The vast majority of MSBP cases resolved through investigation have implicated the victim's mother as the sole offender. The following list includes common characteristics of maternal perpetrators:

- Have backgrounds as health professionals (80%)
- Manifested Munchausen syndrome (self-inflicted injury) themselves (80%)
- Received psychiatric treatment prior to diagnosis (80%)
- Attempted suicide (60%)

Although the mother is a common perpetrator of MBSP, perpetrators can be either inside or outside the victim's family structure. Other perpetrators may include fathers, grandmothers, aunts, or even babysitters. In rare cases, medical professionals could be on the list of potential suspects. By inflicting MSBP and then saving the child, these medical professionals hope to excel within their fields and win acceptance by their peers. All offenders have one thing in common: each acted as the victim's primary caregiver.

15.5.2 Motivational Factors

Most offenders crave the attention provided by hospital staffs, doctors, and family members. Some offenders may be gratified by the idea that they have fooled the doctors. They derive enjoyment from knowing what is wrong with the child while medical experts remain baffled. An offender who is praised as a hero for saving a child may wish to re-create that euphoria by fabricating subsequent incidents. Some offenders may fear a normal daily routine without being the center of attention. Even a minor crisis—such as the fear of being left alone or of the child being released from the hospital—could trigger a new attack.

The manner in which charges of MSBP originate must be considered in the investigation. Child custody cases often generate charges of child abuse. Sometimes, offenders accuse the other parent of abuse in order to mask their own wrongdoing and to keep custody of the child. If a noncustodial or estranged parent reports abuse, the question of role reversal should be considered as an alternate reason for the child's ailments.

This type of issue often arises in contested divorce situations involving minors and may also be linked to parental kidnappings. The underlying rationalization for the actions of MSBP offenders stems from their desire to regain lost custody through outward expressions of love. It appears that the longer offenders are separated from victims, the more desperate and determined they become to regain custody.

15.5.3 MSBP Warning Signs

The following list contains warning signs for MSBP:

- Mysterious and prolonged illness that baffles experienced doctors
- Frequent hospitalizations and extensive medical tests that do not produce a diagnosis
- Lack of response to therapy

- Symptoms that dissipate when the victim is away from the suspected offender
- Symptoms that do not make medical sense
- Mothers who do not seem worried about their child's illness but are constantly at the child's side while in the hospital
- Mothers who have an unusually close relationship with the medical staff
- Family history of SIDS
- Mothers who have previous medical experience and a history of the same illness as their child
- Parents who welcome medical testing, even if it is painful for the child
- Caregivers attempting to persuade the medical staff that the child is still ill when they have been told the child will be released from the hospital
- A model family that would typically be above suspicion
- Past history of Munchausen syndrome
- A caregiver who adamantly refuses to accept the suggestion that the diagnosis is nonmedical

15.5.4 Investigative Guidelines

Despite seemingly strong circumstantial evidence present in some cases of apparent MSBP abuse, law enforcement officers must make every effort to refrain from making false allegations. Accusations based on insufficient investigation and absent forensic analysis can have disastrous consequences. Investigators need to explore all avenues when suspicion of MSBP arises, and the importance of medical evaluation cannot be overstated. Without proper medical documentation to support the suspicion of MSBP abuse, it is unlikely that prosecutors can establish probable cause for custodial arrest.

Keeping the victim safe during the investigation is paramount. Offenders typically deny allegations, blaming the child's illness on unknown causes and attempting to prove the illness by increasing the severity of the victim's symptoms. Unfortunately, the child may not be able to withstand the escalating abuse or the increased treatments prescribed to address the symptoms. Investigators must quickly close the case once they have confronted the suspect.

Accordingly, case guidelines regarding evidence collected should be established prior to informing the subject of the investigation. Careful planning in this area can be critical; research indicates that between 9% and 31% of MSBP victims die at the hands of their abusers.

Some offenders may react to allegations by relocating with the victim and other family members. If the courts do not prevent a suspect from relocating with the child, the cycle of MSBP will likely continue. Investigators should take protective measures via social services or judicial avenues before confronting the subjects.

Offenders who believe that they are suspected may become more careful, but only temporarily. The child's illness may stop until the offender believes it is safe to resume the abuse. Offenders may wait a reasonable time and then readmit the child into the hospital.

The needs-oriented behavior of such offenders is comparable to that of a drug addict. Through cycles of abuse and nurturing, MSBP offenders seek to satisfy an ever-increasing need for attention and self-validation. Some experts believe that unlike most drug addicts, MSBP offenders cannot be rehabilitated.

With suspected MSBP, investigators should take the following actions:

- Review the victim's medical records.
- Ask medical personnel about the parents' concerns and reactions to the child's medical treatment.
- Compile a complete history of the family, including deaths of other children in the family and social history.
- Interview family members, neighbors, and babysitters.
- Utilize video surveillance within the hospital (make certain that all laws, rules, and regulations are strictly adhered to when using video surveillance).
- Utilize a search warrant for the family's residence.
- Question potential victims.

Some of these actions are further explained below.

15.5.4.1 Interviews   During interviews, investigators should not express any signs of disbelief; they should convey that they are keeping an open mind about the case. Expect sound rationalization on the part of offenders, as well as a series of open-ended allegations that cannot be substantiated. Segregate family members from one another during the interview process as relatives will probably voice support and disbelief in the allegations if the suspect is present. In those cases where obvious inconsistencies exist, family members may view facts differently when questioned away from the suspect.

15.5.4.2 Previous Deaths   Identified MSBP offenders may be linked to the deaths of their other children. Investigators should examine related children's medical records. Original medical examiners may have incorrectly identified deaths caused by MSBP as SIDS. If possible, exhume children's bodies for forensic testing. Forensic pathologists may be able to uncover evidence pointing to homicide.

15.5.4.3 Questioning Victims   Because of the lifelong nature of MSBP, the victim may believe that whatever action is being done to cause the illness is normal. This misunderstanding of normal behavior with the attention given by the offender can skew the child's viewpoint— the child may believe that the offender is an ideal caregiver, even if the abuse is blatant.

Whether the child actually knows that the offender has induced the illness depends on the child's physical age and the offender's covert skills. The longer the abuse continues, the more likely it becomes that the victim will understand the offender's actions.

Even if a victim is old enough to talk, the child may not be able to assist officers verbally. Additionally, there are potential consequences should the child be told that a trusted caregiver is, in fact, an abuser. For these reasons, elicit the help of professionals to lessen the possibility of further traumatizing the victim.

15.6 Sexual Abuse

There are two types of pedophiles. Understanding their characteristics may help you protect children.

- Regressed Pedophile—In this type of pedophile, the psychosexual development of the offender was normal beyond the adolescent stage. The offender regresses when feelings of inadequacy intrude. The regressed pedophile is a situational child molester who has been traditionally involved with adults in normal relationships. The offender commits the act when some stressor causes regression. During these times of stress, the regressed pedophile is temporarily more comfortable with a child, and as a result, sexual victimization is more likely to occur. If he or she kills his or her victim, it is out of fear and panic. The body will be dumped in some fashion. This is a result of his or her lack of organization as well as a reaction to fear, guilt, and panic.

- Fixated Pedophile—This person has not experienced a normal sex life or been married. The offender's job or recreational activities place him or her in situations where he or she must deal with children. Statistically, an offender who commits fixated pedophile murders is between 45 and 55 years old.

Bibliography

Westveer, A.E., Jr. (2002). *Managing death investigations*, Vol. 1 (Fifth ed.). Washington, DC: U.S. Department of Justice Federal Bureau of Investigation. (Used with permission.)

16

FEMALE SEXUAL PREDATORS

16.1 Overview

Although the criminological world accepts that females can be serial killers, the idea of a predatory female sex offender is more controversial—especially a serial sex offender. However, while there are substantially fewer of them than male sexual predators, some females can be just as criminally sexually aggressive. Most of their victims are children. From teachers who seduce underage students to incestuous mothers to abusive nuns, females can be chemically conditioned into violating others. Neurological studies over the past decade have focused on the brain's role in addictive aggression (inhibition dyscontrol), and it could be the case that many initiators of sexual abuse suffer from mild to significant neurological impairments. This research, with case illustrations, provides a framework for discussing how women can become behaviorally conditioned toward sexual trespass.

16.1.1 Research

Throughout the literature on female sexual offenders, there is a dearth of controlled studies, especially for trend analysis and threat assessment. Few studies have compared female sex offenders against non-sexual offenders so as to identify causal factors in female deviance, although a Swedish study comparing female sex offenders to women in the general population found a significant percentage had been hospitalized with psychiatric problems or substance abuse disorders. In 2007, a study for the U.S. Department of Justice indicated that female sexual offenses have been significantly underreported, surmising reasons from victim embarrassment (especially male victims who did not wish to admit a female could make them vulnerable) to professional biases that reject female predators to cultural stereotypes about women that dilute legal charges.

At times, victims who did come forward were dismissed by law enforcement and even by mental health experts. As a result, their experiences were not included in databases. To date, no database has been systematically developed for female sexual predators. However, some studies—and single-case analyses—still offer insights.

16.1.2 Lack of Consensus

It seems that the experts disagree about how pervasive the problem really is. One researcher states that females represent as many as 10% of sex offenders, while another places the percentage at 4% to 5%. Psychologist Eric Hickey (among others) cites contradictory studies that undermine the possibility of even stating a specific percentage with certainty. National criminal justice statistics show females committed less than 10% of sex offenses, with only 1% involving forcible rape. (This study fails to differentiate actual predators from other types of offenders.) The Center for Sex Offender Management's report states that the study of female offenders is in its infancy; there was no helpful consensus. Researchers Johansson-Love and Fremouw (2006) located just 13 studies between 1989 and 2004 that examined samples of female offenders larger than 10, and only 8 of them had used control groups. It seems that contradictions, poorly designed studies, small or unrepresentative samples, and the lack of clarity (or seriousness) about victim statements have collectively thwarted the attempt to be statistically definitive about female sexual predators.

16.2 Typologies

Several researchers have devised typologies for female sex offenders to attempt to identify specific psychological dynamics, the first of which was from a study in 1989. Based on 16 cases, Mathews et al. (1989) identified five types:

- Male-coerced
- Predisposed (due to early abuse or incest)
- Teacher/lover (initiators)

- Experimenter or exploiter (a babysitter)
- Psychologically disturbed (encompassing delusional mental illness)

Psychiatrist Janet Warren, with psychologist Julia Hislop, also offered a typology (Warren & Hislop, 2001):

- Facilitators help men gain access to children.
- Reluctant partners seek to maintain a relationship with an abusive male.
- Initiators perform the abuse themselves or inspire someone to do it for their entertainment.
- Seducers develop an intense sexual interest in underage adolescents.
- Pedophiles exclusively target children.
- Mentally ill females have a condition that triggers inappropriate sexual contact.

The most dramatic and clearly delineated distinction for a study on distinct psychological dynamics is females who act alone (predatory initiators) versus females who co-offend as part of a team or group (most typically as compliant accomplices with a predatory dominator). Solo initiators are more often mentally ill, delusional, narcissistic, and psychopathic than are those women who comply with a co-offender out of fear, submissiveness, dependency, or abuse patterns.

16.2.1 Lone Operators

Lone offenders often suffer from a psychiatric disorder or have developed a sadistic type of paraphilia, which can pressure them to become coercive. Anger and/or the need for control usually fuel their abuse. Within this category, we find caretakers who violate children in their charge, as well as the growing category of teacher-predators and adult women (including mothers) who seduce underage boys. They tend to be secretive and may resort to threats or seduction to keep a child compliant.

16.2.1.1 Caretakers Caretakers are often not related to their victims. Although adolescent babysitters are more likely to molest children in their care than adult caretakers do, a historic but dramatic case involved a predator in France named Jeanne Weber. She liked to choke children to achieve orgasm. Trial records show Weber became so compelled by her paraphilia that she often put herself at risk of arrest. This case also demonstrates clear bias by male authorities against females' capability of being sexual predators.

The first murder came to the attention of Parisian authorities on April 5, 1905, when a woman brought her distressed baby to a hospital. The doctor found a reddish mark on the child's neck and learned that among this woman's relatives, four babies had died from apparent suffocation. Jeanne Weber, the mother of three dead children, was the common factor. In addition, 3 years earlier, two other children had died in her care with diagnoses ranging from diphtheria to convulsions to cramps.

Weber was arrested and charged with murder. A renowned pathologist, Dr. Leon Thoinot, examined the exhumed corpses of several of the children. Familiar with studies of manual strangulation, he stated that he had found no such marks on them. Weber was acquitted. However, Weber continued to choke children and got arrested; in each case, but Thoinot insisted that she was not a killer. Then in 1908, Weber was caught choking 7-year-old Marcel Poirot to death.

The examining doctor made an exhaustive photographic documentation of the boy's body, but Thoinot decided that this incident was merely the result of stress from earlier accusations. Still, it was clear from the crime scene that Weber's motive had been sexual ecstasy, so Thoinot declared her psychotic. No one at that time could admit a woman could be a serial sexual predator, killing for an erotic thrill.

16.2.1.2 Mothers   Although the Center for Sex Offender Management study indicates females who offend against their relatives are often co-offenders, there are mothers in the group of lone offenders sometimes. Mothers have the easiest access to children, so if they are inclined to abuse, they are also in the best position to carry it out and coerce the child into keeping it secret. They usually suffer from a psychiatric condition or severe personality disorder.

A famous case involved Shirley Ardell Mason, also known as Sybil. The subject of a best-selling book and two movies, her case became a model for the syndrome of multiple personality disorder caused by childhood abuse. At the age of 31, Mason came under the care of psychologist Cornelia Wilbur, complaining of blackouts, anxiety, and other emotional difficulties. Under hypnosis, she described experiencing horrendous acts of sadistic physical and sexual abuse at the hands of her mother, Martha Alice "Mattie" Hageman. Allegedly, Hageman had probed Mason's vagina with a knife and a buttonhook, causing enough damage to prevent her from having children. Hanging her upside down, Hageman had used an enema bag to fill Mason's bladder with ice-cold water. This had supposedly caused the child to psychologically fragment into 16 different personalities to better deal with the trauma. Dr. Wilber also believed that Hageman had suffered from paranoid schizophrenia.

Forensic psychologist Larry Morris describes the case of "Virginia," a 41-year-old mother of five who had been incarcerated for child molesting (Morris, 2008). Virginia had grown up with a sexually abusive father. Like many girls in such situations, she had experimented sexually at an early age with several acquaintances and became promiscuous. She seemed to combine sex and love, as if engaging in one would get her the other. She married three times, always to abusive men, including one who molested her daughters.

Virginia took up with an inmate and, at his request, sent him photographs of her children. Some were normal, but others included Virginia in the nude with her naked children. She had also engaged in sex acts with each of them while someone took pictures. Then, she took pictures of two of her children having sex with each other. She claimed that the children did not care that she sent these photos to her prison pal because he was "part of the family." Morris found that Virginia was intellectually challenged and seemed unable to perceive social situations accurately. She did not understand the error of what she had done and seemed confused when her children testified against her at her trial. She clearly had a cognitive distortion, possibly neurologically based.

16.2.1.3 Other Authority Figures   Besides babysitters, other types of abusive caretakers can be significant figures of authority in a child's life. Typically, these authority figures start the abuse gradually, with grooming behaviors that engage a child's trust and make the child feel good.

A recent rise in the number of female teachers seducing students is currently under study. In a study commissioned by the U.S. Department of Education, Shakeshaft (2004) indicates that among the seductive behaviors teachers use are deception, gift-giving, isolation, and friendship, gradually moving on to inappropriate touching and methods that will make the student feel complicit. It is a desensitization process common to pedophiles and involves tests along the way to see if the potential victim can be trusted with a secret. Often, the teacher will provide additional help that leaves the child alone with them, creating an atmosphere of a special relationship. They will exercise their considerable power and may also manipulate the child to feel indebted.

When children do report such abuse, they may find that they are not believed, further isolating them. The report states that this fear is top on the list of reasons children have offered for why they did not report abuse.

A case that brought media attention to the issue was that of Pamela Ann Smart, who was convicted of being an accomplice in first-degree murder. She had seduced a 15-year-old boy in the school where she worked as a media services coordinator. Once she had sexual leverage, she threatened to end their liaison if he did not kill her husband. On May 1, 1990, he enlisted three friends, and they carried out the crime.

In another case, Mary Kay Letourneau, a teacher at Shorewood Elementary School in Burien, Washington, first noticed Vili Fualaau when he was in the second grade. Five years later, when he was 12 and she was 34, she seduced him. Despite being married and the mother of four children, Letourneau started to groom Vili. She rewarded him for good grades by taking him to dinner. Soon, she engaged him in light petting and then sexual intercourse, which resulted in pregnancy.

A relative reported them to child protection services and on February 26, 1997, Letourneau was charged with child rape. She pled guilty to two counts of second-degree statutory rape. The judge suspended her sentence on the condition that she take medication, attend a sex offenders' treatment group, and have no further contact with the boy. She agreed but was soon meeting the child again, and she became pregnant again and returned to court.

In her background was a father who had carried on an illicit affair with a student and had two illegitimate children. A specialist on sex offenses, Susan Moores stated that Letourneau showed a deviant sexual arousal pattern and knew what she had done was wrong but seemed unable to stop. Letourneau went to prison but illegally kept in touch with Vili. After her release, they married in 2005.

Some teachers are serial predators. Washington State grade school teacher Jennifer Rice dallied with a 10-year-old student. When his parents barred her from their home, she kidnapped him, drove him to a highway rest stop, and had sex with him. At the time, Rice was 31 and a married mother of three. In April 2009, Rice was convicted of having sexual relations with two underage boys. Court documents indicate that she also had molested her victim's 15-year-old brother.

In California, serial predator Sarah Bench-Salorio, 28, had numerous sexual encounters with an 11-year-old student at Santiago Charter Middle School before he ended it. She moved on to another school and seduced a 13-year-old, but this boy informed his mother. The police arrested Bench-Salorio just as she was about to consummate her third such conquest. Her seduction method involved sending her victims e-mails, inviting them to dinner, and gradually getting them under her power.

Most targets for this type of offender are boys, but several female teachers have been caught having unlawful sexual contact with girls. Amy Gail Lilley, 36, got involved with a 15-year-old girl in Florida, receiving house arrest and 8 years of probation. In Michigan, Elizabeth Miklosovic pleaded no contest to assaulting a 14-year-old girl, whom she apparently married in a pagan ceremony in 2004. The female authority figures least suspected of child abuse are nuns, yet as the child victims of nuns grow up and decide to take their abusers to court, many cases have come to light. Thanks in part to cultural stereotypes about dedicated brides of Christ, such allegations often seem shocking, but in a survey of nuns who themselves have reported being sexually abused, 3% identified a nun or female religious leader as their abuser.

Among the accused is Sister Norma Giannini. She had been the principal of the grade school for St. Patrick's congregation in Milwaukee, Wisconsin. Two men in their 50s brought the complaint against her. One had been 12 years old when the abuse began and the other 13. Both claimed sexual contact had occurred hundreds of times in a variety of places, including bedrooms. Both described how their lives had been adversely affected, including experiencing unemployment, migraine headaches, insufferable guilt, and substance abuse. One man also described another of Giannini's victims who committed suicide.

16.2.2 Co-Offenders and Collaborators

Co-offenders who have active or tacit support from one or more people show greater variation. Such women generally do not initiate the abuse, but once it begins, some become enthusiastic participants. Co-offending females tend to have more victims, victimize females or both genders (rather than males only), and target their own relatives. They are also more likely to be involved in simultaneous nonsex crimes than solo female offenders. Some operate within a permissive group culture (a cult), but more often they comply with or complement a dominating male. The dominant person guides the rules of behavior, luring a weaker person into a shared sense of reality based on his or her sexual desires.

Researchers have found many sexually criminal co-offenders develop along one of two patterns: they become so intimate or co-dependent that when one feels safe enough to share a violent fantasy the other listens, or the weaker person discovers the dominant person's secret activities and complies out of fear. In either scenario, the dominant person then manipulates the other to gradually accept it.

Dominators socially isolate their accomplices, getting them dependent in order to reshape their sense of right and wrong while maintaining psychological control.

16.2.2.1 Group Culture   In history, there have been cultures in which aristocratic individuals exploited their lack of accountability to commit sexual atrocities, often on children. Because these offenders were nearly untouchable according to a permissive social protocol, they often grew increasingly more deviant.

Among such aberrant, predatory females was a Hungarian countess, Erzsebet Bathory. Born in 1560, she molested and participated in the murder of untold numbers of young girls. Bathory represents the type of person whose inert criminality needed only the right trigger to be fully expressed. Some type of disorder appears to have been involved in her behavior. As a girl, Bathory experienced uncontrollable seizures and often flew into intense rages. She then married a sadistic man who involved her in sadistic activities. After he died, she continued to torture and kill. She sacrificed children in occult rituals, binding them and beating them with whips until their skin split open. Finally, authorities arrested her. A handwritten register in her home indicated that she might have maimed and killed as many as 650 victims.

Today, such group cultures are generally part of a subculture or cult and are more secretive. A good example is the adolescent sex offender who finds support for criminal acts from a friend or peer group. Between 1997 and 2002, cases of female adolescent sex offenders rose significantly. There was a 6% increase in forcible rapes committed by girls, 62% more violent sex offenses other than rape, and 42% more nonviolent sex offenses. Several studies indicate female juvenile offenders are typically younger than males when they start offending and have more abuse in their background. They often suffer from depression, suicidal ideation, and substance abuse, and tend to turn their aggression on younger relatives or acquaintances, including children in their care. Common to these offenders is a background of sexual victimization, a dysfunctional family, psychiatric disorders, and post-traumatic stress.

An example is Mary Bell. When she was 11 years old, she, along with an older girlfriend, lured two young boys to their deaths in 1968. On May 25, 1968, 4-year-old Martin Brown was discovered strangled in Newcastle, England. Two months later, 3-year-old Brian Howe was found strangled and sexually mutilated. His killer had used a razor to carve *M* into his stomach. Mary Bell was arrested and she gave a detailed statement about how she and her friend had killed the boys. Mary was convicted of manslaughter and sentenced to a period of incarceration. Author Gitta Sereny located Bell after her release. Sereny (1998) discovered Bell's mother, a prostitute, had subjected young Mary to repeated abuse, making her engage in sexual acts with men when she was only 5. The mother had twice attempted to kill Mary. It was unsurprising that Bell had developed a thick skin, a precocious sexual awareness, and indifference about aggressing against weaker children. With her friend's support, Bell had acted out her own victimization on others. Without a companion, she might still have been aggressive but, perhaps, not predatory or a killer.

16.2.2.2 Capitulators Warren and Hazelwood (2002) studied 20 female accomplices in sexual assault and murder. They identified the male as the person responsible for a process of gradual reshaping. However, Warren and Hazelwood did not distinguish among the accomplices who capitulate out of fear, devotion, or mental illness, and females who are "awoken," or encouraged toward an equal partnership. The potential for the latter's sexual criminality is easily actualized, and the extent of her depravity may even surpass that of the initiator. In either scenario, capitulators take the path of least resistance.

When she met Ian Brady in 1961, Myra Hindley was an impressionable, naive 18-year-old who loved children. Brady recognized her as an easy mark, and she soon became infatuated with him. She wrote in a diary that Brady had persuaded her that morality was relative. Then, he got her to doubt her religious beliefs. He described to her the violent hedonistic philosophies of the Marquis de Sade and eventually fertilized in her the same cynical attitude that he held toward people. When he thought she was ready, he proposed they enrich themselves through crime. Step by step, he involved her in illegal activities until she became an equal party to the rape and murder of several children.

The pair's modus operandi involved Hindley driving a van while Brady lured the victims inside. He forced them into pornographic poses for photographs before he raped and killed them. This team was caught after their attempt to include another accomplice backfired, and the man turned them in. In 1966, Hindley and Brady were given life sentences.

At first, Hindley viewed their criminal activities as part of their love pact. She stated that without her involvement, the murders might never have been committed. However, after she reverted to her former beliefs, she blamed Brady for corrupting her. He had sought to commit the perfect murder, and she feared that if she did not help him acquire victims, he would kill her or her grandmother.

When Brady learned this, he implicated her equally in everything. In a book he wrote, Brady (2001) described the team dynamic in criminal enterprises as a shared delusion known as *folie à deux*, an intellectual conversion of one partner by another. It can occur, he stated, only if the target person is fertile soil. In other words, the criminal desire must already be present. Although he had devised the plans for abuse and murder, he stated that Hindley had been a willing participant.

16.2.2.3 Latent Criminals   Latent criminals are different from capitulators in that they typically have a criminal record or have fantasized about committing crimes. Thus, when the partner arrives, the latent criminal is ready to be involved. In teams comprising initiators and latent criminals, the participants share a strong intimate attraction and decide to spice things up by coercing one or more third parties. Some are married or romantically involved, some are related, and some met in prison. The dominant person introduces the other to the details based on his specific sexual fantasy. Once the act is accomplished, both then want to repeat it. No more persuasion or intimidation is necessary.

A case in point features Doug Clark and Carol Bundy, who were responsible for the Sunset Strip Slayings in Hollywood in the early 1980s. Clark had fantasized about sexual murder before they met, and he wanted a partner. He met Bundy in a bar and moved in with her. To get her ready, he encouraged her to reveal her darkest sexual fantasies and then described his dream of grabbing young girls to torture and turn into sex slaves. After getting Bundy used to this idea, he persuaded her to help him with his necrophilic fantasy: He wanted her to shoot a prostitute while he had sex with her, so he could experience the victim dying.

Bundy found the idea stimulating and a way to bond with her lover. Their mutual victim was a teenage prostitute, although Clark ended up killing her when Bundy got clumsy. Bundy also lured an 11-year-old girl from the neighborhood for Clark's sexual enjoyment, sometimes taking pictures and sometimes joining them. In addition, Bundy murdered and beheaded one of her former lovers on her own. When arrested with Clark, she adopted the pose of a coerced capitulator, but her gruesome lone murder, her willing abuse of a child, and her revealing letters to Clark while they were both in prison undermined the ruse. Together, they were charged with six counts of murder—five females and one male. Bundy got life in prison, and Clark received six death sentences.

Another example is Canadian Karla Homolka. Just 17 when she met 23-year-old Paul Bernardo, she allowed him to do whatever he desired with her, and his sexual demands became increasingly brutal. Nevertheless, her love notes urged him to continue. In 1990, as a gift to Bernardo, Homolka drugged her 15-year-old sister Tammy with an animal tranquilizer. When the girl passed out, they took turns having sexual contact with her, including rape. They made a videotape so they could relive the pleasure later, but Tammy vomited and then suffocated.

Bernardo and Homolka moved in together, and Bernardo raped and killed 14-year-old Leslie Mahaffy. Her body was found dismembered and cemented into blocks of concrete submerged in a lake. Then, Bernardo and Homolka together abducted another schoolgirl, Kristen French. They molested her on videotape before killing her and dumping her body. As police closed in, Homolka struck a deal to save herself. In exchange for a short prison term, she described what Bernardo had done to the murdered girls. He was arrested, tried, and convicted.

Then, incriminating videotapes revealed Homolka's involvement in the French abduction. In addition, it was clear that her sister's death had been no accident. That she could kill her sister and then participate in more rapes and murders with her sister's co-killer indicates a personality primed for crime. She was also caught on videotape telling Bernardo she wanted to get many more young virgins for him.

16.2.2.4 Female Team Leaders   A rare example of a dominant female in a co-offending team was Judith Neelley. In 1980, when she was a teenager, she eloped with Alvin Neelley, a car thief 12 years her senior. Together, they robbed convenience stores and gas stations from Georgia to Texas, as well as cashing stolen checks. Then, their crimes became more serious. Judith grabbed 13-year-old Lisa Millican and kept her captive as a sex slave for 3 days before killing the girl. In another incident, Judith shot a couple, and the male survived to finger her.

When the Neelleys were arrested, Alvin claimed that Judith had instigated the crimes and was responsible for eight murders. She liked having power over others, he said, and the surviving victim corroborated this. Yet Judith claimed she was a victim of domestic abuse.

Female leaders or initiators also turn up on all-female co-offending teams. Catherine Wood was a supervisor at the Alpine Manor in Walker, Michigan, where she became lovers with Gwendolyn Graham. During a session of rough sex, Graham suggested killing patients in their care. This excited Wood, so in 1987, they devised a fatal sex game. The elder care facility routinely recorded the names of deceased or discharged patients in a book. Wood and Graham wanted to kill people whose first initial, when read down the list, spelled "murder." They then proceeded to carry out this plan. The game became fodder for heightening their pleasure as well as a way for each to manipulate the other.

16.3 Developmental and Neurological Issues

16.3.1 Development of an Abuser

Psychologist A. J. Cooper states that the reasons that females become sex offenders are incompletely understood, but he surmises that it is a combination of hypersexuality, associations with early sexual experiences, and imitation of abuse perpetrated on them (Cooper, 2000). Sexual abuse expert Dr. Julia Hislop adds that many abusers were sexually traumatized as children (Hislop, 2001). Hislop also recognizes the influence of a lack of a sense of appropriate boundaries, poor relationship skills, releasing stress, relieving depression, distorted sense of normalcy, lack of self-worth, and sexual preoccupations.

In a comparison of 60 female sex offenders in a Georgia prison to a matched group of 70 female nonsex offenders, there was a significant difference in incidence of childhood sexual trauma, as well as of feelings of sexual adequacy, but there was no significant difference for substance abuse, personality disorders, neediness, or cognitive distortions. However, this is a small and unrepresentative sample.

Many of these offenders suffer from anxiety or depressive disorders, have troubled relationships with their fathers and husbands, and have a grandiose image of themselves. If married, they often believe that their husbands fail to give them the type of attention they crave. Teachers who become erotically entangled with their students, for example, have described the allure of a secret, a feeling of entitlement, a false belief that the student is mature, and the naive notion that there are no victims. Being with a boy, some have said, makes them feel young and desirable. They also like being in charge. Often, their husbands are controlling.

16.3.1.1 The Role of Stress   Dr. Helen Smith, a forensic psychologist, has evaluated thousands of mentally disturbed children and adults. She states that criminal trespass in the form of violence or abuse

derives from the accumulation of stressors, the inability to manage stress, and the maintenance of distorted thoughts (Smith, 2000). Anyone who participates in criminality to solve a problem has already had a number of such thoughts. They perceive their environment and their situation in such a way that, to them, their criminal act seems to be the best option. They may have role models in relatives or peers who have demonstrated this to them, which is to say that offenders become gradually predisposed to offend. They do not just snap; they develop their readiness to act out over time. They have a restricted view of others' rights. They also fail to absorb and manage frustration in appropriate ways.

16.3.1.2 Culture Cultural factors also play a role. Paul and Linz (2008) evaluated the influence on behavior of exposure to erotic images of children under 18. They found that both males and females exposed to these images recognized sexual words at a faster rate than controls who were not exposed. The researchers suggested that media consumption influenced cognitive processing in terms of developing mental schemas through which ambiguous images are more readily interpreted in a sexual manner. That is, if youth are portrayed in media as sexually aware and ready, females who come to believe this notion will more readily see signs of sexual receptivity in children. Implicit theories, coupled with explicit cultural reinforcement, help to disinhibit potential offenders who already hold certain ideas. Rehearsal fantasies reinforce these ideas.

16.3.1.3 Victimized Aggressors When Johansson-Love and Fremouw (2009) compared a sample of 31 female sex offenders against 31 male sex offenders, and 31 violent female offenders against 31 violent male offenders, the female sex offenders reported the highest rate of having been sexually victimized themselves. A cycle of violence, as victims become victimizers, may feed off the dynamic of addiction. Strickland (2008), too, found severe childhood trauma and deprivation distorted sexual values and knowledge. These factors also enhanced neediness and dependency, which thwarted the formation of normal partnerships. Thus, abusing children themselves provided an easier way to meet their needs.

16.3.1.4 A Case Deborah Lafave, a 25-year-old female teacher convicted of sexual contact with an underage boy, participated in an interview with a news magazine show to offer a public self-reflection on how she became an offender. She was caught in Terrance, Florida, when the victim's mother discovered the teacher's relationship with her 14-year-old son. Lafave's husband indicated that she had groomed the boy and cultivated the relationship until she finally had a chance to get her target alone. Then, she took him to her home and performed oral sex on him; this soon led to a fully sexual relationship. On November 22, 2005, Lafave pleaded guilty and received 3 years of house arrest and 7 years of probation.

Lafave cited abuse in her background. She claimed her boyfriend had raped her when she was 13, and during high school, she had undergone therapy for being involved with another girl. She also admitted to a bipolar disorder, causing her judgment during manic phases to be skewed. She had experienced anxiety disorders ranging from panic attacks to obsessions and had developed substance abuse and eating disorders. During college, she had suffered from depression, especially after the death of her sister. Lafave got married but had a difficult time being a wife. She found her work as a teacher to be a rewarding outlet, and her energetic periods caught the attention of the boys in her class. She liked that they thought she was attractive. This positive attention became her new addiction, especially from one boy in particular. Despite her litany of issues, at no time did she accept responsibility. When asked, she refused to admit she was a sex offender.

The excuses initiating female predators use are common from one case to another, similar to the way male offenders try to mitigate their crimes. Among them are as follows:

- The victim pursued her.
- She was in love.
- She was depressed and the sexual act made her feel better.
- She was on medication and did not know what she was doing.
- Her husband was controlling and having sex with a younger person made her feel more in charge.
- She was just getting revenge for having been abused or betrayed.

These offenders are self-centered, insecure, and aggressively needy. They fail to recognize a child's inherent vulnerability and inability to make adult decisions about sex. They also fail to grasp the unfair power differential except to exploit it.

16.3.2 Violence and the Brain

Dr. Adrian Raine studied neurocriminology at the University of Pennsylvania in Philadelphia with the goal of identifying the causes of criminal behavior. With positron emission tomography during the 1990s, he found deficits in the brains of violent offenders, specifically in the limbic system, the corpus callosum, the left angular gyrus, and areas of the prefrontal cortex, where executive decisions are made and inappropriate behavior is inhibited (Raine, 1991). Abnormalities in these brain areas allow people to be impulsive, fearless, less responsive to aversive stimulation, and less able to make socially appropriate decisions about aggression toward others.

Yaling Yang et al. (2008) published a survey of the results of different types of brain imaging on a large population of inmates diagnosed with antisocial personality disorder (APD). These people had an impaired ability to respond to the threat of punishment, make clear moral judgments, and grasp the emotional implications of their behaviors. However, this did not prevent them from understanding that predatory sexual behavior that trespassed on others' rights or harmed them was wrong. The prevalence of APD in females in studies of female sex offenders is unclear due to different studies offering different conclusions.

Some female sexual predators are psychopaths. Recent work in neuropsychology has initiated studies on the brains of male psychopaths, and presumably, these results could apply to females as well. Although they can make accurate judgments about moral violations, they lack the emotionality necessary for inhibiting immoral behavior. Researchers Kiehl and Buckholtz (2010), for example, found this to be consistent with the hypothesis that psychopaths overfocus on items of immediate interest and effectively ignore other input. Psychopaths appear to lack access to their own feelings, thus failing to internalize. This, too, is consistent with highly developed sense of external focus.

If their attention is engaged, they block other information, even risk cues from the environment.

Glenn et al. (2009) used fMRI to reveal that psychopaths had reduced activity in the amygdala during emotional-moral decision-making activities, and those who were the most manipulative—one of the factor quadrants on the Psychopathy Checklist-Revised—showed reduced activity in the entire neural circuit that was related to moral behavior. After testing psychopaths on 10 different moral dilemmas, they argued that emotion is necessary for motivation to act within moral boundaries. Amygdala activity is disrupted in psychopaths during moral decision making, and it appears to be the core deficit in this condition. The researchers interpreted this as reduced responsiveness to the thought of harming others. Without normal amygdala activity, psychopathic individuals had no sense of deterrence and a poorly developed emotional perspective.

16.3.2.1 Inhibition Dyscontrol With impulsive behavior, under conditions associated with the interaction of behavioral inhibition and aggression, some subjects show decreased ventromedial prefrontal activity in the brain compared with healthy subjects. In essence, moral aspects of decision making fail to affect positive and prosocial self-control.

16.3.2.2 Addiction We can link this to what we also know about how the brain choreographs the body's information-processing system via neurotransmitters, which is implicated in addiction. Dopamine floods the system during novel or exciting situations, triggering the brain's reward system. Research indicates that people possessing fewer dopamine receptors than normal are prone to craving stimulation, and the excess of unabsorbed dopamine appears to make them vulnerable to compulsive pleasure seeking. Offenders often achieve this with a perverse desire. The more they enjoy it, the more the brain strengthens the requisite neural pathways. This can develop into an addiction.

Research from Vanderbilt University involved 30 volunteers who were not substance abusers but who scored high for antisocial impulsivity. The results suggest that their brains are wired to keep seeking a reward, no matter the potential cost. That is, the reward value outweighs consequences. Narcissistic offenders are drawn toward self-enriching rewards, and they minimize the costs to others.

16.3.3 Orgasmic Conditioning

16.3.3.1 Definition   Orgasmic conditioning is a developmental process involving self-stimulation to gain sexual satisfaction. If satisfaction does occur, the person is likely to repeat whatever it took to achieve it. If it involves associating stimulation with an image or a paraphilia, the individual's sexual evolution incorporates the image or paraphilia into a masturbatory stimulus and eventually depends on it for arousal. Sometimes, more stimulation is desired as the sex drive matures or levels off or boredom sets in. Thus, the perverse desire is intensified.

16.3.3.2 History   In 1965, psychologists proposed a conditioning theory as they studied the way masturbation assisted the formation and maintenance of deviant behaviors. They hypothesized that whatever was associated with the pleasure of achieving an orgasm, whether it be an image or object, the stimulation is physiologically recorded. The more regularly an image or experience is associated with arousal and climax, the more likely it is to become a sought-after erotic trigger. Successive researchers have found similar results among sex offenders.

16.3.3.3 Paraphilias   Whether abusers operate alone or co-offend, any perpetuation of their activities derives from the pleasure they achieve. This may be in the form of relief from anger or anxiety, a sense of correctness in pleasing a partner, a paraphilia, or the narcissistic satisfaction of controlling or harming a weaker individual. Because the number of cases of female sexual offenders is low, there have been so few focused studies, and the studies contradict one another, it is difficult to know how female and male sexual offenders differ or overlap in their development and behavior. It seems true that female sex offenders rarely use pornography as a stimulus. In fact, when it does appear, it is usually a factor for team offenders, and the male member has introduced it. Still, if they do develop an addiction, as some of the cases suggest, then the concept of orgasmic conditioning applies.

When such lusts are facilitated with drugs or alcohol to relax inhibitions, the impulse to sexually offend strengthens. If the person lacks social bonding, the resulting isolation could inspire a greater dependence on a fantasy. The images can then incorporate more coercive behaviors, more fetish items, and more rituals that could lead to sexual compulsions. When sexual addiction outweighs social restraints, the person may victimize someone.

16.4 Treatment Issues

16.4.1 Victim-Focused Treatment

What many female sex offenders elect to ignore is that these cases are not just about their issues. Failure to grasp consequences to their victims would impede the effectiveness of treatment. The victims and their families do suffer, often much longer and more profoundly than the predator ever will. In some cases, the predator even allowed others to watch, which compounded the victim's psychological issues.

Despite a widespread social belief that females who molest boys are just giving the boys what they want and that no real harm occurs, molestation does cause psychological harm that bleeds into the child's adult life. This can include difficulty in forming long-term relationships, sexual risk-taking later in life, physical ailments, depression, and suicide. "A thirteen-year-old boy will seldom grow up thinking how cool it was that he had sex with his teacher," says sex crimes researcher and criminologist Eric Hickey, "especially as they begin to understand terms such as sexual assault and child rape. Sexual violation of a child is traumatic, regardless of who commits the act" (Hickey, 2006).

Mental health experts Warren and Hislop agree. They found children who have been abused by females have often experienced significant difficulties, and other researchers echo this concern (Warren & Hislop, 2001). In one study, boys said that the immediate effects of being molested by women were devastating. Other studies turned up adjustment disorders and problems in later relationships or with parenting. Many also experience sexual identity issues or become abusers with victims around the age when they were abused.

16.4.2 Treatment Programs

According to the Center for Sex Offender Management, more than 500 programs around the country provide services to female sex offenders (adult and juvenile). A report from this same organization listed the differences between lone offenders and those who co-offended with a partner, based on a sample of 200. The latter were more likely to have had multiple victims, victimized females, and to have participated in nonsex crimes.

There are few data about treatment options and outcomes for female sex offenders. However, those that are currently in place have recognized that ideas about sex offenders derived from studies with males may not apply. These female-oriented programs are more likely to address sexual victimization in the offenders' backgrounds, to encourage emotional expression, to check for psychiatric disorders, and to emphasize developing better relationship skills. Most researchers would agree that, thus far, we have not placed enough emphasis on who these women and girls are and how best to treat them or even prevent them from become sexual offenders.

16.5 Summary

Although there are differences between lone and co-offending female sex offenders, as well as between those who offend once versus those who offend multiple times with different victims, there are overlapping issues. A significant percentage of these women were victimized as children or were subjected to conditions that made them vulnerable to becoming aggressors. In addition, we have more knowledge about neurological factors that can condition people into acting on desires for inappropriate sexual trespass.

Despite social stereotypes about females as nurturers, female sex offenders can be sexually aggressive, addicted, and predatory. Women can be chemically conditioned into violating others. Recent neurological research reveals how dyscontrol in sexual aggression can be a factor in sexual offending. Although results from studies about female sexual offenders have been contradictory and unrepresentative, increased awareness of this population is producing better research designs.

Treatment options with male sex offenders do not necessarily apply to females, so data must be derived from female-oriented programs. To date, there has been insufficient emphasis on how best to study and treat female sex offenders, but the situation is improving. Detailed case studies show us important differences among females who initiate abuse versus those who comply with co-offenders. They also reveal developmental factors, such that the details from numerous case studies can be joined for at least a qualitative analysis of how females can become predatory sex offenders.

Bibliography

Acocella, J. (1998, April 6). A Reporter at Large: The politics of hysteria. *The New Yorker*.

Brady, I. (2001). *The gates of Janus: Serial killing and its analysis*. Los Angeles: Feral House.

Briken, P., Hill, A. & Berner, W. (2007, February–March). Abnormal attraction. *Scientific American Mind*, pp. 58–63.

Buckholtz, J.W., Treadway, M.T., Cowan, R.L. et al. (2010). Mesolimbic dopamine reward system hypersensitivity in individuals with psychopathic traits. *Nature Neuroscience*, Vol. 10, pp. 10–38.

Cauffiel, L. (1992). *Forever and five days*. New York: Zebra.

Cook, T. (1990). *Early graves: The shocking true-crime story of the youngest woman ever sentenced to Death Row*. New York: Dutton.

Cooper, A.J. (2000). Female sexual offenders. In L. Schlesinger (Ed.), *Serial offenders: Current thoughts, recent findings*, pp. 263–288. Boca Raton, FL: CRC Press.

Denov, M. & Cortoni, F. (2004). Women who sexually abuse children. In C. Hilarski & J. S. Wodarski (Eds.), *Comprehensive mental health practice with sex offenders and their families*, pp. 71–99. New York: Haworth Press.

Denov, M.S. (2004). *Perspectives on female sex offending: A culture of denial*. Aldershot, Hampshire, England: Ashgate.

Englade, K. (1991). *Deadly Lessons*. New York: St. Martin's Press.

Fazel, S., Sjostedt, G., Grann, M. & Lamgstrom, N. (2010). Sexual offending in women and psychiatric disorder: A national case-control study. *Archives of Sexual Behavior*, Vol. 39, No. 1, pp. 161–167.

Federal Bureau of Investigation. (2006). *Crime in the United States 2005: Uniform Crime Reports*. Washington, DC: U.S. Department of Justice.

Frasier, D.K. (1996). *Murder cases of the twentieth century: Biographies and bibliographies of 280 convicted or accused killers*. Jefferson, NC: McFarland & Company, Inc.

Glenn, A.L., Raine, A. & Schug, R.A. (2009). The neural correlates of moral decision-making in psychopathy. *Molecular Psychiatry*, Vol. 14, pp. 5–6.

Hickey, E.W. (2006). *Sex crimes and paraphilia*. Upper Saddle River, NJ: Pearson Education.

Hislop, J. (2001). *Female sex offenders: What therapists, law enforcement, and child protective services need to know*. Ravensdale, WA: Issues Press.

Ivanov, I., Schultz, K.P., London, E.D. & Newcorn, J.H. (2008). Inhibitory control deficits in childhood and risk for substance use disorders: A review. *American Journal of Drug and Alcohol Abuse*, Vol. 34, No. 3, pp. 239–58.

Johansson-Love, J.M. & Fremouw, W. (2006). A critique of the female sexual perpetrator research. *Aggression and Violent Behavior Journal*, Vol. 11, pp. 12–26.

Johansson-Love, J. & Fremouw, W. (2009). Female sex offenders: A controlled comparison of offender and victim/crime Characteristics. *Journal of Family Violence*, Vol. 24, pp. 367–376.

Johnson, S. (2004). *Mind wide open: Your brain and the neuroscience of everyday life*. New York: Scribner.

Kiehl, K.A. & Buckholtz, J.W. (2010, September). Inside the mind of a psychopath. *Scientific American Mind*, pp. 28–34.

Lafave, O. (2006). *Gorgeous disaster: The tragic story of Debra Lafave*. Beverly Hills, CA: Phoenix Books.

Lynn, A. (2009, April 21). Former teacher guilty of rapes. *News Tribune*.

Mathews, R., Matthews, J. & Speltz, K. (1989). *Female sexual offenders: An exploratory study*. Brandon, VT: The Safer Society Press.

McGrath, R.J., Cumming, G.F. & Burchard, B. (2003). *Current practices and trends in sexual abuser management: The Safer Society 2002 Nationwide Survey*. Brandon, VT: The Safer Society Press.

Meyer-Lindenberg, A. & Buckholtz, J.W. (2006). Neural mechanisms of genetic risk for impulsivity and violence in humans. *Proceedings of the National Academy of Science*, Vol. 103, No. 16, pp. 6269–6274.

Morris, L. (2008). *Dangerous women: Why mothers, daughters, and sisters become stalkers, molesters, and murderers*. Amherst, NY: Prometheus.

Olsen, G. (1999). *If loving you is wrong*. New York: St. Martin's Press.

Paul, B. & Linz, D.G. (2008). The effects of exposure to virtual child pornography on viewer cognitions and attitudes toward deviant sexual behavior. *Communication Research*, Vol. 35, pp. 3–38.

Penrose, V. (2000). *The bloody countess: The atrocities of Erzsébet Báthory*. Clerkenwell, England: Creation Books.

Perri, F.S. & Lichtenwald, T. (2010). The last frontier: Myths and the female psychopathic killer. *The Forensic Examiner*, Vol. 19, No. 2, pp. 50–67.

Purcell, C. & Arrigo, B. (2006). *The psychology of lust murder: Paraphilia, sexual killing, and serial homicide*. Burlington, MA: Academic Press.

Raine, A. (1999, April 1). *Murderous minds: Can we see the mark of Cain?* The Dana Foundation. Retrieved from http://www.dana.org/news /cerebrum/detail.aspx?id=3066.

Rieber, R. (1998). Hypnosis, false memory and multiple personality: A trinity of affinity. *History of Psychiatry*, Vol. 10, No. 37, pp. 3–11.

Sereny, G. (1998). *Cries unheard: Why children kill: The story of Mary Bell.* London, England: Macmillan.

Shakeshaft, C. (2004, June). *Educator sexual misconduct: A synthesis of existing literature.* U.S. Department of Education.

Smith, H. (2000). *The scarred heart: Understanding and identifying kids who kill.* Knoxville, TN: Callisto.

Snyder, H. & Sickmund, M. (2006). *Juvenile offenders and victims: 2006 National Report.* Washington, DC: U.S. Department of Justice Programs.

Strickland, S.M. (2008). Female sex offenders. *Journal of Interpersonal Violence*, Vol. 23, No. 4, pp. 474–489.

Thorwald, J. (1964). *The century of the detective, translated by Richard and Clara Winston.* New York: Harcourt, Brace & World, Inc.

Vandiver, D.M. (2006). Juvenile female and male sex offenders: A comparison of offender, victim, and judicial processing characteristics. *International Journal of Offender Therapy*, Vol. 50, No. 2, pp. 148–165.

Warren, J. & Hislop, J. (2001). Female sex offenders: A typological and etiological overview. In R. Hazelwood & A. Burgess (Eds.), *Practical aspects of rape investigation*, pp. 423–431. (Third ed.). Sarasota, FL: CRC Press.

Warren, J.I. & Hazelwood, R. (2002). Relational patterns associated with sexual sadism: A study of twenty wives and girlfriends. *Journal of Family Violence*, Vol. 17, pp. 75–89.

Williams, S. (1996). *Invisible darkness: The strange case of Paul Bernardo and Karla Homolka.* New York: Bantam.

Yaling Yang, B.S., Glenn, A.L. & Raine, A. (2008). Brain abnormalities in antisocial individuals: Implications for the law. *Behavioral Science and Law*, Vol. 26, pp. 65–66.

17

CYBERPREDATORS

Cyberpredators come in all shapes and sizes. They actively seek out multiple victims—exploiting and harming them for personal gain. Whether they are bankers, teachers, preachers, coaches, or serial killers, they share a common goal: to plunder others. Thus, they devise tricks, deceptions, deflections, and other behaviors that will assist in their focused stealth and thievery.

17.1 Categories of Cyberpredators

Although terrorists may be considered a form of cyberpredator, this chapter focuses on more typical forms: identity thieves, sexual predators, con artists, and killers.

17.1.1 Predator Psychology

Most predators have developed an attitude of possession and entitlement that affirms their behavior. Since greed and compulsive addiction typically drive predatory behavior, those who complete a first predatory act will most likely repeat it. Persistent offenders may satisfy their needs without considering the consequences. Many commit their full resources to their fantasies, often using the Internet to remain anonymous while they seek out vulnerable prey.

17.1.2 Predatory Development

Predatory deviance is developed and practiced largely in secrecy. Thus, people whose fantasies involve victimizing others are usually skilled at hiding their intent and behavior. As difficult as it can be to recognize them, they do give off signals through certain patterns of behavior, which can help targeted victims spot the danger before it is too late.

17.2 The Internet's Role in Predatory Behavior

People who understand the various Internet tools these offenders use to groom potential victims, gain their trust, and gradually seduce them are better prepared for finding and stopping predators. When we think of cyberpredators or online stalkers, we typically envision pedophiles seeking vulnerable children. However, adults have been victims as well, especially with the increased popularity of social networking.

17.2.1 Websites for All Occasions

Predatory activity can take many forms, including stealing identities or snatching a child for a pornography film. In addition, some websites cater to people with intense and deviant interests. Cyberspace is an easy hunting ground for offenders who pretend to play by the rules but do not.

17.2.2 Ease of Finding Prey

Anything that normal people find useful and positive can also attract predators. Cyberspace is an information and communication highway connecting millions of residences and offices around the world and offering opportunities to meet people from all over the globe.

Since it is easy for predators to present themselves in any way they want, including using false photos, names, and profiles, cyberspace has become a sinister playground for predators. People desperate for love or connection may accept whatever they are told and are often willing to meet strangers in person. This can result in being conned, robbed, raped, stalked, or murdered.

Three examples are listed below.

In Slovakia, Matej Curko searched online for people who wanted to commit suicide, and he invited them to let him consume their bodies. After a potential partner backed out and turned him in, authorities found a grave containing two females.

Another example is John Edward Robinson, one of the oldest-known serial killers on record when caught—59 years old—and the first documented Internet serial killer. A narcissist, he initiated his criminal career with white-collar crimes. After he learned how to use a computer, he lured vulnerable women he met online to become his sexual slaves.

He had a knack for finding women who willingly walked into his traps. Robinson entered bondage-oriented chat rooms as *Slavemaster*, a moniker that proved enticing to women who wanted to be sexually dominated. Robinson soon had them meeting him off-line and signing slave contracts that granted him total control. He found plenty of women looking for this experience, but most expected this to be about role-playing, not outright slavery.

Serving time for a petty offense, Robinson seduced prison librarian Beverly Bonner, and when he was released in 1993, she left her husband for him. Bonner became the fourth woman associated with Robinson to vanish. However, the police had no evidence against him. A mother and a daughter also fell into his net, and Robinson fraudulently collected the daughter's disability checks.

In 1997, he developed a relationship with Izabela Lewicka, a woman interested in exploring sadomasochism. She joined him in Kansas City, Missouri, and filed for a marriage license; then she disappeared.

Something similar happened to Suzette Trouten; however, her family insisted on a full investigation. Not long afterward, while Robinson was under surveillance, Vickie Neufeld filed a complaint against him for theft and sexual assault. The police found items in his possession that linked him to missing women; a computer expert examined his files and e-mail.

Detectives learned that Robinson owned several storage units in Missouri, as well as a vacant property at La Cygne, Kansas. There, cadaver dogs led them to two 85 gal drums, each large enough to hide a body. Inside were the remains of Suzette Trouten and Izabela Lewicka. Three barrels from Robinson's storage units back in Missouri yielded the remains of Beverly Bonner and Sheila Faith and her daughter.

A Kansas jury found Robinson guilty of the murders of three women and sentenced him to death. To avoid the death penalty in Missouri, Robinson acknowledged that prosecutors had enough evidence for five murder charges total, although he did not actually plead guilty. He remains on death row in Kansas.

Robinson is the first serial killer who utilized the anonymity and wide-ranging facility of the Internet to prowl for victims. His case brought attention to the dangers of meeting strangers off-line, especially within a frame of sadomasochism.

Authorities learned Robinson had covered his tracks by faking letters from the victims to their families, so at the time they had disappeared, there was no clear way to prove he was responsible.

The third example is of several Craigslist murders. Craigslist, an online marketplace for goods and services, is a website that has been exploited by several murderers. It appears that at least four New York–area prostitutes met their killer online, and he dumped their bodies on an isolated stretch of land on Long Island. In 2007, Katherine Olsen walked right into the arms of her 19-year-old killer, who thought taking a life would be funny.

A sexual encounter arranged through Craigslist ended the life of a radio reporter who was stabbed 50 times, and a massage appointment trapped Julissa Brisman in a hotel room with a thief who shot her three times. This led to the arrest of a Boston University medical student, Phillip Markoff, who was about to get married. Markoff was traced to an Internet address he had created for predatory activities. In 2010, while awaiting trial, he killed himself.

17.2.3 Social Networks and Children

Of great concern are predators who prey on children. With the rise in popularity of social networking sites like Facebook, MySpace, and their derivatives, it has been quite easy for coercive pedophiles to befriend future victims. Children spend hours in chat rooms or on social sites talking with strangers. They often miss the signals of deception as they seek an innocent adventure.

17.3 Sexuality and Predatory Deviance

Predatory deviance often arises from sexual fantasies that develop over time. Essentially, individuals become predators through mental rehearsal that helps to prepare them for opportunities and empowers them to act. Because sexuality is a complex human experience, it manifests in patterns unique to each person, deriving from the way the imagery merges with an individual's sexual, social, and emotional development.

17.3.1 Template for Sexual Offenses

Through a gradual process of enactment, these impressions provide a template for the future pattern of sexual offenses. They influence the choice of victim, approach, preferred sexual activities, pre- and post-offense rituals, and decision whether to complete the act with murder.

17.3.2 Psychiatric Categories versus Psychosexual Disorders

Deviant sexual desires have been organized into psychiatric categories known as paraphilias, or recurrent, intense urges or behaviors that focus on objects, situations, or activities for sexual gratification. The current edition of the *Diagnostic and Statistical Manual of Mental Disorders* (*DSM-5*) lists many of these conditions and offers criteria for each, but this nomenclature is not exhaustive.

There is a difference between paraphilic excitement that engenders crime and paraphilic excitement that is a victimless personal preference. There is also a difference between sexual offenders and sexual predators. Other lists developed by sexologists and criminologists include even more psychosexual disorders. These psychosexual disorders are not sex crimes. Most are not even criminal acts, but they can fuel predatory criminal behavior, especially as they grow into addictions.

17.3.3 Paraphilias

Paraphilias are primarily, but not exclusively, male disorders, many of which begin in childhood or adolescence and persist into adulthood. They generally derive from what any given society views as abnormal for sexual orientation, which can change from one society to another. Examples of paraphilias are listed below:

- Sexual arousal from objects such as shoes, underwear, candles, or ropes
- Forcing sexual partners to expose themselves in public or to have sex with others

- Deriving principal gratification from erotic pictures
- Sexual gratification from listening to stories with sexual content
- The desire to expose one's genitals to others
- A sexual fixation on oneself, often accompanied by self-strangulation that produces a loss of consciousness
- Touching or rubbing one's body surreptitiously against another person, usually a stranger in a crowded public place
- Arousal from making obscene phone calls to strangers to hear their reaction
- The focus of sexual attention involving children typically aged 13 or younger either as pornography or as molestation of actual victims
- Gaining sexual pleasure from being hurt or humiliated via verbal abuse, bondage, and even being beaten, whipped, or cut
- Gaining sexual arousal from handling or having intercourse with corpses
- Sexual excitement over the taste and smell of excrement
- Sexual pleasure from dominating, torturing, or abusing others via activities such as verbal abuse, whipping, burning, stabbing, raping, choking, and killing

Whenever paraphilias involve nonconsenting partners (including animals) or when there is a resulting harm to others or destruction of property, a paraphilia becomes a crime. Clearly, given the sexual source of energy, paraphilias can trigger both addictive and predatory behavior. Thus, when a child becomes the focus of a predator's coercive paraphilia, the hunting behavior can be quite persistent.

As an example, Jeff Doland entered into a chat room for underwater asphyxial fantasies (NecroBabes) and began a discussion with a woman whom he had learned was the mother of two girls, ages 9 and 12. They exchanged e-mails for a few months, and this married man and stepfather of two sent his correspondent pictures of children being tortured. He also described his ultimate sexual fantasy, which was to watch young girls being submerged underwater, struggling for air until they passed out. He was aroused by the bubbles rising to the surface.

He offered the mother $550 for the opportunity to fulfill his fantasy in real life. She accepted, so they set a date. Then in July 2007, he packed up his scuba gear, told his wife he was going scuba diving, and boarded a plane bound for Miami.

However, Doland's correspondent was an undercover agent for the Secret Service. When Doland arrived in Miami he told his plan to yet another undercover agent and the Child Predator Cybercrime Unit, along with the Miami–Dade police, moved in to arrest him. Doland was charged with the selling or buying of minors, a first-degree felony, and with promoting the sexual performance of a child.

The school district where he had worked on computers cut all ties with him, and administrators assured worried parents he had no direct contact with children. While Doland's targets never actually existed, they might have, and authorities could only wonder how many people have managed to broker and complete such exchanges.

17.3.4 Types of Sexual Predators

Although children are generally savvier about online socializing than their parents, they often fail to realize that making their personal information freely available is a red flag to a predator. Prowling among them are people who mean to exploit them for self-gratification. According to the National Center for Missing and Exploited Children, sexual predators looking for children are generally male and between the ages of 13 and 65. Some of the adults are married, although most are single, and they have been classified into four operational types:

- Collectors—These are predators who start on static sites by collecting photos and pornography but who generally graduate to dynamic sites, or real-time chat areas where they can meet potential victims and devise ways to entice them.
- Travelers—The most dangerous type, these men will go great distances to meet their prey (even to other countries) to get what they want, generally sending gifts and using other enticements to draw their targets into their nets. They will spend large amounts of money as well. They are quite persistent and skilled and look for vulnerable, lonely children who crave attention. They can often establish a relationship within two chats.

- Manufacturers—They distribute pornography to others and sometimes partake themselves, but are mostly in it for the money. Their danger lies in luring kids for films they may make, but most are merely distributors.
- Chatters—They like to engage children in chat rooms and talk about sex but do not often graduate to meeting off-line.

17.3.5 Appeal of Anonymity

For many young people, the appeal of online socializing is its anonymity and even the opportunity to role-play. It can also be a forum in which to admit things they do not want to say to people they personally know, especially their parents. This kind of interaction can help kids figure out who they are and what they want to do about it. Unfortunately, it also gives predators informational bait for their hooks.

17.3.6 Hunting Their Prey

Cyberoffenders look for children with low self-esteem, family troubles, uncertainty about their sexuality, frustration about parents or teachers, and other issues common to the transitions of adolescence. These predators will go where they are likely to encounter a large pool of kids.

Sometimes, they will offer a mentoring relationship; other times, they act as if they are the same age as their contact. Online, predators can achieve a faster sense of intimacy than they can face to face, especially if they are self-conscious or unattractive because they have more time to calculate and can use clever phrases to convince a child that they actually care.

They study children to get the right phrasing so they can come across as an equal in the child's cadre of friends. They also develop a relationship prior to any visual interactions, which can establish a degree of trust that undermines basic gut instinct—young people who meet them already view them as friends or mentors.

The truth is the Internet allows kids of all ages much more access to sexually charged subjects and more opportunities to explore them.

Investigators and psychologists who specialize in Internet predation offer a series of red flags for parents to be aware of the following:

- Gifts sent to a child from someone the parents do not know (especially a cell phone or paid phone card)
- Phone calls from unknown adults for the child
- A child who spends a lot of time online but does not say much about it
- A child who tries to hide what he or she is doing online
- A child using someone else's online account
- Evidence of pornography on the child's computer
- A child who begins to behave differently, especially more aggressively

17.4 What to Do

While the laws governing cyberspace are just catching up, law enforcement has devised some ways to help protect kids. Many jurisdictions have devoted significant resources to special teams. Cybercrime units spend hours in chat rooms looking for pedophiles by posing as children or potential buyers of child pornography to trap them in an illegal act. Such units have cracked extensive international pornography rings.

Still, Internet predators pose challenges to public safety officials because they remain many steps ahead in their grasp of predatory technology, and they far outnumber law enforcement officials. They seem to hover and wait undetected for anyone posting his or her age, and then subsequently move in; one agent who posed as a 14-year-old boy received a query within a couple of hours, asking if he was really 14.

17.4.1 Increase of Numbers

Despite how many sting operations are now in place, the predators have multiplied and become more creative. In the past decade, arrests for underage soliciting have quadrupled to more than 3000 nationwide, but agents still feel overwhelmed. In 2008, the National Center for Missing and Exploited Children received more than 94,000 reports of predators in the cyberworld; most were for child pornography, but about one-tenth were regarding online solicitations.

Some estimates reveal that 40% of children and adolescents have reported an online solicitation. Predators know that cops are overwhelmed, and the odds are in their favor. More are getting caught, but many more are learning how to successfully exploit Internet resources.

17.4.2 Sophisticated Predatory Techniques

Predators have developed sophisticated techniques using traditional methods paired with ever-evolving technology to reach children.

17.4.2.1 Instant Messaging (IM) and Webcams   Predators initiate the enticement process with real-time conversations, often an IM posting. Participants post profiles that list things about themselves, such as their gender, favorite movies, hobbies, and what they like to do for fun, giving predators a way to introduce themselves by saying they have something in common.

Children may also include their photos or use webcams to show themselves in action. They may offer a cell phone number, which gives sophisticated predators a way to get all the information they need, as well as the ability to send text messages and listen in on private conversations.

17.4.2.2 Social Networking   A teenager might post a picture of his or her new car, and it could show a license plate number. Often, young people signal on Facebook their plans to travel to some foreign location, often with minimal supervision. Through one child, predators can learn about other children who might not even go online.

17.4.2.3 Building Emotional Connections   When sexual predators find exactly what they seek, they hone in. If such a child tells of conflicts with adults, depression, abuse, loneliness, or the need for love, that is all a predator needs to start manipulating. They offer emotional support and gradually work their way into inviting the child to meet them off-line.

They make certain that the child keeps the secret, and they use specific tactics to isolate their prey from friends and family. Often, they will send gifts, particularly webcams or paid phone cards, and they will do whatever they believe it will take to seem trustworthy. It is known as the *candy* ploy.

17.4.3 Networks of Predators

Attorney Monique Ferraro and forensic examiner Eogahn Casey discuss in *Investigating Child Exploitation and Pornography* how the Internet has impacted every significant human endeavor, including how predators operate (Ferraro & Casey, 2004). The Internet, they state, has created a trade in child pornography that stays several steps ahead of law enforcement and legislative regulation. It has even encouraged communication and networks among child molesters who might otherwise have remained solitary wolves. They pass around ideas and describe new opportunities, as well as support each other in criminal activity. Child porn networks have grown enormously, expanded internationally, and become quite lucrative.

17.4.4 Parental Roles

To ensure a child's safety, parents must set up clear rules about Internet use and remain firm in these rules, engage in regular periods of monitoring, keep open communication with children, and discuss the reality of Internet dangers. There will still be enticements for some children who are determined to defy their parents or try something dangerous, but other children, when educated, may be deterred. The fact is, sexual aggression is a persistent crime, and cyberpredators have found a viable avenue for locating vulnerable children. However, they will avoid children who are clearly protected if easier targets are available.

17.4.5 Study of Bait Behaviors

Like adults, children can inadvertently assist a predator with certain behaviors that act as bait. A team of researchers from Internet Solutions for Kids conducted a study in 2005 in which they phoned young people nationwide between the ages of 10 and 17. Most subjects were white, and the pool was evenly split between male and female.

In the initial results, the team had nearly 1500 kids in their sample population. They then did another survey with an equal number of participants, as well as talking with more than 600 officials in federal, state, and local law enforcement who dealt with these crimes. In this combined study, they found that there were five specific behaviors that stood out among those who had reported an encounter with a sexual predator:

- Making contact with people in a wide variety of online venues
- Talking specifically about sex with strangers
- Allowing strangers to be part of their personal buddy list or social network
- Making rude or vulgar comments online
- Intentionally visiting X-rated sites

These activities are erotic markers to predators trolling for child victims. Often, the child does these things while in the company of peers, and a high percentage of those experiencing unwanted sexual attention online reported having serious problems with parents, incidents of sexual abuse, and difficulty with bullies at school. They generally do realize that they are speaking with an adult rather than being duped by an adult posing as a person of the same age, but they willingly meet new online buddies off-line. Youth who engaged in at least four of these risky behaviors were most likely to become victims of sexual predators.

17.4.6 A Case: Christina Long

In May 2002, Christina Long, age 13, vanished. She was an honor student, altar girl, and cheerleader in Danbury, Connecticut. She was also actively seeking adults with whom to have sexual encounters and was hiding her password from her aunt, who had temporary custody of her.

On the day she disappeared, her aunt had dropped her off at a mall. A search of her home computer revealed she had exchanged sexually explicit e-mails with "Hotes300," or Saul dos Reis, a married 24-year-old Brazilian man who lived nearby. They had initially met online and had already met face to face for sex.

After dos Reis was arrested, he confessed to having sex with Christina, but insisted he did not know she was underage. He said her heart gave out during rough sex, so to avoid a mess for himself, he had dumped her body in a nearby ravine. He showed police the spot, and they found Christina faceup, lying in a stream. She had been strangled. Dos Reis received a 30-year sentence for manslaughter.

This fatal attraction had begun as a simple IM communication wherein people can seek out others who share the same interests and have quick and easy conversations; they are linked via the profiles they fill out with their personal information, a searchable user profile, or by becoming friends on Facebook (kids who view the number of friends they acquire as a sign of popularity or success will often allow anyone to be on their personal page).

This was not the first man with whom Christina had hooked up. Her aunt had warned her about strangers online, but the girl had ignored her. Yet her aunt had believed Christina was safe because she was on her computer at home. "You don't realize that a computer predator is practically in the same room as your child," the aunt said.

17.4.7 Sexting

Another behavior that puts children at risk is known as *sexting*, or sending sexually explicit images of themselves via cell phones. One study found that one in five teenagers is a participant, but this is probably an understatement. These images can be sent to others or posted on the Internet. Kids seem to lack any notion of how their information, photos, and videos can end up where they would never want them; however, once the photos are posted or sent, they have no more control. The same is true of cell phone technology.

Many think a cell phone is private, but predators can use software to tap into a cell phone and download images, listen in on conversations, and acquire personal information. In addition, despite being erased, the images remain in the phone's memory. Predators can even tap wireless networks to spy inside houses to locate a child's bedroom.

17.4.8 Parental Education

Parents who become educated about these issues are better equipped to thwart predators, and police officers can help by holding community forums on the subject. The more people are aware, the better. Predators will always find ways to be creative, but they do not like too many hurdles.

17.5 Identity Thieves

Another area of active and increasing predation is identity theft, which thrives on the pervasive availability of personal information, from bank accounts to social security numbers to home addresses. Thanks to cloud technology, online participants are especially vulnerable. Thieves can also use an old-fashioned method of simply going through people's trash for credit card statements or stealing bills from mailboxes.

These thieves may purchase information from others or sell it. There has been concern, for example, that increasing numbers of methamphetamine addicts, who can stay awake for days, are turning to the Internet to support their habits with computer crimes. They move stolen goods on auction sites, use e-mail scams to phish for victims, and break into company computers to steal credit card information. Nondrug users often employ them because during their manic stages they can complete menial tasks, such as testing credit card validity, for hours at a time.

Once thieves access even a small amount of personal information, they can use it to get more. They may call a credit card company with an unsuspecting person's number and change the address, and then run up bills before anyone can catch them. They can also open a new account with someone else's information. They may take out mortgages and fail to pay them or purchase cars, porn, expensive gifts, or weapons; they may open a bank account and write bad checks. Their crimes are accomplished anonymously, with a devastating impact on the victim who could spend years trying to rectify the situation and restore his or her credit status.

Crimes like these have a high probability of going cold, in part because the criminals can be difficult to catch and because institutions that become victims are reluctant to report it. Some—especially large corporations that can absorb it—decide it is more costly than what it is worth to pursue it.

Identity theft is the primary way terrorist groups that have targeted the United States have managed to get professional training, driver's licenses, bank accounts, and access to sensitive information.

Anyone can be a victim of identity theft—even a deceased person. Investigating this crime is more time consuming than actually committing it because with the Internet, the criminal can be in many places at once and can cost victims much more than they will ever recover.

17.6 Summary

Predators have always mingled in the human community, seeking ways to profit from what others have or to feed their deviant appetites. The Internet has expanded their scope and repertoire of tools. Tech-savvy predators have many advantages in cyberspace, but laws and law enforcement resources are catching up. Individuals must do their part to get educated because awareness of how predators operate is the best defense.

Bibliography

Bower, B. (2006, June 16). Growing up Online. *Science News*.

Dam, C.V. (2006). *The socially skilled child molester: Differentiating the guilty from the falsely accused*. New York: Haworth Press.

Douglas, J.E. & Singular, S. (2003). *Anyone you want me to be: A true story of sex and death on the Internet*. New York: Scribner.

Ferraro, M. & Casey, E. (2004). *Investigating child exploitation and pornography: The Internet, law, and forensic science*. Amsterdam, Netherlands: Elsevier/Academic Press.

Hickey, E.W. (2006). *Sex crimes and paraphilia*. Upper Saddle River, NJ: Pearson Education.

Monsewicz, L. (2007, July 26). *Busted: Scuba diving pervert wanted to drown young girls*. Cyber Diver News Network (CDNN).

Montero, D. & Fanelli, J. (2009, April 26). Craigslist "killer" warns: There is more coming out. *New York Post*.

Richmond, T. (2009, March 23). More Internet predators are challenging agents. *Associated Press*.

Snyder, H. & Sickmund, M. (2006, March). *Juvenile offenders and victims: 2006 national report*. National Center for Juvenile Justice.

Wolak, J., Finklehor, D., Mitchell, K. & Ybarra, M. (2008). Online "predators" and their victims: Myths, realities, and implications for prevention and treatment. *American Psychologist*, Vol. 63, No. 2, pp. 111–128.

SECTION IV
PRACTICE TEST

1. It is estimated that there are _____ injuries per year as the result of women being abused by their significant others.
   a. 1,000,000
   b. 2,000,000
   c. 3,000,000
   d. 4,000,000

2. Which of the following is a characteristic of mental sexual abuse?
   a. Forced sex
   b. Unwanted sexual advances
   c. Attacks on the breasts
   d. Rape with objects

3. Seductive behaviors teachers utilize are deception, gift-giving, _____, and friendship.
   a. sexual relations
   b. isolation
   c. threats
   d. intimacy

4. In a survey of nuns who have reported being sexually abused, 3% identified a _____ as their abuser.
   a. priest
   b. parent
   c. babysitter
   d. nun

5. The _____ is the area of the brain where executive decisions are made and inappropriate behavior is inhibited.
   a. prefrontal cortex
   b. corpus callosum
   c. angular gyrus
   d. limbic system

6. It is true that female sex offenders rarely use _____ as a stimulus.
   a. fetishism
   b. masturbation
   c. violence
   d. pornography

7. The most accurate word for the killing of one human being by another is _____.
   a. *murder*
   b. *homicide*
   c. *fratricide*
   d. *euthanasia*

8. As U.S. jurisdictions adopted common law concepts, various degrees of intent, _____, and justification were considered for sentencing.
   a. aggravating circumstances
   b. exceptional circumstances
   c. mitigation
   d. deliberation

9. Most criminologists have designated _____ as the minimum count for a mass murder.
   a. two
   b. five
   c. four
   d. three

10. _____ is the ability to understand something immediately, without the need for conscious reasoning.
    a. Intuition
    b. Reasoning
    c. Extrasensory perception
    d. Clairvoyance

11. What do all offenders of Munchausen syndrome by proxy (MSBP) have in common?
    a. They are all the same race as the victim.
    b. They are all in some sort of financial trouble.
    c. They have all attempted suicide at some point in their life.
    d. They all acted as the victim's primary caregiver.

12. The average age at death for a neglected child is _____ months.
    a. 5
    b. 11
    c. 16
    d. 20

13. What do identity thieves know about stealing from large institutions or corporations?
    a. Businesses that consider identification and prosecution more costly than it is worth fail to protect themselves from criminal activity below their radar.
    b. Institutions that become victims are highly motivated to report identity theft because it makes the company look more sympathetic to clients.
    c. Large institutions and businesses have detailed anti-identity theft measures in place that keep this type of criminal activity from happening.
    d. It is more cost effective to steal from individuals than from large institutions or corporations.

14. What is sexting?
    a. Sending text messages about sex to others via a cell phone
    b. Sending sexual or nude photos to others via a cell phone
    c. Chatting about sex in a teenage-only website
    d. IMing friends about sexual websites

15. What is the typical profile of an online sexual predator?
    a. 13–65, female, single
    b. 13–65, male, single
    c. 20–35, male, married
    d. 20–35, male, divorced

See page 529 for answer key.

SECTION V
INJURIES
AND FATALITIES

Section V details injuries victims may receive and different causes of fatalities investigators may see. The chapter on injuries details the different types of injuries and how to recognize them. The types of fatalities included in this section are homicide, SIDS, asphyxia, drowning, fire, drugs, poisoning, sex-related homicide, autoerotic fatalities, and suicide. See page 459 for questions reviewing the material in Section V.

18

INJURIES

Law enforcement officers are called upon to investigate injuries of all kinds. It is important for investigators to be familiar with the different types of injuries people experience—the characteristics of each type of injury, how each type is created, and what to look for when foul play is suspected. Falls, altercations, and abuse are some of the most common types of injuries investigators face. They must be able to tell the difference between these injuries.

When people fall and get injured, they typically injure protuberant, or prominent, areas. People can fall while standing at ground level, or they can fall off something higher. When this happens, tibiae (shinbones) may be driven through the soles of the feet; this is characterized by overstretching of skin. If a person falls and hits his or her head, a large abrasion with radiating fracture lines may surround the laceration.

When people are involved in some type of altercation, they can injure protuberances as well as recessed areas. When a person receives a blow, he or she may have linear lacerations with fine marginal abrasions, a depressed skull fracture, or coup cerebral contusion. Altercations may include physical abuse, which will include a history of multiple injuries over a period. The common types of abuse are child abuse, domestic abuse, and elder abuse.

This chapter identifies and explains some of the most common injuries with which investigators deal.

18.1 Blunt Force Injuries

The following are types of blunt force injuries:

- Abrasion—An abrasion is a scrape or brush that partially removes the epidermal surface. This is indistinct when the body is wet; when it dries, it is brown or black. Abrasions can happen either premortem or postmortem. They can be grazes, scratches, brush burns (which cover a broad surface area), and rope burns (which indicate friction). Abrasions also can be from ligatures or bindings, which leave an impression or incision in the skin. They can be superficial or deep.

- Contusion—A contusion is a bruise with damage to subcutaneous tissues and vessels; the skin will remain intact. Dating contusions by their color is possible and may be useful. However, this is a guide only. Within hours of the injury, the contusion is light blue or red. If it has turned purple, it is less than a week old. If the contusion is changing from green to yellow, it is approximately a week old. After a week it turns brown. It disappears within 2 to 4 weeks. An artifact, a type of contusion, is a tear in blood vessels. It is usually found in the upper extremities in the obese. A true hemorrhage will infiltrate all layers of the skin.

- Laceration—A laceration is a rip or tear in the skin due to a shear or crush at the point of impact. The edges generally are ragged with tissue bridging.

- Split—A split is a rip or tear in the skin due to the tension adjacent to the impact point.

18.1.1 Force Used

The energy of motion, kinetic energy (KE), is dependent on the mass of an object (m) and the speed at which the object is moving (v). Thus the formula for describing such energy is $KE = 1/2mv^2$. Force, however, is difficult to assess to an exact degree because many things modify the force: the tissue that is struck, intervening materials, weapon characteristics, relative deceleration, the impact area, victim factors, and decomposition.

It is possible to determine the direction of force used. In abrasions, there may be a heaped margin at the opposite side of initial impact. A laceration may have an abrasion border wider on the margin of initial impact and undermining on the edge opposite the initial impact.

The distribution of force is the total surface area involved in energy exchange. It is more severe with a smaller impact point because this concentrates the amount of force.

18.1.2 Types of Blunt Force Injuries

Abrasions cause a stamping of the impact area into the skin's surface. Contusions cause an outline of blood forced on impact point. Lacerations may contain elements of the forming object (embedded trace materials from the object that formed the wound).

18.1.2.1 General Tissue Reaction

The following is a timeline of tissue reaction after a blunt force injury:

- <2 hours—No reaction
- 4 to 6 hours—Perivascular polymorphonuclear leukocytes (PMNs)
- 8 hours—PMN zone subjacent (beneath wound)
- 12 hours—Three layers (fibrin/red blood cells, PMNs, collagen)
- 12 to 30 hours—Collagen infiltrated by PMNs
- 3 to 72 hours—Epithelial regeneration
- 3 to 5 days—Granulation
- 12 days—Remodeling

18.1.2.2 Defense Wounds of Extremities

There are ways to tell if a person received a blunt or sharp force injury while defending himself or herself. Defense wounds typically are abrasions or contusions, but they may be fractures or sharp force injuries as well. They are usually on the dorsolateral (side and back) of the upper extremities. If these wounds are on the lower extremities, the wounds are likely from self-defense. If the victim is deceased, investigators consider sexual homicide if such injuries are present.

18.1.2.3 Common Injury Indications

These are common injury indications:

- Fat emboli—These fat particles found in blood do not preclude immediate death. Autopsy findings include petechiae (tiny reddish or purplish spotting) in the armpits, palpebral conjunctivas (mucous membranes that line the inner surface of the eyelids), brain, and kidneys; pulmonary edema; and generalized visceral congestion.

- Deep-vein thrombosis—These blood clots form in leg veins due to immobilization. They can break free, traveling to the lungs and causing death.
- Crush syndrome—This results in acute tubular necrosis.

18.1.2.4 Modifiers   Some findings may modify how to recognize a blunt force trauma. Decomposition of the body may obliterate wound detail. Also, diseases such as alcoholism may modify some things. Alcoholics often have multiple injuries of varied ages, especially injuries involving joints and protuberant areas. They often have little external injury, and they may have clotting factor abnormalities, such as extensive hemorrhaging.

18.1.3 Evidence

Blunt force trauma evidence must be documented with tools such as photographs, videos, and computer enhancement. The unique aspects of the wound help investigators interpret evidence. It might be possible to identify the type of weapon used based on the wound: it could be a complicated or multifaceted weapon with unusual features.

18.2 Sharp Force Injuries

A large percentage of police injuries are from edged weapons resulting from disturbance calls. Sharp force injuries are often a component of sexual homicide. The most common weapon utilized to inflict these injuries is a screwdriver; pencils are also common. The minimum safe distance from an assailant wielding an edged weapon is 21 ft. Edged weapons inflict wounds by stabbing, incising, and chopping.

Here are the types of sharp force injuries:

- Incision—This is a cut longer than it is deep. It may be caused by implements such as razor blades, sharp glasses, and knives. Incisions have structures similar to those of stab wounds.
- Stab—This is a penetrating wound that is deeper than it is long. Stab wounds sometimes have a track or a path corresponding to the stab. It may be caused by implements such as files, knives, scissors, hatpins, needles, screwdrivers, axes, and

pitchforks. Stab wounds can be homicidal, suicidal, or accidental. They can cause death due to hemorrhage (when a massive, vital structure is perforated or penetrated), air embolism, pneumothorax, infection, or asphyxia (due to blood aspiration). The instrument used, the direction of the wound track, the depth of penetration, the width of the instrument, and the number of wounds may be of medicolegal importance, so they should be documented. It is also important to know that serrated knife wounds and non–serrated knife wounds are not always distinguishable from one another. Additionally, the same knife may produce wounds with different appearances. Wounds that are angled may result from separate thrusts, twisting of the knife, or the victim twisting after the knife entered the body.

- Hilt mark—This is an abrasion corresponding to the handle guard impacting the skin. This is a misnomer since knives do not have hilts (it is actually the edge of the handle at the blade).
- Chop wound—Some wounds are made by a chopping or cutting action. These wounds appear to be incised (clean or well defined) on a quick glance and typically are caused by a dull blade, such as the blade of a machete, ax, bayonet, propeller, meat cleaver, angel iron, or pry bar. The structure of chop wounds is obvious. Chop wounds include decapitation.

Sharp force injuries can cause internal bleeding, blood leaking into the pericardial sac, and hemorrhage into tracheobronchial tree, which blocks air from entering the lungs. These injuries may also allow air to get into the vessels keeping oxygen from tissue and allowing blood and air to enter the chest cavity, which causes the lungs to collapse.

18.2.1 Characteristics of Wounds

18.2.1.1 Measurements Taking multiple measurements of each wound increases the accuracy of the measurements. A single sharp-edged blade typically produces a wound with one sharp and one blunt edge. The width of the blunt edge of the injury (from the flat side of the blade) corresponds to blade thickness. The only thing not affected by the angle at which the blade enters the body is the thickness of the wound. Some other aspects may change the size or shape of a wound, however.

18.2.1.2 Wound Reconstruction Methods A reapproximated wound is typically longer than it was when gaping open. Reconstruction methods include using tape or superglue. The pathologist may retain involved fragments for later tool mark comparison. Fascia and organs may be used to estimate the thickness of the blade. The heart, the liver, and the brain are especially valuable in this estimation. Note that clothing may maintain weapon characteristics better than the skin does. This is especially true of leather and synthetics.

18.2.1.3 Atypical Stab Wounds Movement may create relative motion between the blade and the skin. This may occur with weapon entry and exit (twisting of the blade) and with victim or assailant motion (struggle). This may show up as a wound with a dog-ear—one end of the wound jutting out to the side, perpendicular to the rest of the wound.

18.2.1.4 Penetration Penetration gives relative idea of blade length. Usually the depth of a wound exceeds actual blade length, and the track may be greater than, less than, or equal to actual blade length. Less than 2 lb of force is required for skin penetration. Tissues are elastic, and the body surface can be indented when penetrated.

Hilt marks (contusions adjacent to the stab site) and rib fractures adjacent to the stab site suggest that the blade penetrated to its maximum depth. Shallow and deep wounds are caused by similar forces. Full penetration is not an indicator of extreme force; things such as blade sharpness, clothing, and track length can affect the depth of the injury.

It is important to remember the organs may not be in the same location in life as at autopsy. When the body is standing erect, gravity pulls tissues downward; during the autopsy, the body is horizontal.

18.2.1.5 Direction of Wound The direction of the wound is determined with certainty only at the autopsy. To discover this, investigators dissect down to and follow the wound track. The hilt mark may also suggest direction.

18.2.2 Scene Investigation

The scene of a crime may provide a better indication of the activities than an autopsy. Investigators should consider the degree of incapacitation caused by the wounds and the effects on potential activity. Ideally, all blood evidence should be typed by serology/DNA, though this is seldom practical or warranted. Circumstances of individual cases indicate relative needs of evidence processing.

18.2.2.1 Weapon   Weapons are usually present at a suicide scene and absent at a homicide scene. Rarely is a knife left inside a body. The weapon may be one of opportunity (found by the assailant at the scene) or intent (brought to the scene).

To determine whether a weapon was used to create the injury, investigators first need a suspect weapon. Then they can discover whether the wounds are consistent with the weapon. This can be difficult to ascertain. The blade may twist or enter at an angle, which would make the wound larger than the weapon. The only way to identify a suspect's knife for certain is if a piece of the weapon breaks off in the wound.

18.2.2.2 Order of Wounds   Discovering the order in which wounds are inflicted is a limited interpretation at best. Investigators may be able to discover whether the wound is prior or recent. There is a sequence of wounds occurring premortem, agonal, and postmortem. Wounds from the postmortem period may ooze blood, but it is a small quantity compared to blood from premortem wounds. When trying to discover the order wounds were inflicted, investigators consider incapacitation and survivability. The wound may not be immediately incapacitating.

18.2.2.3 Blood Evidence   At the scene, blood spatter may be minimal unless the wound is on the head or the neck. Blood infiltrating tissues is the best indicator of a premortem wound. Blood may leach out of tissues with submersion.

18.2.2.4 Attacker Handedness and Position   It is difficult to scientifically defend an absolute opinion on this. A weapon may be held in either the dominant or the nondominant hand. The blade may extend medially or laterally from the hand. The attack may occur from above or below or from the front or rear.

18.2.2.5 Altercation   If an altercation takes place, there may be fingernail scratches and superficial incisions. Investigators collect fingernail clippings as evidence. There may also be wielding in altercations. Most homicidal slashing, part of wielding, occurs from behind. Sometimes it is impossible to implicate a specific weapon or determine the direction. There may be a superficial incision at the trailing end when the injury happened due to a confrontation.

Defensive wounds, often a result of altercations, are more consistent with warding off blows or grabbing the blade. If these are on the upper extremities, it may be on the dorsolateral area, including ulnar and extensor forearm. There may also be injuries on the palms or fingers from gripping a blade. If wounds are on the lower extremities, especially for female or nude victims, sexual assault should be considered.

18.2.2.6 Homicide   This often involves a domestic relationship, such as a spouse or lover. It may involve other elements, however, such as hate crimes, stimulant drugs, or a psychotic person. Homicide may involve mutilation. This may be psychiatric or sexual in nature, or it may simply be a way to hinder identification. Patterns include injuries from an ax, a handsaw, or a chainsaw.

18.2.2.7 Suicide   A person who has committed suicide may have multiple sharp force injuries. This is usually on a nondominant extremity, such as the flexor/radial forearm. There may also be hesitation marks, which are superficial sawing motion marks on the wrists or neck or multiple superficial punctures with one or two deep stabs. On the other hand, there may be marks of the person's determination. Slashing marks are possible, although these are uncommon. There also may be scars from a previous suicide attempt. Finally, there may be sympathy cuts, which are often seen in drug addicts who are attempting to get pain medication.

18.2.3 Complications of Sharp Force Injuries

There are many problems that can arise in the victim of a sharp force injury. Victims are in danger of bleeding to death, cardiac tamponade (blood in the pericardial sac around the heart), getting an air embolism (often seen with major neck wounds where air gets into vessels, resulting in oxygen not being delivered), hemopneumothorax (blood or air in chest cavity), asphyxiation, or infection.

18.2.4 Atypical Weapons

The following is a list of atypical weapons that can cause sharp force injuries:

- Serrated blade—A wound from a serrated blade may appear similar to a wound from a typical blade, but trailing or leading serrations may leave a pattern.
- Screwdriver—A screwdriver may leave a marginal abrasion. A wound from a Phillips-head screwdriver may appear similar to the wound from a standard head screwdriver.
- Survival knife—The serrated spine of a survival knife may abrade the skin as the flat edge passes the surface. Protrusions or recesses may create adjacent wounds.
- Scissors—Opened scissors create overlapping, oblique angles in a wound. Wounds from closed scissors are rectangular with abraded edges. There may be a central marginal abrasion corresponding to the screw.
- Fork—Wounds from forks may have a pattern corresponding to the number of tines. The relative distance between the tines may indicate direction. Kitchen forks do not generally penetrate skin.
- Ice pick—A wound caused by an ice pick may resemble a central line stick or a small pocketknife. It causes an ovoid or slit wound.
- Stick—A stick can cause a puncture wound with abraded edges.
- Broken glass—Broken glass can cause a sharply incised and ragged gaping wound. The wound may have abraded edges and grouped wounds. Foreign material may be embedded in the wound.

18.3 Closed Head Injuries

Coup-type injuries are those produced by focal compressions of the skull (with or without the area of impact). The smaller the acted-upon area, the greater the likelihood of a coup contusion. The effects are immediate, producing contusions (bruises) and hemorrhages. An impact from a flat surface usually does not cause a coup contusion. They are typically caused by a blow to the resting, movable head.

Contrecoup brain contusions occur opposite a point of cranial impact, independently of skull fractures. They are sustained when a moving, falling, or accelerating head strikes a solid object. There is no proof that human coup–contrecoup injuries are ever produced by any mechanism other than impact of the moving head against a solid object.

A blow to a resting head produces brain contusions beneath the point of impact (coup-type injuries). A moving head striking a firm or unyielding surface results in brain contusions opposite the point of impact (contrecoup-type injuries). A moving head will rarely suffer more than mild coup-type injuries, if any, when impacting against another surface. A resting head sustains mild or no contrecoup-type injuries (with rare exceptions) from an impact. The typical contrecoup lesion has never been produced in humans unless the head was in motion. Occipital trauma (hitting the back of the head) to a moving head often results in frontal and temporal (contrecoup) brain injury. Frontal trauma (hitting the front of the head) to a moving head rarely results in occipital (contrecoup) brain injury. A head fixed against a firm surface will sustain both coup and contrecoup type injuries when struck on the free surface (this is related to the elastic properties of the skull). When trauma is sustained to the upper jaw or temple in a moving head, the major lesions are always contrecoup. Contusions of the brain surface can result from the edges of fractured bones impacting the brain surface. In severe skull fractures, differentiating fracture contusions from coup–contrecoup injuries may be difficult or impossible.

18.4 Firearm Injuries

There are many misconceptions about firearm injuries. Some misconceptions are as follows:

- An entrance wound is always smaller than an exit wound.
- An exit wound never resembles an entrance wound.

- Right-handed individuals always commit suicide by shooting themselves in the right side of the head.
- Multiple shots indicate murder, not suicide.

There are many different factors that affect the damage firearms can cause. For instance, the penetration of the projectile will affect what tissue is damaged. Here are some terms relating to firearm damages:

- Permanent cavity—This is the volume of space once occupied by tissue that has been destroyed by the passage of the projectile. It is the hole left by the passage of the bullet.
- Temporary cavity—This is the expansion of the permanent cavity by stretching due to the projectile's passage.
- Fragmentation—This refers to the projectile pieces or secondary fragments of bone that are impelled outward from the permanent cavity and may sever muscle tissues and blood vessels apart from the permanent cavity.

18.4.1 Types of Powder Residue

There are three types of residue that can be left at the scene of a firearm injury: flake, flattened ball, and ball. Flake residue may be deposited between 18 and 24 in. from the muzzle of the weapon. Flattened ball residue may be deposited up to 35 in. from the muzzle. Ball residue may be deposited between 28 and 42 in. from the muzzle of the weapon.

18.4.2 Types of Wounds

Listed below are the various types of wounds associated with firearms:

- Entrance wounds—These wounds can be affected by hot gases, charring, singeing, burning, smoke and lead vapors, bullet and barrel lubrication, the abrasion collar of the bullet, and powder grains (unburned, partially burned, or burning).
- Exit wounds—These wounds are usually stellate or star shaped.
- Perforating wounds—These are also known as through-and-through wounds. These wounds happen when a projectile passes all the way through the body. They include entrance and exit wounds.

- Penetrating wounds—In the case of penetrating wounds, the projectile enters the body and lodges inside. The projectile only leaves if there is an exit wound.
- Grazed wounds—These can cause abrasions or tears.
- Rifle wounds—These wounds can cause beveling of bone and keyhole wounds. These wounds detect where entrance and exit wounds overlap—one end of the perforation will resemble a typical entrance wound, while the other end will show external beveling consistent with exit holes.

18.4.3 Investigation of Firearm Deaths

18.4.3.1 Gunshot Autopsy   When completing an autopsy after a gunshot, investigators must discover whether the injuries were produced by bullets, whether the victim died as a result of the gunshot or the victim had been dead before the shot was fired, the cause of death, whether there were other injuries, and whether all injuries were produced by one bullet. Investigators always examine the victim's hands to look for soiling, burns, or other injuries. They also look for the following evidence:

- Entrance and exit wounds
- Distance between the weapon and the victim
- Direction of gunfire
- Location of bullets, pellets, or shotgun
- Type and characteristics of weapon used
- The projectile
- Powder on the victim's clothing

There are many common failures in investigating firearm deaths, such as failing to perform a complete autopsy. It is important to look for gunshot wounds in unexpected locations such as the mouth, eyes, vagina, or axilla (armpit). If necessary, an X-ray or fluoroscopy is used. It is common to misinterpret lacerated wounds as exit wounds. Grease and other bullet fouling can be misinterpreted as powder residue. Bullets should be examined for ricochet. Other failures include incorrectly identifying the larger wound as the exit wound solely based on size and the wound with marginal abrasion as the entrance wound. Premature release of information before correlating all findings is also considered a failure.

18.4.3.2 Evidence of Gun Discharge Materials are often left behind on the barrel and cartridge case when a gun discharges. When a gun discharges, the bullet, gas, powder, soot, bullet and jacket fragments, and primer compounds (lead, antimony, and barium) leave the barrel. Each of these might be left behind as evidence. Copper, brass, and nickel leave the cartridge case of a gun on discharge.

18.4.3.3 Wound Evidence There are different types of wounds: contact wounds, intermediate wounds, distant wounds, entrance wounds, exit wounds, and bullet wounds of bones. Each of these wounds has different types of evidence.

18.4.3.3.1 Contact Wounds In contact wounds, the muzzle is in contact with the victim's body. In all contact wounds, the following evidence will be present:

- Scorching of the wound edges
- Soot deposited on the wound margins
- Soot and powder particles driven into track
- A muzzle impression due to blowback of the skin

In contact wounds over bone (hard contact wounds), as in the head, soot usually is deposited on the outer table of the bone around the entrance in the bone. Soot may also be on the inner table of the bone and on the dura. There may be discontinuous skull fractures and a stellate entrance wound.

Loose contact wounds (contact wounds not over bone) differ from hard contact wounds in that there is an area of soot around the entrance wound not confined to the edges of the wound. Also, stellate entrance wounds usually do not occur.

If the contact wound is over clothing or hair, the clothing or hair may absorb all the external soot and powder. Powder grains and soot may still be found inside the wound track, however.

18.4.3.3.2 Intermediate Wounds In intermediate wounds, the muzzle is still close enough to cause powder tattooing of the skin, despite there being no contact. This occurs as a result of the impaction of grains of powder in the skin. The maximum ranges of powder tattooing from handguns are 24 in. for flake powder, 35 in. for flattened ball powder, and 48 in. for ball powder. The diameter and density of the powder tattoo pattern can determine range. Powder tattooing cannot be wiped off. Soot (powder blackening) is also present on close-up gunshot wounds from 6 to 10 in. away. Hair and clothing may interfere with powder to some degree. All clothing should be examined for evidence.

18.4.3.3.3 Distant Wounds   In distant wounds, there is no soot or powder tattooing. The range is too great, although an exact range cannot be determined. In distant wounds, an entrance wound can be differentiated more easily from an exit wound.

18.4.3.3.4 Entrance Wounds   These have an abrasion ring due to the bullet scraping the margins of the bullet hole as it enters the skin. These wounds tend to be small, circular, and regular. In most cases, symmetrical abrasion rings suggest a head-on shot and oval rings an angular shot. A bullet's course can be determined only by internal examination.

18.4.3.3.5 Exit Wounds   These are usually larger and more irregular than entrance wounds because they lack the support or reinforcement of the skin. They also are larger because of bullet tumbling and deformation. There is usually no abrasion ring. These occur on exit wounds only when the exit is firm against an object such as a belt or wall.

18.4.3.3.6 Bullet Wounds of Bone   In these wounds, the entrance wound is a punched-out, circular or oval hole with sharp edges. The opposite surface is beveled. In the skull, for example, the entrance bullet hole is beveled on the internal table. The exit wound is beveled or cratered. In skulls, the exit hole is beveled on the outer table.

18.4.3.4 Bullet Wipe   The bullet wipe is a gray ring around the entrance hole in skin or clothing, appearing when bullet grime is wiped on the skin or cloth as the bullet enters. It is more common with wounds caused by revolvers and should not be mistaken for soot on the wound margin.

18.4.3.5 Caliber of a Bullet   X-ray distortion makes it impossible to tell the caliber of a bullet by x-raying it in the body, nor can the caliber be determined by the entrance hole in the skin.

18.4.3.6 Trajectory Trajectory through the body depends on the positions of the victim and the assailant and the angle at which the weapon was held.

18.4.3.7 Notes about Suicide Contrary to popular belief, right-handed people may steady a gun with their right hand and fire with their left. Also, multiple bullet wounds do not rule out a suicide.

18.4.3.8 Firearm Evidence Firearms evidence can prove whether a bullet or casing was fired from a class of firearms or one specific firearm, whether multiple bullets or casings were fired from one firearm or multiple firearms, or whether bullets or casings recovered from multiple scenes were fired from one firearm. It can also show if a defendant knew how to use a pistol and if the defendant handled individual rounds.

18.4.4 Information on Firearms

18.4.4.1 Shotgun Shells Shotgun shells contain the following elements:

- Casing, usually made of plastic or paper, occasionally made of metal
- Lead or steel shot
- Powder
- A primer of large size
- An overpowder/undershot wad made of plastic or paper (wadding is sometimes found inside the body)

18.4.4.2 Rifle Actions Manufactured Today Here are the types of rifles manufactured today:

- Automatic—An automatic rifle cycles the action and fires rounds as long as the trigger is pulled. It is sometimes referred to as a machine gun.
- Bolt action—With this, a turn bolt or straight pull bolt is operated manually.
- Lever action—In a lever action rifle, the breech mechanism is cycled by a manually operated lever.

- Semiautomatic—A semiautomatic rifle cycles the action and fires one round with each release and pull of the trigger. It is often referred to as an autoloader.
- Slide—In a slide rifle, the breech mechanism is cycled by a manually operated forearm moving parallel to the barrel. It also is known as a pump action.

18.5 Injuries and Fatalities from Automobile Accidents

Transportation fatalities are the most common cause of blunt force injury. The following are three stages of impact: primary, secondary, and tertiary. In the primary stage, the vehicle impacts a relatively stationary object. In the secondary stage, the victim impacts a relatively stationary object. In the third stage, viscera (internal organs of the body) impacts a relatively stationary object. At this point, deceleration is complete.

18.5.1 Accident Reconstruction

Reconstructing an accident is important to investigate what happened. When reconstructing an accident, investigators must remember that eyewitnesses are unreliable. Instead, investigators should use police accident reports. All available information should be considered. Drawing definitive conclusions from injuries to reconstruct events must be avoided. It is not always possible to determine the specific cause for each and every wound.

18.5.2 Automobile Fatalities

Automobile accidents are a representation of interaction between the kinetic energy and the object or victim. Less extensive injuries are seen upon the victim striking a close object as opposed to a distant one. The use of restraints and an intact cabin result in a marked decrease in motor vehicle collision fatalities.

Investigators should use caution when determining the identities of the driver and passengers because they might have been thrown about the cabin. Besides placement of victims, shoe prints may give clues as to the identity of the driver. The driver sometimes leaves a shoe print on the brake pedal from emergency braking prior to the collision.

Therefore, it is important to examine the bottom of the shoes of the victims. Listed below are the common causes of motor vehicle collisions:

- Drugs and alcohol—More than 50% of drivers who are killed in a collision are driving while intoxicated. Between 10% and 15% of deceased drivers have a positive drug screen result. It is important to test for the presence of drugs in all vehicle occupants. If doing an external exam only, femoral blood is the desired sample. Vitreous fluid (eye fluid) can also be tested. Even when testing blood obtained at a hospital, investigators must be sure to keep the chain of custody. Finally, testing a subdural clot yields the blood alcohol level when the clot formed, not what it is currently.
- Carbon monoxide—When this causes an accident, it is usually a result of defective vehicle exhaust system. This is often overlooked as a factor contributing to an accident.
- Human error—Many people are not cautious when driving. Things like high speed, reckless driving, and fatigue cause many accidents.
- Environment—The environment can also cause accidents. Deer, downed trees or power lines, and events such as tornadoes and thunderstorms can cause automobile accidents.
- Disease—This uncommon cause of vehicle accidents usually results in no severe injuries because the driver usually slows in anticipation.

18.5.3 Common Injuries

The following are common injuries associated with automobile accidents:

- Cabin violations—Cabin violations can cause a crush with pelvic injury or traumatic asphyxiation.
- Restraint injuries—Restraints rarely cause significant injury and generally decrease fatalities and serious injury. The lap belt can lacerate the mesentery (bowel) or cause abrasions or contusions. The shoulder belt can cause abrasions or contusions. These injuries are minor, however, and the benefit from these restraints outweighs the risk these injuries pose.

- Air bag injuries—Air bags protect the chest and prevent whiplash in frontal impact accidents. However, they deploy at very high speeds. This is certainly unsafe with children in rear-facing child seats in the front seat. They may also be dangerous to very short individuals.
- Dicing injuries—These injuries result from shattered tempered glass. These cause angled superficial cuts usually on the head and upper extremities.

18.5.4 Victims

One of the important responsibilities of responders to vehicle accidents is to identify the driver and the passengers. The following are ways victims are impacted by automobile accidents.

18.5.4.1 Driver Drivers often have fairly uniform injuries, such as injuries from impacting the steering wheel. These injuries result in flail chest or sternum fractures and possible microscopic heart injury. Facial lacerations, especially below the nose, result when an unrestrained driver hits the steering wheel. Belt injuries result from intracabin protrusions, such as door handles and window cranks.

18.5.4.2 Passengers Passengers' injuries are less uniform than the driver's. However, if they receive dash injuries, they may be similar to the injuries of a driver hitting the steering wheel.

18.5.4.3 Ejected Occupants When dealing with an ejected occupant, investigators try to determine which injuries were from the crash and which were from the ejection. Lethal injuries often result from the head impacting the ground during an ejection.

18.5.4.4 Pedestrians Understanding possible evidence present when a vehicle impacts a pedestrian is important. If a pedestrian is involved in the accident, investigators examine the clothing of pedestrians for trace evidence that might have been exchanged between the vehicle and the victim. They look for paint chips, glass fragments, hair, fibers, and grease.

Investigators should pay attention to tread marks. Sometimes there is a pattern to the injury that corresponds to the tires. They look for tread marks opposite brush abrasions. Investigators document suspect vehicle tires with a scale. There may be a shearing of the skin flap from fascia and overstretched striae.

If the vehicle is traveling at a high speed, the accident is often characterized by late or no braking, causing the victim to be thrown into the air. The victim may land on the roof, trunk, or rear bumper of the vehicle or behind the vehicle. There is often a dent in the bumper or hood. The injuries sustained by the pedestrian are often extensive, involving mutilation and striae of the groin and neck skin opposite the impact point.

When a child is hit by a car, he or she is propelled forward and down, which often leads to the child being run over. This happens because children have a low center of gravity. If the driver brakes hard, the bumper drops and the child may remain on the impact surface and carried for a short distance. If an adult is hit by a car, he or she is propelled upward because of the higher center of gravity. An adult victim may be struck below the center of gravity. In such cases, the vehicle would have been traveling at a moderate speed or the driver braked hard. The victim might be scooped onto the hood and could slide onto the windshield. If a truck or bus is involved, the impact point is always above the center of gravity.

Table 18.1 shows the correlation between vehicle speed and pedestrian injury.

Table 18.1 Vehicle Speed versus Injury

SPEED (MPH)	VEHICLE DAMAGE	PEDESTRIAN INJURY
<25	Not significant	Thrown forward and sideways
25–30	Dent in hood, broken windshield	Thrown up and slide off → ground impact
50–60	Dents in bumper, grill, fender	Thrown up and over → ground impact

Source: Westveer, A.E., Jr., *Managing Death Investigations*, Vol. 1, Fifth ed., U.S. Department of Justice Federal Bureau of Investigation, Washington, DC, 2002. With permission.

Injuries commonly suffered by pedestrians in accidents are listed below:

- Brush abrasions—These are a common injury to pedestrians when involved in a vehicle accident. These are superficial scraping abrasions due to friction with the road surface. They usually involve protuberant areas and have no hemorrhage.

- Bone fractures—An extremely common injury to pedestrians is bone fractures from the bumper of the car. Elderly victims fracture even when hit at lower speeds, whereas healthy, young victims fracture less frequently. Even at 14 mph, though, a young adult would fracture his or her legs. There would be multiple fractures at 25 mph or more. For male pedestrians, the bumper strikes roughly at the knee. Fractures typically involve the midcalf to lower calf, with an average bumper height of 14 to 15 in. The most protuberant area of the bumper is at about 18 to 19 in. on average. Fractures are photographed with a yardstick or tape measure. Investigators also measure the pedestrian's footwear heel thickness. This is important because the driver usually brakes, which makes the front of the car dip, creating a lower impact point. If the car has poor shock absorbers, the impact may be at the victim's heels. If the victim is walking, the fracture level will be different on each leg. The weight-bearing leg usually has a higher level of injury. The victim may have no grossly apparent injury. Soft tissue/ muscle bruises and lacerations are documented. The area may be protected by clothing. If there is no bumper injury, the pedestrian ran into the side of the car. Wedge fractures at the tibia have the apex indicating direction of force and often are displaced fractures with lacerations opposite the impact.

- Pockets—These injuries are on the upper thigh, buttocks, or hip and happen because of a tangential force. The victim usually is walking with one leg pivoted around the axis of the weight-bearing leg. The injury causes subcutaneous shearing, which, in turn, creates a large pocket. There may be copious hemorrhage. This injury is especially prominent in obese individuals. The injury may not be visible but is easily palpated, and it may entrap trace evidence within the pocket.

- Overstretching of the skin—This injury is caused by rear impact. If the vehicle is traveling at low speeds (less than 30 mph), it can cause striae, or stretch marks. If the vehicle is traveling at high speeds (over 45 mph), it may cause lacerations or have associated avulsion of viscera.
- Pelvic fractures—The victim can have a shattered pelvis laceration if the vehicle is traveling at speeds more than 45 mph. A fracture of the pubic ramus is a fracture of the buttock or hip bone opposite the point of impact. A fracture of the ilium (especially sacroiliac joint) is the same side as the impact.
- Whiplash—This injury occurs with a rear impact. It can be associated with upper cervical atlantooccipital injuries.

18.5.5 Lethal Injuries

The most common lethal injuries are injuries to the central nervous system or brain; these account for 85% of fatalities. These include head injuries, cervical spinal fractures or subluxation (partial dislocation), and visceral injuries. Frontal impact is the common cause of fatal injury, which can be induced by the following implements.

18.5.5.1 Windshield Windshields are made of safety glass, which has two glass panes with a central plastic core. The glass is designed to prevent ejection of passengers through the windshield. The side and rear windows are still made with tempered glass, which shatters.

In windshield injuries, there are often facial cuts characterized by superficial parallel vertical incisions on the forehead and the nose. Often the windshield is impacted and the glass may shatter. It can create deep incisions.

18.5.5.2 Steering Wheel Impacting the steering wheel can cause transverse sternum fractures, bilateral rib fractures, and cardiac contusion, which is often the cause of death. It can also cause visceral lacerations and a descending aorta horizontal transection. The liver or spleen might be affected by an acute abdominal or gradual subcapsular bleed with a possible delayed rupture. This slow bleed increases the pressure, which leads to rupture.

18.5.5.3 Dashboard   Hitting the dashboard can cause lower extremity fractures and subluxations. This is true for the patella, which acts as wedge between distal femur malleoli (ankles) and the femoral neck (proximal thighbone).

18.5.5.4 Seat   The seat can cause fracture or subluxation of ankles or feet due to sliding forward.

18.5.6 Types of Accidents

The following details different types of impact:

- Side impact—This type of accident typically is seen at intersections. It causes more severe injuries than other types of impacts, especially to the driver and passengers of the impacted vehicle. The driver of the impacted vehicle usually has the most severe injuries. This person may suffer from aortic transaction; visceral lacerations on the heart, the liver, the spleen, or kidneys and basilar skull or neck fractures. Seat belts are less effective in side impact accidents than frontal impact accidents. Also, partial or complete ejection from the vehicle is possible.
- Rollover—Rollover accidents are even more lethal than side impact accidents. Those in the vehicle are fairly unrestrained, so there is unpredictable movement within the cabin. Complete or partial ejection is possible.
- Rear impact—Rear impact accidents are the least fatal. The impacting vehicle occupants often have less injury than the occupants of the impacted vehicle. These accidents often cause whiplash.

18.5.7 Special Considerations of Automobile Accidents

Other causes of accidents are listed below:

- Sudden natural death—Sometimes accidents of relatively minor extent are caused by the sudden natural death of the driver.

- Vehicular suicide—When there is a head-on collision into fixed objects, vehicular suicide must be considered. Investigators check the driver's shoes for pedal imprints to see if he or she attempted to stop or if he or she sped up. The absence of breaking, possible psychiatric history, or prior suicide attempts give hints of a vehicular suicide.
- Multiple vehicle strikes—When a pedestrian has been hit, investigators look for multiple vehicle strikes. They establish the presence or absence of a typical impact point. The victim most likely was standing for the initial impact and down for any subsequent strikes. Investigators look for a bumper fracture, stretch strikes, or pattern injury. If there were multiple hits, it must be determined if the victim was dead before the second hit.
- Vehicular fire—A fire in a vehicle sometimes occurs. Investigators determine whether the injury, the fire, or the death occurred first. Vehicular fires are very uncommon, with only 0.5% of accidents including fire. Usually these fires are fuel fed in rollover or rear impact accidents. In these situations, death is usually from blunt force injury. Flash fire is rare with accidents; carbon monoxide may be from exhaust rather than from the fire.

18.6 Motorcycle Accidents

18.6.1 Causes

Motorcycle accidents are usually caused by alcohol or drugs, recklessness, other drivers, or the environment.

18.6.2 Injuries

In motorcycle accidents, occupants are always ejected. The passenger may be tossed from the motorcycle before the impact. The following are the most common injuries received in motorcycle accidents:

- Head injuries—Head injuries are very common and are usually the cause of death in motorcycle accident fatalities. Typically, the skull fractures because of ground impact. It may be a sagittal (forehead) impact, or a transverse (temporal or chin) impact.

- Whiplashes—Whiplashes often occur due to rapid deceleration. There may be instant death with a pontomedullary rent.
- Pattern injuries—The driver's legs may be forced into the gas tank. The handlebars may lacerate viscera. Occupants may also receive chain abrasion, muffler burn, or décollement—shearing off a layer of skin.

18.6.3 Safety Devices

Wearing safety devices can increase the safety of motorcycles. A helmet provides weak front protection. If the motorcycle is traveling at low speeds, it can significantly decrease chances of receiving a head injury. If it is traveling at a high speed, a helmet offers little protection. Wearing leather can decrease brush abrasions.

18.7 Train Accidents

Mass disasters may occur with accidents involving trains or any mode of mass transit. Because of the marked kinetic energy of a train with a large mass, extensive injuries are present. When a vehicle is involved, side impacts are typical from hitting the vehicles of drivers trying to beat the train or a car stalling on the track. These accidents often involve an intoxicated driver.

18.8 Plane Accidents

With light, noncommercial planes, victims typically are seen by a nonmilitary medical examiner. Major concerns are identifying the deceased and determining why the crash occurred. Investigations are similar to larger disasters but with fewer victims under relatively good conditions.

Drugs and alcohol are sometimes a factor in plane crashes, as are poor judgment. Human error accounts for more than three-quarters of all plane crashes. These often involve civil litigation. Also, light planes may be used for suicide. The survivability of a plane crash depends on cabin compromise and crash force.

18.9 Injuries to Specific Body Parts

Below are examples of injuries to different body parts:

- Bones—Basically, a fracture is a laceration of bone. Fractures can be used to assess the degree of osteoporosis.
- Pelvis—The pelvis is a ring that must break in at least two places to be fractured.
- Ribs—A rib is a pliable and discontinuous ring. It fractures less often in young people. The following are some types of fractures that may happen to a person's ribs:
  - Iatrogenic—From resuscitation efforts
  - Pathologic—From underlying prior disease
  - Direct—From local trauma applied
  - Indirect—Distant trauma with force transferred via bone
  - Compression—Usually lateral
  - Directional—Usually midline
- Chest—Other chest structures besides the ribs also may be damaged: the chin, sternum, and heart. The chin–sternum–heart syndrome happens when there is an impact causing a severe neck flexion injury. The chest and heart may be injured by driving the jaw into the sternum.
- Aorta (transverse laceration)—The arch of the aorta, which is right outside the heart, can be compressed by a force, putting pressure on the aorta and possibly blocking the blood supply to the brain. A transverse laceration is a common injury to the descending aorta. This is a blunt force cutting across the aorta. Transverse lacerations often are caused by automobile accidents.
- Lungs—The surface of the lungs can burst, causing them to collapse. Resuscitation can also cause an iatrogenic injury. Lung trauma also can happen as a result of contusions. When energy is transferred from an impact, lacerations or punctures may cause the lungs to collapse.
- Abdomen—Evidence of a traumatic event to the abdomen may not be obvious. There are various types of injuries that may happen in the abdomen. An iatrogenic injury is an injury caused by something a doctor has done diagnostically or operatively. It is usually not an injury to the spleen, but it often

may be a colon injury from a colonoscopy, for example. Solid organs, such as the liver, the spleen, and kidneys, are commonly injured by lacerations. Hollow organs, including the stomach, the small intestine, the large intestine, the gallbladder, and the descending aorta can be easily ruptured. Hollow organs are more vulnerable when distended.

Bibliography

Westveer, A.E., Jr. (2002). *Managing death investigations* (Vol. 1, Fifth ed.). Washington, DC: U.S. Department of Justice Federal Bureau of Investigation. (Used with permission.)

19

DEATH INVESTIGATION

19.1 Medical Terminology

19.1.1 Anatomy

- Anterior—Toward the front
- Aorta—The large artery in the heart that distributes blood to the other arteries
- Cardiac—Related to the heart
- Cerebral—Related to the brain
- Cholecystic—Related to the gallbladder
- Dorsal—Related to the back of the body or the back of the hand or foot
- Gastric—Related to the stomach
- Hepatic—Related to the liver
- Peritoneum—The abdominal cavity
- Pleura—The chest cavity about the lungs
- Pulmonary—Related to the lungs
- Renal—Related to the kidneys
- Ventral—Related to the abdomen or the front of the body

19.1.2 Diseases

- Cirrhosis—A chronic disease of the liver with scarring and reduced function
- Emphysema—A chronic disease of the lungs reducing a person's ability to breathe
- Infarction—Dead tissue in an organ due to insufficient circulation of blood
- Jaundice—Yellow pigmentation of skin, commonly resulting from liver failure

- Myocardial infarction—Heart attack; death of an area of the heart muscle
- Necrosis—Death of tissue
- Peritonitis—Inflammation in the abdominal cavity
- Phlebitis—Inflammation of the veins
- Pleuritis—Inflammation in the chest cavity
- Pneumonia—Inflammation in the lung
- Thrombophlebitis—A blood clot in an inflamed area
- Thrombosis—Blood clotting inside the blood vessels, often in leg veins
- Uremia—Toxic condition resulting from kidney failure

19.1.3 Injuries

- Bruise—A bluish swelling of blood beneath the skin
- Comminuted fracture—A break of a bone with separation of the broken ends, or a fracture in which the bone is splintered or crushed
- Contusion—Essentially the same as a bruise
- Hemorrhage—Bleeding or the abnormal flow of blood
- Laceration—A tearing of the skin
- Subarachnoid hemorrhage—Bleeding between the brain and its covering arachnoid membrane
- Subdural hemorrhage—Bleeding between the brain covering dura mater and the arachnoid mater

19.1.4 Medical Procedures

- Autopsy—An examination of the body of a deceased person for the purpose of identifying the cause of death
- Bronchoscopy—Looking into the bronchi with the aid of a metal tubular instrument
- Craniotomy—An operation in which the skull is opened
- Electrocardiogram—Shows the electrical activity of the heart
- Electroencephalogram—Shows the electrical activity of the brain
- Laparotomy—An operation in which the abdominal cavity is opened

- Laryngoscopy—Looking into the larynx with the aid of a metal instrument
- Lumbar puncture—Placing a thin needle in the lower back and withdrawing fluid; also called a spinal tap

19.2 Coroner and Medical Exam Systems

To help solve a crime, an examiner (usually a pathologist or a coroner) will evaluate the body to determine the cause of death. A coroner is a public official who investigates, by inquest, any death due to unnatural causes. Such an examination or an autopsy can reveal crucial information in a case.

19.2.1 Forensic Sciences in Antiquity

The earliest account of forensic medicine had to do with the prohibition of suicide. It was believed the individual who committed suicide was possessed by evil spirits and could pass them on to the community.

Suicide was condemned in ancient Greece because people were considered servants of the gods and self-destruction was rebellion against them. Therefore, medicolegal personnel reviewed suicide cases to determine whether a penalty was in order. Soldiers who committed suicide in ancient Rome were considered deserters. Likewise, criminals who committed suicide in order to escape punishment were condemned. In England, suicide was a crime under the common law during the 10th century. In 1184, the canon law of the Roman Catholic Church condemned suicide.

There was a postmortem exam in the ancient world. The *Hsi Yuan Lu* (or *Instructions to Coroners*), a Chinese handbook published circa 1250, lays out guidelines for the postmortem examination of bodies. This included descriptions of wounds caused by sharp instruments in comparison to wounds caused by blunt instruments.

19.2.2 Early Advances in Autopsy

Written records of forensic pathology in Europe began in 1407 when the Bamberg Code appeared. Later, a more extensive penal code, the Constitutio Criminalis Carolina, was issued by Emperor Charles V.

Both documents portray the importance of forensic pathology. Under these codes, law enforcement personnel would call physicians to help solve fatal crimes.

Ambroise Paré performed some of the first official medicolegal autopsies in the late 16th century. His reports covered his findings in sexual assault cases and in the lungs of smothered children.

The first formal lectures on forensic pathology where held at the University of Leipzig in Germany. These lectures helped advance the knowledge of European police and judicial authorities.

19.2.3 Early Systems in England and America

The English coroner system was developed nearly 600 years before the first such system in America. Early American colonists brought the English system over with them to the New World, modifying it over the centuries.

19.2.3.1 Coroner System in England   In 1877, a law was passed in England that required an investigation when a coroner suspected a violent or unnatural death or when the cause of death was unknown. In 1888, an appointee system for coroners developed in which the head of local government appointed the coroner. Originally, there were no minimum qualifications to be coroner. In 1926, regulations were established. Candidates needed 5 years of experience as a medical practitioner or lawyer to be considered for a coroner position.

19.2.3.2 Forensic Pathology in America   The following timeline tracks the development of the forensic pathology system in America:

- In 1635, a coroner in New England found that John Deacon died as a result of fasting and extreme cold, which caused bodily weakness.
- Some of the earliest American autopsy records were filed in Massachusetts as far back as 1647.
- In 1890, two physicians in Baltimore were appointed as medical examiners and assigned all autopsies requested by the coroner or state attorney.

- In 1915, New York City eliminated the coroner's office and created a medical examiner system. Dr. Charles Norris was the first chief medical examiner in America and was empowered to order an autopsy when he thought it necessary. Thus, the first proficient medical examiner's system was established, allowing for a variety of cases to be investigated and the capability to order autopsies if public interest demanded it.

19.2.4 Determining Cause

An autopsy can be used to determine the cause of death. The determination of the cause of death involves consideration of the following possible causes:

- Homicide
- Suffocation
- Fire
- Drowning
- Drugs
- Poisoning
- Sex-related homicide
- Autoerotic fatalities
- Suicide
- Injuries from external mechanical violence
- Injuries from sharp external violence
- Bullet injuries
- Explosion injuries
- Electric currents

This section gives some details about death from mechanical and sharp external violence, electric currents, bullet injuries, and explosions. The following sections will detail the other possible causes of death.

19.2.4.1 External Mechanical Violence   Death by injuries from external mechanical violence (made by either blunt or sharp instruments) can be from the following types of injuries:

- Abrasions—From an abrasion, it is possible to determine from which direction the violence occurred and what caused the injury.
- Contusions or bruises—At the autopsy, it is possible to determine whether the contusion was produced shortly before death or if it resulted in the death.
- Crushing wounds—In crushing wounds, an impression of the object that produced the wound often can be found on the body.
- Bone injuries—The direction of the crack usually can determine the direction in which the violence originated.

19.2.4.2 Sharp External Violence   Deaths due to sharp external violence can be from the following types of injuries:

- Cutting wounds—It is difficult to determine if these wounds occurred during life or after death. Murder typically is suspected if the wound is very deep or irregular or if the wound does not correspond with a natural hold of a weapon.
- Stab wounds—Stab wounds are usually larger than the width of the blade. Murder typically is suspected when wounds are scattered and not concentrated on one area of the body.
- Chopping wounds—These are usually produced by an ax or by a blow with another edged tool. Typically, murder can be assumed in cases of chopping wounds. Suicide with an ax is rare.

19.2.4.3 Bullet Injuries   In soft parts of the body, the bullet can produce an explosive effect. The bullet may split into several parts, creating multiple exit wounds. To be immediately fatal, a shot through the head must have a bullet producing a bursting effect or injure an artery of the brain or a vital brain center. Thus, a shot to the head is not always fatal.

19.2.4.4 Explosion Injuries   Fragments from an explosion can perforate the brainpan and penetrate the body, producing severe damage. Explosions in close proximity can be fatal because of the air pressure alone. At greater distances the explosion can cause injury from the resulting fall.

19.2.4.5 Electric Current Injuries These can occur from an electricity supply or from lightning. Current marks are visible injuries on the body and are found at the points of entry and exit of the current.

19.3 The Death Scene

First responders are often exposed to traumatic situations; thus, it is important for them to control their attitudes and emotions. They need to maintain their cool, stay calm, and remain detached. It is important to be thorough and professional when processing the death scene.

19.4 Victim Personality Assessment

A victim personality assessment is designed to obtain accurate answers to significant questions pertaining to a victim. The personality assessment can be beneficial when investigating ambiguous death cases. Ask the exact same questions about the victim to all who are interviewed, and indicate—on the record and verbatim—the responses of each person being interviewed. The list below details the information that should be documented:

- General background
  - Name
  - Aliases
  - Gender
  - Date of birth
  - Place of birth
  - Citizenship
  - Race
  - Height
  - Weight
- Family
  - Socioeconomic status of family
  - Number, names, and ages of siblings
  - Status of parents (living/deceased, ages, health, married/ divorced, employment)
  - Religion of the family and degree to which it is practiced

- The biggest influence in the subject's life
- The subject's rapport with his or her parents and siblings (include the frequency of contact with each family member and any important changes in the relationships in recent years)
- General data
  - The most important things in the subject's life
  - Residence and description of neighborhood
  - Significant days to the subject
  - The subject's current financial status
  - Recent changes in his or her finances (changes in bank accounts, names on accounts, etc.)
- Marital status
  - Whether the subject is single, married, divorced, or separated
  - Description of current marriage and significant relationships
  - Names and dates of birth of the subject's children
  - Description of the nature of subject's involvement with his or her children and the overall relationship maintained with children
  - Description of any changes in these relationships
- Employment
  - The subject's present employment, time spent there, attitude about the job and his or her coworkers
  - The subject's job competence and his or her reputation in the workplace
  - The subject's significant prior employment
  - Reasons for job changes
  - The impact the subject would have experienced from a job loss
- Education
  - The subject's formal educational background
  - Other specialized training the subject received (e.g., firearms, defensive tactics)
  - Nature of any problems the subject experienced in a formal academic setting
  - Significant academic achievements and/or failures

- Health
  - The subject's health status
  - The subject's attitude about health and fitness
  - Significant injuries and illnesses during his or her lifetime which may have a current impact
  - Mental health history
  - Any known or suspected substance abuse
  - The subject's usual eating and sleeping habits
- Appearance
  - The subject's usual appearance
  - Any recent changes in weight and when these took place
  - Any physical characteristics that could be viewed as unusual
  - The usual mode of transportation and types of vehicles owned or used
  - The subject's attitude about his or her appearance
- Personality and behavior
  - A description of the subject from those who know him or her
  - The type of person the subject would select as a friend
  - Strengths and weaknesses of the subject
  - The subject's life ambitions
  - The subject's life failures
  - The subject's intelligence level
  - The subject's criminal history and attitude toward law enforcement
  - The subject's reaction to stress
  - Stresses in the subject's life
  - Significant mood changes
  - The subject's religious beliefs and to what level he or she practiced and portrayed those beliefs
  - Recent changes regarding his or her religious beliefs
  - The subject's sexual habits, practices, and attitudes
  - If the subject accepts responsibility for his or her actions or places blame elsewhere
  - The subject's trustworthiness

- Interests
  - The subject's hobbies and pastimes
  - Types of literature, movies, and music the subject enjoys
  - Groups and organizations the subject belongs to now or has belonged to in the past

19.5 Criminal Investigative Analysis (CIA)

CIA is the study and analysis of a person's secret life as opposed to his or her public or private life. The following section outlines the process by which investigators utilize CIA.

19.5.1 CIA Services

Listed below are services offered to law enforcement through crime scene analysis:

- Crime analysis
- Description of offender characteristics in unknown offender cases
- Investigation strategy
- Interviewing techniques
- Search warrant information
- Prosecution strategy
- Expert witness testimony
- National Center for the Analysis of Violent Crime (NCAVC) Coordinator (at least one profile coordinator trained through the NCAVC is assigned to every FBI field office)

19.5.2 Homicide Classification

The following list characterizes the different homicide classifications used in CIA:

- Single—A single homicide involves one victim.
- Double—A double homicide involves two victims during one event at a single location. The victims are usually related or socially acquainted.
- Triple—A triple homicide involves three victims killed during one event and at the same location. The victims likely are related or acquainted with one another.

- Mass—A mass homicide involves four or more victims killed in the same location at the same time. The offender is often located on site and may surrender to authorities or commit suicide.
- Spree—This involves victims at multiple locations with no cooling-off period between homicides. The time between homicides can be minutes or days. The offender is often characterized as having ongoing high levels of excitement. Spree homicide may involve fugitive situations.
- Serial (classic)—This involves two or more victims killed in separate events. The perpetrator is usually acting alone. The homicides are committed over a period ranging from hours to years. Frequently, the method is predatory or stalking with a psychological motive. The offender's behavior and evidence at scenes often reflect sadistic sexual overtones.

19.5.3 Victimology: Key to Crime Analysis

The following information about the victim is key to criminal investigation analysis:

- Age
- Sex
- Race
- Marital status
- Any recent changes in status
- Intelligence
- Lifestyle
- School achievements
- Personality style or characteristics
- Demeanor
- Residence in relation to crime scene
- Sexual adjustment

Analysts try to determine answers to the following questions about the victim:

- Why was the victim selected?
- Why was the victim lured by the method used by the serial killer?

- What feeling was the victim expressing?
- What were the victim's travels or activities prior to death?
- Where was he or she employed?
- Where did he or she live?
- Where was he or she last seen?
- Where was the crime scene?

19.6 Criminal Profiling

Several elements of the crime scene can provide clues to the identity of the killer and his or her motives. This is an important part of catching and convicting a perpetrator.

19.6.1 Profilers versus Detectives

Profilers write detailed profiles, recall a great number of details, describe the suspect in a sex offense more accurately than in a homicide offense, and examine each detail to determine the reason and motivation for an act. Detectives look more to the motivation of the act without looking at the individual reasons.

19.6.2 Investigative Approach to Profiling

When investigators approach profiling, they look at the presentation of the crime scene. It sometimes can be tainted by personnel. The neighboring and surrounding areas also must be examined. Racial, ethnic, and social data are also considered. Photographs are taken of the crime scene, and a color photograph is taken of the victim. Larger photos are better, focusing on the extent of the wounds. The position of the body is photographed from different angles. If the scene is indoors, investigators photograph other rooms and include a sketch or floor plan of the building. The exterior of the building is photographed, including an aerial shot.

Information for a complete profile includes the following items:

- Photographs of the crime scene
- Information on the complex and neighborhood
- Medical examiner's report

- Map of the victim's travels prior to death
- Investigative report of the incident
- Background on the victim

The medical examiner's report should contain the following items:

- Photos to show full extent of the damage
- Number of stabs and cuts
- Number of gunshots wounds and their locations
- Bruises
- Lividity
- Toxicological reports (drugs, alcohol, sperm)
- Wounds and whether they are premortem or postmortem
- Medical examiner's opinion

19.7 Offender Profile Analysis

Analyzing an offender requires an investigator to surmise his or her psychological state, decide whether the crime is an organized or disorganized one, and whether the motives are sexual in nature. Asking the questions listed below is a good way to begin the analysis:

- What method did the offender use to assault the victim?
- Why was that particular victim selected?
- What were the feelings of the offender before and during the attack?
- Why did the offender make the decision to allow the victim to live or die?

How the body is displayed and the psychological profile of a perpetrator are both considered. Displaying a body suggests that the attacker wanted the body found. The way in which the body is displayed indicates whether the perpetrator's desire is to taunt the family, the friends, the police, or the community or whether it is to have the body found out of concern for the victim or the family.

When looking at the psychological profile of a perpetrator, investigators determine his or her characteristics, including the following:

- Sex
- Age range

- Marital status
- Education level
- General employment
- Reaction to police questioning
- Degree of sexual maturity
- Whether the individual might strike again
- If he or she has committed a similar crime in the past
- If he or she has a police record

To determine if the perpetrator has a mental abnormality, investigators complete the following actions:

- Study the nature of the act and the types of people who have committed this offense.
- Analyze the crime scene.
- Examine the background and activities of the victims and those of any known suspects.
- Formulate probable motivating factors.
- Develop a description of the perpetrator based on the characteristics associated with his or her probable psychological makeup.

19.8 Modus Operandi (MO) versus Signature

19.8.1 Modus Operandi

The MO is the behavior that is necessary to successfully commit the crime. It is considered a learned behavior and is developed through trial and error. The MO can be used as a clue for serial crimes, but serial crimes should not be matched by MO alone.

The MO might include a trick to lure the victim into a vehicle or the use of specific restraints when a victim falls asleep. The purpose of the MO is to ensure the success of the crime, protect the offender's identification, and affect the offender's escape. The development of the MO depends on dynamic changes, experience, education, and offender age.

19.8.2 Signature

A signature is that behavior which is unnecessary to commit the crime. It is the subject's "calling card." The signature aspect of the crime should receive greater consideration than the victims' similarities. It can include the use of pornography, restraints, or torture.

The signature introduces the offender's personality into the crime. It may include unusual behavior characteristics (unique or ritualistic) and repetitive behavior. It may be verbal or nonverbal. Here are some examples of signatures:

- Posing
- Foreign object insertion
- Overkill and/or mutilation
- Crime scene adjustment
- Excessive bondage
- Scripting (verbal behavior)

19.9 Organized versus Disorganized Crimes

19.9.1 Organized Crime

Whether the criminal is organized or disorganized depends much on the state of the scene. The following characteristics are indicative of an organized crime scene and criminal:

- Location—The organized perpetrator kills at one location and may move the body to another location (mobility and adaptability). The body may be blatantly displayed, or there may be a concentrated effort to conceal it.
- Weapon—There is typically one weapon of choice. The killer brings it to and takes it away from the scene.
- Souvenir (trophy)—The perpetrator may take a trophy to psychologically relive the crime. He or she may give the item to a significant person in his or her life. Usually this item has intangible value. Sometimes it involves amputation, which may delay identification of the victim. The clothing is sometimes removed and taken as a trophy.
- Miscellaneous—An organized crime may involve penis penetration, sexual experimentation, or psychological or physical torture prior to death. The perpetrator leaves little or no evidence.

Organized criminals are developed. Those who commit organized crime often internalize hurt, anger, and fear. They may have a superior attitude and do senseless acts to overcompensate. The organized criminal is likely described as a troublemaker who is angry at himself or herself, his or her family, or society in general. Often the person acts out in anger. He or she is often in the late teens or early 20s. The person may commit arson or be cruel to animals. He or she selects victims that can be manipulated and dominated.

An organized crime offender is often indifferent to the welfare of society; instead, he or she is irresponsible and self-centered. He or she may have a chameleon personality. This criminal is methodical and cunning and easily and regularly manipulates people. He or she lives some distance from the crime scene and fits into society well. This person is often of above-average intelligence. He or she is sexually competent and may have had inconsistent childhood discipline. The person controlled his or her mood during the crime and may use alcohol during the crime. He or she cruises for victims, but they are chosen randomly. He or she personalizes the victim and controls their conversation. The offender often demands a submissive victim and may use restraints. Overall, the crime scene reflects control.

19.9.2 Disorganized Crime

Listed below are the characteristics found at a disorganized crime scene:

- Location—The victim is killed and left at same location and little effort is given to conceal the body. The scene will be close to the offender's residence or job.
- Weapon—The perpetrator typically uses a weapon of opportunity, and it is often left at or near the scene. The cause of death is often strangulation or blunt trauma. Sometimes there is mutilation of the body with a sharp weapon following death.
- Souvenir—This is usually an object or article of clothing taken as a remembrance (fantasy).
- Miscellaneous—The perpetrator often uses stabbing or slashing to hurt, kill, or mutilate the victim. There may be bite marks on the breasts, buttocks, neck, thighs, or abdomen, and these may have happened postmortem. Sometimes the

perpetrator dissects the body, making an exploratory examination after death or when the victim is unconscious. There may also be blood smearing.

Disorganized criminals are developed over time, and like the organized criminal, they often internalize hurt, anger, and fear. They may become secluded and isolated from the world, rejecting society. They may have a poor self-image and feel inadequate. These criminals often take part in arson, substitute sex, voyeurism, and fantasy. They may be described as nice, quiet, shy, or strange. They commit crimes against the weak and helpless, such as the young or the elderly.

The offender may have a social aversion and find interpersonal relationships difficult. He or she is likely of below-average intelligence, has low birth order status, and may have received harsh discipline as a child. He or she is anxious during the crime but abstains from using alcohol. This type of criminal lives alone, possibly near the crime scene. He or she may have minimal interest in the news and media. He or she depersonalizes and does not talk with victims. He or she may feel rejected and lonely and lacks cunning. This person often commits the crime in frenzy and in close proximity to his or her residence. He or she may be strange in appearance and behavior. He or she usually does not use restraints and may commit a sexual act on the body after death. The crime scene is generally random and sloppy.

19.9.3 Organization to Disorganization

Some factors might transform a crime from organized to disorganized. The reverse does not happen generally. Some of the factors that may cause this transformation are listed below:

- Causal factors
- Youthfulness of the offenders
- Ingestion of alcohol
- Ingestion of drugs
- Lack of criminal experience
- Multiple offenders

Table 19.1   Comparison of the Conditions in Which George Russell's Victims Were Found

	VICTIM 1: MARY ANN POHLREICH	VICTIM 2: CAROL MARIE BEETHE	VICTIM 3: ANDREA S. LEVINE	SIGNATURE ASPECTS CONNECTING DEATHS
Body posed	Yes	Yes	Yes	Yes
Foreign object inserted	Yes	Yes	Yes	Yes
State of dress	Nude	Nude	Nude	Yes
Head/face covered	Yes	Yes	Yes	Yes
Postmortem activity	Yes	Yes	Yes	Yes
Cause of death	Blunt force to head	Blunt force to head	Blunt force to head	Yes
Item(s) taken	Yes	Yes	Yes	Yes
Semen identified	Yes (vaginal)	No	No	No

19.10 Serial Homicide Examples

The following are examples of serial homicides committed in Bellevue, Washington, in 1990. George W. Russell was convicted of these crimes and sentenced to two life sentences plus 28 years in 1991 (*State of Washington v. George W. Russell*, 1994). The case was appealed unsuccessfully in 1994. Table 19.1 provides a chart comparing the conditions in which the victims were found.

Based on this information, the signature aspects of the deaths mentioned in Table 19.1 are the following:

- Foreign object insertion
- Bodies posed nude
- Blunt force to head
- Postmortem activity
- Significant amount of time spent with the bodies
- Bodies not concealed and posed to shock
- Head and face covered—lid/pillow, plastic/sheet
- Items taken from each scene

Bibliography

Ressler, R.K. & Burgess, A.W. (1985). Crime scene and profile characteristics of organized and disorganized murders. *FBI Law Enforcement Bulletin*, Vol. 54, No. 8, pp. 18–25. Retrieved from https://www.ncjrs.gov/pdffiles1 /Digitization/99114-99117NCJRS.pdf.

State of Washington v. George W. Russell, 125 Wn. 2d 24 (1994).

Vecchi, G.M. (2009, Summer). Principles and approaches to criminal investigation (Part 1). *Forensic Examiner*, Vol. 18, No. 2, pp. 8–13.

Vecchi, G.M. (2009, Fall). Principles and approaches to criminal investigation (Part 2). *Forensic Examiner*, Vol. 18, No. 3, pp. 8–12.

Vecchi, G.M. (2009, Winter). Principles and approaches to criminal investigation (Part 3). *Forensic Examiner*, Vol. 18, No. 4), pp. 10–15.

Vecchi, G.M. (2010, Spring). Principles and approaches to criminal investigation (Part 4). *Forensic Examiner*, Vol. 19, No. 1: pp. 10–15.

Westveer, A.E., Jr. (2002). *Managing death investigations* (Vol. 1, Fifth ed.). Washington, DC: U.S. Department of Justice Federal Bureau of Investigation. (Used with permission.)

20

DEATH BY HOMICIDE

20.1 Death Scene Analysis

Crime scene analysis is a combination of criminalistics and criminology. Criminalistics is the application of science to physical evidence, such as bloodstains, DNA, and bullet trajectories. Criminology is the psychological angle, which involves studying crime scenes for motives, traits, and behaviors that help interpret the evidence.

20.1.1 Outside versus Inside

Outdoor body discovery scenes are categorized by how the body is found: buried, exposed, or submerged in water. If the body is buried, soil samples must be tested for the presence of added substances, such as quicklime. Bodies found in water must be handled with special procedures. Corpses left outside may have undergone changes unrelated to their demise. The science of taphonomy (the study of decomposition) can assist with complex cases, since it coordinates several areas of forensic science specifically for outdoor death investigations.

With indoor body discovery scenes, the crime scene is generally more preserved. However, the corpse may have been dismembered and stored for a long period. Bodies have been found in freezers, attics, and storage facilities.

20.1.2 Cause and Manner

Death investigation involves determining how the death occurred, when it happened, and what caused it. The cause of death is whatever led to it, such as a lethal knifing, fatal bullet wound, or asphyxiation by strangling. Pathologists are concerned with both the proximate cause (the chain of events leading up to the death) and the immediate cause (the injury or disease that killed the person).

The manner of death falls into one of five categories:

- Natural—The victim died in a nonhostile environment.
- Accidental—The person fell victim to a hostile environment.
- Suicide—The person caused his or her own death.
- Homicide—Someone else caused the victim's death.
- Undetermined—Some deaths fit easily into one of these categories, while others might require a thorough investigation before a determination is made.

20.2 Reconstruction: The Pyramid Approach

Incident reconstruction involves identifying, locating, and examining potential evidence to determine what happened and in what order it occurred. Detectives look at all the pieces and try to form a coherent and accurate puzzle. Along the way, they must properly record and file chain of custody forms for the evidence, so that it is available for reexamination. A clue might be as fragile as dust particles from a foreign environment or as obvious as large, gaping wound patterns from a specific type of weapon. Sometimes the evidence is sparse; other times it is overwhelming. Detectives must use logic to make their way through it all to arrive at the proper conclusions.

The process of investigation moves through several stages of a pyramid as it crystallizes and becomes more refined (see Figure 20.1). The pyramid's base is knowledge, which involves gathering information from many sources, including careful observation. As things stand

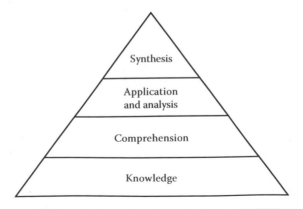

Figure 20.1   The process of investigation.

out, the next level is comprehension. Following this is application and analysis. By the time investigators arrive at the top of the pyramid, investigators are working on synthesizing what they know. They have considered all investigative processes to derive a specific understanding of the incident. The goal is to pull everything together into a single theory without violating known facts or leaving out anything significant.

20.2.1 Solvability Factors

Former homicide detective Robert Keppel undertook a study to address empirical research for specific solvability factors. He found that the more information there is on the times and distances that separate a murder victim from where he or she was last seen, the location of the contact between the killer and the victim, where the fatal assault occurred, and where the body was discovered, the more likely it is that the crime can be solved and the killer identified. Thus, the careful, comprehensive collection and organization of information is crucial for case management.

20.2.2 The Murder Book

A murder book is a case file that provides the framework for a given investigation. It contains the crime scene photos, autopsy reports, witness statements, crime scene map and sketches, investigative notes, and forensic reports. It also identifies computer support and technology needs along with the results of any database searches.

Murder books also may offer a set of core procedural requirements about handling and storing evidence and working with a task force. They can provide protocol for handling the media in the event of a high-profile incident. As incidents grow more complex, either because there are multiple victims or because the investigation crosses jurisdictions or periods, the need for clear guidelines is imperative.

Although currently there is no standardized model for homicide investigations, several researchers have identified the need for a best-practices approach for processing and organizing information efficiently. There should be a murder book protocol that can be applied universally.

20.3 The Initial Call

When a potential homicide initially is discovered, a call goes out to authorities, generally via 911. A dispatcher notifies patrol units, who arrive and decide whether they need other personnel (e.g., paramedics and homicide unit). They note the time and record any other pertinent observations.

20.4 The Scene

Investigators must assume that whoever was at the scene has left something there or has taken something from the scene—probably both. This is known as Locard's exchange principle: every contact leaves a trace.

If a perpetrator is present, the officer makes an arrest. Any and all suspects are detained. Otherwise, the officers control the scene by marking the perimeter with tape or a clearly marked barrier and by keeping everyone clear of the defined area. This prevents the destruction of evidence. If a body must be moved for any reason, then the officer must make accurate notes, photograph the pose of the corpse when found, and transport the body in that same position, if possible.

20.4.1 Evidence Collection

Under the direction of the detective, crime scene technicians generally search for evidence in a way that clears a path to the body. The officer in charge also directs the coroner or medical examiner through the scene and to the body. The body is removed by lifting and wrapping it in a clean, white sheet to preserve evidence.

Evidence collected at the scene may serve several purposes:

- Prove that a crime has been committed
- Indicate the key aspects of the crime
- Establish the identities of the victim or suspect (or determine what kind of investigation must be done to identify them and how the two interacted)
- Corroborate (or not) any testimony given by witnesses
- Help to exonerate a suspect who is innocent
- Provide leads for further investigation
- Pressure suspects into giving confessions

20.4.2 Behavioral Evidence Analysis

The homicide narrative shows up most clearly in behavioral clues. Specialists who can accurately interpret this behavior are increasingly in demand. This can mean evaluating behavioral patterns that link one crime to another (as with serial murder, arson, or rape) or interpreting psychological aberrations.

In the United States, there are two basic types of behavioral consulting for homicides—behavioral profiling and psychological autopsy—to help determine the manner of someone's death. Both involve the interpretation of behavior evident at a scene in an attempt to resolve an open question relevant to making decisions in an investigation.

Criminal profiling, used most often with multiple homicides, is a process used to analyze a specific crime or a series of crimes in order to develop a behavioral composite of an unknown offender. The underlying assumption is that personality dictates behavior. Therefore, what an offender shows at a crime scene is what he or she will show in other facets of his or her life. In truth, there is generally a wide range of behaviors to interpret in any given crime scene.

20.4.3 Development of a Theory

Cases are assigned on a rotating basis or based on an officer's area of expertise. Once assigned, the lead detective follows through until the case is solved with a conviction or shelved as a cold case. Homicide detectives form initial hypotheses that become guiding theories for organizing and prioritizing leads. They attempt to determine the following information:

- Who committed the homicide
- Who else might have been involved
- What happened
- When it happened
- How it happened
- Where it happened
- Who the victim was
- Why the crime was committed
- What evidence is there to help prove the motive and establish the crime

The incident is assigned a case number to keep evidence organized and the chain of custody intact. Decisions about what to do next depend on the type of crime committed.

20.5 Legal Requirements

Everything homicide investigators do is potentially for exhibit and cross-examination in a courtroom. They work for the state, so they have a legal goal: find evidence that will prove a case against a perpetrator within legal guidelines. The court system and its rules of admissibility are always in the background, influencing the evidence collection process. Fact finders must feel confident of the evidentiary process. Evidence handled badly can be successfully challenged, letting a dangerous killer walk free. Thus, part of the training should involve education about legal demands.

20.6 The Body

Homicide detectives have access to unique forms of evidence such as bodies. Victims of homicide offer a microcosm of evidence that can help reconstruct the homicide narrative. Often, detectives attend the autopsy to see the primary items of interest on the body itself.

20.6.1 The Autopsy Procedure

The medical examiner or coroner decides whether there is to be an autopsy, which generally occurs for any unattended death and always for a homicide. The assumption of homicide may be mistaken, but it is better to assume it and operate accordingly than not. If insects are present, investigators work with an entomologist. If the corpse is deteriorated to skeletal form, they rely on a forensic anthropologist.

Before anything is done, the body should be photographed in various states: both clothed (if it was clothed when found) and unclothed, and both dirty and cleaned up. It is x-rayed, weighed, fingerprinted, and measured, and identifying marks are recorded. Old and new injuries are noted, along with tattoos and scars. Trace evidence, such as hair and fiber, is collected off the body and from under the fingernails. The wrapping sheet, along with clothing and trace evidence, is stored to be sent for analysis. Anything that is wet is air-dried. In cases of suspected suicide by gunshot, hands are swabbed for gunpowder residue.

20.6.2 Wound Analysis

Injuries are generally categorized as blunt force trauma, gunshot, sharp force trauma, and asphyxiation. In all cases, the number of wounds is recorded, and each wound is carefully measured and its characteristics are described.

A blunt force injury comes from impact with a blunt object—something with no sharp edges. The autopsy shows the direction of impact, the type of object that caused it, and how often the contact was made. A suspect weapon may or may not be available. If it is, wound patterns can be matched to the weapon.

Blunt force injuries can cause lacerations, which are tearing injuries from impact and have ragged or abraded edges and bruising. There may also be abrasions, which are friction injuries that remove superficial layers of skin. Contusions are ruptures of small blood vessels.

Crushing wounds can result from blunt force violence where the skin is close to bone, and these wounds tend to bleed into the tissues. Often they are made by blows from an implement such as a hammer. Bite marks also are a form of a crushing wound and can be crucial evidence.

With gunshot wounds, the pathologist looks for tattooing and stippling (burns from gas and powder residue) or fouling (soot) around the wound. The pathologist measures the size of the exit and entry wounds and extracts any bullets left in the body to determine the type of gun from which they came. Photos are taken to estimate how close the shooter was to the victim. The broader the area of stippling, for example, the further away the gun was held. Contact wounds, in which the gun was held against the skin, often leave an imprint from the muzzle and more powerful guns cause gaping wounds with powder residue and blowback—hot gases from the gun that fail to penetrate the body and blow back to the exterior, ripping the skin.

Rifled weapons (rifles and many handguns) fire single bullets, stabilizing their trajectory with grooves in the barrel. Unless they are too damaged, bullets will show some characteristics of the grooves. The weapon also may eject identifying shell casings. If no casings are found at the scene, it may indicate use of a revolver. Smoothbore weapons, such as shotguns, have no grooves and often fire multiple pellets.

Entrance wounds generally are round and surrounded by some abrasion. Exit wounds are irregular and bruised, lack stippling, and are larger (typically) than the entrance wound. They can also show protruding skin. However, there are cases where the two types of wounds look too similar to tell which is which. Detailed work on the trajectory path inside the body might be required.

Knife or incised (sharp force) wounds pose a puzzle. The pathologist must make a distinction between cut wounds and stab (or puncture) wounds and between different types of piercing implements, such as an ice pick and a small knife. A cut is longer than it is deep, while a stab wound is deeper than it is long. Some wounds are defensive, such as cuts made on the palms or fingers of a victim's hands. Cuts associated with suicidal gestures are known as hesitation wounds, made as the person attempts to inflict self-damage.

Asphyxiation results from cutting off oxygen to the brain. Before a homicide can be ascertained in such cases, another possibility must be eliminated: autoerotic hypoxia. Hanging by the neck, obstruction of airways with an object, smothering, and strangulation can cause asphyxia. Each has specific manifestations. Carbon monoxide poisoning also can cause asphyxia.

20.6.3 Postmortem Interval

If insects are present (typical of bodies left outside but sometimes also on bodies left inside), investigators work with an entomologist. Due largely to more than 30 years of work done at the Forensic Anthropology Center in Knoxville, Tennessee, quite a bit is known about the progression of insect activity and rates of decomposition under diverse conditions.

At the scene, the homicide detective and a medical examiner or coroner make an informed guess at the approximate time when the individual expired. This is known as the time of death determination, which differs from the time-since-death, or the postmortem interval. Time-since-death is the amount of time that has passed between when the decedent died and when he or she was found. Thus, if someone died on Monday and was not found until Friday, the time-since-death would be 5 days, and the time of death would be between 10:00 a.m. and 2:00 p.m. on Monday. Both determinations are important for incident reconstruction, as well as supporting or breaking a suspect's alibi. Many of the factors involved in these determinations overlap.

Time of death can be difficult to state with certainty unless there was a witness who looked at a watch. No single factor is wholly reliable, since all are affected by diverse conditions, but taken together they can provide a fairly reasonable estimate of the time–since-death. Specifically, these factors include the following:

- Body temperature (algor mortis)—After death, bodies stop breathing, and without oxygen, they cannot maintain the normal temperature of 98.6°F. Typically, a body cools at the rate of approximately 1 to 1.5°F per hour until it takes on the temperature of its surroundings. However, if the weather is cold, the body temperature may drop more quickly. An obese person tends to cool more slowly than someone with little body fat. Layers of clothing can insulate a corpse, and other factors (e.g., exercise) can raise the body temperature just prior to death.

- Discoloration (livor mortis)—Also known as postmortem lividity or hypostasis, this refers to the dark purple color of the body part that is found closest to the ground where it is lying. It appears about 1 to 2 hours after death and becomes fixed within 8 to 10 hours. Lividity is caused by the cessation of the heart's pumping action, which allows the red and white blood cells to separate. The red cells then settle into the lowest parts. Discolored skin that blanches when touched indicates that lividity is not yet permanent. The death was more than 2 hours earlier but probably not as long as 10 hours earlier.

- Rigor mortis—Immediately after death, bodies go limp, but within 15 minutes to 15 hours (with average time being 2 to 3 hours), accumulating waste products stiffen the muscles. It first shows in the face, lower jaw, and neck. Over the next 12 to 18 hours, it spreads throughout the body, lasting as long as 36 hours. Beginning in the head and neck area, the body loosens up again. This process may take as long as 10 hours from start to finish.

- Ocular—If the eyes remain open after death, a thin film forms on the surface. The potassium content from the breakdown of red blood cells enters the eyes and within 2 to 3 hours, the eyes look cloudy. Eyes that are closed develop the same conditions, but it takes much longer.
- Food digestion—This is based on an assumption that the stomach digests food and empties into the intestines at a predictable rate, but many things can influence the amount of time this process takes. The type of food, the body's metabolizing rate, the presence of drugs or medication, and the person's emotional condition prior to death may all have some effect on how quickly food is processed. A light meal may remain in the stomach for about 2 hours; a heavy meal may remain for 4 to 6 hours. Examination of the small intestine traces the path of the food.
- Personal factors—Other factors during the investigation may also play a part. If a witness can place the person alive at a specific time in a specific place, then that person was not deceased at that time.
- Decay or decomposition rates—Because bodies may be found at any time from seconds after death to years later, death investigators must be familiar with the stages of decomposition. The rate at which these stages occur depends on certain environmental factors, such as air temperature, whether the body was buried in earth or left in water, whether it was exposed to the sun or wrapped in a blanket, or whether it was placed in a cool cellar. Injured areas decompose more quickly than other areas, especially if there is insect activity.

20.6.4 Stages of Decomposition

Aside from those indicators mentioned above, the stages of decomposition take place as follows:

1. When the heart stops beating, the skin starts to look waxy.
2. The eyes flatten, and the extremities turn a bluish color.
3. Desiccation occurs on drying mucous membranes.
4. The body then putrefies, which is signaled by a greenish discoloration in the skin. About 2 or 3 days after death, putrefaction,

caused by the proliferation of bacteria, starts in the lower abdomen. Soon this will spread over the rest of the abdomen and into the thighs and chest. The face will swell and become unrecognizable.

5. A foul odor develops. Bacteria in the intestines produce gases that bloat the body and, eventually, turn the skin black. By the second week after death, bloating makes the tongue, breasts, scrotum, and eyes protrude and pushes the intestines out through the rectum.

6. Soon the skin blisters and detaches. Then internal organs break open and liquefy.

7. Under certain conditions, such as bodies submerged in water, a cheesy substance called adipocere forms, while fatty tissues harden and keep the body preserved.

Left alone in a warm and moist climate, a body can decompose to a skeleton within a few weeks, while in other conditions it can take months or even years. Water preserves twice as long as open air, and burial extends that time frame by several weeks. In a hot, dry climate, some bodies merely mummify. Although the postmortem interval determination increasingly gets more difficult to ascertain as time passes, decomposed bodies that have tissue or hair intact can be subjected to toxicology analysis for potential cause of death.

Bibliography

Geberth, V. (2006). *Practical homicide investigation: Tactics, procedures, and forensic techniques* (Fourth ed.). Boca Raton, FL: CRC Press.

Keppel, R.D. & Birnes, W.J. (2003). *The psychology of serial killer investigations: The grisly business unit.* San Diego, CA: Academic Press.

Ramsland, K. (2007). *Beating the devil's game: A history of forensic science and criminal investigation.* New York: Penguin Publishing.

Sachs, J.S. (2001). *Corpse: Nature, forensics, and the struggle to pinpoint time of death.* New York: Perseus Publishing.

Weis, J.G. & Keppel, R.D. (Eds.). (2010). *Murder: A multidisciplinary anthology of readings* (Fourth ed.). Hoboken, NJ: Wiley.

Zugibe, F. & Carroll, D.L. (2005). *Dissecting death: Secrets of a medical examiner.* New York: Broadway Books.

21

SUDDEN INFANT DEATH SYNDROME (SIDS)

SIDS, the most common cause of death for those under 1 year old, can be characterized as a situation where a well-cared-for infant between 1 and 6 months old is found unresponsive in his or her bed. The infant may have exhibited mild cold symptoms, but a thorough autopsy reveals no adequate cause of death.

The definition of SIDS has changed over time. SIDS used to be the death of an infant in apparent good health who dies suddenly and in whose case an autopsy does not reveal a commonly accepted cause of death. The current definition of SIDS is the sudden, unexpected death of an infant under 1 year of age that remains unexplained after a complete postmortem investigation, including autopsy, examination of the death scene, and review of the case history.

When autopsies are performed on SIDS victims, the findings are nonspecific. They often find petechial hemorrhages and pulmonary congestion. SIDS is not caused by suffocation, vomiting, or choking. It is not contagious, and it cannot be predicted. It does not cause pain or suffering to the infant.

A diagnosis should not be made without a full examination and investigation. For instance, death due to child abuse can easily be and is often mistaken for SIDS. This is why investigating the death is so important.

SIDS can occur in every situation. Here are some statistics about SIDS:

- SIDS occurs in 1 in 1000 live births in white babies.
- SIDS occurs in 11 in 1000 live births in nonwhite babies.
- Male–female ratio = 3:2.
- 85% of SIDS cases occur between birth and 6 months.

Although SIDS occurs in all socioeconomic groups, the most common backgrounds include children from overcrowded urban areas, children living in poverty, and children with reduced prenatal care. Also, illegitimate children die from SIDS more often than other children do.

21.1 SIDS or Child Abuse

Investigators look for signs to determine if the infant died as a result of SIDS or child abuse.

With SIDS death, the victim appears to be asleep. The victim may be twisted in his or her bedclothes. Also, there may be purple-spotted markings on his or her head and facial areas. The victim may have frothy or blood-tinged mucus or vomit present in or around the nose or mouth.

In cases of child abuse or neglect, the caretaker's story does not feel right to the investigators, and it may not account for all of the baby's injuries. The victim may have disfiguring welts, bumps, or broken bones. The siblings of the victim may also show signs of child abuse. There may also be evidence of neglect, such as malnourishment.

21.2 Investigating SIDS

The following lists outline the information and evidence that should be collected when investigating a possible SIDS death.

21.2.1 Evidence

- Infant's bedding (sheets, blankets, etc.)
- Objects in crib (toys, bottles, etc.)
- Unusual or dangerous items found near the death scene (plastic bags, sharp objects, paint chips, etc.)
- Medications—even adult medications (investigators should take these with them to the hospital)

21.2.2 Identifying Information

- Name
- Date of birth

- Age
- Race
- Sex
- Address
- Names of mother and father
- Telephone number

21.2.3 Scene Information

- Address
- Time of last feeding
- Time last seen alive, by whom, and the activity in which the deceased was engaged at the time
- The person who found the deceased and this person's relationship to the deceased

21.2.4 Caretaker Demeanor

- Orientation
- Responses and if they were appropriate to the situation
- If medicated or intoxicated

21.2.5 State of Bedding

- Type of bed (water bed, crib with wide side rails or slats, lax or improvised bed, playpen, parent's bed, etc.)
- Type of sheets (plastic, cloth, etc.)
- Type of mattress
- Presence of pillows or blankets
- Position of infant in relation to the mattress, aid rails, toys, and bedcovers
- Compression of face, neck, or chest
- Environment
- Cleanliness and organization level
- Thermal state
- Presence of vermin
- Presence of food

21.2.6 Resuscitation Efforts Made

- Cardiopulmonary resuscitation, tube, or intravenous therapy
- Given by whom

21.2.7 Mother's Pregnancy History

- Previous births—Note if they were premature, stillbirths, or parity.
- Complications—Note any hypertension, infection (type), severe vomiting, ruptured membranes and bleeding, diabetes, medications, and illegal drugs, alcohol, or smoking (amount).
- Delivery details—Note the gestation, whether it was multiple births (twins, triplets, etc.) or a single birth, if it was a vaginal or cesarean birth, if the baby was breech, the names of the hospital and physician, and the duration of labor.
- Prenatal details—Note the birth weight, infant response, if special care was needed, and the length of stay and treatment.

21.2.8 Details about the Infant

- Formula or breast-fed
- Appetite
- Last feeding
- Immunizations (Ask about diphtheria, pertussis [whooping cough], and tetanus vaccine, hepatitis B vaccine, and *Haemophilus influenzae* type b vaccine; when they were given; and if there were any fever or seizures afterward.)

21.2.9 Evidence of Recent Illness

- Duration
- Appetite during illness
- Distention of abdomen
- Recent medications (of infant and caretaker)
- Medical attention
- Recent falls and injuries

- Type of illness
  - Upper respiratory—Note if there was a stuffy nose, wheezing, congestion, or cough, and note the type of cry.
  - Intestinal—Note if there was vomiting (color, duration), diarrhea (color, duration), or fever.
  - Rashes—Note when, where, and the duration.
  - Allergies—Note if the skin, lungs, or bowels were affected.
  - Seizures—Note when they occurred, the type of seizure, and the treatment given.

21.2.10 Family History

- Age and health of the victim's parents and siblings
- Family history of SIDS—Note when it happened, the age of the person who died from it, the diagnosis received, the relation to the victim, and if there was any heart or lung disease present.

21.2.11 Development of Victim

- Type of eater (good, slow, fussy)
- Irritability
- Looks at parents
- Holds head up
- Rolls over

21.2.12 Caregiver Information

- Name
- Age
- Address
- Experience

21.2.13 Physician or Institution Caregiver

- Name
- Address

- Phone number
- Compare growth chart (present) and physician data with information given by child's caregiver.

Bibliography

Westveer, A.E., Jr. (2002). *Managing death investigations*, Vol. 1. (Fifth ed.). Washington, DC: U.S. Department of Justice Federal Bureau of Investigation. (Used with permission.)

22

DEATH BY ASPHYXIA, FIRE, AND DROWNING

22.1 Asphyxia

Asphyxia is defined as a lack of oxygen or an excess of carbon dioxide in the blood. It is usually caused by an interruption of breathing that causes unconsciousness and death.

Pressure to the neck can cause death by asphyxia. Unconsciousness begins in a matter of seconds. The heart may continue to beat for 15 to 20 minutes. Physical force placed on the base of the neck may cause the tongue to project between the teeth with the exposed portion becoming dry and dark (postmortem artifact).

Broken bones or cartilages are rarely caused by asphyxia except in judicial hanging where the cervical vertebrae are fractured and death is instantaneous. In all cases of asphyxia, the face tends to be to be congested or discolored (cyanosis). Petechial hemorrhage may be observed in the face, conjuncture of the eye, and the mucous membrane of the mouth and throat.

Asphyxia can happen in a homicide or suicide, but it can also be from natural causes, such as heart failure or pneumonia, or be accidental, such as an allergic reaction. There are various types of asphyxia examined below.

22.1.1 Compression of the Neck

Compressing the neck is one type of asphyxia. The amounts of pressure necessary to cause asphyxiation are listed below:

- Jugular veins—4 to 5 lb
- Carotid arteries—11 lb

407

- Trachea—33 lb
- Vertebral arteries—66 lb

22.1.2 Hanging

Hanging is the suspension or partial suspension of the body. The body provides the restricting force for cutting off oxygen. The blood supply to the brain ceases very quickly, and the airway is generally obstructed in hangings. Respiration ceases quickly. A narrow depression, or furrow, on the neck of the victims tends to angle toward suspension point. There may be abrasions or contusions, and fingers may be trapped under the ligature (this is different from manual strangulation). In hangings that are not total suspension, internal bleeding or local hemorrhage is uncommon. If a fall is involved, as in judicial hangings, some tearing of internal muscles, organs, and blood vessels may occur, and there may be some bone fractures or damage to the cervical vertebrae.

Most hangings are typically suicides, and investigators look for the hanging groove—a distinct mark on the neck full of details (twisting, knots, irregularities, width of the rope). Murder by hanging is considered rare, and if used, it is typically on children or unconscious individuals. The murder usually takes place first, and then the murderer hangs the individual to give the appearance of suicide.

This is a common form of suicide in inmates. Those who are arrested while intoxicated and those who are recently incarcerated are at a higher risk of suicide, especially within the first 24 hours. If jailers consider an inmate a potential risk, suicide precautions should be implemented by regular observation and removing anything that an inmate can use to harm himself or herself.

When an inmate does commit suicide, families are often highly upset. The death occurred while the decedent was under another's care (jailers), and the family was denied access to the subject. The family is often angered at the jailer for not being able to prevent the death. Sometimes, there are allegations that the police murdered the subject. These cases should be treated as homicides at the outset. It is highly unlikely that an investigation will uncover a homicide. If it does, another inmate is usually the one who committed the crime. Officers in charge of jails and prisons contact an outside agency to lead the investigation. They also try to disturb the scene as little as possible. A medical examiner is used to process the scene and complete the autopsy to exclude trauma.

22.1.3 Strangulation

Strangulation is the squeezing of the neck arteries, causing an interruption of the supply of air to the lungs. A struggle is generally a precursor to strangulation, so injuries can usually be found on other parts of the body as well. There are two types of strangulation: manual and ligature.

22.1.3.1 Manual Manual strangulation is done with the hands (throttling) or arm. In manual strangulation, death can immediately occur from shock. Investigators look for fingernail marks on both sides of the throat. From the number of marks on each side of the throat, an investigator can typically determine if the perpetrator is right- or left-handed. In cases of manual strangulation, the autopsy finds the face suffused with blood and conjunctival petechiae, which is most visible above the compression point. There may also be abrasions to the face, fingertip bruises (oval bruises less than 1 in. in diameter), injury to the neck, and fingernail marks from the struggle. Vertical marks may be from the assailant's hand in the act of strangulation, while horizontal marks may be from the victim trying to remove the assailant's hands. Manual strangulation is often seen in sexual homicide.

22.1.3.2 Ligature When a ligature is used in strangulation, hemorrhage may be present between the strap muscles and the ligature. Abrasions may be present due to a struggle. There will usually be a furrow or groove on the neck that is lower than that of a hanging. When done with a rope or cord, strangulation is generally considered murder, but there is a possibility of suicide.

22.1.4 Obstruction of the Airway

Obstruction of the airway is caused by choking or a blockage of the internal airway by a foreign object. This is often accidental, such as adults choking in a restaurant or children choking on marbles or balloons.

22.1.5 Smothering

Smothering is the blockage of the internal airway or the nose and mouth. This is more common in infants. Suffocation occurs when a pillow or other soft object is pressed against the face. When an object with soft material is used, there are typically no marks on the victim, but an investigator may find saliva or mucus on the object that could prove useful in determining the perpetrator. If a hand is used, an investigator may find scratches on the face of the victim. Plastic bags or gags are also used to smother victims.

22.1.6 Compression of the Chest

Compression of the chest is essentially being squeezed to death. When the chest is compressed, the normal mechanism for respiration cannot occur. This is generally considered to be an accident (e.g., trampled by a crowd or buried by a heavy object). External injuries from squeezing are considerable and easily interpreted.

22.1.7 Depletion of Oxygen

A depletion of oxygen happens when there is a sudden loss of cabin pressure at high altitudes or when a person has already consumed the available oxygen in a sealed space.

22.1.8 Replacement of Oxygen

This is the replacement of oxygen in the body, also known as chemical intoxication. Different types are explained below:

- Carbon monoxide (CO)—This restricts red blood cells from carrying oxygen to the tissues of the body.
- Cyanide intoxication—This prevents body cells from utilizing the oxygen carried to them by the blood.

- Central nervous system depressants—These inhibit the respiratory centers, causing respiratory depression.

22.1.9 Positional Asphyxiation

In most cases, positional asphyxiation occurs in victims who are intoxicated. The victim is inverted so that the lungs cannot amply exchange air. This may also happen in police in-custody deaths when an officer is hog-tying a criminal. This is an effective method of restraint where an officer ties together the feet and hands of the prisoner, usually behind the prisoner's back. It helps control combative individuals but has led to deaths.

In cases of positional asphyxiation, the autopsy finds hemorrhage in soft tissues of the chest and the abdomen and fascial or conjunctival petechiae with acute congestion. There may be rib fractures. These symptoms may also be found in death cases of smothering or deaths of infants while in bed with an adult. In infant death cases, SIDS must be excluded, which is difficult if not impossible.

22.1.10 Cyanide

Cyanide blocks cellular respiration. Death can come rapidly if the victim is in a confined location that has a high concentration of cyanide. Death may take several minutes at a lower concentration. The autopsy will find bright red (cherry red) livor mortis and tissues if cyanide was the cause. The toxicology report will have difficulty proving cyanide levels.

22.1.11 Hydrogen Sulfide

Hydrogen sulfide is commonly used in the petroleum industry. Hydrogen sulfide emits a distinct rotten egg odor. It can be found in wells, sewers, and manure pits. In these cases, the autopsy will find dark livor mortis and tissues (cyanotic). Use extreme caution if there are more than two dead animals or humans on the scene with no visible injuries evident to explain sudden death.

22.2 Death by Fire

Fire can cause death in many different ways. Victims can die from heat, flames, toxic gases, and asphyxiation. When a victim dies from a fire, investigators may see a contraction of muscles, fractures in large bones or the skull, and a splitting of the skin. Two-thirds of all fire fatalities are the result of asphyxiation. This likely happens because CO is produced in most fires since the oxygen level is too low to allow complete combustion of all available carbon compounds. CO combines with the blood to form carboxyhemoglobin, which restricts the amount of oxygen carried by the blood. Here are the human reactions to different concentrations of CO in the blood:

- 0% to 10%—Slight loss of mental sharpness
- 10% to 20%—Slight headache and dilation of skin
- 20% to 30%—Severe headaches
- 30% to 40%—Severe headache, weakness, dizziness, confusion, nausea, vomiting, and collapse
- 40% to 50%—Fainting, rapid breathing, collapse, and possible death
- 50% to 60%—Fainting, rapid breathing, possible coma, convulsions, irregular respiration, and possible death
- 60% to 70%—Convulsions, depressed heart action, and death
- 70% to 80% (and higher)—Weak pulse, respiratory failure, and death

There are also different classifications of burns that victims might receive in a fire:

- First degree—Burned area is red, swollen, and painful.
- Second degree—Burned area is typically sun blistered; scarring may occur.
- Third degree—Entire thickness of the skin is destroyed; scarring is usual.
- Fourth degree—There is complete destruction of the skin and charring of underlying tissues.

The severity of these burns depends on the intensity of the heat and flames, the length of time the victim was exposed, and any chemical components present in the fire.

22.2.1 Investigation of Fire Deaths

There are various manners of death associated with fire: homicide, suicide, accidental, natural, and undetermined. An investigation is required to determine which of these happened in each specific case.

Here are some terms related to fire investigations:

- Accelerant—Any substance used to accelerate the fire
- Arson—The crime of maliciously and intentionally or recklessly starting a fire or causing an explosion
- Burn patterns—Damage created by flame
- Fire—Rapid oxidation with the evolution of heat and light
- Fire cause—The circumstances under which fuel, air, or oxygen and an ignition source come together
- Plant—Items used by arsonist to increase or boost the fire intensity (flammable liquid-soaked clothing, cans of gasoline, etc.)
- Point of origin—The exact physical location where a source of ignition and a fuel come together
- Pyrolysis—The transformation of a compound into one or more substances by heat alone
- Pyromaniac—A pathological fire setter
- Serial arsonist or fire setter—A person who has set three or more separate fires at different times
- Source of ignition—A heat-producing device or substance
- Trailer—Item used by an arsonist to carry the fire from one area to another (flammable liquid, smokeless gunpowder, newspaper, etc.)

22.2.1.1 Investigative Tools   The history, autopsy, toxicology reports, and investigation of the scene are the main tools to start an investigation. When examining the scene, investigators use photographs and sketches. Bodies must be examined and moved very carefully. The debris under the body is sifted through for evidence. Clothes or cloths smelling of accelerants should be collected and placed in a clean, airtight container (a new, metal paint can-style container). Firefighters, police officers, forensic pathologists, toxicologists, radiologists, odontologists, and anthropologists are included in the investigation.

22.2.1.2 Identification of the Victim   If remains are human, investigators determine if the victim is male or female. It is not unusual for male genitalia and female breasts to be destroyed by fire, so this may not be easy. The internal sex organs are used to determine this. Also, investigators determine if the victim was alive at the time of the fire. If soot deposits are discovered within the larynx and the trachea, the victim was alive during the fire. The bones, blood, organs, hair, and teeth are examined to identify the victim. Weight and length are unreliable factors because these can change in the fire. The teeth are the most reliable form of identification. It is essential to determine the specific cause and manner of death and the reason the victim did not escape. Below are reasons the victim may have failed to escape:

- Blocked escape routes
- Heavy smoke
- Overpowering fumes
- Explosion
- Intense heat
- Drug or alcohol use
- Physically or mentally unable

Everyone involved in the investigation should help determine the answers to these questions.

22.2.2 Arson Filicide

Arson filicide is a parent killing his or her children through fire. There are three types of arson filicide:

- Acutely psychotic
- Spouse revenge
- Murder for profit (collect life insurance)

22.2.2.1 Characteristics of Arson Filicide   The victims of arson filicide are often very young children. The crime generally takes place at night or early in the morning. It may be staged (e.g., the children had been killed before the fire began and then placed in bed). Oftentimes, a flammable liquid or accelerant is used on the fire; this is very crucial to the case. Sometimes, the escape routes are blocked. The perpetrators often think that the fire will destroy this evidence. The homes are often rented. The parents are typically in the mid-20s to mid-30s. In some cases, the mother (typically older) may have had other children who died in deaths indicated to be SIDS.

The perpetrator may also be a stepparent or a parent's lover. The parent figure will state he or she was in bed when the fire occurred and then utilized halfhearted rescue attempts. The parents often show the following signs that may indicate arson filicide:

- No sign of exposure to fire—No heat exposure, watering eyes, red skin, or singed hair
- Inappropriate behavior (front lawn scenario)—Little or no grief exhibited, little said about victims, much said about material losses (clothes, stereo, TV, etc.), declarations about the future
- Little mistakes—Careless comments made with neighbors before the fire occurred or not being appropriately dressed for having been awakened by a fire (not in nightclothes, hair and makeup are fixed, etc.)
- Little income—Families usually known to social service agencies, indicating a lack of income

22.2.2.2 Investigation of Arson Filicide   Begin the investigation with various interviews. Investigators should interview firefighters, witnesses, neighbors, friends, and relatives of the parents, as well as the parents of the children's playmates. These people should be interviewed separately from each other. The interviews cannot be too detailed. Investigators go step by step through the process of the fire, beginning with how the person became aware of it and what happened next. They focus on the smallest details, such as time or duration, making note of any observations they may have and considering a walk-through of the scene. Microinterview techniques—going through what the witnesses heard, saw, felt, or smelled—may also be used. Details of the interview are documented.

Then, investigators move on to background checks of the parents. If the parent is unmarried, the insurance coverage on the children is checked. It is also determined if a boyfriend or girlfriend is in the picture. If so, he or she must be interviewed. Investigators ask about the relationship between the couple and the person's attitude toward the significant other's children. If the parents are married, investigators ask about problems in the marriage, financial difficulty, or if either spouse has ever expressed the desire to be free of children.

Often, foul play is not suspected when it should be. Cremation of the victims should be delayed until the lab results are returned and the interviews are completed. When the remains are autopsied, investigators must insist upon photographing each victim separately. X-rays and blood tests are also performed on the victims.

22.2.3 Heat-Related Illnesses

Listed here are heat-related illnesses of which investigators should be aware.

22.2.3.1 Heat Exhaustion   Heat exhaustion is characterized by hyperthermia, heat cramps, progressive lassitude, vomiting, tachycardia, and hypotension. The body temperature may be normal or slightly elevated. Heat exhaustion happens because of water and salt depletion.

22.2.3.2 Heat Stroke   This life-threatening emergency is characterized by severe central nervous system disturbances, hyperthermia (105.8°F to 109.4°F), and hot, dry skin.

22.2.4 Cremation of the Human Body

When a body is cremated, it should be exposed to a well-ventilated, constant fire for 1 to 2 hours at 1800°F to 2200°F. Approximately 6 to 9 lb of bones will remain. Fires are fueled by high-temperature accelerants (between 2500°F and 5500°F). Temperatures in this range can reduce the human body to a few pounds of calcium and silicon salts.

22.3 Drowning

People drown from submersion, partial submersion, or immersion in water. It is usually accidental, and very few cases are suicides. Death in the water can be due to natural causes, such as a heart attack or cerebral hemorrhage that occurred while the victim was swimming.

Drowning happens because the inhalation of water results in absorption of the water into the blood. The changes caused by this absorption materially contribute to death by drowning. The victim must have inhaled enough fluid and survived long enough for absorption and electrolyte exchange to take place.

In the United States, approximately 7000 to 8000 deaths by drowning occur annually. Drowning is the fourth leading cause of accidental death in the United States. Sometimes, spontaneous recovery can happen in a drowning victim. In 10% to 12% of all drowning deaths, asphyxia will take place. When this happens, spastic closure of the airway will not be evident in the autopsy.

22.3.1 Phases of Drowning

Only when the drowning victim has exhausted his or her energy does the actual drowning begin. The phases of drowning are listed below:

1. Holding breath
2. Swallowing liquid, coughing, vomiting, and advancing into unconsciousness
3. Muscle spasms and profound unconsciousness with heart failure following
4. Permanent changes in the brain and death occur

22.3.2 Drowning Factors

It takes less time to drown if the victim is submerged suddenly. If the victim is submerged suddenly in cold water, the cause of death may actually be cardiac failure. The elements that affect drowning time include the circumstances of submersion, the characteristics of the victim, and the victim's reactions to the submersion. There is the possibility of instantaneous death due to cardiac inhibition.

Those who do not know how to swim, are out of shape, or panic will drown more quickly. Drowning can be accelerated in a victim with a preexisting injury or even a cramp. Unreliable respiratory distress in a cold water immersion can cause the victim to inhale water. Unconsciousness generally ensues 2 to 10 minutes after submersion. Before death, there may be a period of suspended animation during which the victim can be resuscitated. Resuscitation is possible even if the victim has been submerged for as long as 30 minutes. There may be a brief convulsive phase, followed by suspended animation and death.

There is wide variation in the number of times a person may sink before remaining submerged. The body eventually sinks and remains on the bottom until putrefaction sets in, causing the formation of gas, which in turn causes the body to float. This occurs 7 to 14 days after death.

22.3.3 Freshwater versus Saltwater

In a freshwater drowning, low salt absorption (0.5%) into the circulation takes place. This results in the dilution of the blood along with an abrupt, violent increase in blood volume. This causes pulmonary edema and overloading of the heart. Arrhythmias of the heartbeat lead to death within 3 to 5 minutes of submersion. An adult may inhale and absorb 6 pt or more of liquid.

Seawater has a content of 3% sodium chloride. The high salinity of the water draws fluids from the blood into the lung tissue. This causes severe pulmonary edema. Saltwater drowning resembles an asphyxial death more than a freshwater drowning. It takes longer than a freshwater drowning, and a person drowning in saltwater is more likely to be resuscitated.

22.3.4 Signs of Drowning

There are consistent signs of drowning. The special difficulty in interpretation is distinguishing between accidental, suicidal, and homicidal drowning. For this reason, all available information concerning the death must be given to the pathologist prior to the autopsy. There are both external and internal signs of drowning.

22.3.4.1 External Signs of Drowning Although it may be difficult, it is important to distinguish between the changes that are due to drowning and the changes that are solely the result of submersion in water. Each of the following signs indicates the body was submerged in water; however, this does not mean the victim drowned:

- Body temperature—The body temperature will fall 5° per hour and will reach its surrounding temperature in 5 to 6 hours. Water cools at about twice the rate of air. Most bodies are cool or cold when recovered.

- Skin color—Exposure and oxygenation will frequently cause the head, neck, and front of the chest to turn bright pink.
- Putrefaction—This is often present and the skin may appear to be green, bronze, or exceptionally dark.

The following are signs that the victim actually drowned instead of merely being submerged after death:

- Pulmonary edema—The presence of foam at the mouth or nostrils is a sign of drowning. Pulmonary edema foam is caused when fluid enters the air passages to form mucus, which, when mixed with air, forms a foam. This can also be caused by strangulation or seizure.
- Instantaneous rigor—This is rare and may be a result of submersion.
- Presence of weeds or sand—Weeds or sand may be clutched in the hands or feet, which is evidence that the victim was alive at the time of submersion.
- Inhalation of sand—A person may inhale a thick suspension of sand in seawater. This could happen if the person was knocked down by a wave or hit his or her abdomen on a surfboard. Death occurs with appalling suddenness in these circumstances.
- Chemicals—Although chemicals in water may not contribute to the cause of death, their detection in the body of the victim can confirm the fact of drowning in that fluid.

22.3.4.2 Internal Signs of Drowning   If putrefaction is present, it will eliminate the internal signs of drowning. If it is not present, the following signs will help determine if drowning has occurred:

- Presence of foam and water—If foam is present in different amounts in the air passages, it is a sign of drowning. The air passages may be completely or partially filled. Water will also be present in the air passages. This may be abundant and escape from the mouth when the body is turned.
- Congestion—The larynx may appear to be congested.
- Bulky lungs—The lungs will be bulky or ballooned. There may be rib marking on the lungs.

- Blockage of the pulmonary circulation—This results in distention of the right side of the heart and great veins, which are filled with dark blood.
- Fluid blood—Blood is likely to remain fluid. Dilution of the blood is responsible for the prevention of coagulation.

Bibliography

Westveer, A.E., Jr. (2002). *Managing death investigations*, Vol. 1. (Fifth ed.). Washington, DC: U.S. Department of Justice Federal Bureau of Investigation. (Used with permission.)

23

DEATH BY DRUGS AND POISONING

23.1 Drugs

Toxicology is the study and analysis of poisons and their actions. When interpreting these data, it is important to have all of the available information. When completing an autopsy on a potential victim of substance abuse, investigators obtain samples of blood, liver, bile, and stomach contents. A complete autopsy must be performed.

When investigating a possible overdose, investigators collect a medical history, time the person was last seen alive, a list of mediations the person was on, any pill containers found at his or her home, and any notes that may be found.

23.1.1 Types of Drugs

The following are types of drugs and some of their effects.

23.1.1.1 Narcotics   Narcotics include the following drugs:

- Morphine
- Heroin
- Demerol
- Codeine
- Dilaudid
- Darvon
- Talwin

Narcotic abuse can cause many medical complications, including the following diseases:

- AIDS
- Hepatitis
- Syphilis
- Tetanus
- Heart infection
- Malaria
- Gangrene

23.1.1.2 Depressants   Depressants cause respiratory depression. These are often synergistic drugs, or various drugs combined and taken at the same time. Sometimes, a person can die from the withdrawal effects of depressants. Below is a timeline of sedative withdrawal:

- 12 to 16 hours—Improvement and alertness
- 16 to 24 hours—Shakes, tremors, and insomnia
- 24 to 72 hours—Delirium and convulsions

23.1.1.3 Stimulants   The various types of stimulants include amphetamines, cocaine, caffeine, and strychnine. Overdosing on these stimulants can cause mania, aggression, fever, convulsions, unconsciousness, and even death.

23.1.1.4 Hallucinogens   The various types of hallucinogens are listed below:

- Lysergic acid diethylamide
- Phencyclidine
- Tetrahydrocannabinol (marijuana)
- Mescaline
- Glue and solvents (sniffing)
- Over-the-counter drugs

Hallucinogens can cause panic, paranoia, flashbacks, and death. If the hallucinogen is sniffed through an aerosol or solvent, it can cause respiratory damage.

23.1.1.5 Antidepressants   Various types of antidepressants are available, including the following drugs:

- Amitriptyline
- Imipramine
- Doxepin
- Loxapine
- Elavil
- Tofranil
- Sinequan
- Loxitane

Antidepressants can cause changes in body image, disorganization of thought, estrangement, hostility, apathy, and negativism. Antidepressants can begin to have an effect within 2 to 5 minutes. The effect reaches a plateau within 15 to 30 minutes. The person should be back to normal within 24 to 48 hours.

Tricyclic antidepressants are a group of antidepressants that includes amitriptyline. The following are indications of tricyclic use:

- Psychiatric history
- Prior suicide attempts
- Depression

The following are effects of tricyclic intoxication:

- Coma
- Seizures
- Fever
- Arrhythmias
- Respiratory depression

23.1.1.6 Diluents Types of diluents include procaine, mannitol, and talcum.

23.1.2 Investigation of Drug-Related Homicide

The following list outlines the types of homicides typically related to drugs and drug usage:

- Drug hits—These are premeditated murders intended to eliminate competition or enforce control over a drug cartel.

Victims may have been selected because they provided information to authorities or were potential witnesses and considered to be risks to the business. Murders that occur during drug rip-offs also are considered drug hits.

- Interpersonal drug disputes—These are homicides that occur spontaneously, usually without any premeditation. Such murders take place during drug-related disputes between those who are under the influence of drugs or are involved in illicit drug activity.

- Murder of innocent bystanders—This includes those caught in a shooting cross fire or hit by random shots fired between rival gangs or participants during drug-related disputes. The number of civilian casualties, especially within the inner cities, has dramatically increased with the proliferation of drugs and the high-powered weaponry utilized by drug dealers.

- Drug assassinations—Premeditated murders directed toward government and law enforcement personnel are drug assassinations. Such attacks are a form of terrorism and are intended to discourage active drug enforcement policies and create the impression that the drug groups or cartels are as powerful as authorities. Drug assassinations rarely occur in the United States.

Authorities should implement an enforcement strategy that addresses three distinct phases of the drug-related murder investigation. The three phases are below:

- Phase one—The application of procedural and forensic techniques and investigative resources to the homicide crime scene and murder investigation
- Phase two—The evaluation of intelligence resources with the objective of cultivating reliable sources whose information can effectively be corroborated with the information developed at the homicide crime scene
- Phase three—Completion of the crime clearance procedures, which allows authorities to clear a case without an arrest

The rationale of a three-phase strategy is based on the idea that most drug-related homicides result from ongoing criminal ventures.

The solvability of each case depends on the factual information developed at the time of the event and current information intelligence.

23.2 Poisoning

The 430 poison control centers throughout the United States report 1.5 million calls yearly in which potentially toxic substances were involved. Of the 1.5 million incidents, 91% happened at home and 60% of victims were under 7 years old. From 1979 to 1982, 21,600 children between birth and 9 years of age were hospitalized for poisoning.

Medication accounts for about 40% of exposures in children under the age of 5, followed by cleaners, polishes, and plants. Vitamins account for 14.1% of exposures. The kind of drug that poisoned the victim depends on what area of the country the victim is in. For example, in 1978, Boston reported that salicylates were the drugs involved in most cases, followed by diazepam, acetaminophen, and vitamins.

Poisoning patterns have dramatically changed as a result of the availability of new drugs and the passage of the child-resistant packaging law.

In 1980, there were 10,968 poisoning deaths reported in the United States. Out of those, 4331 (39.5%) were accidental deaths and 5453 (49.7%) were suicides.

23.2.1 Cases of Poisoning

There have been many cases of poisoning throughout history (Table 23.1). In ancient Greece, a toxic poison was delivered through an arrow shot at its victim. The following cases illustrate more recent poisoning homicides.

23.2.2 Types of Poisons

23.2.2.1 Thallium Discovered in 1861, thallium was utilized as a medical agent to treat venereal disease, ringworm, gout, dysentery, and tuberculosis. Its recent use includes the manufacture of imitation jewelry pigments, optical lenses, and low-temperature thermometers.

Table 23.1 Poisoning Cases from History

PERPETRATOR	MOTIVE	POISON	VICTIM(S)	TIME	LOCATION	OUTCOME
Edward William Pritchard, MD	Unknown	Antimony	Wife and mother-in-law	1865	Glasgow, Scotland	Executed by hanging
George Henry Lamson, MD	Money (morphine addiction)	Aconitine (given in Dundee cake)	Brother-in-law	December 1881	England	Executed by hanging, April 28, 1882
Johann Otto Hoch	Money (an opportunist)	Arsenic	12 to 24 wives	1892–1905	Various U.S. states	Executed by hanging in Chicago, February 23, 1906
Arthur Warren Waite (oral surgeon)	Money and mistress	Arsenic	Mother and father-in-law	January to March 1916	New York	Executed by electrocution at Sing Sing, May 24, 1917
Christa Lehmann	Wanted free of husband and revenge	E-605 (parathion) in chocolate truffles	Neighbor (also husband and father-in-law)	February 1954	Worms, Germany	Life imprisonment
Ronald Clark O'Bryan (the Candy Man)	Insurance money ($65,000)	Potassium cyanide (in Pixy Stix candy straws)	Son (8 years old)	October 31, 1974	Pasadena, Texas	Executed by lethal injection, March 31, 1984
T. George Trepal	Bothered by neighbors	Thallium in bottles of Coke Classic	Peggy Carr and attempted on six other family members (one son was permanently disabled)	1988	Bartow, Florida	Convicted March 6, 1991; awaiting execution

Its use as a rodenticide was banned in 1965 because of accidental and suicidal exposures and its severe toxicity.

The average lethal dose for an adult is 1 g. The onset of thallium poisoning is insidious, reaching a maximum in 2 or 3 weeks, followed by gradual resolution or death.

The following are the physical effects of thallium:

- Immediate (3 to 4 hours)—Mostly gastrointestinal symptoms such as nausea, vomiting, and diarrhea and hematemesis may occur.
- Intermediate (hours to days)—Central nervous system disorientation, lethargy, coma, convulsions, psychosis, thirst, insomnia, cerebral edema with central respiratory failure, peripheral nervous system combined motor and sensory neuropathy, including severe hyperesthesia of palms and soles, autonomic nervous system tachycardia, hypertension, fever, salivation, and sweating may also occur.
- Late (24 weeks)—Dry scaly skin, white stripes across nails (Mee's lines), and loss of scalp and facial hair are evident.
- Residual (months)—Central and peripheral nervous system abnormalities may persist, including ataxia, tremor, foot drop, and memory loss.

23.2.2.2 Arsenic Arsenic is an odorless, tasteless compound. Americans ingest an estimated 1 mg of it daily in the water they drink. It is the most common cause of pesticide-induced deaths in children and is the most common cause of heavy-metal-related deaths, second only to lead. Ant pastes are a major source of exposure. The clinical presentation of arsenic poisoning may be divided into three forms:

- Acute massive—This occurs following the ingestion of large doses of soluble arsenic typically on an empty stomach. Absorption of arsenic is typically very quick, causing an almost immediate onset of cardiopulmonary symptoms similar to shock. Gastrointestinal symptoms are not usually present, although in some cases the ingestion of huge doses of arsenic may produce immediate vomiting.
- Gastrointestinal—This is the most common clinical presentation following acute ingestion. Severe gastric disturbances

predominate, including nausea, vomiting, diarrhea, and burning abdominal pain or cramps. The onset and severity is dependent upon the dose and whether the stomach was empty or full. Generally, symptoms occur within 30 minutes of ingestion, but they may be delayed for hours.

- Chronic intoxication—This results from a rather continuous exposure to low concentrations of arsenic or repeated ingestion of small doses over varied intervals of time. Nonspecific complaints of anorexia, weight loss, weakness, and general malaise predominate. Over time, dermatopathology characterized by thickening of the nails and the skin of the palms of the hands and soles of the feet may occur.

23.2.2.3 Selenium   Selenium toxicity resembles arsenic toxicity. Stupor, respiratory depression, hypotension, and death can result several hours after ingestion. Acute ingestion of selenium is almost always fatal. Effects of selenium ingestion include the following:

- Hair loss
- White horizontal streaking on fingernails
- Paronychia (nail infection)
- Fatigue
- Irritability
- Hyperreflexia
- Nausea
- Vomiting
- Muscle tenderness
- Tremor
- Light-headedness
- Facial flushing
- Garlic odor on breath
- Metallic taste

23.2.2.4 Water Intoxication   Excessive water intake may result in severe neurologic symptoms, death, and hyponatremia (abnormally low sodium concentrations in the blood).

In infants, water intoxication can be caused by feeding mismanagement, swimming lessons (with water swallowing), or vigorous hydration (such as in the use of diluted formula). In adults, water intoxication can be caused by professional weight-loss programs (8 to 12, 8 oz servings of water per day), excessive water intake after accidental ingestion of a caustic substance, psychogenic polydipsia, excessive beer drinking, or the use of 5% dextrose in water as a vehicle for oxytocin for therapeutic abortions.

23.2.2.5 Strychnine   Strychnine is an alkaloid extracted from the dry seeds of the nux vomica tree, found in Southeast Asia. It is a colorless, crystalline poison. The estimated lethal dose in humans is 5 to 8 mg/kg. Small children may develop symptoms with only 15 to 20 mg; adults may develop symptoms with 30 to 80 mg, and death occurs from 100 mg doses. Half of the dose is distributed to tissues in 5 minutes. Symptoms rapidly begin (within 5 to 60 minutes) and last 15 to 20 minutes.

A person affected by strychnine experiences apprehension, fear, nausea, muscle twitching, depersonalization, and hyperreflexia within 1 hour. Severely affected persons progress to extensor spasm and opisthotonos, causing interference with breathing without loss of consciousness. Spasms occur at 5- to 10-minute intervals and last between 1 and 2 minutes. The patient may remain conscious, but coma can follow. The presence of symmetrical seizures, trismus, opisthotonos, and risus sardonicus in awake patients suggests strychnine poisoning. There is no specific antidote available, nor are there any effective elimination methods.

23.2.3 Treatment of Poisoning

Typically, a doctor considers poisoning as a cause of the patient's ills only if the patient's occupation brings him or her into contact with toxic substances. Self-poisoning is common today. However, murder by poison is rare. Persons who resort to the use of poisons are usually either very unintelligent or quite clever.

There are basic actions that can be taken for poisoned patients. First, the patient must be stabilized. Then, medical personnel obtain the complete patient evaluation (history, physical examination, laboratory tests). Appropriate treatment is given to reduce absorption, and appropriate measures are taken to improve elimination of the toxin. Antidotes are used, if possible.

Many symptoms of poisoning can also be caused by disease. However, there are symptoms that render a poisoning diagnosis moderately certain, such as the onset of symptoms immediately after eating or drinking, rapid progression of symptoms, and rapid death (bacterial food poisoning has a delayed onset of symptoms). When poisoning is suspected, investigators note the following information:

- Time medical personnel arrived
- The signs and symptoms of intoxication
- Condition of the pupils
- Pulse and respiratory rate
- Convulsions or paralysis
- Stomach pain
- Time the symptoms started and their order
- Smell and color of the subject's vomit or breath
- Time of death
- All statements made by the victim

23.2.4 Investigation of Poison

Investigators typically practice the following guidelines when investigating a possible poisoning death.

23.2.4.1 Evidence Ascertaining the right information and collecting the necessary evidence is key to starting an investigation into a possible poisoning.

Investigators obtain the following information:

- Everything the deceased ingested within the past 24 hours (collect, if possible)
- Time of last meal or beverage
- The victim's state of health prior to symptoms
- Others who shared the deceased's last meal, if they became sick, and their symptoms
- Suicide attempts made by the subject
- Location where possible poisons and medications were kept
- All pertinent medical information

The following items are collected and placed in separate containers, closed, sealed, and labeled:

- All medicine bottles, hypodermic syringes, etc.
- All empty or opened containers of poisons or medicines
- All food the victim recently ate
- Any items recently used for eating
- Garbage left from the victim's last meal
- Vomit, urine, and excretion of the victim prior to death
- Soiled linens or clothes of the deceased

23.2.4.2 Postmortem Examination of the Body   The pathologist can recognize the effects of certain types of poisons during an autopsy. For example, strong acids and alkalines may cause extensive burns on the surface of the body and severe destruction of the tissues, and phosphorus causes gross fatty degeneration of the liver. It is possible that metallic poisons can cause intensive damage to the gastrointestinal tract, liver, and kidneys.

Most drugs and poisons do not produce trait pathological lesions. These drugs will be uncovered only by a toxicological analysis. In many cases, the value of the pathologist's examination is the establishment that death was not due to natural causes or traumatic injury, thus meaning there is no evidence for death except from possible poisoning.

23.2.4.3 Toxicological Examination   Death due to poisoning cannot be established without contention unless the agent can be demonstrated in the body by chemical methods of isolation and identification. The stomach and the intestines are legally considered outside the body. The presence of the poison must be established in blood, liver, or other tissues in the body. Poison in the urine indicates only that it was at some time present in the body.

There are thousands of compounds that are lethal if ingested; therefore, it is imperative that the investigators supply the toxicologist with as much information as possible. The possible identity of the poison in question would greatly help.

Embalming and putrefaction may greatly hinder the toxicologist's work. Many poisons are rapidly biotransformed or excreted; in such cases, only the biotransformation products (metabolites) or low levels of poisons may be detected. Some poisons can be detected for years after death, such as arsenic.

To complete a toxicological examination, specimens must be collected. Each specimen should be placed in a separate container, either glass jars with screw tops or plastic bags. Each container should be labeled, and the identification should bear the following information:

- The date and time of collection
- The name of the victim
- The identity of the sample
- The signature of the law enforcement person or pathologist
- The initials of the person who sealed and collected the sample

When exhibits are handled by several persons and when they are accepted by the analyst, a written receipt that can be produced in court must be obtained.

23.2.5 Analysis of Postmortem Specimens

23.2.5.1 Inner Body Specimens Blood, bile, gastric content, tissue, vitreous humor, and urine are tested in the toxicology examination (Table 23.2). An explanation of each is below:

Table 23.2 Toxicology Testing

SPECIMEN	QUANTITY NEEDED	TOXICANT SOUGHT
Adipose tissue	200 g	Insecticides, thiopental
Bile	All available	Codeine, morphine, benzodiazepines
Blood	15 mL	Alcohols, all toxicants, carbon monoxide
Brain	500 g	Volatile poisons
Kidney	One whole organ	Heavy metals, most toxicants
Liver	500 g	Most toxicants
Lung	One whole organ	Drugs, gases, inhalants
Stomach contents	All available	All toxicants taken orally
Urine	All available	Most toxicants and/or metabolites
Vitreous humor	All available	Alcohol, digoxin, electrolytes, glucose
Hair	Pull from scalp	Metals, drugs of abuse
Nails	Pull whole, fingernails	Metals
Maggots	10–25 g	Drugs

Source: Westveer, A.E., Jr., *Managing Death Investigations*, Vol. 1., Fifth ed., U.S. Department of Justice Federal Bureau of Investigation, Washington, DC, 2002. With permission.

- Blood—This is a valuable specimen for most analyses. Drug concentrations in blood are more likely to correlate closely with drug effects than other specimens. Most of the interpretations of analytical data have been based on blood concentrations. For example, pathologists analyze 15 mL of blood, and specifically look for alcohols and carbon monoxide.

- Bile—All bile present in the gallbladder is collected at all autopsies for toxicological testing. Bile is particularly useful for the detection of opiates, benzodiazepines, and other drugs of abuse. Pathologists analyze all of the bile available, looking for codeine, morphine, and benzodiazepines.

- Gastric content—The stomach may contain large amounts of substances taken orally. Undissolved tablets, the color of the fluid, and any particulate matter may indicate oral overdose. Stomach content may have distinct odors such as those produced by alcohol, methyl salicylate, paraldehyde, nicotine, ethchlorvynol, petroleum products, halogenated hydrocarbons, or cyanide.

- Tissues—About 50 mg of liver is obtained and stored. These are not to be cut on a dirty block nor contaminated with stomach content. Drugs are present in the liver in concentrations greater than in blood and most other specimens. Parts of the liver can be available even in decomposed bodies when blood is unavailable.

- Vitreous humor—This clear, colorless jelly that fills the eye is particularly useful in that it is anatomically isolated and protected from putrefaction, charring, and trauma. Volatile poisons, particularly ethanol, are readily detected in vitreous humor. Other drugs may be detected, but the interpretation of vitreous drug findings is questionable.

- Urine—The entire urine content of the bladder is collected for testing. Urine is not always available at autopsy, but even a small amount can be helpful. Screening for a wide range of drugs is possible with as little as 1 to 2 mL of urine. Drugs and metabolites may be found in urine that are no longer present in the blood.

23.2.5.2 Miscellaneous Specimens   Other types of specimen are also collected:

- Hair—Samples of hair are preferred to differentiate acute from chronic heavy metal poisoning. The analysis of sections of hair provides reliable correlation to the pattern of heavy metal exposure. Metals in the blood are deposited in the hair follicle and carried up the follicle in the growing hair. Normal metal content of hair varies; however, concentrations have been established for a wide variety of exposure situations.
- Maggots—The fundamental premise underlying maggot analysis is that drugs or intoxicants detected could have originated only from tissues upon which the larvae were feeding. Analysis of maggots is straightforward, requiring no special methodologies beyond those routinely applied in toxicology laboratories.
- Premortem specimens—Premortem blood, serum, plasma, and urine are important if the deceased had been hospitalized and lived for some time after taking an overdose. Special efforts are made to obtain these samples by promptly requesting them from the hospital laboratory.

23.2.5.3 Specimen Collection in Challenging Cases   The list below explains some challenging cases:

- Exhumed bodies—For embalmed or exhumed bodies, fixed tissue samples from the major internal organs are collected. Investigators also collect peripheral fluid specimens such as spinal fluid or vitreous humor. Hair is also collected. Any fluid or soil in the coffin may be collected and submitted to the laboratory.
- Decomposed bodies—Soft tissues and specimens such as vitreous humor, spinal fluid, and hair are collected. A large quantity of maggots and soil adjacent to the visceral tissue should also be collected. The quantitative results of testing decomposed tissue are of limited usefulness; however, qualitative results do demonstrate drug use.

- Skeletal remains—Drug identification in skeletal remains is not hopeless. Any muscle tissue available is analyzed. Investigators collect both rib and long-bone specimens. Numerous drugs have been successfully identified in bone marrow and bone washings. Hair is also collected for a drug analysis.

23.2.6 Interpretation of Toxicology Results

23.2.6.1 Blood and Tissue Concentrations The physiological effects of most drugs correlate with their concentration in the blood. Interpretation of blood or tissue values may be divided into four categories:

- Normal—This is the concentration of a substance found in the general population that has no toxic effect on the body. For example, cyanide is widely known as a highly poisonous chemical; however, minute quantities of cyanide are generated through certain foods. Many heavy metals, such as lead and mercury, are present in the general environment through food, drink, and air.
- Therapeutic—This is the sufficient amount of a drug necessary to treat a disorder.
- Toxic—This is the concentration of a drug that is associated with harmful effects and may or may not be life threatening.
- Lethal—This is the concentration of a drug consistent as the cause of death in documented and investigated cases.

23.2.6.2 Postmortem Changes Toxicologists must be aware of chemical changes that occur during decomposition. The autopsy or toxicological analysis should be started as soon after death as possible. The natural decomposition processes may destroy a poison initially present or may produce substances with chemical physical properties similar to common poisons. Decomposition turns phenylalanine, a normal amino acid of the body, to phenylethylamine, which is similar to amphetamine. The ethyl alcohol and cyanide content of blood may change depending upon the degree of putrefaction and microbial activity. Poisons such as arsenic, barbiturates, mercury, morphine, and strychnine may be detectable years after death.

23.2.6.3 Factors Influencing Toxicity   Factors that may influence the response of an individual to a given toxicant concentration include age, sex, and body weight, as well as nutritional, genetic, and immunological status. Also, the presence of disease or specific organ pathology and central nervous system activity (depression, stress, etc.) must be considered.

The case history is reviewed, accounting for all toxicity factors and comparing the results with similar cases before investigators develop a final interpretation.

23.2.6.4 Evidence Relating to the Victim   The following is evidence to be collected relating to the victim:

- Medical history—The complete medical records of the victim are obtained.
- Signs and symptoms of poisoning—If the victim is treated either in the emergency department or by a family physician, the signs and symptoms of the poison will be established through the medical records.
- Smell and odor of vomit—Some classic poisons may produce a characteristic smell on the breath, around the mouth, or in the stomach contents of the victim.
- Treatment administered by medical personnel—If the victim is treated in the emergency department or survives for a while, all drugs administered by the medical personnel should be documented.
- Time of the last meal—The time of the victim's last meal may be important in a sudden, unexpected death. The time after eating and the time of the onset of fatal symptoms may establish when and how the poison was administered.
- Time of death—If the victim dies under direct medical management, the time of death will be established.
- Death of pets—In the investigation of several poison homicides, pets had died unexpectedly some time prior to the symptoms of the victim.
- Victim's statements and psychiatric history—Note if the victim was ever treated for psychiatric problems such as depression or anxiety. Suicide is often a defense in trial.

23.2.6.5 Prosecution of a Murder by Poison For successful prosecution of a suspect, law enforcement officers must establish that the suspect was aware of the lethal effects of the poison, had access to a supply of the poison, and had opportunities to administer the poison to the decedent.

23.2.6.6 Lack of Suspicion That Murder Has Occurred The lack of suspicion of murder by poisoning is due to several factors:

- The rarity of murder by poison
- Difficulty in the clinical diagnosis of poisoning
- The lack of specific organ pathology from poisoning

Bibliography

Westveer, A.E., Jr. (2002). *Managing death investigations*, Vol. 1. (Fifth ed.). Washington, DC: U.S. Department of Justice Federal Bureau of Investigation. (Used with permission.)

24

SEX-RELATED HOMICIDE AND AUTOEROTIC FATALITIES

24.1 Sex-Related Homicide

Sex-related homicides often begin with rape and turn into a homicide. It often involves the elderly. The word *rape* is a legal term, not a medical term. It requires three elements:

- Penetration—It is the slightest violation of any orifice; it may include penetration by foreign bodies.
- Force—It is the use of force that may be actual or threatened or physical or mental.
- Lack of consent—This may be due to age, mental incapacitation, or lack of volition.

24.1.1 Sex-Related Homicide in the Elderly

Crimes against the elderly tend to be more serious than those against younger persons. Older victims are most likely to be victimized in their own homes, less likely to protect themselves, and more vulnerable to injuries. Elderly victims are much more likely to be injured or killed than younger victims during a sexual assault. When a rapist attacks an older woman, the rape or sexual assault is likely to be exceptionally vicious and provoked by anger, power, or cruel goals. Many elderly women are unaware of their vulnerability to sexual assault.

Offenders rarely seek sexual gratification, but rather seek to punish, dominate, and control because the elderly (females in particular) may represent an authority figure over whom the assailant wants power. Offenders see sexual assault as a method to effect revenge, utilizing physical force and killing their victims in 60% of elderly rape cases.

According to the FBI, there were 812 elderly homicide victims in the United States in 1999; more than half of this total (499) were identified as females. The FBI also states that elderly female homicides constituted just more than 3% of all homicides in the United States in 1999. Other statistics are listed below:

- 81% of the victims are white.
- 45% of offenders are white; 55% are nonwhite.
- Predominant weapons include hands, fists, and feet.
- The assailant is a stranger 54% of the time.
- 92% of the cases involve rape with 8% involving some other sexual offense.
- On average, the offender is 27 years old.

24.1.2 Investigation of Sex-Related Homicides

High-profile crimes such as sex-related homicides often shock and outrage the community and offend public sensibilities. These crimes require diligence by investigators because the cases and the evidence are potentially open to intense scrutiny.

24.1.3 Evidence

There are several areas on the body in which to examine and look for key evidence.

24.1.3.1 Neck
Strangulation is often correlated with sexual homicide. There may be layered dissection, even if strangulation is not suspected. Neck examination is the final aspect of the autopsy; other organs, including the brain, should be removed first. Documentation of injuries is taken in two different forms: photographic and microscopic. The medical examiner may potentially age hemorrhage within neck muscles.

24.1.3.2 Genitalia
Obviously, the genitalia may hold evidence in a sex-related homicide. When examining genitalia, investigators give special considerations for the elderly and the sexually immature. The elderly have atrophied skin and mucosae. They are prone to injury

and bleed with less force than others. The young are prone to acute trauma injury as they are unprepared for penetration. The hymeneal ring should be examined to note if injuries are recent or old. Wounds may have resulted from the same or another assailant. Wounds may be from penile or other penetration. Injuries may arise from forcible sexual or foreign body penetration. Bleeding into a wound (wound hematoma) indicates a premortem wound. Direct wounds to genitalia may be from within the body. If bleeding is absent from wounds, it can be from either a postmortem injury or an agonal injury. Postmortem injuries appear yellow. Agonal injuries occurred as the person was dying, resulting in low blood pressure from shock, bleeding, or insufficient pressure or blood to bleed into tissue.

If ejaculation occurred but evidence is not present, this may mean that the offender used a condom or ejaculated onto the victim's body or into a tissue. The offender may also clean the orifice in an attempt to conceal evidence. Even if the body has been cleaned, an investigator should collect samples. If no ejaculation occurred, either no sexual act took place or the offender performed a sexual act but did not ejaculate. One-third of all rapists do not ejaculate during forced sexual interaction with their victim.

While a positive DNA (sperm) sample may be significant, it does not *prove* rape. Investigators must listen to the suspect's explanation about why their sperm was found in, on, or near the victim. A negative sample is equivocal.

There is other crucial evidence in proving case. The type and nature of injuries may suggest use of force. Genital injuries suggest forcible intercourse. Clothing disarray, damage, or absence suggests use of force. None of these in and of themselves may be critical pieces of evidence, but together, they may suggest rape.

24.1.3.3 Bite Marks   Bite marks are potentially highly incriminating evidence, but it does not prove the suspect committed the full attack. Other assailants may have acted subsequently. Bite marks may definitely be from the suspect or they may be consistent with the suspect but not exclude others. It may be impossible to determine who made the bite mark, or it may exclude the suspect of the full attack entirely.

Bite marks are valuable because the pattern of the teeth may be unique, aiding in the identification of an assailant. Also, saliva that can be used for DNA testing may be deposited on the skin.

24.1.4 How to Handle Evidence

Properly handling evidence is absolutely vital. First, investigators examine the scene for evidence of a struggle (torn clothing, missing buttons, ripped textiles, marks on the ground, and blood spatter).

The victim's clothing may hold significant evidence. Each piece of the victim's clothing is to be packaged in a separate container. The suspect's body should be examined for any fingernail scratches, bite marks, or other indications of a violent struggle. In addition, hair and blood samples should be obtained legally.

Seminal fluid must be collected immediately. Bloodstains, spittle, and hair are obtained at the scene. Trace evidence found on the victim or the victim's clothing is collected. Bruises and marks on the victim, including sadistic injuries, should be recorded. The body is examined for bite marks. When found, investigators complete saliva washing of the bite mark area for a blood grouping. They use 100% cotton dampened in distilled water. It is also important to get a control sample from another area of the body. The bite mark is photographed in black and white as well as in color. A measurement instrument is used in the photograph and an anatomical landmark is obtained. A casting (if possible) using dental materials is also obtained.

Fingernail scrapings are collected for an analysis of any blood, skin, or hair from the perpetrator. Investigators must ensure specimens are taken from the body (hair) as well as anal, nasal, and oral swabs.

If the victim is female, vaginal washing may also be needed by inserting saline or sterile water into the cavity and then removing and containing the solution.

Other key evidence includes the following: an excessive number of wounds, marks from ligatures (if the victim was immobilized with binding ties), signs of torture (burn, electrocution, and sadistic or repetitive wounds), torn or disheveled clothing, a disrobed victim, if the victim is weak (elderly adult, child, mentally handicapped individual), and toxicology reports for both the victim and the suspect (especially the presence or lack of a date rape drug).

Other significant clues should not be overlooked. For example, the scene and clothing of the victim may offer insight. The victim's body, the injuries he or she received, and his or her position offers clues. The victim and suspect profile and the surrounding area should also be considered.

Common wounds include manual or ligature strangulation; sharp force injuries such as cuts or stabs; blunt force injuries such as contusions, abrasions, or lacerations; or combinations of each. There may also be defense wounds to the arms or legs. If there is postmortem mutilation or injury to the breasts, penis, genitalia, or buttocks, this is further evidence that it was a sex-related homicide.

Every effort should be made to preserve evidence and minimize contamination of the evidence. The body is placed in a clean sheet or body bag. The hands of the victim are placed inside paper bags.

24.1.5 Evidence Collection Procedures

The following is an outline of how evidence should be collected and processed.

24.1.5.1 Trace Evidence The following list details trace evidence that needs careful handling:

- Fingernails—Investigators bag the victim's hands at the scene with clean paper bags or envelopes. They check for a possible physical match to broken-off fragments. If nails are extremely short, they are scraped with a clean wooden stick. Any defects, tears, or missing nails are documented and photographed; they offer possible DNA evidence if later recovered.
- Pubic hair—The pubic hair is combed with a clean plastic comb. Pulled pubic hair is collected and retained for later analysis if needed. Investigators take 25 to 50 individual hairs with roots attached.
- Scalp hair—Pulled scalp hairs should be collected—25 to 50 individual hairs with roots attached.
- Clothing—Investigators check for soil, grass, blood, or biological fluid stains. Foreign material such as grass, hair, or fiber may also be important. They look for defects caused by a

weapon or struggling. There may also be drainage of ejaculate from the vagina or anus on the undergarments.

- Proffered (suspect) weapons—Blood or biological material may be present on these weapons. Even small quantities can be used for DNA analysis. Pattern wounds may be present.
- Fingerprints—The body surface (especially legs) may have latent prints on the skin. Iodine fuming and other techniques may allow visualization of latent prints.

24.1.5.2 Serology Evidence   Serology is the study of serums such as blood and other human fluids. Human blood can be grouped into distinct types (A, B, AB, and O). In a large part of the population (80%), blood type can be detected in blood as well as other bodily fluids, such as ejaculate and saliva. This can be very useful in an investigation. Blood at a crime scene could be from the victim or the assailant. Collecting samples from suspects can help eliminate people from the crime. Control samples should be taken from known victims, assailants (if possible), and any suspects. If a suspect's blood type does not match that of the blood at the crime scene, he or she is probably not the assailant.

At a crime scene, investigators also collect cigarette butts, tissues, drinking glasses, and partially consumed food items. These may have saliva on them, which can possibly reveal the suspect's blood type. This can also help eliminate suspects or identify possible leads.

Below is the serology evidence that should be collected:

- Sexual intercourse evidence—To collect evidence of sexual intercourse, investigators use cotton-tipped swabs. Samples are collected as soon as possible. Proteins degrade with time and temperature, and bacteria may accelerate normal degradation.
- Sperm evidence—Best results are from the cervical canal (vagina). Slides are prepared to examine this evidence under a microscope. Washings and other samples should be examined for motile sperm (sperm with tails). Typically, sperm lasts an average of 3 to 4 hours, but it can last from 1 to 6 hours. This may be affected by the postmortem environment. Anal samples can be tainted by leakage from the vagina.

- Ejaculate—Acid phosphatase, enzyme secretion from normal tissues, is elevated in seminal fluid (ejaculate). Life span in the vagina ranges from 8 to 24 hours. Concentration falls with time; the level may suggest a general idea of the time that intercourse occurred. Highest levels are during the first 12 hours postcoitus. Subsequently, levels fall in the vagina over the next 12 hours. There is a longer duration if the area dries. A component of semen produced by the prostate gland (specific for men) called P30 glycoprotein may be present even if sperm is absent.

24.1.5.3 Oral Act Salivary amylase is a normal enzyme secreted by tissues. Any site acted on with saliva is a potential positive, such as sexually significant areas, the extremities, or bite marks. Collect suspected saliva from bite marks, sexually significant areas (breast, etc.), uninvolved areas for negative control, and the victim's mouth (buccal mucosa).

24.2 Autoerotic Fatalities

It is difficult to gather statistics regarding autoerotic fatalities because there is a lack of established criteria to identify and label this type of death. Because of this, it is difficult to categorize the manner of death. There is also a lack of access to large numbers of these cases in order to study them in depth. When there are cases to study, samples are collected unsystematically. The topic is also taboo, and secrecy is common. All of these make it difficult to research autoerotic fatalities. The information available on this topic is examined in the following section.

24.2.1 Autoeroticism

Autoeroticism is a solo sexual activity that combines ritual and endangerment with erotic gratification through fantasy. It includes masturbation, voyeurism, pornography, erotic literature, fantasies, cross-dressing, exhibition, bondage, sadomasochism, sex with animals or dead bodies, and the use of props such as inflatable dolls or mannequins.

Autoeroticism is often chosen because no sex partner is available, but sometimes there is no preference or desire to have sex with another person. These people often feel a need to be in total control during sex. They may feel shame or embarrassment over sexual desires due to moral or religious beliefs, or they may just be experimenting.

Paraphilia may be included in someone's autoerotic practices. This is a sexual variant in which unusual objects, rituals, or situations are required for full sexual satisfaction to occur. People with paraphilia often have an impairment in their capacity for reciprocal affectionate sexual activity. Psychosexual dysfunctions are also common, especially emotional issues and personality disturbances.

Those who have paraphilia will lie somewhere on a four-point spectrum:

1. Slight sexual arousal toward some particular object or activity
2. Stronger arousal toward object or activity but able to perform sexually with a member of the opposite sex
3. No sexual activity or orgasm can occur without the object or activity
4. Object or activity is substituted for his or her living sexual partner

24.2.2 Fatalities

The FBI completed a study of autoerotic deaths in 1981. Here are the results of that study:

- Victims' ages range from 9 to 77 years old (most in teens or twenties).
- 45% were married.
- Most were middle class.
- 63 were white males.
- 3 were black males.
- 3 were white females.
- 1 was a black female.

The manner of death during an autoerotic activity is usually accidental, although it can be natural, suicide, or even homicide. One natural cause of death that may occur during an autoerotic activity is a heart attack. Accidental deaths often occur because of neck compression (including hanging or strangulation), airway obstruction (including suffocation and choking), chest compression, and oxygen exclusion.

There may be atypical autoerotic fatalities, or fatalities outside the norm. Some examples of these are listed below:

- A bondage practitioner dies of exposure when he is unable to remove his bindings and is forced to remain seminude in a cold, remote area.
- A man dies of electrocution when the wires he was using to induce electrical current into his genitals become short-circuited.
- A man dies of peritonitis after inserting and losing a large soda bottle up his rectum.
- A man bleeds to death after accidentally stabbing himself while using a knife for autoerotic stimulation.
- A man dies of a gunshot wound after he "loses" a game of Russian roulette he was playing with a partially loaded revolver during autoerotic activity.

Autoerotic fatalities sometimes result from complex behaviors. Complex behaviors include an apparatus that alters the physiological state and, because of its potential lethality, a self-rescue mechanism relying on a practitioner's judgment. Death may result from failure with the physiological mechanism of the self-rescue device or failure to control a dangerous fantasy.

A person engaged in autoerotic activity may decide at some point to commit suicide. This point of decision may be prior to engaging in the activity. The person may then deliberately decide to incorporate his or her autoerotic activity into the suicide, or vice versa.

An individual engaged in autoerotic activity may also become the victim of a homicide. The autoerotic activity may have nothing to do with the homicide. The victim, for example, coincidentally may be found engaged in autoerotic activity when the killer strikes. A homicide scene may also be deliberately staged to appear to be an accidental autoerotic death.

24.2.3 Investigation of Autoerotic Fatalities

In an investigation, there are two major areas to evaluate: the crime scene or death scene and the victim's history. The investigator should also have some knowledge of sexually associated factors, such as sadism or masochism, bondage, fetishism, transvestism, ritualism, and fantasy. An investigator should know what a typical autoerotic death scenario looks like and be aware of methods of escape and evidence of prior autoerotic activities. Also, an investigator should have a victim profile, an evaluation of the victim's history, and a psychological autopsy. Investigators interview friends, relatives, and coworkers of the victims, and find any diaries, writings, or recordings from the victim.

There are four criteria for determining death during an autoerotic practice:

- Evidence of solo sexual activity
- Secrecy
- Victim moved away from residence—woods, hotel, locks on doors
- Evidence of sexual fantasy aids (fantasy plays a key role)

Evidence that the victim has had prior experience with autoeroticism is a strong indicator that the death was an autoerotic fatality. If there is evidence of neck compression, often taking the form of hanging, the victim may have prior experience. The victim is checked for abrasions from previous autoerotic episodes. The complexity of the physiological apparatus involved is important; a more complex apparatus suggests prior autoerotic practice. Also, investigators look for confirmation from others that the victim practiced autosadistic activities. This confirmation usually comes from a spouse or a significant other. Additional fantasy aids are discovered elsewhere, such as the victim's car, home, or closet.

It is important to rule out suicide for this death. If everyone who knew the victim is very surprised to hear about the death or the psychological autopsy suggests that there was no suicidal intention, it was likely not suicide.

There are problems in ruling a death an autoerotic fatality because there is a general lack of knowledge about this. It is often misdiagnosed as a suicide or homicide. There may be false or misleading information, and the death scene may be altered by those who do not understand its importance. To discover the truth, the investigator must be able to recognize and converse professionally with the public, the victim's family, and insurance companies.

Bibliography

Westveer, A.E., Jr. (2002). *Managing death investigations*, Vol. 1. (Fifth ed.). Washington, DC: U.S. Department of Justice Federal Bureau of Investigation. (Used with permission.)

25

SUICIDE
AND EQUIVOCAL DEATHS

25.1 Suicide

Suicide is a person's genuine and sincere form of self-analysis and critique and often is seen as the only solution to whatever is bothering him or her. Parasuicide is a nonfatal act in which a person deliberately causes self-injury. This happens two to eight times as often as suicide. A suicidal gesture is self-mutilation for secondary gain.

Suicide is viewed differently by different cultures. In the Roman Empire, suicide was viewed as a crime against the state. In the Far East, suicide is accepted and considered appropriate under certain conditions, such as when the person has disgraced his or her country.

Here are some statistics about suicide:

- Around 200,000 individuals attempt suicide every year.
- Five million living Americans have made a suicide attempt at some time in their lives.
- Every year, there are more than 35,000 successful suicides in the United States.
- Suicide is the third leading cause of death among 15- to 24-year-olds.
- Suicide is the fifth leading cause of death among 25- to 44-year-olds.
- The most common method of suicide for both men and women is the use of firearms.
- The highest suicide rates are for persons over the age of 65.

The peak age range for individuals attempting suicide is 24 to 44. For Americans ages 15 to 24, suicide was the third leading cause of death, behind unintentional injury and homicide. Teenage suicide has tripled in the past 20 years. More than 5,000 teenagers successfully commit suicides each year. As many as 500,000 teenagers attempt suicide each year.

Those at high risk for committing suicide include those who are 65 years of age and older, alcoholics, ex–mental patients, physicians, dentists, lawyers, psychologists, and law enforcement officials.

25.1.1 Myths of Suicide

The first myth about suicide is that those who threaten to commit suicide do not actually follow through with it. The reality is that 60% of people who commit suicide give direct threats. Another 20% give indirect threats, while only 20% give no indication.

Here are some other common myths about suicide:

- Suicide is always committed without warning.
- Only people of a certain social class commit suicide.
- Belonging to certain religions is a good predictor that a person will not commit suicide.
- The motives for suicide are easily established.
- All those who commit suicide are depressed.
- A person with a terminal physical illness is unlikely to commit suicide.
- A person has to be insane to commit suicide.
- The tendency to commit suicide is inherited.

25.1.2 Suicide Indications

There are usually some indications of suicide before it takes place. The traits listed below affect the suicide potential of a particular individual:

- Age
- Sex
- Symptoms
- Stress
- Suicidal plan
- Resources
- Prior suicidal behavior

- Medical status
- Communication aspects
- Reaction of significant other

There are also suicidal clues such as the lethality or seriousness of a person in committing suicide and the intent or chance of rescue. The more precise the death plan, the more lethal the intent. Listed below are some key indicators, motives, and personality traits that might point to suicide or an impending attempt.

25.1.2.1 Precipitating Events   Certain stressors and situations can precipitate the act of suicide:

- Stressors—These can be financial, family, workplace, or relationship stressors.
- Situations—This means that the potential suicide victim has the means, opportunity, motive, role of victim, and peer influence.

25.1.2.2 Warning Signs   The warning signs listed below are serious and should not be taken lightly:

- Change in mood
- Depression
- Withdrawal
- Neglecting personal hygiene
- Loss of interest or energy
- Threats
- Feelings of hopelessness, haplessness, or helplessness
- Loss of family
- Loss of a love interest
- Loss of social status
- Financial difficulties
- Incarceration

25.1.2.3 Extreme Danger Signs   Extreme danger signs include a person suddenly becoming cheerful or calm after a depression or experiencing a sudden burst of activity. The person may have resolved the inner conflict by deciding to take his or her own life. This person may give away prized possessions or speak of life in the past tense, for example, "I've loved you," or "You've been a good mother."

25.1.3 Suicide Motivations

The following list includes possible motives for attempting suicide:

- Depression
- Guilt
- Drug usage
- Alcohol usage
- Fear
- Anger
- Hostility
- Illness
- Loss of a loved one
- Severe emotional or psychological crisis
- Financial problems
- Teenage problems
- Loss of employment
- Despair or inability to cope with life

Because depression is a possible suicide motivation, signs of depression are important to know. Those with depression often have physical complaints such as pain, headaches, tension, or fatigue. They may also have sleep difficulties, such as being unable to fall asleep, waking up early or often, or sleeping too much. They may lose their appetite, have problems tasting food, or have problems with indigestion, heartburn, gas, or cramps. They may have abdominal issues such as nausea, vomiting, bowel disturbances, diarrhea, or constipation. They may have either a decreased or an increased sex drive.

25.1.4 Communication of Suicide

Those who commit or attempt to commit suicide may communicate in four ways: directly, indirectly, by cryptic message, or by a suicide note. About 24% of people who commit suicide leave notes that are mailed to someone or found near the body. This does not exclusively determine that suicide has occurred, but it does give insight into the person's psyche.

25.1.5 Investigation of Suicide

All death investigations should be handled as homicide cases until the facts prove otherwise. The resolution of the mode of death as suicide is based on a series of factors that eliminate homicide, accident, and natural causes. Investigators establish suicide by three factors:

- The presence of the weapon or means of death at the scene
- Injuries or death wounds that are obviously self-inflicted or could have been self-inflicted
- The existence of a motive or intent on the part of the victim to take his or her own life

The following sections detail factors investigators should consider.

25.1.5.1 Crime Scene

- Intent/lethality
- Overall scene
- Weapon/method
- Wounds
- Messages

25.1.5.2 Personality Assessment A psychological autopsy should be conducted based on the deceased person's thoughts, feelings, and behaviors. The following information is important in assessing the situation:

- Birth date
- Birthplace
- Physical characteristics and health
- Family information
- Personal information (aspirations, type of friends, etc.)
- Assessment information
- Education
- Employment
- Hobbies
- Behaviors
- Marriage

25.1.5.3 Interview of Witnesses, Friends, and Family   A structured interview follows a predetermined plan where all persons will be asked the same questions. Some questions to ask are listed below:

- Type of association with the victim—How long the two have known one another, how often they interacted, and how good their relationship was.
- Description of the person's behavior—List any behavioral changes. Describe them and what attributed to them.
- Problems or concerns in the victim's personal life—What type of problems? When did these problems occur? What was the severity of these problems? Did he or she make any suicidal statements?
- The victim's life at the time—This may include any major upset such as a divorce or a change in lifestyle.
- Prior actions or events—List precipitating life stressors, absence of emotional expressiveness, extreme preoccupation, or socially inappropriate behavior.
- Behavioral or emotional changes—What change did you notice? When did this occur?

25.1.5.4 Evaluation of the Wounds   Could the deceased have caused the death? Sometimes, it is necessary to re-create the act utilizing props to confirm that a suspicious death is even mechanically possible as self-inflicted based on the evidence and body position, including the physical characteristics of the victim. Investigators determine if the person was physically able to accomplish the act. The wounds must be within reach of the deceased, and they may be grouped together in suicide. There may also be hesitation marks in suicide. The nature and position of the victim's injuries are described.

25.1.5.5 Psychological State of the Victim   A background of the victim is obtained from family and friends, including medical and social information. Investigators ask if there were any recent deaths in the family or if there were any warning signs from the victim. A sample of the victim's handwriting is obtained for analysis. This should be done even if a note is not found—one may show up later. Close friends are interviewed as soon as possible.

25.2 Equivocal Deaths

This section summarizes how to handle undeterminable deaths or deaths of an uncertain nature or classification. The cause of death may include a gunshot wound or a heart attack. The death may be natural, accidental, homicide, suicide, unexplained, or undetermined.

Deaths that are questionable are listed below:

- Occupational
- Fire deaths
- Overdose
- Firearm
- Vehicular
- Drowning
- Cutting
- Stabbing
- Falls
- Electrical

To try and determine the cause of death, investigators complete a psychological autopsy and interview family, friends, coworkers, and anyone else who may be connected with the person or the death in some way.

Bibliography

Westveer, A.E., Jr. (2002). *Managing death investigations*, Vol. 1. (Fifth ed.). Washington, DC: U.S. Department of Justice Federal Bureau of Investigation. (Used with permission.)

SECTION V
PRACTICE TEST

1. Which of the following is often exhibited by organized crime scenes?
   a. There are indications that the victim was not a stranger.
   b. The assault and disposal site of the body are the same.
   c. There are signs of postmortem sexual activity.
   d. The victim was transported.
2. Which of the following is an example of a serial murder?
   a. Oklahoma City bombing
   b. Columbine school shooting
   c. Charles Manson murders
   d. Ted Bundy murders
3. Which type of violent crime involves three or more victims, one offender, one location, and a single event lasting minutes, hours, or days?
   a. Spree murder
   b. Serial murder
   c. Fratricide
   d. Mass murder
4. _____ is the base of the investigation pyramid.
   a. Comprehension
   b. Application and analysis
   c. Knowledge
   d. Synthesis
5. Typically, how old is a victim of sudden infant death syndrome (SIDS)?
   a. 1–6 months
   b. 6–9 months
   c. 9–12 months
   d. over 1 year

6. Which of the following is/are the fourth leading cause of accidental death in the United States?
   a. Motor vehicle accidents
   b. Poisoning
   c. Firearms
   d. Drowning

7. When immersed in water, how fast does body temperature fall?
   a. 5° per hour
   b. 10° per hour
   c. 15° per hour
   d. 20° per hour

8. How many hairs should be collected for DNA analysis?
   a. Only 1 is needed
   b. 13–25
   c. 25–50
   d. 50–100

9. Which of the following do offenders of sexual assault against the elderly rarely seek?
   a. Punishment
   b. Control
   c. Domination
   d. Sexual gratification

10. The more _____ the death plan, the more lethal the intent of suicide.
    a. malicious
    b. precise
    c. destructive
    d. ambiguous

11. The definition of parasuicide is _____.
    a. the act of intentionally ending one's own life
    b. a deliberate intervention undertaken with the express intention of ending a life to relieve intractable suffering
    c. a suicide method in which a suicidal individual deliberately acts in a threatening way with the goal of provoking a lethal response from a law enforcement officer
    d. a nonfatal act in which a person deliberately causes self-injury

12. Which of the following is amitriptyline considered to be?
    a. Stimulant
    b. Antidepressant
    c. Hallucinogen
    d. Diluent

13. What is the most common cause of death in an autoerotic fatality?
    a. Neck compression
    b. Chest compression
    c. Smoking
    d. Choking

14. When experiencing sedative withdrawal, what happens at the 24- to 72-hour marker?
    a. Improvement
    b. Tremors
    c. Insomnia
    d. Delirium

15. Two-thirds of all fire fatalities are the result of _____.
    a. asphyxiation
    b. burns
    c. heat exhaustion
    d. toxic gases

16. In contact wounds, which of the following will always be present?
    a. A muzzle impression
    b. Scorching of the wound edges
    c. The bullet itself
    d. Soot on the skin adjacent to the wound

17. In a hanging, suspension or partial suspension, what is the restricting force for cutting off oxygen?
    a. The rope
    b. The body
    c. The airway
    d. How long the body has been suspended

18. The presence of _____ suggests that a blade penetrated to its maximum length in a stabbing.
    a. ripped clothing
    b. the blade's sharpness
    c. a hilt mark
    d. tissue resistance

19. If a vehicle were to hit a pedestrian at about 25–30 mph, what would be damaged on the vehicle?
    a. No significant damage
    b. A dent in the fender
    c. The windshield breaks
    d. The vehicle would be totaled

20. Relatively, if a contusion is a dark purple color, how old is it?
    a. A few hours
    b. Less than a week
    c. One week
    d. More than one week

21. The purpose of a modus operandi is to ensure the _____ of the crime.
    a. cause
    b. quality
    c. success
    d. victim

22. When putting together a personality assessment, which of the following should you ask about the subject's marital status?
    a. How the subject and the spouse met
    b. The religion of the spouse and if it is the same as the subject's religion
    c. If the subject is single, married, divorced, or separated
    d. Where the spouse works

23. The vitreous humor is a good specimen to obtain when attempting to find which of the following toxicants?
    a. Volatile poisons
    b. Insecticides
    c. Carbon monoxide
    d. Metals

24. Of all the calls made to poison control centers involving potentially toxic substances, about how many happen in the home?
    a. 52%
    b. 68%
    c. 74%
    d. 91%

See page 533 for answer key.

SECTION VI
THE PSYCHOLOGICAL AUTOPSY

Section VI is about psychological autopsy. It specifies what psychological autopsy is used for, its history, how it has changed over time, and its use in forensics. See page 519 for questions reviewing the material in Section VI.

Chapter 26: Psychological Autopsy

26

PSYCHOLOGICAL AUTOPSY

26.1 Introduction to Psychological Autopsy

26.1.1 Overview

A middle-aged man was found dead in his home. He lay supine on the floor, under a heavy chairbed in his study. Blankets covered his head, and he was dressed in boxer shorts and pajamas. A rubber slipper lay between his throat and one leg of the chair, which pressed on his bruised neck. An iron support bar lay across his chest, keeping the furniture frame elevated off the floor. Analysis showed that this man had died from asphyxia due to external compression, and no substance was present in his blood. Investigators discovered that the victim had cancer, so it looked like an odd form of suicide. However, it turned out that he was seeing a psychiatrist about his odd habit of placing heavy objects on himself as part of a practice of masochistic sexual gratification. He was worried that he could not achieve an intimate relationship with a woman. It was difficult to know whether this death was an autoerotic accident or a suicide—or both.

In the United States, there are two basic types of crime reconstruction consulting in which psychological experts participate: behavioral profiling and psychological autopsy. The former attempts to narrow the pool of suspects in a possible homicide, while the latter helps determine the probable manner of someone's death. For some incidents, such as the above case, mental health experts possess the best background for this work. Both areas involve the interpretation of human behavior as evidence to attempt to resolve an open question relevant to making decisions and devising leads. Both also involve extensive victimologies, although a psychological autopsy generally is more detailed, diagnostic, and penetrating.

A medical autopsy establishes a cause of death by examining the physical condition of the body. In cases where the manner of death is unexplained and it is not clear what actually happened, a psychological autopsy may assist in clearing up the mystery. Over the past 50 years, practitioners have worked on revising and refining this approach.

26.1.2 Labels and Concepts

26.1.2.1 Definition   When the circumstances surrounding a death can be interpreted in more than one way, psychologists can compile information retrospectively about the victim's past behavior, most recent psychological state, and potential motives. If an analysis of the decedent's state of mind is requested for other issues, a biographical type of psychological autopsy can be compiled. If an incident appears to be a homicide, especially a staged homicide, a psychological autopsy can assist with details for incident reconstruction, an area in which typical law enforcement investigators are not trained.

Psychological autopsy has been called *psychiatric autopsy, retrospective death assessment, reconstructive evaluation,* and *equivocal death analysis.* The phrase refers to a specific method used for examining a person's life and personality—specifically, the most recent life aspects of a decedent. Depending on the purpose, it may be used for a variety of evaluations, from testamentary capacity while drawing up a will to the state of mind of the victim during the days or hours before death. There is a strong reliance on the discipline of suicidology. Some psychiatrists say a psychiatric autopsy adds more medical and genetic details, but reviewers of those claims believe that there is little real difference.

26.1.2.2 Psychological Knowledge   To give an example of the value of psychological knowledge, a woman who had disappeared for 30 years was found dead from apparent suffocation. The prosecutor suspected her husband, an angry recluse, had kept her prisoner and, eventually, had murdered her; he was arrested and tried. Each day during the 8-day trial, the defendant brought in a large suitcase. His defense attorney hired a medical expert to show that the woman could have had an epileptic seizure in bed, smothering herself while faced down on her pillow. Then, the defendant opened the suitcase; inside were more than 10,000 pages of his wife's writing, which matched writing all over the walls of their home. Included were letters of love and devotion, her daily activities, recipes, and Bible verses. She had suffered from agoraphobia and hypergraphia (compulsive writing), disorders a psychologist could have explained to investigators, and she had been relieved her husband had protected her from the outside world. He was acquitted. With psychological assistance on the investigation, he might never have even gone to trial.

26.1.3 NASH Categories

There are three key issues for death certifications: the cause, the mechanism, and the mode or manner of death. The cause is the instrument or physical agent used to bring about death (for example, a heavy weight compressing the throat), the mechanism is the pathological agent that resulted in the death (oxygen deprivation), and the manner, according to the NASH classification, is considered to be one of the following: natural, accident, suicide, or homicide.

Even when the cause and mechanism of death can be determined, sometimes, the manner cannot be determined because the circumstances are ambiguous. Thus, it becomes an undetermined death, and among those, some may be labeled *undetermined*, *pending*, meaning that further investigation is warranted. Some coroners have also proposed suicide by cop as its own unique category.

26.1.4 Statistics

Depending on the research consulted, anywhere between 5% and 20% of deaths in the United States are either equivocal or erroneously labeled, and most are unclear as to whether a seeming suicide was an accident. Sheleg and Ehrlich (2006) found numerous cases of supposed suicide that were clearly autoerotic accidents. Thus, it is difficult to definitively state how much error might exist in death statistics, especially in jurisdictions lacking resources and education about unusual death events.

26.1.5 Timing

26.1.5.1 Identification of the Victim and Time of Death Estimates   When a corpse is discovered, a coroner or medical examiner is called to the scene. A coroner will generally bring the body to a forensic pathologist for an autopsy unless a doctor can be found to acknowledge that the individual was ill, the death was from natural causes, and the corpse was not dangerous to the community. A medical examiner, who generally has more medical training than a coroner, may make a cursory examination at the death scene.

The first step is to identify the deceased. Sometimes, an identification is on the body (a wallet or purse), but sometimes, the body itself serves as the means for identification. Generally, the teeth offer this, in terms of the records a dentist may have. Sometimes, a scar, distinctive mole, or tattoo can assist, as well as broken bones matched to X-rays. Fingerprints may be on file, and at the very least, a DNA profile can be extracted. Any reports of missing people will be checked as well, both in local news and on national databases.

Even as the process of identification is going on, the time of death must be established in the event that the death was the result of a homicide. An investigation can place victims with a suspect at a certain time, eliminate suspects via alibis, or break alibis altogether. It can also help to get a killer arrested.

26.1.5.2 Postmortem Interval Estimate (PMI)   Historically, the PMIs, or time-since-death estimations, have been based on a variety of changes following death—lividity, rigor mortis, rate of digestion, body temperature, insect activity, etc.—because they were observed to proceed in a predictable order. None of these is wholly reliable since diverse internal and external factors affect them, but taken together, they provide a reasonable estimate. Time of death may be something like "between midnight and 6:00 a.m.," while the PMI would involve the passage of time since the death occurred (24 to 48 hours ago).

26.1.6 Importance of the Manner of Death

Barring some religious beliefs, most families would rather know the death of an adolescent was an accident instead of a suicide, even if it involves an embarrassing sexual practice. Also, an insurance payment can depend on the manner of death, since many policies will not pay if the death was a suicide. If the case is a homicide but is not sufficiently clarified to pursue, a killer could go free and, perhaps, even kill again. In addition, if the death is a surprise, the surviving friends and relatives seek closure.

26.2 History of Psychological Autopsy

26.2.1 Origins of Psychological Autopsy

The practice of psychological autopsies began during the 1930s with the systematic examination of 93 suicidal deaths among New York City police officers during a 6-year period. However, as a methodology for psychology professionals, the origin is more accurately pinpointed to the late 1950s. The Los Angeles medical examiner Theodore Curphey had to account for the manner of death in an unprecedented number of drug-related deaths. Any of them could have been an accidental overdose, suicide, or even homicide, and he was overwhelmed.

Curphey heard about the Los Angeles Suicide Prevention Center (LASPC), which had opened in 1958 in a former tuberculosis center on the grounds of the Los Angeles County Hospital. He invited Edwin S. Shneidman and his codirectors, Norman Faberow and Robert Litman, to assist him. Thanks to a grant, they were able to collaborate.

Shneidman and Farberow had just edited and published an anthology, *Clues to Suicide*, including a paper they wrote based on 721 suicide notes from people ranging in age from 13 to 96 they had discovered in 1953 in the basement of the Los Angeles coroner's office. Shneidman had been asked to write condolence letters to family members of two suicide victims, and while researching the cases, he discovered this collection in a vault. In their article, Shneidman and Faberow (1961) wrote that there were three types of raw material for understanding suicide: psychiatric case histories, psychological test results, and suicide notes. They looked for control data for each of these categories in order to make statistical comparisons. They founded the discipline of suicidology, which is further described below.

26.2.2 Approach to Suicide

26.2.2.1 *Early Efforts* To structure their approach for replication in research, Shneidman and Farberow obtained the names of adult male suicide victims from the coroner's weekly lists from 1944 to 1953. Then, they located 32 case histories of white males who successfully had completed suicide, 32 cases of attempted suicide, 32 who had threatened suicide, and 32 who had no suicidal behavior. The ages ranged from 20 to 69, with most under age 40. The researchers applied more than 100 different social, cultural, economic, and psychological categories—family history, marital status, employment history, and possible psychiatric diagnosis.

They also collected test results from the Rorschach inkblot test, the thematic apperception test, and the Minnesota Multiphasic Personality Inventory (MMPI), where available. In addition, they had their collection of 721 suicide notes.

Shneidman and Farberow found that it was nearly impossible to distinguish a potentially suicidal person from case details alone, except for certain red flag conditions such as paranoid schizophrenia and reactive depression. Almost three-quarters of those who completed the act had attempted or threatened it in the past. About 50% of those who killed themselves after being discharged from a hospital accomplished the act within three months.

On the psychological tests, individuals who have threatened suicide instead of attempting it showed more guilt, agitation, and aggression in their responses. They were more emotionally disturbed. This may seem obvious, but in the 1950s, little was known about suicidal minds.

26.2.2.2 Scene Investigation   For Curphey, the LASPC devised an interdisciplinary approach. First, they had a police officer write a report on the scene, which he submitted to them. The LASPC also sent a nonmedical investigator to the scene to write a second report. Eventually, this would save the medical examiner a trip. He would perform an autopsy only if reports indicated a need. If a suicide note was found, the LASPC asked a handwriting expert to confirm its authorship. If there was no note and the case was equivocal, then they would set up a death investigation team.

This team involved several psychologists who would check one another, and may also involve the occasional specialist. The mental health professionals would interview people who had known the decedent in an attempt to reconstruct the life narrative. During this process, they looked for known clues to suicide. They used a probability analysis to make a scientific extrapolation. Then, they discussed their ideas about the death in a conference before writing a final report for the medical examiner. In many cases, details were sketchy, but this approach assisted them to develop a better database.

26.2.2.3 Categories   The researchers grouped the type of information they used into four categories:

- Life history
- Psychological/psychiatric data
- Communication information
- Nonpsychiatric data

Seeing an opportunity for advancing their work on suicide, Shneidman sought to formalize the process of psychological autopsy, and in a 1961 article, he and Farberow explained what was involved. They interviewed individuals who had attempted suicide to gain an in-depth perspective and then described their focus on the deceased person's intention in relation to his or her own death. They found only a few rare cases of suicide lack evidence in the life history and also noted that the process of a psychological autopsy offers a secondary benefit: comfort to surviving relatives.

26.2.3 Fifteen Areas of Evaluation

Within the 4 categories, Shneidman, Litman, Farberow, and their colleagues identified 15 distinct categories for evaluation:

- "Identifying information for the victim (name, age, address, marital status, religious practices, occupation, etc.)
- Details of death (cause, method, etc.)
- Historical information (sibs, marriage, medical illnesses, medical and psychotherapy, suicidal attempts or gestures)
- Death history of victim's family (suicides, cancer, other fatal illnesses, age at death)
- Description of personality and lifestyle
- Victim's characteristic reactions to stress
- Any recent upsets, pressures, tensions, or anticipations of trouble
- Role of alcohol or drugs in overall lifestyle and death
- Nature of victim's interpersonal relationships
- Fantasies, dreams, cognitions, premonitions, or fears relating to death, accident, or suicide
- Before-death changes in habits, hobbies, sexual pattern, or other life routines

- Information about upswings, successes, plans
- Assessment of intention
- Rating of lethality, i.e., intent to die in terms of low, medium, or high
- Reaction of informants to victim's death"

They also proposed a four-level scale of lethality related to the decedent's knowledge and intent. In simplistic terms, Shneidman proposed that psychologists explore the *why, how,* and *what,* with special reference to the timing of the death. It might have occurred on an important anniversary (especially of a loss), or have been due to a prolonged illness or a session of unrelenting bullying. Their analysis was based on probability, and they had only the barest databases against which to test their criteria. In fact, the study of suicide had long been discouraged in the profession. However, they were determined to make the study of suicide more scientific. By 1961, they had set up a National Advisory Board of the Suicide Prevention Foundation, and in 1962, they established the Center for the Scientific Study of Suicide.

26.2.4 *State of Mind*

Shneidman classified motives as intentional, subintentional, or unintentional. He found that just 20% to 30% of suicides had left a note explaining their act. Another early study found that 62% had communicated their intent to at least one person. These fatal acts are clearly intentional, but Shneidman noted that with some people, it is not obvious. Their death wish is suppressed, so their self-destructive intent is subtle. In addition, there was this third category: those people who engage in something they know could be fatal but did not necessarily intend to die while doing it, such as racing a car on slick pavement.

Litman emphasized an aspect of state of mind he called the *suicidal crisis,* which was a temporary state through which people can pass. With help, they can avoid killing themselves and will eventually move on and resume their lives. Shneidman would later state that quite a few suicidal people experienced this temporary phase, which gave hope to mental health experts that many of their patients could be guided away from self-destruction.

26.2.5 Death of a Celebrity

26.2.5.1 The Suicide Panel   Los Angeles officials found this collaboration to be productive, and they continued to consult with the mental health experts on equivocal deaths. They established a *case of the week* conference, which was well received. Then in August 1962, they had a rather stunning case on their hands that put their new ideas to the test.

The world-famous actress Marilyn Monroe was found dead in her bed. She was just 36. On the bed stand were empty bottles of recently filled prescription drugs, and given her general emotional instability and trouble with depression, it seemed like a clear case of suicide. However, more than 4 hours had passed between the housekeeper discovering her and the call to police. In addition, her body appeared to have been posed, and the housekeeper was doing laundry when the police arrived. These events were troubling to investigators.

26.2.5.2 Monroe Autopsy   Deputy Medical Examiner Thomas Noguchi performed an autopsy and found Monroe had died from acute barbiturate poisoning, specifically an overdose of Nembutal and chloral hydrate. Curphey had specifically assigned the autopsy to him, and he believed that it was because he had a science background. He had sent samples of several of Monroe's organs to the toxicology lab, but they dropped the ball and performed only a partial analysis (a blood and liver test). Believing that the case was closed, they quickly destroyed the untested organs. Due in part to this, as well as resistance from those who knew Marilyn, rumors began to swirl that President John Kennedy and his brother, Robert Kennedy, were implicated— especially when Monroe's diary went missing. It was not long before conspiracy theories arose that Monroe had been murdered, and a cover-up that included the death investigators was underway.

Curphey gathered his consultants, which the media dubbed a *Suicide Panel.* Shneidman, Farberow, and Litman were all members, but they worked as much as possible in secrecy. They ensured those they interviewed the entire process would remain confidential. They spoke with Monroe's agent, former husbands, business associates, friends, housekeeper, and psychiatrist, as well as all of the investigators involved. They specifically looked for factors that indicated

Monroe was capable of suicide and had been depressed recently, but tried not to form tunnel vision that would neglect other aspects of her state of mind.

26.2.5.3 Marilyn's Psychache   Ultimately, the panel concluded that she fit the profile for suicidal depression. She had been fired from a movie set, gone through three failed marriages, had a drug addiction, had two devastating miscarriages, and had serious attachment issues from having a severely mentally ill mother. She had overdosed before death on a drug that one must take in large quantities to be fatal. In addition, the door and window to her bedroom had been locked from the inside.

Yet Monroe also had reasons to live. She had made significant plans, and many who saw or spoke to her the day before she died had failed to see signs of depression. In fact, she had seemed fine to them. In addition, those who knew her well were aware of how often she forgot which drugs she was mixing with liquor. To them this overdose seemed accidental. She had not been hopelessly depressed. Even the psychiatrist who came to her home that day and spent several hours with her was not entirely convinced of suicide.

Still, the panel determined Monroe's death was a probable suicide. Noguchi concurred based on his findings.

26.2.5.4 Revisiting the Case   Noguchi was mystified, when called to a new investigation 20 years later, that people had not accepted his determination, although he admitted to several puzzling elements— notably the lack of capsules in Monroe's stomach. He decided her stomach had quickly kicked them to the intestines, which had not been properly examined. However, he did not explain why she was found neatly laid out in bed rather than in the sort of convulsed position that most overdoses cause, nor did he know why so much time had passed before the authorities were called.

Marilyn Monroe's death still attracts theories about conspiracy and murder. The case presents a good lesson about being thorough, especially for deaths that will be highly scrutinized. In fact, in 2005, a former Los Angeles prosecutor, John Miner, who had been present at the autopsy, revived notions about murder after he exposed a secret he had carried for years. Monroe's psychiatrist, Dr. Ralph Greenson, had allowed Miner to hear tapes that Marilyn had sent to him of their therapy sessions. Miner had heard nothing on the tapes that supported a finding of suicide. He had taken extensive notes, and in 2005, he allowed them to be published in the *Los Angeles Times*. (Greenson was dead by then.)

Miner thinks Marilyn had been drugged via a drink during the evening and then given an enema that contained the lethal dose of Nembutal. He called for a reautopsy. The current district attorney (DA) believes that there is insufficient evidence for this. Nevertheless, the Los Angeles office now admits that the overdose could have been accidental rather than intentional. Despite the thorough investigation performed by the Suicide Panel, they did not have facts that have emerged since 1962.

26.2.5.5 Mode Conference   Dr. Noguchi later became the chief medical examiner, and he dubbed the process of a team-based psychological autopsy a *mode conference*. He was able to charge a small fee for participation. He also streamlined the effort by encouraging phone interviews rather than face to face. It is still called a *mode conference* today.

26.3 Psychological Evidence

26.3.1 Deceiving Appearances

Kristen Rossum called 911 on November 6, 2000, to report her husband, Greg deVillers, was unconscious. She thought that he had committed suicide. The dispatcher instructed her in cardiopulmonary resuscitation, and the paramedics arrived in less than 5 minutes. Kristen indicated that Greg had been despondent over marital problems. Investigators noticed that there were rose petals scattered around the double bed and a wedding photo nearby. Kristen said Greg was romantic like that and suggested that he might have taken some of her old prescriptions.

Investigators looked into their background. The two had been married for less than 2 years, and Greg was just 26. He had rescued her from a downward spiral of drug addiction. Shortly after they married, she took a job as a chemist with the San Diego County Medical Examiner's Office. There, she got involved with her supervisor, 31-year-old toxicologist Michael Robertson. During the police interview, Kristen admitted that she had told Greg about "someone else" who made her happy, and this had been the reason for his suicide. However, she said a number of things during the interview that, according to his relatives, contradicted her husband's character. In addition, there were odd things at the death scene that failed to add up to a suicide. For example, there was no source for the drugs—no empty pill bottles. Also odd was the fact that Kristen said she had taken a long bath before discovering her husband dead, but investigators found no stopper for holding water in the tub. She also claimed that she had fixed Greg lunch during the day, but his boss had called the house at that time, and no one had answered the phone. Greg's boss said that if Greg had been able to eat, he would have definitely called in. Kristen said that Greg had been up and around, but his boss had phoned several times without getting him. Kristen's idea that the rose petals were Greg's "melodramatic suicide note" struck detectives as an unlikely act for a male. In addition, she said that she had found them on his chest, but there was no trace of rose petals in the bed in which he died. She also said that the petals were from roses he had bought for her birthday weeks earlier, but the petals were fresh. There were enough puzzling aspects to this case to perform a more thorough investigation. Kristen's affair alone made it worth pursuing.

26.3.2 Suicide Disconfirmation

The toxicology report indicated Greg had three drugs in his system: OxyContin, clonazepam, and fentanyl. These same three drugs were missing from the inventory at the medical examiner's office, and Kristen was in charge of the drug inventory. She and her lover, Michael Robinson, had been to a toxicology seminar a month before Greg's death, where they had attended a lecture on fentanyl's lethal effects. This lecture included the fact that it was not routine to test for this drug during a death investigation. This made fentanyl a perfect murder weapon. In addition, Kristen had purchased a single rose the day before Greg's death, a reference to a scene from her favorite movie, *American Beauty*, that involved rose petals strewn around a character. In addition, Kristen had tried to donate Greg's skin and eyes immediately after the autopsy and had asked for a cremation.

This was suspicious enough that his family sought an independent autopsy. Their investigator who examined Greg's body found an unexplained needle puncture.

Kristen was arrested and her attorney offered a new angle: Greg had killed himself but had hidden the evidence so as to get revenge on Kristen by making his death look like a murder. However, contrary to a finding of suicide for any reason, Greg's friends, family, and associates all said that he had been looking forward to a trip, he had been excited, and he had not been depressed. Thus, investigators had a case of ambiguity; the facts seemed sufficiently malleable to support either story.

26.3.3 Psychological Interpretations

Psychological evidence can take many forms, some of them ambiguous. The arrangement of rose petals (an intentional behavior) may be interpreted as either a suicidal note or a killer's flourish. The type of behavior that is considered evidence has to do with motive, scene reconstruction, deception, inconsistency in statements, inconsistency in normal behavior, decision making, and the types of disorders evident in an incident. We typically rely on psychological evidence in a forensic context to explain something, to undermine a proffered explanation, or to predict future behavior.

Interpreting psychological evidence relies on knowledge about disorders or about phenomena in social or cognitive psychology. It also involves skilled observation, especially if expected evidence is absent. For example, with a suicidal drug overdose, we would expect to see empty pill bottles and perhaps a suicide note. If suicide is by firearm, we expect the gun to be there. Its absence would undermine a suicide theory unless the decedent (or someone else) had staged his or her suicide as a murder (to frame someone in revenge, for example).

Interpretation of psychological evidence is based on probability: What is the likelihood that this is a suicide staged to look like murder versus an actual murder poorly staged to look like a suicide? In this case, the interpreter must have experience with suicide cases. It also helps to look at statistics in a database. Essentially, we develop an inner sense of logic in terms of what we expect about a given incident and what we can predict based on our common experience of human behavior. Occasionally, a death will be so unique that someone with a particular type of expertise may have to help interpret it.

26.3.4 Scientific Analysis

Psychological information can have a significant impact on the final death determination. Nearly half of the country's medical examiners (195 out of 400) participated in a 1986 study. They each received scenarios from both typical and equivocal death cases. In addition to standard information about the death circumstances, half received information from a psychological autopsy on factors about the decedent, such as history of depression, signs of a significant life change, signals about closure, or a lack of suicidal ideation.

Although receiving this information failed to influence medicolegal decisions in unequivocal cases, it had a significant impact in the equivocal cases: The medical examiners more often decided on a definite manner of death in seemingly equivocal cases rather than leaving them undetermined. This underscores the importance of gathering psychological information that could become evidence in support of a determination.

In the case of Greg deVillers's death, the totality of circumstances helped to gain a conviction for Kristen Rossum. Her description of what happened was uncorroborated by many other factors, on scene and off, and this undermined her credibility. The probability of a male leaving a symbolic suicide note with rose petals was too unlikely, and the fact that Rossum was having an affair and the drugs in Greg's system had come from her office, supported a guilty verdict. Reconstruction involved psychological evidence to understand the physical evidence, which could have supported two different analyses.

26.4 Suicidology

26.4.1 History

A French alienist, Jean Esquirol, was a leader in making insanity a medical concern rather than a purely religious one. During the late 18th century, he devised a classification of mental disorders that gave suicide a prominent place. The earliest notions about suicide were that the reasons were obvious: psychosis or concern over one's health.

Sociologist Emile Durkheim published *Le Suicide* in 1897, while Freud's followers examined what they called self-focused aggression during the following decade. Yet it was not until the 1950s that suicide studies became more visible. This was due to the seminal work, mentioned above, of Shneidman, Farberow, and Litman at the LASPC. Its doors opened in 1958, and the staff were soon assisting the coroner on equivocal death analyses. Shneidman coined the term *suicidology* for this emerging discipline.

26.4.1.1 Formalizing Suicide Research Shneidman and Farberow's research, along with the collection of papers in their first anthology, formed the basis for the discipline of suicidology. Scholars in this field met in 1968, as Shneidman founded the American Association of Suicidology; its members established a journal, which inspired many more professionals to conduct research and consult on cases. In 1987, the American Suicide Foundation began to fund suicide research. Advances in psychopharmacology offered therapeutic drugs to treat depression and suicidal delusions.

Although getting actual clinical data is difficult, there is a great deal to be learned from postmortem idiographic research. For example, although common sense says a person intent on suicide will, if thwarted, just find another place, a study of 515 people who had been blocked from jumping off San Francisco's Golden Gate Bridge revealed that just 4.8% had taken their lives in another way. Six people who had survived the jump said they had not attempted to kill themselves again. One even said that after he had jumped, he suddenly realized all of his problems were fixable (except his most immediate one—the jump).

26.4.1.2 Suicide Statistics Suicide holds steady as the 11th leading cause of death in the United States. Anywhere between 1 in 20 and 1 in 30 attempts succeed (depending on the report), with the elderly being the most successful (1 in 4). Among people aged 15 to 24, suicide is the third leading cause of death, with about 5000 deaths every year. Around 90% of people who commit suicide have a mental illness, with clinical depression as most common. Low levels of serotonin are often present in the brains of those who have killed themselves. Other mood disorders, as well as substance abuse, are also factors. Although there are spontaneous suicides, in which a person who died surprised everyone, more often, there have been prior signals.

Suicides spike during certain seasons, but not in winter or during the holidays, as many imagine; they spike during the spring and have done so for centuries. Monday is the day most commonly chosen, and in the United States, nearly half of self-annihilators use a firearm. Men take their lives at nearly four times the rate of women and account for 79% of all suicides in the United States. However, three times more women than men make a suicide attempt, especially when their estrogen levels are low. In recent years, more females have used weapons than in the past.

Suicidology, the scientific study of suicide risk and prevention, offers a growing body of research findings. For example, although only a quarter of successful suicide victims leave an explanation, 80% gave obvious clues. More than 60% who threaten to kill themselves either make an attempt or complete the act. However, most people are ambivalent about suicide. They just want the pain to stop. In a study of suicide attempt survivors, only 4% indicated their intent had been "very serious."

The risk for suicide does not necessarily disperse with an improved state of mind. The highest rate occurs within about 3 months after an apparent improvement because sufferers have gained the energy and focus to carry it out. It is common for them to have recently seen a doctor. In addition, a past attempt is the best predictor of a future attempt. Around 80% of people who commit suicide have made at least one previous attempt, although it is not true that most will keep trying until they succeed. The fact that someone attempted suicide is more significant for risk assessment than the method.

26.4.1.3 The Desire for Death   Suicidologist Thomas Joiner believes that there are two primary psychological states that support a desire for death: perceived burdensomeness and a sense of low belongingness. He has made a study of the myths that float around about suicide, and among the erroneous beliefs that people hold, he lists the following (Joiner, 2005):

- Suicide is an easy escape; it is for cowards.
- Suicide is an act of anger or revenge.

- If people intent on suicide are stopped, they will just go elsewhere.
- People seriously considering suicide do not make life plans.
- People often die by suicide on a whim.
- Most suicides leave a note to explain it.
- Most suicides look terribly depressed before they do it.
- Children cannot form suicidal intent.

Shneidman would add a few more myths:

- People who talk about suicide do not commit suicide (in fact, 70% to 80% do).
- Suicide usually happens without warning.
- People who kill themselves were fully intent on doing it.

26.4.2 Recent Findings

People who are vulnerable to suicidal thoughts vary with age, gender, social demographic, and ethnic group. Some reports state that risk factors often occur in combinations. One study from Australia found more that 70% of those who had survived a suicidal jump were psychotic. Often, they were undiagnosed, suggesting that more suicidal jumpers than originally thought have a form of psychosis.

Also, German researchers examined autopsies of people diagnosed with bipolar disorder or schizophrenia and found that the 9 people who took their own lives (versus 30 who died naturally) had more densely packed von Economo neurons in their brains. These cells have receptors for neurotransmitters that help to regulate emotion. Scientists believe that because humans have the highest density of these cells of all animals, the cells may be involved in complex social processes, such as guilt, empathy, and shame. Suicidal people may be especially sensitive, but further research is warranted in this area.

26.4.3 Risk Factors

Risk factors include having a history of one or more suicide attempts, having a family history of mental disorder or suicide, being a victim of abuse, having a chronic physical illness, having been incarcerated, and having been closely exposed to the suicidal behavior of others. An adverse life event can be the tipping point.

Immediate warning signs include the following:

- Talking about death or suicide
- Having severe, unresponsive clinical depression
- Having a death wish manifested in high-risk behavior
- Losing interest in things he or she once cared about
- Making comments about being hopeless or worthless
- Putting affairs in order, tying up loose ends, or changing a will
- Saying things such as "I'm worth more dead than alive," or "I want out"
- Having a sudden switch from sadness to calmness, or even happiness
- Visiting or calling people to say good-bye
- Obsessing over a grievous loss
- Changing religious habits, sleeping habits, or eating habits
- Giving important things away and closing accounts
- Reading or listening to music about suicide

26.4.4 Suicide Notes

26.4.4.1 Context Philosopher and prize-winning author Albert Camus once said that suicide was the one truly serious philosophical question. It forces one to ask why life is worth living. "There are many causes for a suicide," he wrote in *The Myth of Sisyphus*, "and generally the most obvious ones were not the most powerful. Rarely is suicide committed (yet the hypothesis is not excluded) through reflection. What sets off the crisis is almost always unverifiable."

Suicide notes can offer valuable information (but not always) about the reasons people kill themselves and their psychological state at the time of death. Sometimes the motive is spelled out; sometimes it is clear only indirectly. Note-leavers feel a need to say something to someone they have left behind, whether a harsh word, an apology, an explanation, or just a list of tasks that must be done. It may be a single phrase, several pages, a series of Post-it notes, or even a videotape. As mentioned above, a study of suicide notes launched the formal field of suicidology.

26.4.4.2 Actual Notes   A divorced woman, age 61, wrote in a suicide note: "You cops will want to know why I did it, well, just let us say that I lived 61 years too many. People have always put obstacles in my way. One of the great ones is leaving this world when you want to and have nothing to live for. I am not insane. My mind was never more clear. It has been a long day. The motor got so hot it would not run so I just had to sit here and wait. The breaks were against me to the last. The sun is leaving the hill now so hope nothing else happens."

Some of the sentiments expressed are below:

- I cannot find my place in life.
- This is best for all concerned.
- I do not want to go but there is nothing else to do. I have never been much good.
- The only thing you never called me was crazy. Now you can do that.
- I am all twisted up inside.

As mentioned, Shneidman and his colleagues examined 721 suicide notes. This represented nearly all of the notes collected by the coroner between 1944 and 1953, but this meant that only about 15% of suicidal decedents had left notes.

26.4.4.3 Notes Analysis   To study the notes, Shneidman used the discomfort relief quotient to compare the amount of *discomfort thought units* with the mount of *relief thought units*. Generally, whatever feeling was expressed—rage, hatred, vengeance, fear, or self-loathing—was intense. But some notes were neutral; they gave lists, admonishments, or instructions. A number of note-writers simply expressed relief over having made the decision.

Shneidman discovered difficulties in finding control data; first, because people who survive generally destroy the notes they had written. Thus, the researchers looked for people who matched many characteristics of the successful suicides and asked them to write hypothetical notes, imagining they were going to commit suicide. (The researchers employed screening tests and other safeguards to avoid upsetting participants.) Thirty-three male, white, married, Protestant, native-born genuine suicide note-writers were matched against 33 males of similar characteristics. All were from southern

California. (The researchers understood the study would not be representative, but believed it would be a tentative first step in a continuing study. In an appendix, they offered examples of the genuine and simulated notes for readers to see for themselves.)

The final stage of research was to compare actual notes with the simulated notes. The comparison was a qualitative analysis (based on John Stuart Mill's method of difference) that formed comparison categories from discomfort thought units, relief thought units, and neutral thought units. Shneidman and Farberow defined a thought unit as "a discrete idea, regardless of number of words." Obviously, this became a matter of interpretation.

26.4.4.4 Findings   The researchers found that there were significantly more thought units in the genuine notes, compared with the fictitious notes. "The genuine note writers apparently feel the need to say more in this last communication." There also were also more discomfort units among the genuine suicide notes, and these notes were more emotionally intense (especially for hatred, self-blame, and vengeance). There was no quantitative difference between the note-writers on relief statements.

However, under the neutral category, they found the most dramatic difference. The genuine note-writers had many more neutral content thought units. Usually, these units involved giving instructions or listing things to do (such as who gets this or that from the decedent's possessions).

Shneidman and Farberow concluded that genuine note-writers had accepted the fact that within a brief time frame, they would be dead, something missing from the controls' frame of reference. This sense of imminent absence that inspired things like admonitions to the living was absent from the fictitious notes. It seemed that the suicidal person was trying to exercise one last bit of power in the world, as if his or her death added weight to his or her requests and requirements. The researchers believed that this reflected paradoxical and illogical motivations.

Since then, no study has found the rate of note leaving to be more than 50% and in most studies, this figure is below 40%. It is often as low as one in four, which holds steady even when suicide rates climb.

26.5 Autoerotic Complications

26.5.1 Definition

Investigators who are not familiar with cases of autoerotic fatalities (AEFs) may confuse an accidental autoerotic death with a suicide. Autoerotic asphyxiation is a self-induced reduction in oxygen to produce a state of hypoxia. It results in feelings of elation, exhilaration, and heightened sexual pleasure. In the *Diagnostic and Statistical Manual of Mental Disorders, Fourth Edition, Text Revision*, or *DMS-IV-TR*, AEF is included under the description for the paraphilia, sadomasochism. In psychoanalytic terms, the activity is viewed as an expression of weakness and the need to overcome the threat to life in order to achieve a sense of success.

Sometimes, AEFs have obvious autoerotic features, such as sexual paraphernalia, neck padding, transsexual clothing, and pornography, but not always. The victims are predominantly adolescent males but women and even children have engaged in this practice as well.

Although autoerotic asphyxia generally refers to the use of a ligature apparatus around the neck during self-gratification rituals, it can be performed in other ways. For example, there is a phenomenon called *cocooning*, in which a person uses plastic sheeting to restrict airflow during masturbation. In 2002, a man in Maine encased his entire body in shrink-wrap, using a diver's snorkel as a limited airway. However, he lost his grip on the snorkel and was unable to free himself, so he died. Others have used bags over the head, chest compression, submersion, and chemical inhalation. Death occurs when some part of the mechanism fails. Such fatalities are considered accidental (unless they are used during the course of a clear suicide).

26.5.2 Atypical Autoerotic Death

In rare instances, the sexual activity is performed underwater while holding one's breath to produce hypoxia. A 25-year-old man went into water in a homemade plastic bodysuit with his genitals wrapped separately in a plastic tube. He wore a hockey helmet, and over the bodysuit was a snowmobile suit and ski boots. He was bound with an elaborate setup of mesh and chains, which were padlocked at his groin. He was found completely submerged, with an air tube running from his mouth to a floating plastic container. However, he had apparently miscalculated, using a tube too narrow for both the intake and the expulsion of air. His air supply was significantly fouled with carbon dioxide, killing him. Another indicator that this was not a suicide was his membership in an online autoerotic practitioner's club.

Besides the scene that one typically finds in autoerotic deaths, there are a variety of atypical scenes, which make the death investigator's job more difficult. One man, 19, died from a massive compression of the thorax when he dressed in a pressure suit for military pilots, covered his head with three masks and a helmet, bound his arms and legs, and turned on a 12 V air compressor. It inflated the suit to the point that the pressure stopped his ability to breathe, and he lost consciousness.

Most of those who engage in autoerotic activity are male, but there are some female cases. A 19-year-old woman had placed a rope around her neck and attached it to her legs, easing the knot's pressure by bending her legs. However, her hair got caught in the mechanism, which caused it to fail, so she died.

Former special agent Roy Hazelwood, who in 1983, coauthored the first textbook devoted to autoeroticism, *Autoerotic Fatalities*, specialized in trying to understand this area of death investigation. He and his coauthors examined 150 deaths and found that most were acting out masochistic fantasies. He selected some of the more fascinating cases for *Dark Dreams*.

"I was surprised by the variety of means in the ways they died," Hazelwood said. "It wasn't just hanging. We had nitrous oxide. We had suspension around the abdomen, in which they suffocated. We had one kid who slipped into a garbage can. The neighbors thought they heard a dog howling all night long and it actually was him in this garbage can. There were simplistic ways, such as lying down beside a chest of drawers, pulling out the lower drawer, laying it across your carotid artery, and dying in that passive position. And then there were violent ways, with things like electrocution. I had one guy who drove out to a park in the middle of the night, undressed, redressed in female clothing, got into the back seat, and played Russian Roulette."

Another unusual case he described featured a man who had decided on autoerotic suicide. He left a note describing the pleasure he anticipated as he died. He set fire to a woman's slip that he was wearing, padlocked a chain around his wrists, and kicked over a chair to ensure that he hanged. "I come wildly, madly," he wrote. "The pain is intense as my clothes start burning my legs." He definitely wanted to end his "nightmare life," but he wanted to do so while enjoying maximum sexual pleasure.

Another case involved a young man who was found hanging from a metal ladder, nude, inside a tall, vertical sewer pipe. His mouth and eyes were wrapped in duct tape. He had wrapped a bicycle cable around his arm and neck, and his grandfather's pocket watch was in his mouth. His clothes lay at the bottom of the pipe. Detectives did not know what to call this death. The victim had been a thrill seeker, and nothing about his manner of death was consistent with known homicides or suicides. The duct tape would have enhanced sensory deprivation, and other victims of autoeroticism gone wrong often used timing devices to tell them how much time had passed.

26.5.3 Developmental Factors

A more recent book devoted entirely to the subject is *Autoerotic Asphyxiation: Forensic, Medical and Social Aspects* by Sergey Shelog and Edwin Ehrlich. It provides a history of asphyxiophilia (or hypoxyphilia), dating back to 1856. A summary of psychiatric knowledge from 1968, which still holds true, offers clues for death investigators. The following facts are signs of autoerotic fatalities:

- The deaths were a complete surprise to relatives.
- There was no known psychiatric history or obvious motivation for suicide.
- Preparation and bondage activity suggested habitual practice.
- The victim was typically an intelligent Caucasian male.

As the person grows older, his technique often becomes more elaborate and involves bondage. It may also become more extreme as the initial edginess wears off. One man had created a Russian roulette setup, which did finally kill him. Prior to his death, however, the very possibility of annihilation had enhanced the intensity of his masturbatory experience. Most such death scenes include props, female clothing, pornography, bondage materials, and hanging or smothering mechanisms. Among the latter may be plastic bags or gas masks. Aerosol inhalants such as CO_2 or nitrogen may also be present.

Many autoerotic accidents are clearly associated with paraphilias, some of which are unique. When a man went missing in Pennsylvania, police went to his home. They saw stacks of magazines and porno-graphic videotapes about mud eroticism. They also found several empty 5 gal cans of plaster. Nothing appeared to be missing and the resident's keys and wallet were visible in the bed. In the bathroom was a large trash receptacle filled with hardened plaster. They might not have given it a second thought except for the plaster-encrusted hand that reached out. They had found their missing person. A TV set was on and a pornographic video was playing in a continuous loop. The trash can was hauled into the morgue for the removal of the body. There was no evidence that someone had killed him and dumped him into the can. The posture in which it had hardened suggested that the man was planning an autoerotic session, using plaster in place of mud, but had slipped, gone deep into the plaster, and aspirated it into his lungs. The manner of death was classified as an accident.

26.6 Modern Changes in Psychological Autopsy

26.6.1 Updated Criteria

Ebert (1987) published a guide in which he reviewed professional writing about psychological autopsies. He pointed out that the technique had been used to analyze aircraft crashes, homicide investigations, hospital deaths, and complex legal questions. Ebert also included more categories than Shneidman, for a total of 26. Confirming Shneidman's lethality scale, Ebert called his list a practical guide for the working professional, wherein a professional can change the coro-ner's process "from guessing to educated guessing."

Ebert's 26 criteria are as follows:

- Alcohol history
- Suicide notes
- Writings
- Books read
- Relationship assessments
- Marital relationships

- Mood
- Psychosexual stressors
- Presuicidal behavior
- Language (references to suicide; changes in language)
- Drugs used
- Medical history
- Reflective mental status exam of deceased's condition before death
- Psychological history
- Laboratory studies (from evidence at scene)
- Coroner/medical examiner report
- Motive assessment
- Reconstruction of death event
- Feelings regarding death; preoccupations and fantasies
- Military history
- Death history of family
- Family history
- Employment history
- Educational history
- Familiarity with death methods
- Police report

Within each category, Ebert lists more specific aspects for 100 separate factors. For motive assessment, he suggests making a chart for each of the NASH categories on which to record data in support of one or another manner of death. Although there is no benefit of direct observation, he states that a psychological autopsy often gathers more information about psychological states than standard assessments.

Ebert states that professionals conducting a psychological autopsy should review the police and coroner's report and examine the decedent's educational history and preoccupational fantasies, military history, and familiarity with methods of death.

26.6.2 Sufficient for Suicide

To consider a death as a potential suicide, there must be evidence that a wound could have been self-inflicted and some way to determine whether the victim understood the consequences of what he or she was doing. This involves compiling information about the person's last hours, days, and weeks. A close examination of the death scene may indicate the degree of intent and lethality—a secluded place and the use of a weapon indicating a higher degree of both than using slow-acting pills in a place where the victim is likely to be discovered. Also, people who knew the deceased might have motives for concealing what happened, so the investigator needs to be proficient in deception detection as well. One man who had reported his wife's suicide claimed that he had found her in the shower after he had heard the water running for some time. He had not even cut her down, but instead got neighbors to assist him to place her on the floor. But the investigator realized that there was no evidence of water on the floor, in the tub, or on the body. An investigation produced the husband's marital affair.

It has been more than two decades since Ebert's article was published, but there is yet to be an agreement among professionals to adopt this approach nationwide.

26.7 Methods and Reports

26.7.1 Methods

26.7.1.1 Initial Indicators   Appearances can be deceiving. One case initially looked like a fatal sexual assault. Neighbors found a 39-year-old woman dead on her living room floor after they heard a lot of banging that sounded like an attack. Her hands were covered in scratches. Police found her pet cat in the kitchen, disemboweled, with its tail hacked off, and lying on the stove. The victim's pants were pulled down to her knees so it appeared that she had been raped. Yet the autopsy revealed this woman's stomach was full of cat intestines, adipose tissue, and strips of fur-covered skin. An intact left kidney and adipose tissue were lodged in her throat just above her epiglottis. The end of the cat's tail was damp and it tested positive for saliva. After a complete investigation turned up a background of bipolar disorder and no evidence of a break-in, the cause of death was determined to be asphyxia by smothering due to animal tissue. It was assumed that the decedent had tried to dislodge the items stuck inside her throat with the cat's tail. Despite appearances, the death was considered accidental.

26.7.1.2 Intent and Lethality   At times, the results will be clear; while at other times, the decedent's state of mind prior to death cannot be known with certainty.

26.7.1.3 Timing   Some mental health professionals estimate a comprehensive psychological autopsy could take around 20 to 30 hours to develop, but the amount of time depends on the goal and, often, the time and funds available for it. Some professionals have remained interested beyond the initial assignment.

26.7.1.4 Sources   To compose an understanding of a person's final days and hours, an investigator may use any number of the following sources, with the awareness any interviewee could thwart as easily as facilitate the process:

- Interviews with eyewitnesses or police officers at the scene
- Medical autopsy reports (which can reveal things about the victim, such as substance abuse, that even close friends did not know)
- An examination of the death scene, either at the scene or via photographs
- Journals/correspondences/suicide note associated with the victim
- Types of books the victim read, music preferred, or video-games played
- Behavior patterns noted by others, especially unusual recent behavior
- Records (school, military, phone, employment, medical, psychiatric)
- History of medication, if any, including recent changes
- Digital habits (online social networks, computer journal, texting, cyberbullying)
- Recent comments on social network sites or in texts
- The results of a formal suicide assessment instrument (licensed clinicians only)

- Reports about conflicted relationships or other stressors (life events that precipitated a loss of hope, or psychache)
- Sudden and significant changes in wills or life insurance policies
- Death legacy or mental illness in family

26.7.1.5 Interpretation Psychological investigators will then compile and interpret the collected information to determine a number of factors about the decedent. For this, they will focus on personal information, details about the death, indications of the decedent's familiarity with death methods and access to them, stress reaction patterns, and recent stressors. If they are known to drink or take drugs, this will become part of the study, as will any significant changes in routines. For example, if the person does not usually go to church but suddenly starts attending regularly (or vice versa), this can indicate depression or thoughts about death and the afterlife.

Changes in a significant relationship can also be a factor, especially an unwanted divorce or sudden unexpected death. On the other hand, if associates or relatives react strangely to news about the death, the death could have been something other than a suicide.

26.7.2 The Report

The final report that accompanies a psychological autopsy should present an accurate sense of the decedent's personality, habits, and behavior patterns, specifically including any recent changes. Often, the likely manner of death will emerge from these facts, but the problem with ambiguous situations is that each new factor can shift the theory back and forth. Ebert (1987) offers the example of a person falling from a plane. He or she wore a parachute, but it did not open. Did he or she fall accidentally? Was he or she pushed? Did he or she jump and the parachute did not open, have a heart attack before pulling the cord, or jump and decide not to open the parachute?

26.8 Psychological Autopsy in Forensic Contexts

Despite attempts over the years to formalize this approach, even today, the profession has adopted no standard procedures. This has caused trouble with some assessments, especially one well-known case that involved a number of professionals.

26.8.1 A Controversial Case

Forty-seven sailors were killed aboard the battleship *USS Iowa* on April 19, 1989, and the Navy invited members of the FBI's BSU, now BAU, to offer a behavioral profile. Special Agents Roy Hazelwood and Richard Ault were assigned. The Navy gave them the details from its own investigation.

During training in the Caribbean, an explosion had occurred in one of the gun turrets, sparking a series of deadly fires, and after a 5-month investigation, the Navy identified its chief suspect as Gunner's Mate Clayton Hartwig, who was among the dead. Unfortunately, the best eyewitnesses to the central incident had perished in the blast. The Naval Criminal Investigative Service (NCIS) ruled out accidental causes. The agents were told that Hartwig had made a statement about dying in an explosion in the line of duty so he could be buried in Arlington National Cemetery. They also learned about some of his troubled relationships.

Special Agents Roy Hazelwood and Richard Ault relied on the Navy's stash of letters, journals, reading material, song lyrics, and bank account balances associated with Hartwig, as well as interviews the Navy had conducted with Hartwig's friends, relatives, and fellow sailors. It seemed that Hartwig had an interest in explosives, and he had possibly been depressed over a failed relationship with another sailor. He had taken out a life insurance policy, naming this man as a beneficiary (although he claimed there had been no relationship).

From the start, it was clear that the agents were there to consider only the NCIS's hypothesis about an intentional act and to decide on a finding of suicide, homicide, or a combination of the two. Accident was not part of the equation.

However, it was known the ship had problems, having been through two wars, and some conditions on it were dangerous. Nevertheless, the BSU agents found that Hartwig had exhibited emotional instability. They concluded that Hartwig had been an angry, suicidal loner who had a history of deception. They decided that he had acted intentionally, killing himself and the other men in a suicide/homicide.

Hartwig's family mounted a campaign to clear his name. Congress organized a subcommittee for the Armed Services to look into the case. Twelve psychologists from the American Psychological Association, along with two psychiatrists, were asked to review the FBI profile. The panel included experts in suicidology, forensic psychology, personality assessment, psychopathology, and risk assessment.

Their job was to examine the methodology of psychological autopsy, which Hazelwood and Ault firmly defended. The committee examined the validity of the report's conclusion, how exhaustive the investigation had been, viable alternative conclusions, and the limitations of a postmortem analysis of personality and motives. The glaring weakness was the fact the Navy had provided the documents rather than allowing an independent investigation.

Ten of the professionals rejected the approach of psychological autopsy as having no basis in science. They could not support the degree of confidence with which the agents had filed their report, although four of them accepted the Navy's conclusions about Hartwig's suicidal state of mind as appropriate. Even so, this did not support an intentional act of homicide.

Ault and Hazelwood testified before the Armed Services subcommittee hearing at the end of 1989. Ault indicated that an equivocal death analysis utilizes all possible resources and generates a number of hypotheses before deciding on which one best encompasses the evidence. Hazelwood testified about how they had applied these principles to the USS Iowa case. They were challenged on their degree of confidence at offering their findings, and Ault took issue with the academic analysis, because the psychologists who had offered their opinions did not work in the field and, therefore, could not draw solid conclusions about investigations.

Given the diversity of opinions among the experts, the House Armed Services subcommittee faced a difficult task. Aside from the BSU agents, nearly every expert had been tentative. Nevertheless, it became clear there was no scientific validity backing up a psychological autopsy. Thus, until this procedure had better backing, its use in a forensic setting was deemed inappropriate. In the end, the committee members found that the evidence was insufficient to draw a definitive conclusion about the cause of the explosion.

26.8.1.1 What the Courts Accept   It has been more than two decades since the *USS Iowa* case. Since then, there has been a decision about the admissibility of scientific evidence.

In 1923, in *Frye versus United States*, the judge decided scientific claims must be "sufficiently established to have gained general acceptance in the particular field in which it belongs." Later revisions included the Federal Rules of Evidence 702, which appeared to drop general acceptance in lieu of knowledge, skill, training, or experience, and allowed judges to decide on relevance. This opened the door for inventors to claim that novel methods unknown to their peers were nonetheless scientific.

Just after DNA analysis emerged as a viable forensic tool, another case changed admissibility standards. Jason Daubert was born with a birth defect. In a suit against Merrell Dow Pharmaceuticals, the boy's parents alleged the Bendectin that his pregnant mother had taken had caused it. The drug company's expert testified about published studies that showed no fetal malformations, while the plaintiffs' eight experts offered the unpublished results of test tube and animal studies.

The parents lost, so they appealed, but in 1993, the U.S. Supreme Court affirmed the trial court's decision. It also ruled that judges should be more diligent as gatekeepers in blocking unreliable findings. By the new guidelines, scientific methods and procedures should be clearly established in the field. Judges should determine whether the theory is testable, its potential error rate is known, it has been peer-reviewed, and it is relevant to the case.

The *Daubert* standard replaced the *Frye* standard in federal courts and many states. Two subsequent cases, *General Electric Co. v. Joiner* and *Kumho Tire Co. v. Carmichael*, clarified the judge's role and applied the criteria to specialized knowledge and technical expertise. They were tasked with ensuring that the science is testable, has an error rate, is peer-reviewed, and is relevant to the case at hand. In other words, it is consistent, reliable, and testable.

Psychological autopsy, as behavioral science, had an uphill battle. Nevertheless, psychological analysis does assist with reconstructions when cases are difficult to interpret from physical evidence alone.

26.8.1.2 Suicide or Homicide?   In a bedroom of his mobile home, Robert Perry was found shot to death on March 29, 2001. He was 83 and had been suffering from terminal throat cancer. His 57-year-old nephew, Craig Perry, claimed to have found him while Craig's girlfriend, Carol, called 911 to report a suicide. The police arrived and filmed the scene for analysis, but did not do a homicide investigation.

Robert Perry was in the back of the trailer, on the floor, facing the bed. Blood was coming from the back of his head and a .22-caliber long-barreled pistol lay near his feet. A deck of playing cards were scattered on the floor near him and in his right hand, he clutched an oxygen tube.

Craig and Carol, who lived with him as caregivers, gave statements. Craig indicated his uncle had made an earlier comment that he was going to end it, and Craig had tried to dissuade him. It sounded simple, but they also changed their story. They said they had found him on the floor, but then said he had been slumped over on the bed. Carol indicated that Craig then went to embrace the man, and finding him dead, laid him on the floor. Craig said they had heard one loud pop, while Carol described two.

The story did not add up, especially because Robert had taken two bullets in the back of the head—a possible but improbable area for self-infliction. Craig Perry was charged with second-degree murder. He took and passed a polygraph, but several forensic science experts believed the scene supported a finding of homicide.

Craig's attorney defense insisted that Robert had killed himself because he felt like a burden. The case involved analyses of motive, wound pattern, blood spatter patterns, and victim background; however, the pistol was not tested for fingerprints, and no tests were done for gunshot residue in the bedroom or on Craig Perry, so important evidence for accurate reconstruction was lost.

Since the wound pattern and blood spatter experts on both sides disagreed about how to interpret the evidence, making either homicide or suicide a possibility, psychological evidence about the decedent's state of mind was central. However, this, too, proved ambiguous, as he had expressed at separate times both suicidal despair and a determination to live.

Craig claimed that he had no motive to kill his uncle. Robert had no money or insurance, and Craig had loved him like a father. In fact, after his own father had died, Robert raised him—others supported this story. Medical records indicated Robert's illness had grown worse, and his home nurse reported that he had rejected traditional cancer treatment. Two days before he died, he had coughed up blood and gone to the hospital, where doctors could do nothing more for him. Hours before he died, Carol had reported that he was having trouble breathing. She also stated that Robert had been depressed.

Numerous character witnesses testified that Craig was a peaceful man who had loved his uncle and would not have shot anyone. He paid his uncle's expenses and took care of his needs, from feeding him to getting him into bed. There was no evidence that he considered his uncle a burden.

But there was one more clue, which was perhaps the most significant one: police had found a newspaper article about assisted suicide in a suitcase, along with power of attorney documents signed by Robert, giving Craig the power to make his decisions.

This was a tough case, as there was no motive to kill Robert, but a finding of suicide was not clear, either. The jury acquitted Craig Perry of murder, but the likely finding is assisted suicide, which is still a homicide. It is not difficult to see which factors would have been important in the conclusion: Craig's motive, his uncle's state of mind and physical health, the probability that a man shooting his uncle and staging it as a suicide would shoot twice, and Craig's attitude about caring for the man. While assisted suicide is a strong possibility, outright homicide without the uncle's cooperation seems unlikely.

26.8.1.3 Staged Crimes Death investigators must learn the basic red flags that indicate a crime has been staged. A staged scene has been altered by someone to appear to be something other than what it is. The intent is to misdirect. When parents discover the autoerotic activity of their deceased son, for example, they might remove the embarrassing paraphernalia before calling it in. There are also apparent suicides that turn out to be homicides, and even some seeming homicides or accidents turn out to be suicides. Some scenes are staged ad hoc, while some staging is premeditated. The former is a deflection, while the latter involves focusing attention directly on the staged "evidence." In addition, some staged scenes are done accidentally, by moving something or someone (thus, they are artifacts), while others have a clear purpose. Any indicators of staging must be seriously considered during a psychological autopsy, since they can shift the final interpretation.

26.8.2 Toward Legal Admissibility

One issue is that many malpractice suits have been launched against care providers over attempted or completed suicides, often based on negligence or poor treatment. Thus, psychological autopsies can help decide if a caregiver met the standards of care. This would occur in a civil suit, as would evaluations for insurance claims and testamentary capacity.

Oddly, there have been cases in which an accused murderer claimed the victim participated in the fatal incident because he or she wanted to die. A case in Germany in which Bernd Brandes answered an ad placed by Armin Meiwes had bizarre repercussions. The ad requested volunteers for an act of cannibalism. Brandes wanted to be eaten, and Meiwes obliged. He killed Brandes slowly, and they consumed pieces of his body together before he finally expired. Meiwes was arrested and at trial, his defense was that he was guilty only of killing on demand, or assisted suicide.

The lack of reliability and validity studies for psychological autopsy is its central criticism, and this significantly affects legal admissibility. Both Shneidman and Ebert offered their guidelines merely as suggestions. Thus, questions have been raised as to whether psychological autopsy can rise above the level of junk science. The fact that the methodology appears to differ from one practitioner to another makes this a viable concern.

26.8.3 Legal Obstacles

Without minimum standards established, there are no legal safeguards and, thus, no means for adequate scrutiny. Psychological autopsies are based largely on clinical assessment; poor quality evidence from partial interviews or inexperienced clinicians easily can be introduced. In addition, it is difficult to decide who is or is not an expert in this area. Shneidman insisted a psychological autopsy could not be properly undertaken by a detective, a prosecutor, or a psychologist acting as a hired gun for one side or the other. However, who is to stop them from doing it and using the results in court? There is no authoritative body. Although there is a certification program associated with a suicidology association, the courts have not recognized it. Yet if psychological autopsy is barred from a proceeding, this may prevent certain defendants from putting on their best defense. Thus, we turn to the next suggestion.

26.8.4 Qualitative Analysis

Examples of psychological autopsy can be found in case law dating back to the 1930s, especially in civil proceedings. However, courts have rejected it in a number of criminal proceedings. In *Jackson v. Florida* (1989), an appellate court upheld a decision to admit a psychological autopsy. The justices considered the process to be similar to a clinical sanity evaluation. In fact, some death scenes literally beg for a psychological autopsy because without it, no sense can be made of the death incident.

Bullis (2012) makes the case that because investigations and courtrooms rely so strongly on narratives, the psychological autopsy should be accepted more readily as a methodology based in narrative. Since narratives and narrative analysis already play an extensive role in court and jury decision making, there should be room for psychological autopsy as a form of narrative. He describes it as "narrative DNA." Such narratives are found in confessions, witness testimonies, attorney presentations, and jury deliberations.

Forensic narratives are stories used in the legal setting to make sense of an incident. Both sides form narratives through which to interpret available facts. They help to resolve a mystery. Narratives are a jurisprudential norm, supported with research. Neuroscience shows human beings are hardwired to think in narrative logic. We hear a story and expect a beginning, a middle, and an end, with appropriate buildup and closure. Narrative structures organize the data, as well as engage listeners both cognitively and emotionally. Story shapes how we think and apply, or evaluate, meaning.

Psychological autopsy reports can be expert testimony or circumstantial testimony. Based on professional research, the investigator tells the decedent's story. Qualitative analysis, which embraces narrative truths, is an accepted form of scientific investigation. A narrative approach to a death incident improves juror comprehension. Bullis suggests standards that could be applied by the court, along the lines of *Daubert*, including coherence, consistency, completeness, and plausibility.

Researchers who belong to certifying organizations could establish a protocol, so some authority could adhere to the clinician presenting a psychological autopsy. As this develops, authority would gain acceptance. A skills-training program could also be set up, both for the collection of information for a psychological autopsy and for presenting it in court. This has happened for clinicians offering other types of testimony. Neuroscience could enhance the testimony with hard data.

26.9   Psychological Autopsy Uses

Aside from determining the manner of death, psychological autopsies serve other purposes as well:

- In the event of suicide, it determines the triggers.
- In the event of homicide, it helps with crime reconstruction and block attempts by a defendant to raise the victim's suicide as a defense.
- It answers questions about testamentary capacity prior to death.
- It offers postvention for survivors (helping survivors deal with grief and loss).
- It gains actuarial information about behavior, for improving databases.
- It assists with a trial strategy.

Below are some illustrations.

26.9.1 Clarifying a Confusing Case

On November 12, 1995, David Wahl, 27, and Linda Stangel, 23, went drinking and then for a drive. They ended up in Oregon's Ecola State Park. This is a rugged area with high cliffs, and can be a dangerous place to walk after a night of drinking. More than 300 ft over the ocean, the rocky path has no guardrail. The following morning, David turned up missing.

Linda stated to his family that while they were sitting in the van, David had decided to take a short walk, saying he would be back in 10 minutes. He was not dressed for much more than that on that brisk morning. He took a can of beer and left. She waited in the car. David failed to return, so Linda finally left the area to return home and wait for his call. However, their relationship had been in serious trouble, so this disappearance was suspicious. The police, volunteers, and David's family searched the park (Linda did not join them), but found no sign of David.

A month later, a headless male corpse washed ashore 60 mi north. A fingerprint and a partial jawbone were matched to David Wahl, so his death was declared a suicide, with the assumption that, despondent over his crumbling relationship, he had jumped into the ocean.

The Wahls were unhappy with this decision. They insisted that he would not have killed himself, and they demanded an investigation. Detectives brought Linda in for further questioning, although she had already passed a polygraph. They took her out to the park and up the precarious trail to get her to help them reconstruct the incident. They thought they might be able to spot from her behavior if she had been deceptive. Upon on the cliff, she gave an entirely different scenario.

David had returned to the car that morning, she admitted, and they had gone up the trail together to see the cliff. He had fake-pushed her to playfully scare her, and she had pushed him back, inadvertently causing him to lose his balance in a precarious place. To her horror, David had fallen to his death on the rocks below. Linda feared she would be blamed, so she made up the other story. Back at the police station, Linda repeated this new story on tape, and told it later to the DA.

Now David Wahl's death, formerly a suicide, was considered accidental. Yet in light of Linda's lies and inconsistencies, as well as her failure to report the incident, the DA charged her with first-degree manslaughter. Thus, the suicide-turned-accident was now a homicide.

However, Linda had a surprise defense. With backup from an expert in coerced confessions, she stated that she had fabricated the story about fake-pushing David because she was deathly afraid of heights, and she had wanted to get off the cliff. She had repeated it two more times likely because she had already changed her story once, and she wanted them to believe her.

The jury did not accept her new explanation, especially after seeing evidence that she was not afraid of heights. Linda was convicted of second-degree manslaughter. Thus, acquiring a full victimology, plus details about Linda, assisted to clarify the probable manner of death as a homicide.

26.9.2 Disconfirming Suicide

Christopher Vaughn was driving his Ford sport-utility vehicle with his wife, Kimberly, and their three children in Washington State in June 2007. On their way to a water park, they stopped on an isolated stretch of Interstate 55. Within moments, the entire family, except Vaughn, was dead. Vaughn called police and told them Kimberly had shot at him, but he had jumped from the truck. She then shot the children before killing herself. She had been distraught over an affair that she had discovered between her husband and another woman.

Police were suspicious of a father who would abandon his children rather than protect them. Although an investigation did turn up evidence Vaughn had spent thousands of dollars on exotic dancers, there was no evidence Kimberly would slaughter her entire family over it. In fact, she had been upbeat the evening before. Vaughn had taken out a $1 million life insurance policy on Kimberly just more than 2 years before her death, and the policy stated he could not collect it if Kimberly committed suicide within the first 2 years they held the policy. At the time of her death, he was eligible for the payment. Also, Vaughn had constructed a survival guide and posted e-mails and Internet messages about becoming a recluse in the Canadian wilderness. It was Vaughn who had initiated the surprise trip for his family on June 14, the day of their deaths, not his wife. Vaughn had also visited a gun range to practice shooting just the day before the family's deaths. There was also a magazine in his home with an article about how to make a murder look like a suicide.

These facts assisted investigators to do a more thorough forensic examination. A ballistics and blood-spatter expert analyzed the interior of the Vaughn's Ford Expedition to the stains on Vaughn's jeans and the holes in his jacket where Kimberly had allegedly grazed him with bullets. He found the pistol Kimberly had allegedly pressed beneath her chin failed to display the appropriate pattern of blood droplets typical for a self-inflicted wound. In addition, the gunpowder burns on Vaughn's jacket and jeans indicated a pistol had been pressed against his leg and jacket.

Also, burn marks and the bullet trajectories for each of the three children (who were all shot in the chest and head) indicated that the gun barrel was only inches away from each. It was not where one would expect from someone in the front passenger seat. Two shell casings in the front contradicted Vaughn's account as well.

Psychological and physical evidence together developed a narrative that fully undermined the story that Vaughn had given to the police. It took 5 years to get the case to trial, but Vaughn was finally convicted.

26.9.3 Testamentary Capacity

The wealthy Howard Hughes was an aviator, a businessman, and a movie producer. As an ambitious perfectionist, he sought to perform the most impressive demonstration of a given medium in everything he undertook, but he also suffered from a severe compulsive disorder that worsened as he aged. Toward the end of his life, he became a mysterious, eccentric recluse with money to pay for privacy, and the license to fully indulge in bizarre behaviors, such as sitting naked in a locked room with his feet encased in tissue boxes. He died from natural causes on April 5, 1976, at the age of 71.

Although there was no mystery about the manner of his death, he was nearly unrecognizable due to drug use and personal neglect. He had a long beard, fingernails, and toenails, and he had lost a considerable amount of weight. He was severely malnourished, so the FBI used fingerprints to identify him.

About 3 weeks after Hughes' death, a handwritten will was offered as proof that he had left his considerable fortune to various charities, with some for his two former wives. A court determined the will was a forgery, so Hughes had died intestate. Due to the aura of mystery about his life and death, a law firm representing the Hughes family estate decided to retain a psychologist as an expert witness for a legal proceeding. They required a postmortem personality assessment. Attorney George Dean recommended Dr. Raymond Fowler, chair of the Psychology Department at the University of Alabama.

Fowler was hired to undertake the assessment. He called it a psychological autopsy, with the intent to clarify Hughes' state of mind at various junctures of his life. Fowler had studied substance abuse, personality assessment, and criminal psychology, and he had helped to design a computer program for analyzing the MMPI. He had also assisted with prison reform programs.

Spending a year on the psychological autopsy, and 5 more years out of his own interest, Fowler discovered many stages of Hughes' life had been extensively documented. "His overprotective mother kept notes on his childhood," he later wrote, "especially his health, and during his years as a businessman, his staff recorded practically everything he did, including transcripts of his personal and professional telephone calls." There were also numerous depositions from people who had known Hughes. Fowler took a leave of absence in order to do a thorough job. He added more information from his own interviews and consulted with mental health professionals on diagnostic issues.

When Fowler was writing his autobiography, he described how interesting this process had been, because it had added detective work to the typical psychological evaluation. New clues constantly emerged, but finally he had a legal document that saved the estate from millions of dollars in lawsuits. Later, Fowler (1986) summarized his findings in an article for *Psychology Today*. Fowler had spent several years on this project, and his primary interest lay in looking back over Hughes' life to determine how such a vibrant man had become a paranoid and eccentric recluse.

Born in Houston, Texas, in 1905, "Sonny" was an only child. His mother doted on him with an excessive concern about his health, teeth, and bowels. His father was usually absent. At the time, the public feared the spread of polio, so when young Howard went to camp, his parents wanted assurances he was protected. Finally, Mrs. Hughes decided it was better just to keep him home. Here, Fowler saw the early seeds of Hughes' later germ phobia, which became so extreme that toward the end of his life, he did not leave his rooms. In addition, since he was not allowed to play like other boys, he became an introverted loner.

Fowler learned a great deal from letters Hughes' mother had written to camp counselors. From this information, he diagnosed avoidant disorder, a means of coping in which someone wants friends but is too anxious to make them. He believed Hughes' mother actually exacerbated these problems and used illness to provide the means of escaping social pressures. Howard picked up on this and avoided another year at camp by complaining about headaches and bad dreams.

On the verge of adolescence he became ill, so his mother kept him out of school for most of that year. He developed a paralysis which was never diagnosed and which disappeared after several months. Fowler believed this was psychosomatic. When Hughes was 16, he suffered a terrible loss: His mother died during surgery. Just 2 years later, his father died, precipitating a deep depression and probably a great sense of vulnerability.

However, he had a profitable business to run in Houston based on his father's invention, which had revolutionized oil drilling world-wide. He married without any romantic involvement and divorced after he went to Hollywood, where he took up flying and developed a passion for movies—a budding industry in the mid-1920s.

From this point, a psychologist could ask business associates about Hughes, which Fowler apparently did, adding comments into his report from people who worked with Hughes. It was clear to those who knew him that his ambitions were high—to be the richest man alive and to be a top film producer and a top aviator. He managed all three, winning international fame in his early 20s, so newspaper accounts are widely available about his rise to fame.

A website about social history says, "At various points in his life, he owned an international airline, two regional airlines, an aircraft com-pany, a major motion picture studio, mining properties, a tool com-pany, gambling casinos and hotels in Las Vegas, a medical research institute, and a vast amount of real estate." Yet according to people around him, he was uncomfortable with his public persona. By the time he was 24, Fowler found out, Hughes began to avoid the parties and publicity.

Hughes had three nervous breakdowns over the course of 13 years. In Beverly Hills in 1944, after he had been in several serious accidents in which others had died, Hughes spent most of his time sitting naked in a white leather chair where he could be free of germs (he thought) and where he watched movies endlessly. It was possible he had sus-tained brain damage, evidenced by his sudden habit of repeating him-self. He developed an obsession with details. When he moved to Las Vegas (and bought up hotels and casinos), he also took to watching movies naked, but this time he had developed an addiction to codeine and valium. For one 7-month stretch, he had a pilot secretly fly him around the Southwest, where he would stay alone in darkened motel rooms. "It seems likely," writes Fowler, "that all the stress Hughes was under increased his already high anxiety."

By 1966, at the age of 60, he was the world's wealthiest man, but he had a terror of contagious diseases. People who worked for him had to wash their hands often and were made to wear white gloves. They were not to speak to him or look directly at him. He would go so far as to burn his clothing (which he wore infrequently) if he heard someone he had met had become ill. Clearly, Fowler points out, he had an obsessive-compulsive disorder that disrupted his life.

Hughes left Las Vegas for the Bahamas and then moved to Mexico, reportedly to get codeine more easily. Only his security guards and doctors saw him. By this time, he was injecting codeine and breaking needles into his arms that later showed up on X-rays during the autopsy. He wore tissue boxes on his feet, wore no clothing, and let his hair and nails grow out. Eating candy bars, his teeth rotted and fell out because he never brushed them. He urinated on the floor and never bathed, but might sit on the toilet for 20 hours at a time. He still watched movies obsessively, mostly *Ice Station Zebra*.

In the end, Fowler concludes, Hughes was not psychotic. There was never a time when he could not rouse himself to deal rationally with a situation. "But," he writes, "he was a disturbed man."

26.9.4 Incident Dissection

Sometimes, an analysis on the manner of death is not sufficient, and the death event itself can shed important light on what needs to be done to seek the motive. For example, a psychiatric autopsy was performed in the aftermath of the suicidal mass murder at Columbine High School in Littleton, Colorado, in 1999 to try to determine from the motives some risk factors for similar incidents in other places.

Dylan Klebold, 17, and Eric Harris, 18, were obsessed with violent video games, a fascistic subculture, and paramilitary techniques. They had collected an arsenal of semiautomatic guns and homemade bombs and had plotted a crime they hoped the nation would never forget. If everything went according to plan, they would cause a lot of death and damage, and then they might just fly off together in a hijacked plane to some remote island. Or, more likely, they might die.

One day in April 1999, they sent an e-mail to the local police declaring they were going to do something at the school. They blamed parents and teachers in their community for turning their children into intolerant sheep and then announced their own suicide. Then at 11:30 a.m. on April 20, the boys hid weapons and bombs beneath their long trench coats and walked through the school, yelling at teachers and students and shooting at random. When they reached the library, they cornered and killed their largest number of victims before turning their weapons on themselves. After police got into the building, they counted 34 casualties, with 15 deaths, including the shooters.

Then Harris's diary turned up, which confirmed the elaborate plan. For more than a year, they had worked at it, drawing maps, collecting weapons, and devising a system of silent hand signals for coordinating their moves. Behind closed doors in their parents' homes, they had spoken of death and of their lone wolf idea of heroism. The simple fact that initially emerged is that they were angry, bitter children who had access to guns, who identified with twisted ideas, and who were inspired by images of grandiose violence.

A couple of years later, in September 2001, five members of the Threat Assessment Group (TAG), run by prominent forensic psychiatrist Dr. Park Dietz, came into Littleton for a week to perform a psychiatric autopsy. They were experts in risk management and violence prevention and had worked with many companies on workplace violence.

TAG evaluated the crime scene to see how the school had looked to the boys that morning. They examined home videos the boys had made and considered the way they had thought the entire incident was something about which to joke. They looked at the computer games the boys repeatedly had played and movies they had watched (e.g., *Natural Born Killers*). They considered the boys' diaries and their to-do list for the day of ground zero. At the end of this list, after setting off the bombs, one of the killers had written a psychopathic message: "Have fun."

The original plan had been to set off explosions and wait outside, picking off students as they rushed out. However, when the bombs failed, they went inside. Once they were inside, there would be no getting out. Surviving witnesses reported that Harris and Klebold appeared to be having a good time.

Due to pending lawsuits, many key people did not respond to TAG's requests for interviews—notably members of the Harris and

Klebold families. This was a serious gap in their analysis. Yet more than 50 people agreed to talk. One boy stated that the shooters had often been humiliated (although others have since disputed there had been unusual bullying).

The TAG members looked over the mental health records for both boys. They had been in trouble before in a minor way and had been ordered to go through an anger management program. Harris was taking the antidepressant Luvox, and changes in Klebold's outlook over the 2 years prior to the incident indicated depression as well. They were both quite cynical, with an apparent high level of anger. Harris kept checking to ensure Klebold was holding strong, which marked him as the leader.

While TAG did hear about a recurring dream Eric had told a class about shooting teachers and students, and about Eric's breakup with a girl, the team was denied access to the tapes the boys made in the basement, another major gap. (They have since been revealed in other sources.)

Without all the facts, TAG could only hypothesize that anger grew out of resentment and depression from sadness. These moods were reinforced with immersion in violent imagery, which raised the emotional tone to rage and thoughts of suicide. They had rehearsed extensively for their day of violence. TAG considered bullying to be insufficient to explain the level of violence displayed. Rather, the way the two angry young men had reinforced each other appeared to be a more striking factor. Designating a date, having a clear purpose, gaining access to the weapons, and having no sense of a positive future collectively raised the risk that they would strike. Thus, the postmortem analysis assisted with risk assessment databases and with the management of future school violence. The gaps in knowledge could be filled in when information became available later.

26.10 Historical Analyses

A few psychological autopsies have been performed from sheer curiosity, and increasingly, researchers are examining ambiguous deaths from long past. Psychological evidence has assisted with closure, although at times, it remains conjecture at best.

26.10.1 Malcolm Melville

Edwin Shneidman undertook the psychological autopsy of the 18-year-old son of Herman Melville, author of *Moby Dick*. Malcolm Melville died in 1867 from a pistol wound to the head. At the time, his death was thought to be, alternatively, a homicide, a suicide, and an accident. Since the manner of death was never settled definitively specifically between accident and suicide, Shneidman offered it as an open case to his colleagues at the LASPC. They gathered for their own form of a suicide panel.

Each of them independently examined Malcolm's family life, and Shneidman decided Herman Melville had been *suicidogenic*; that is, he was prone himself to suicidal depressions that could have affected his son, and had been himself a battered child. Melville had also used suicide as a repeated motif. In addition, he was self-centered and monomaniacal about his writing, neglected his four children, and even rejected them—especially his firstborn, the ill-fated Malcolm. This boy may have felt that he would be better off dead; Shneidman thought that he imagined his options for peace of mind as either parricide or suicide.

The result of this exercise was that most of the LASPC's staff believed that the manner of Malcolm's death was suicide. Since the young man had known how to handle a weapon, they had ruled out an accident. There was no evidence for homicide, and depression and despair (psychache) seemed to be the most likely triggers.

26.10.2 Julius Caesar

Some investigators have teamed up with documentary makers to use the tools of psychological autopsy as a way to reexamine cases deep inside history once believed to be settled. Although it is difficult to determine if they have all the facts—and it is more than likely that they do not—some investigators have arrived at provocative conclusions.

Such an undertaking was done for the death of Julius Caesar, to try to determine whether a conspiracy of men had taken him by surprise and killed him, as history tells us, or whether a much more subtle manipulation had occurred.

Julius Caesar, a great Roman dictator and military genius, was slain on the Ides of March in 44 BC by a group of his own senators and one-time friends. He had arrived at the senate that morning without his guards and was quickly overtaken and stabbed to death by an unknown number of men.

An Italian investigator, Colonel Luciano Garafano, reopened the case to use computer-generated models, psychological analysis, and crime scene simulations to try to determine what might actually have happened. To his mind, Caesar had been too astute and well informed to have left himself vulnerable to such an attack.

Garafano used a team of investigators, forensic psychiatrists, and historians to piece together what had happened with an emphasis on the means and motivations of everyone involved—including Caesar. The fact that Caesar had dismissed his guards that morning seemed significant, because he had surely heard the rumors of a conspiracy against him. It was sufficiently strange behavior to look further into Caesar's state of mind during the days leading up to his famous assassination, in so far as that could be known.

Garafano first went to the crime scene, where any investigation begins. Since it is now in ruins, he had to reconstruct via computer what it might have looked like. He knew Caesar had been taken home and autopsied, and a note was found in his hand about the conspiracy. Of the 23 stab wounds, only one was determined to be fatal. A computer helped the team to better see the pattern of the wounds and to set up an incident simulation. Then, Garafano looked into the motives of the reputed ringleaders and found one with a personal grudge who might have persuaded the other conspirators to join him.

Yet, even so, Caesar had to make himself vulnerable to such an attack, so that meant an inquiry into his circumstances. A few weeks earlier, a deputation of senators had pronounced him a god, and he had insulted them by remaining in his seat. This gesture had bred resentment. Yet there was talk that he did not rise to honor them because he had a case of diarrhea. Garafano knew there were rumors of epilepsy, so he consulted with a psychiatrist, who explained how this condition could have affected Caesar's brain. It might have produced attitude changes and exacerbated psychiatric conditions.

Garafano thought Caesar either was losing his mental facilities or had decided to walk into danger. His health was failing, and he risked public humiliation at some point as he aged, so he could have decided to accept a violent end that would have ensured his legacy of greatness and made him a martyr. The evidence was there: A soothsayer and his wife had urged him to be careful on this day. He even received a note warning him away, which was in his hand when he was stabbed. The psychiatric expert believed that he would have read the note: He was a man who wanted to be fully prepared for everything. On this of all days, he would not have been as careless as he seemed.

No one knows for sure, but Garafano's painstaking work at least brings out the possibility Caesar exploited the situation to commit a form of suicide by cop.

26.10.3 Tut

In 2001, the Discovery Channel hired former FBI agents to conduct an investigation into the death of Tutankhamen, or King Tut. Their reasoning was that if recent technology in the field of forensic science can tell us the boy king was murdered, we should change the historical accounts to acknowledge him as a victim. Former Special Agents Greg Cooper and Mike King, both experienced law enforcement officers, claim discoveries made with forensic techniques reveal the real story.

Tut was born in Egypt around 1334 BC, the son of a controversial pharaoh who had angered the priesthood. Around age 9, Tut became king but died 8 years later at a surprisingly young age, given Egypt's high standard of living. He was interred in what for royalty seemed to his discoverers a makeshift, undersized, and unfinished tomb. Egyptologists surmised that Tut's death had been sudden and unexpected. He might have gotten ill or had an accident, but he might have also been murdered. Suicide was the only NASH option not considered.

Howard Carter had discovered the tomb in 1922. The boy king's remains were removed at this time and autopsied. Forty years later, they were X-rayed. At that time, anatomist R. G. Harrison suspected from skull irregularities that the king had died slowly from a blow to the back of the head. He suggested that someone had possibly struck him while he was asleep on his side. Recent reexamination of those X-rays, with better medical knowledge, indicates it was more likely that a backward fall had snapped the brain forward.

Then commenced a psychological autopsy, undertaken by Egyptologist Bob Brier: In short, what was Tut's risk potential for being the victim of violence? Who might have had a motive, the means, and the opportunity to do him harm? Brier identified two primary suspects: Tut's wife, Ankhesenamen, and his advisor, Ay—who upon Tut's death became the new pharaoh. Ultimately, Brier suspected Ay had hired a killer, dispatched the king, and then pressured the young queen to marry him.

King and Cooper added two more possible suspects: Tut's chief treasurer, Maya, and his military commander, Horemheb. For psychological reasons, they eliminated them both. Horemheb seemed unduly loyal (at least from the distant perspective of centuries), and did not take the throne when he could have. Maya, too, had no motive. Ankhesenamen, who apparently had given birth to two stillborn children (buried with Tut), might have been looking for a better stud, but killing the king was not in her best interest. Cooper and King thought they were a loving couple, based on paintings inside the tomb. This left Ay, for the same reason Brier had stated: political ambition.

However, scientific analysis only tells us that Tut may have suffered skull or brain damage. He liked to hunt, so he could have fallen from his horse. Suffering from a possible hematoma does not in itself prove he was murdered.

Yet Cooper and King believe they found more clues that, considered together, go pretty far to establish the death as a homicide. For example, the burial appeared to have been done in haste, using unusual unguents (maybe as a cover-up). There is a note dated around this time from an anonymous Egyptian queen trying to avoid a marriage to a servant, and they believe this links Ay and Tut's wife. A ring bearing her name along with Ay's indicates they might have married, and because she disappeared from the records directly after the marriage to Ay, it is not a long shot to think that she was killed. However, each clue is highly interpretable, and historians consider a reliance on tomb paintings and jewelry to determine the state of mind to be naive.

The case for murder, then, has been made on an accumulation of possibilities and likelihoods. It seems that, for such a distance diagnosis, science and psychology can only go so far. Tut's case is interesting, even suggestive of violence, but not solved.

26.10.4 Charles Francis Hall

In 1871, Charles Francis Hall led an expedition in search of the North Pole, supported with a sizable grant from the U.S. Congress. Hall was experienced in arctic conditions, but not with a haughty crew member, physician, and chief scientist Dr. Emil Bessels. They set anchor for the winter about 500 mi from their goal in a harbor at Greenland. Bessels and another officer insisted that they go south for safety. Hall stood firm on his plans.

On October 24, after drinking coffee, Hall became ill. Bessels gave him medications, but he only grew worse. Hall believed that he was being poisoned, and he died on November 8, before anyone could do anything for him. The crew buried him in Greenland. Later, after an inquiry, it was determined that Captain Hall had died from natural causes.

The case seemed to be closed, but people remained curious. It was nearly a century before another scientist decided to find out if Hall might have actually been poisoned. Over time, scientists had learned human hair roots absorb arsenic like blotting paper, and each dose leaves a permanent and measurable record in every growing strand. If someone dies from arsenic poisoning, there should be a high concentration close to the roots. Fingernails will also provide a record via growth patterns.

Professor Chauncey C. Loomis of Dartmouth College and pathologist Dr. Franklin Paddock formed a team and went to Greenland to exhume Hall's remains. They performed an autopsy right there on the ground, because the coffin was frozen into the earth and the body with it. However, it was remarkably well preserved. Hall's body fat had been converted into adipocere, a substance like soap that had a preservative effect on the internal organs.

The scientists removed various samples from strategic places, including hair samples and fingernails. They also took samples from the soil surrounding the coffin. The procedure they used for analysis separated foreign substances into component parts and made it possible to measure how much had been ingested over the course of just a few days. To the scientists' disappointment, the Greenland soil samples contained a high percentage of arsenic. Yet they could still learn things from the body.

In one of Hall's fingernails, they found evidence that he had ingested a large amount of arsenic during the last 2 weeks before his death. Since the nail had shown differential growth, its condition contradicted the idea that arsenic had leached through the coffin into the body. The hair samples displayed the same thing. Had the arsenic come from the soil, the distribution would have been more uniform. Given Hall's reported symptoms, his suspicions, and the results of the analysis with modern forensic technology, those involved in the investigation agreed the chances were good that Hall had been murdered.

Yet even with the likelihood of murder, there was no telling just who the murderer was. Several people had been at odds with Hall. Despite the obvious suspect, there was no evidence tying Bessels to the crime. He did give Hall medication, but the incident is too far distant in history to say more than Hall's original manner of death was in error.

26.11 Conclusion

26.11.1 Summary

Demand for a psychological autopsy comes from the office of a coroner or medical examiner. Its purpose is to help resolve ambiguities that affect a decision about the manner of death, especially in suspected suicide. Developed more than 50 years ago, psychological autopsy is not yet standardized as a scientific method, but it is gaining ground as a useful tool in death investigations. While a decedent's intentionality can be difficult to determine, the science and databases of suicidology can assist. The more educated investigators become about this approach, the more psychological autopsies can assist in a variety of legal and investigative contexts.

The first generation of psychological autopsies produced detail-rich reports on suicidal state of mind that suffered from inconsistency in methodology. The second generation, starting during the late 1980s, imposed more rigorous controls and standardized procedures. Still, no one made it clear how the qualitative analysis should measure variables. Nevertheless, precursor conditions have been isolated and identified, especially the presence of specific forms of mental illness. The next generation could follow the narrative approach to persuade courts to include such testimony as part of their general reliance on narrative truths.

26.11.2 The Future

In the future, a suicidal state of mind could be linked to specific forms of brain activity. However, this lies much farther along than the results of neuroscience can currently support. It is more likely that professionals who perform psychological autopsies will focus on the reliability of causal connections between precursors and suicide. They will also keep refining the interview protocols. For example, they can establish a time frame for when it is appropriate to approach grieving relatives. Providing interviewees with a better sense of what is at stake could become part of the standard procedure. Specific interview questions may form the core of a psychological autopsy. Whether to have one or more interviewers can be tested.

The concept of a *death panel* is sound, but time consuming for all undetermined deaths, so some form of triage evaluation will likely be devised. In addition, effectively attaching psychological autopsies to sensational cases can endow this method with a recognition and further interest in research. This approach has worked for many other areas of forensic science and psychology.

Bibliography

Aggrawal, A. (2009). *Forensic and medico-legal aspects of sexual crimes and unusual sexual practices*. Boca Raton, FL: CRC Press.

Baumeister, R.F. (1990). Suicide as escape from self. *Psychological Review*, Vol. 97, pp. 90–113.

Biffl, E. (1996, Fall). Psychological autopsies: Do they belong in the courtroom? *American Journal of Criminal Law*.

Bullis, R.K. (2012). Narrative approaches in psychological autopsies: Suggestions for methodologies. *Journal of Forensic Psychology Practice*, Vol. 12, pp. 124–146.

Center for Disease Control. (2012). Understanding Suicide Fact Sheet.

Choi, C. (2011, December 21). Neurons offer clues to suicide. *Scientific American*.

Cliffhanger. (2003, June 9). *Dateline*, Court TV's *The System*.

Coleman, L. (2004). *The copycat effect*. New York: Paraview.

Colt, G.H. (1991). *The enigma of suicide*. New York: Summit Books.

Columbine: Understanding why (2002). Investigative Reports, A&E.

Conner, K.R., Beautrais, A.L., Brent, D.A. et al. (2102). The next generation of psychological autopsy studies. *Suicide and Life-Threatening Behavior*, Vol. 42, No. 1, pp. 86–103.

Ebert, B. (1987). Guide to conducting a psychological autopsy. *Professional Psychology Research and Practice*, p. 18.

Farberow, N.L. & Shneidman, E.S. (Eds.). (1961). *The cry for help*. New York, NY: McGraw Hill.

Fischer, D. (2000, September/October). Equivocal cases of teenage suicide. *The Forensic Examiner*, Vol. 9.

Fowler, R.D. (1986, May). Howard Hughes: A psychological autopsy. *Psychology Today*.

Fowler, R.D. (2006). Computers, criminals, an eccentric billionaire, and APA: A brief autobiography. *Journal of Personality Assessment*, Vol. 87, No. 3, pp. 234–238.

Frye v. United States. 293 F. 1013 (D.C. Cir 1923).

Hazelwood, R. & Michaud, S.G. (2001). *Dark dreams: Sexual violence, homicide, and the criminal mind*. New York: St. Martin's Press.

Isometsa, E. (2001). Psychological autopsy studies: A review. *European Psychiatry*, Vol. 16, pp. 379–385.

Jackson v. Florida, 545 So. 2d 260, 264 (1989).

Joiner, T. (2005). *Why people die by suicide*. Cambridge, MA: Harvard University Press.

Joiner, T. (2010). *Myths about suicide*. Cambridge, MA: Harvard University Press.

Kluger, J. & Dorfman, A. (2002, September 16). Who killed King Tut? *Time*.

Mesoudi, A. (2009). The cultural dynamics of copycat suicide. *PLoS ONE*, Vol. 4, No. 9.

Noguchi, T. & DiMona, J. (1983). *Coroner*. New York: Pocket.

Oregon v. Stangel: Young woman charged with pushing boyfriend off cliff. (2002, November 27). Retrieved from http://www.CourtTV.com /archive/trials.

Proenca, M. (2001, April 7). The psychological autopsy. *Suicide and Parasuicide*.

Ramsland, K. (2011). *The forensic psychology of Criminal Minds*. New York: Berkley.

Reiter, H. & Parker, L.B. (2002). Psychological autopsy. *The Forensic Examiner*, Vol. 11.

Selkin, J. (1994) Psychological autopsy: Scientific psychohistory or clinical intuition? *American Psychologist*, Vol. 10.

Sheleg, S. & Erlich, E. (2006). *Autoerotic asphyxiation: Forensic, medical and social aspects*. Tucson, AZ: Wheatmark.

Shneidman, E.S. (Ed.). (1981). The psychological autopsy. *Suicide and Life Threatening Behavior*, Vol. 11.

Shneidman, E.S. (Ed.). (1993). *Suicide as psychache: A clinical approach to self-destructive behavior*. Northvale, NJ: Jason Aronson.

Shneidman, E.S. (Ed.). (1994). The psychological autopsy. *American Psychologist*, p. 75.

Shneidman, E.S. (Ed.). (1996). *The suicidal mind*. Oxford, UK: Oxford University Press.

Shneidman, E.S. (Ed.). (2001). *Comprehending suicide: Landmarks in twentieth century suicidology*. Washington, DC: American Psychological Association.

Shneidman, E.S. & Collins, J. (1961). Sample investigations of equivocal deaths. In Farberow, N.L. & Shneidman, E.S. (Eds.). (1961). *The cry for help*. New York, NY: McGraw Hill.

Shneidman, E.S. & Farberow, N. (Eds.). (1957). *Clues to suicide*. New York: McGraw-Hill.

Who killed Julius Caesar? (2003). Discovery Network.

Who killed King Tut? (2002). Discovery Network.

SECTION VI
PRACTICE TEST

1. _____ helps determine the probable manner of someone's death.
   a. Behavioral profiling
   b. Forensic examination
   c. Psychological autopsy
   d. Family history

2. The phrase *Postmortem Interval (PMI)* is another way of saying _____.
   a. time-since-death
   b. police response
   c. autopsy
   d. decedent profile

3. Which world-famous actress's death did the Los Angeles Suicide Panel examine in 1962?
   a. Marilyn Monroe
   b. Jane Mansfield
   c. Janis Joplin
   d. Natalie Wood

4. In the late 18th century, suicide was considered a _____ concern rather than a medical one.
   a. mental health
   b. religious
   c. psychiatric
   d. psychological

5. Low levels of _____ are often present in the brains of those who have killed themselves.
   a. fentanyl
   b. serotonin
   c. clonazepam
   d. OxyContin

6. In a study of suicide notes, the _____ note-writers apparently felt the need to say more in their last communication.
   a. fictitious
   b. original
   c. surviving
   d. genuine

7. Autoerotic asphyxiation results in feelings of elation, exhilaration, and heightened _____.
   a. awareness
   b. sensitivity
   c. sexual pleasure
   d. spirituality

8. Regarding malpractice litigation, psychological autopsies can help decide if a caregiver met the _____.
   a. burden of proof
   b. medical requirements
   c. Medicare requirements
   d. standards of care

9. A psychological autopsy conducted on the Columbine killers by the Threat Assessment Group could only hypothesize that anger grew out of resentment, and depression, from sadness. These moods were reinforced with immersion in _____, which raised the emotional tone to rage and thoughts of suicide.
   a. drugs
   b. alcohol
   c. violent imagery
   d. role playing

10. Who can demand a psychological autopsy?
   a. Prosecuting attorney
   b. Law enforcement officer
   c. Circuit judge
   d. Coroner or medical examiner

See page 537 for answer key.

PRACTICE TEST

ANSWER KEYS

Section I

1. Ethical behavior goes beyond simply knowing the difference between right and wrong; it is doing what is _____.
   a. honest
   b. diligent
   c. **right**
   d. discreet

2. Investigators should not allow personal feelings or _____ to interfere with factual and truthful disclosure.
   a. anger
   b. hatred
   c. laziness
   d. **prejudices**

3. In 1994 in the O. J. Simpson murder trial, not only did millions of laypeople learn intimate details about the investigative process, they also witnessed its _____.
   a. **limitations**
   b. influence
   c. importance
   d. complexity

4. Believing that human behavior could be classified with objective tests, _____ was convinced that certain people were born criminals, identifiable by specific physical traits such as bulging brows, long arms, and apelike noses.
   a. Vidocq
   b. Pinel
   c. **Lombroso**
   d. Prichard

5. Colin Pitchfork was the first person convicted for rape and murder based on _____.
   a. fingerprints
   b. **DNA evidence**
   c. blood typing
   d. bite mark evidence

6. A forensic odontologist, a dentist with training in forensic procedures and courtroom testimony, has two primary roles: identification and _____.
   a. **comparison analysis**
   b. reconstruction
   c. testifying
   d. collection

7. The bones of an average, fully mature, adult male weigh about _____ lb.
   a. 20
   b. 15
   c. **12**
   d. 16

8. _____ is a medical specialty that determines the cause and manner of death in situations falling under the jurisdiction of the local medical examiner or coroner.
   a. Forensic investigation
   b. Forensic autopsy
   c. Forensic medicine
   d. **Forensic pathology**

9. _____ states that the decomposition process begins in the face and neck and moves downward through the body.
   a. Hick's hypothesis
   b. The principle of masticular rigidity
   c. Raoult's law
   d. **Nysten's law**

10. A Chapter 11 bankruptcy proceeding helps to _____ a business so that it can settle its debts and get a fresh start.
    a. **reorganize**
    b. dissolve
    c. liquidate
    d. inventory

Section II

1. Blood is a specialized form of _____ involving multiple cells suspended in plasma.
   a. **connective tissue**
   b. liquid that does not contain cells
   c. material that contains only red blood cells
   d. fluid that conforms to Newtonian physics

2. If a bloodstain on a vertical wall measures 3 mm wide and 6 mm long, the blood drop that caused the stain impacted the wall at an approximate _____ angle.
   a. 45°
   b. **30°**
   c. 90°
   d. 60°

3. The pooling of blood as it accumulates at the lowest part of the body is known as _____.
   a. **hypostasis**
   b. plasmorphis
   c. gravitational coagulation
   d. convergence

4. A class of fingerprints that includes ridge patterns that are generally rounded or circular in shape and have two deltas is known as a _____.
   a. loop
   b. **whorl**
   c. bifurcation
   d. arch

5. The _____ should remain in the same condition as it was when the first officer arrived.
   a. victim's body
   b. suspect weapon
   c. suspected point of entry
   d. **crime scene**

6. Obtaining _____ samples is important to later use in comparison with crime scene evidence.
   a. **standard/reference**
   b. blood/semen
   c. hair follicle
   d. soil

7. When conducting a criminal investigation, ensure that witnesses of the incident are identified and _____.
   a. numbered
   b. interrogated
   c. **separated**
   d. catalogued

8. The ABO system is the most commonly used and divides _____ into four different groups.
   a. fingerprints
   b. **blood**
   c. crime scenes
   d. forensics

9. A _____ is a firearm designed to be fired using both hands and has a longer barrel and a larger capacity magazine.
   a. **rifle**
   b. pistol
   c. shotgun
   d. submachine gun

10. Which form of evidence can indirectly prove facts from inference?
   a. Physical evidence
   b. Testimonial evidence
   c. Direct evidence
   d. **Circumstantial evidence**

11. When searching a crime scene, a _____ search can be used for both large and small areas.
   a. grid
   b. strip
   c. **zone/sector**
   d. circle

12. When collecting evidence, what kind of evidence should be given first priority?
    a. Trace evidence
    b. **Fragile evidence**
    c. Evidence that could impede the search of the scene
    d. Circumstantial evidence

13. Blood from a victim who takes blood thinners may have a different hematocrit level from that of blood from a person who has just finished exercising in a gym. Blood thinners and exercise are known as _____ when doing a bloodstain pattern analysis.
    a. parameters
    b. **variables**
    c. raw scores
    d. raw values

14. You measure 40 well-formed bloodstains, calculate the angle of impact values, add them together, and divide by 40 to get a value known as _____.
    a. the standard deviation
    b. the regression coefficient
    c. **mean**
    d. mode

15. _____ evidence refers to evidence in written form.
    a. Text
    b. Graphical
    c. **Documentary**
    d. Binary

16. CDs and DVDs are the safest removable media to handle because they are usually in _____ mode.
    a. encrypted
    b. compressed
    c. rewritable
    d. **read-only**

17. _____ evidence is the statement of a witness under oath, either in court or by deposition.
    a. Documentary
    b. **Testimonial**
    c. Personal
    d. Verbal

18. What hidden area is typically missed by data-backup utilities?
    a. Metadata
    b. **Slack space**
    c. Spool space
    d. File index space

19. Which of the following is considered a responsibility of the coroner or medical examiner?
    a. Determining which items are considered evidence
    b. Determining who the murderer was
    c. **Determining the cause of death**
    d. Determining the next of kin

20. After eating, how long will food stay in the stomach before it starts to empty?
    a. **10 minutes**
    b. 30 minutes
    c. 1 hour
    d. 2 hours

Section III

1. The purpose of _____ is to exonerate innocent individuals through the use of post-conviction DNA testing.
   a. Operation Freedom
   b. wrongful justice
   c. **the Innocence Project**
   d. equal justice

2. In the courtroom, who is expected to remain impartial and
   present unbiased evidence?
   a. The prosecuting attorney
   b. The defense attorney
   c. The judge
   d. **The expert witness**

3. When is the interrogation process used?
   a. **When people are believed to be not sharing information**
   b. When you come across any person involved in an
      investigation
   c. When you are speaking with any witness of a crime
   d. The constitution protects any person from being interrogated

4. Who should you identify yourself as during an interrogation?
   a. **Law enforcement**
   b. Anybody you believe the suspect will talk to
   c. A fellow suspect
   d. Do not identify yourself at all

5. What does a polygraph measure?
   a. Truth
   b. Lies
   c. Deceptions
   d. **Bodily reactions**

6. Which of the following is one of the elements of case
   management?
   a. **Commencing with the initial report**
   b. Allocating supervisorial duties
   c. Giving proper notifications
   d. Dividing responsibilities for case officers

7. Which of the following is an exception to having a warrant?
   a. A canine alert
   b. Probable cause
   c. Intuition
   d. **Consent**

Section IV

1. It is estimated that there are _____ injuries per year as the result of women being abused by their significant others.
   a. 1,000,000
   b. 2,000,000
   c. 3,000,000
   d. **4,000,000**

2. Which of the following is a characteristic of mental sexual abuse?
   a. Forced sex
   b. **Unwanted sexual advances**
   c. Attacks on the breasts
   d. Rape with objects

3. Seductive behaviors teachers utilize are deception, gift-giving, _____, and friendship.
   a. sexual relations
   b. **isolation**
   c. threats
   d. intimacy

4. In a survey of nuns who have reported being sexually abused, 3% identified a _____ as their abuser.
   a. priest
   b. parent
   c. babysitter
   d. **nun**

5. The _____ is the area of the brain where executive decisions are made and inappropriate behavior is inhibited.
   a. **prefrontal cortex**
   b. corpus callosum
   c. angular gyrus
   d. limbic system

6. It is true that female sex offenders rarely use _____ as a stimulus.
   a. fetishism
   b. masturbation
   c. violence
   d. **pornography**

7. The most accurate word for the killing of one human being by another is _____.
   a. *murder*
   b. *__homicide__*
   c. *fratricide*
   d. *euthanasia*

8. As U.S. jurisdictions adopted common law concepts, various degrees of intent, _____, and justification were considered for sentencing.
   a. aggravating circumstances
   b. exceptional circumstances
   c. **mitigation**
   d. deliberation

9. Most criminologists have designated _____ as the minimum count for a mass murder.
   a. two
   b. five
   c. **four**
   d. three

10. _____ is the ability to understand something immediately, without the need for conscious reasoning.
   a. **Intuition**
   b. Reasoning
   c. Extrasensory perception
   d. Clairvoyance

11. What do all offenders of Munchausen syndrome by proxy (MSBP) have in common?
   a. They are all the same race as the victim.
   b. They are all in some sort of financial trouble.
   c. They have all attempted suicide at some point in their life.
   d. **They all acted as the victim's primary caregiver.**

12. The average age at death for a neglected child is _____ months.
   a. **5**
   b. 11
   c. 16
   d. 20

13. What do identity thieves know about stealing from large institutions or corporations?
   a. **Businesses that consider identification and prosecution more costly than it is worth fail to protect themselves from criminal activity below their radar.**
   b. Institutions that become victims are highly motivated to report identity theft because it makes the company look more sympathetic to clients.
   c. Large institutions and businesses have detailed anti-identity theft measures in place that keep this type of criminal activity from happening.
   d. It is more cost effective to steal from individuals than from large institutions or corporations.

14. What is sexting?
   a. Sending text messages about sex to others via a cell phone
   b. **Sending sexual or nude photos to others via a cell phone**
   c. Chatting about sex in a teenage-only website
   d. IM'ing friends about sexual websites

15. What is the typical profile of an online sexual predator?
   a. 13–65, female, single
   b. **13–65, male, single**
   c. 20–35, male, married
   d. 20–35, male, divorced

Section V

1. Which of the following is often exhibited by organized crime scenes?
   a. There are indications that the victim was not a stranger.
   b. The assault and disposal site of the body are the same.
   c. There are signs of postmortem sexual activity.
   d. **The victim was transported.**

2. Which of the following is an example of a serial murder?
   a. Oklahoma City bombing
   b. Columbine school shooting
   c. Charles Manson murders
   d. **Ted Bundy murders**

3. Which type of violent crime involves three or more victims, one offender, one location, and a single event lasting minutes, hours, or days?
   a. Spree murder
   b. Serial murder
   c. Fratricide
   d. **Mass murder**

4. _____ is the base of the investigation pyramid.
   a. Comprehension
   b. Application and analysis
   c. **Knowledge**
   d. Synthesis

5. Typically, how old is a victim of sudden infant death syndrome (SIDS)?
   a. **1–6 months**
   b. 6–9 months
   c. 9–12 months
   d. over 1 year

6. Which of the following is/are the fourth leading cause of accidental death in the United States?
   a. Motor vehicle accidents
   b. Poisoning
   c. Firearms
   d. **Drowning**

7. When immersed in water, how fast does body temperature fall?
   a. **5° per hour**
   b. 10° per hour
   c. 15° per hour
   d. 20° per hour

8. How many hairs should be collected for DNA analysis?
   a. Only 1 is needed
   b. 13–25
   c. **25–50**
   d. 50–100

9. Which of the following do offenders of sexual assault against the elderly rarely seek?
   a. Punishment
   b. Control
   c. Domination
   d. **Sexual gratification**

10. The more _____ the death plan, the more lethal the intent of suicide.
    a. malicious
    b. **precise**
    c. destructive
    d. ambiguous

11. The definition of parasuicide is _____.
    a. the act of intentionally ending one's own life
    b. a deliberate intervention undertaken with the express intention of ending a life to relieve intractable suffering
    c. a suicide method in which a suicidal individual deliberately acts in a threatening way with the goal of provoking a lethal response from a law enforcement officer
    d. **a nonfatal act in which a person deliberately causes self-injury**

12. Which of the following is amitriptyline considered to be?
    a. Stimulant
    b. **Antidepressant**
    c. Hallucinogen
    d. Diluent

13. What is the most common cause of death in an autoerotic fatality?
    a. **Neck compression**
    b. Chest compression
    c. Smoking
    d. Choking

14. When experiencing sedative withdrawal, what happens at the 24- to 72-hour marker?
    a. Improvement
    b. Tremors
    c. Insomnia
    d. **Delirium**

15. Two-thirds of all fire fatalities are the result of _____.
    a. **asphyxiation**
    b. burns
    c. heat exhaustion
    d. toxic gases

16. In contact wounds, which of the following will always be present?
    a. A muzzle impression
    b. **Scorching of the wound edges**
    c. The bullet itself
    d. Soot on the skin adjacent to the wound

17. In a hanging, suspension or partial suspension, what is the restricting force for cutting off oxygen?
    a. The rope
    b. **The body**
    c. The airway
    d. How long the body has been suspended

18. The presence of _____ suggests that a blade penetrated to its maximum length in a stabbing.
    a. ripped clothing
    b. the blade's sharpness
    c. **a hilt mark**
    d. tissue resistance

19. If a vehicle were to hit a pedestrian at about 25–30 mph, what would be damaged on the vehicle?
    a. No significant damage
    b. A dent in the fender
    c. **The windshield breaks**
    d. The vehicle would be totaled

20. Relatively, if a contusion is a dark purple color, how old is it?
    a. A few hours
    b. **Less than a week**
    c. One week
    d. More than one week

21. The purpose of a modus operandi is to ensure the _____ of the crime.
    a. cause
    b. quality
    c. **success**
    d. victim

22. When putting together a personality assessment, which of the following should you ask about the subject's marital status?
    a. How the subject and the spouse met
    b. The religion of the spouse and if it is the same as the subject's religion
    c. **If the subject is single, married, divorced, or separated**
    d. Where the spouse works

23. The vitreous humor is a good specimen to obtain when attempting to find which of the following toxicants?
    a. **Volatile poisons**
    b. Insecticides
    c. Carbon monoxide
    d. Metals

24. Of all the calls made to poison control centers involving potentially toxic substances, about how many happen in the home?
    a. 52%
    b. 68%
    c. 74%
    d. **91%**

Section VI

1. _____ helps determine the probable manner of someone's death.
   a. Behavioral profiling
   b. Forensic examination
   c. **Psychological autopsy**
   d. Family history

2. The phrase *Postmortem Interval (PMI)* is another way of saying _____.
   a. **time-since-death**
   b. police response
   c. autopsy
   d. decedent profile

3. Which world-famous actress's death did the Los Angeles Suicide Panel examine in 1962?
   a. **Marilyn Monroe**
   b. Jane Mansfield
   c. Janis Joplin
   d. Natalie Wood

4. In the late 18th century, suicide was considered a _____ concern rather than a medical one.
   a. mental health
   b. **religious**
   c. psychiatric
   d. psychological

5. Low levels of _____ are often present in the brains of those who have killed themselves.
   a. fentanyl
   b. **serotonin**
   c. clonazepam
   d. OxyContin

6. In a study of suicide notes, the _____ note-writers apparently felt the need to say more in their last communication.
   a. fictitious
   b. original
   c. surviving
   d. **genuine**

7. Autoerotic asphyxiation results in feelings of elation, exhilaration, and heightened _____.
   a. awareness
   b. sensitivity
   c. **sexual pleasure**
   d. spirituality

8. Regarding malpractice litigation, psychological autopsies can help decide if a caregiver met the _____.
   a. burden of proof
   b. medical requirements
   c. Medicare requirements
   d. **standards of care**

9. A psychological autopsy conducted on the Columbine killers by the Threat Assessment Group could only hypothesize that anger grew out of resentment, and depression, from sadness. These moods were reinforced with immersion in _____, which raised the emotional tone to rage and thoughts of suicide.
   a. drugs
   b. alcohol
   c. **violent imagery**
   d. role playing

10. Who can demand a psychological autopsy?
   a. Prosecuting attorney
   b. Law enforcement officer
   c. Circuit judge
   d. **Coroner or medical examiner**

Bibliography

AccessData Corporation (Forensic Toolkit): www.accessdata.com.

Computer Crime and Intellectual Property Section, U.S. Department of Justice: www.cybercrime.gov.

Death Scene Checklist: This is a checklist to help investigators as they deal with a case. It will help ensure nothing is missed during the investigation and everything is documented and reported properly. It can be downloaded for free at www.dsigizmos.com/dscl.

e-fense (Helix): www.e-fense.com.

Federal Rules of Evidence: www.federalevidence.com/rules-of-evidence.

Forensic Focus: www.forensicfocus.com.

Forward Edge II, U.S. Secret Service: www.forwardedge2.com.

Guidance Software (EnCase): www.guidancesoftware.com.

Hakin9 Magazine: www.en.hakin9.org.

International High Technology Crime Investigation Association: www.htcia.org.

Internet Crimes against Children Task Force: www.icactraining.org/default.htm.

Security Distro: www.securitydistro.com.

Techno Forensics Conference: www.technosecurity.com/html/TechnoForensics2009.html.

Wecht, C.H. (Ed.). (2012). *Forensic Sciences*, Vols. 1–5. San Francisco: Mathew Bender & Company, Inc.

Wecht, C.H., & Rago, J.T. (Eds.). (2006). *Forensic Science and Law*. Boca Raton, FL: CRC Press.